FORGOTTEN KINGDOM

BRIGHAM YOUNG, 1857
As he appeared during the Mormon theocracy's
military confrontation with the United States.
Courtesy, Manuscripts Division, University of Utah Libraries.

FORGOTTEN KINGDOM

The Mormon Theocracy
in the American West,
1847–1896

by
David L. Bigler

UTAH STATE UNIVERSITY PRESS
Logan, Utah
1998

LIBRARY OF CONGRESS CATALOG CARD NUMBER 98-10734
ISBN-0-87421-245-6

published by
Utah State University Press
Logan, Utah 84322-7800

This book was first published by the
Arthur H. Clark Company
as Volume 2 in the series
KINGDOM IN THE WEST:
The Mormons and the American Frontier

Bigler, David L., 1927–
    Forgotten kingdom: the Mormon theocracy in the American
West, 1847–1896 / David Bigler.
    p. 416   cm.
Originally published: Spokane, WA: Arthur Clark Co., 1998.
Includes bibliographical references and index.
ISBN 0-87421-245-6
1. Church of Jesus Christ of Latter-Day Saints-West
(U.S.)-History–19th century.   2. Mormon Church-West
(U.S.)–History–19th century.   3. West (U.S.)–Church history–19th
century.   I.   Title
BX8615.W47 B54 1998
289.3'78'09034–dc21   98-10734
                                                   CIP

To Evah
who made it possible

CONTENTS

ILLUSTRATIONS

PREFACE

Is there a secret history of Mormonism? Not really. The lack of access to significant sources held by the Church of Jesus Christ of Latter-day Saints (LDS or Mormon) creates the impression that they are hiding something dark and important, but this is largely an illusion. The institution's First Presidency holds any number of key documents—the minutes of the Twelve Apostles and the Council of Fifty are prime examples—that would be of great interest to scholars, but such sources would likely confirm rather than overturn the conclusions careful historians have drawn regarding of the colorful story of America's "peculiar people."

There are so many sources of information concerning Mormon history that the real problem facing scholars is not what is withheld, but rather simply comprehending the abundance of available material. Unlike the prophets of old, the faith's founder was born in the age of the printing press, and since Joseph Smith released *The Book of Mormon* in 1830, those presses have produced libraries of material on the beliefs, hopes, achievements, and misdeeds of his disciples. The Lord's instruction to Latter-day Saints to keep personal journals sounded a call that even the semi-literate answered as best they could, creating a wealth of first-person accounts describing almost every aspect of the creed's trials and triumphs. The federal government has produced hundreds of executive documents, thousands of court records, and countless manuscript records on the subject. The number of works critical of Mormonism is more than matched by a vast outpouring of "faith promoting" histories. The challenge to historians is not overcoming restrictions on key sources but mastering the staggering amount of material that is available.

David L. Bigler has studied the history of the West and the role of the Mormons in that story all his adult life. This book, *Forgotten Kingdom: The Mormon Theocracy in the American West, 1847–1896*, is an original look at that history; it tells this story as it has never been told before. Bigler rein-

terprets the history of the LDS church in the Rocky Mountains, providing an often-surprising look at the most significant conflict between
politics and religion in American history. The author's scholarly skill is
evident throughout, showing not only a mastery of Utah and Mormon
sources but a wide-ranging knowledge of federal records and the wider
history of the West. His keen understanding of LDS theology and his
insights into the hopes and dreams of the Mormon people in their early
days in the West is simply unsurpassed.

Although Mr. Bigler pursued a career in business, his work in Mormon and Western history has had a great influence on professional historians. He has been a respected activist in Utah's historical community
for more than three decades. Bigler is a founding member and past-pres-
ident of the Oregon-California Trails Association and was instrumental
in the creation of the Utah Heritage Foundation and the Utah Westerners. His tireless efforts have brought forth a bounty of primary
sources that otherwise might have vanished forever in the state's archives
or landfills. He first located, copied, and transcribed many of the original narratives on which this present work is based. Bigler's 1990 edition
of *The Gold Discovery Journal of Azariah Smith* was hailed as a model of its
kind.

His work places the history of Utah and Mormonism in the larger
context of the story of the American Republic. The subject of Mormonism in the West has traditionally been addressed from a Utah-cen-
tric perspective. All too often that perspective fails to connect the
religion's conflict with American law and culture with larger issues of
national significance, often casting the story as a struggle between righteous Latter-day Saints and evil government bureaucrats or vice versa.
This "heroes and villains" approach does a disservice to the many hon-
orable men and women who fought valiantly for the American system in
the nation's most difficult territory.

Bigler ably tells the stories of forgotten leaders whose role in the
Americanization of Mormonism is often overlooked in the traditional
histories. He brings to life such colorful but obscure characters in this
struggle as Robert Baskin, John Robinson, Norman McLeod, James
McKean, and George R. Maxwell, whose concept of what Utah's society could become much more closely matched the realities of the mod-

ern state than did Brigham Young's vision of the Kingdom of God. (It is truly ironic that the accommodations its nineteenth-century "enemies" forced on the LDS church prepared the institution for its phenomenal growth in the second half of the twentieth century.) With equal skill, Bigler introduces a fascinating cast of little-known Latter-day Saints, including Hannah Tapfield King, Joseph Morris, Jeter Clinton, Sylvanus Collett, George Reynolds, Lydia Spencer Clawson, and George Hill, who show both the diversity of opinion within the faith and the devotion of its people to their institutions.

This highly readable narrative is crafted to appeal to a wide readership. Bigler's prose is clear, direct, and never pretentious. He wrote the book with a specific audience—new arrivals in Mormon Country—in mind, recounting the incredible history that created the singular social conditions that still persist in the Great Basin. *Forgotten Kingdom* meets the standards of the most demanding scholarship but tells a story so odd and interesting that it both challenges and entertains. Bigler's gentle wit seldom misses the high irony of a story that has entertained Western observers since Samuel Clemens.

Forgotten Kingdom is an original look at a complex history that will challenge some readers' most beloved beliefs and traditions. Yet all should recognize this book for what it is, a labor of love. David L. Bigler's history presents a lifetime of careful scholarship and the work of a thoughtful and perceptive intellect in a forthright telling of one of the great stories of the American West.

WILL BAGLEY
Salt Lake City, Utah

INTRODUCTION

During the middle of the nineteenth century a theocratic state was established in the American West whose people were governed by inspiration from God to their leaders on earth. The subjects of this American theocracy came from all parts of the United States and northern Europe, and they were zealous beyond the imagination of most members of their faith today.

Whether they wanted to or not, these bearers of the standard of revealed truth, ultimate and final, were compelled to confront and triumph over other systems of belief as a condition of faith. For truth, divinely inspired, must prevail. It cannot compromise with lesser gospels or philosophies without contradicting its own claim of superiority. Moreover it must prevail to universal rule. There is no stopping place short of that destiny.

The members of this unique enterprise called themselves the Latter-day Saints, but they were popularly known as the Mormons, followers of Joseph Smith, Jr., a modern prophet who claimed to have restored the true gospel of Jesus Christ. Unable to coexist with manmade institutions, Brigham Young and his Mormon followers gathered in the Great Basin to establish the most singular form of government ever to exist in North America. This was the Kingdom of God, also known as the "State of Deseret," or Utah Territory, the literal fulfillment of Old Testament prophecy and the answer to the prayer of Christians over the centuries:

"Thy kingdom come, Thy will be done on earth as it is in heaven."

Accepting any suffering or hardship, its people set out to accomplish an incredibly ambitious and confrontational purpose. This was to sweep away all other nations of this world and make ready for the coming of the Lord, and to do this within their own lifetime. For the destiny of the Mormon kingdom was to roll forth to world dominion, to prevail over the kingdoms of the earth, as a condition of Christ's return to inaugurate His millennial reign.

For some fifty years this militant millennial movement engaged in a continuing struggle for sovereignty with an American republic that never quite knew how to take the challenge. In the end, the more irresistible of two incompatible systems proved to be the one founded on ideals of individual freedom and self-rule, which managed to succeed almost in spite of itself. It eventually did so despite the mistakes or good intentions of leaders who consistently underestimated the abilities and convictions of their adversaries.

Out of this conflict came many ironies. Not least of them is that the members of the little theocracy that took on the national government afterward adopted the legacy of its opponent, while those who fought on what they called "the picket line of civilization," to make Utah an acceptable member of the American Union, have since been in the main reviled or forgotten.

The late Theron H. Luke, former city editor of Provo's *Daily Herald* and Utah history teacher at Utah Technical College (now Utah Valley State College), referred to this paradox in the title of a talk he often gave on early Utah history as "Forty Years of Historical Amnesia." To this valued and well-remembered friend, the author is indebted for much, including the title of this work and the perspective it reflects.

Possibly one reason for the loss or distortion of this unique story is that it was first written by historians who were themselves too close to the events to treat them without bias, while many of those who followed have seemed reluctant to stray far from the line they drew. Whatever the reason, an important chapter of American history has largely vanished in a remarkably short time.

Its loss is unfortunate, not only because this story is unique in American history and carries many lessons. It is also essential to an understanding of society today in a place that is one of the nation's fastest growing states, but still reflects and is divided by ideas and attitudes brought forward from the nineteenth century.

The years from 1847 to 1858 were especially significant in shaping Utah's history and culture. These years might be called the "Stone of Daniel Period," when the Kingdom of God existed in its original form, as yet little affected by the outside world. The 1855 call of the Indian missionaries, the Great Reformation and handcart emigration of 1856, and the armed defiance of the United States to the point of bloodshed a year later, are pivotal events in this time. Yet this is the very period that usually receives the least attention from most historians, who must bear a large responsibility for the loss of historical knowledge and cultural awareness.

Nor is this loss limited only to Utah. The Mormon theocracy's battle for independence also had a major bearing on the settlement, creation, and final form of other western states. Nevada became a separate entity because its early settlers rejected theocratic rule and Congress determined to cut Mormon domains back to governable size. Brigham Young's followers were also involved in important historical events in early Wyoming, Idaho, Arizona, California, and elsewhere.

Finally, the disappearance of this story should be regretted because forgotten with it have been some important figures in Utah history who deserve to be remembered for their contributions to the political freedom and the natural family relationships most Utahns take for granted today. They include such names as Patrick E. Connor, Daniel S. Tuttle, Duncan J. McMillan, Charles S. Zane, Robert N. Baskin, Caleb W. West, Clarence E. Allen, and many others whose stories are told in this volume.

Unaware that they are inheritors of a worthy tradition that goes back to Utah's earliest years, those who come to the beehive state may find themselves in a society unlike any they have known in the past. Often feeling like strangers in a strange land, they want to know more about the local culture, how it got the way it is, and where they might belong, if anywhere, in it. Nor is this interest limited only to the growing numbers, including many young professionals, who are coming to the state for the first time.

The author became aware of this interest in Utah's historical roots in recent years when he taught a course on the state's early history in a number of non-Mormon Christian Sunday schools in Salt Lake Valley. The size of these classes and the attention of those who attended for a full hour or more at a time were surprising. Of all their questions, the most often asked was, "Where can I find a book that provides this information?"

A number of modern historians have provided answers to this question in their coverage of important subjects or individuals in this story. But there has not been a single book that looks at the theocratic period of Utah's past as a whole in such a balanced way that a newcomer from Peoria, or any interested reader, might better understand the state and how it became the way it is.

The purpose of this work is to fill that need. It is to tell the story of Mormon theocracy in the American West and the men and women on both sides who took part in its fifty-year quarrel with the American republic, and to do this with honesty and understanding. In so doing, it ventures to begin a restoration of Utah's colorful past and a vanishing chapter of American history.

The author is indebted to many associates who have given freely of their knowledge and professionalism over the years. Rather than attempt to remember them all by name, he prefers only to extend special appreciation to the editor of this series, Will Bagley, for his invaluable contribution; Floyd A. O'Neil, who reviewed this work and made many important suggestions; Harold Schindler, for his long-standing friendship and encouragement; and Dr. Jay Haymond of the Utah State Historical Society, a friend of infinite wisdom and good judgment.

DAVID L. BIGLER
Roseville, California
October 1997

FORGOTTEN KINGDOM

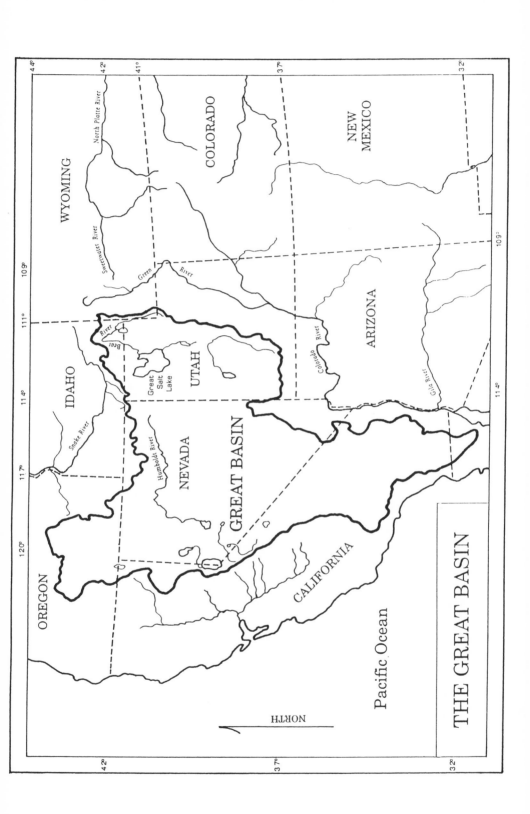

THE GREAT BASIN

A Broad Open Valley

Lo, the Gentile chain is broken,
Freedom's banner waves on high;
List, ye nations: By this token,
Knowing that your redemption's nigh!
—"Mountain Standard"

On July 21, 1847, two men, one mounted and the other on foot, struggled to the crest of a steep hill on the western slopes of the Wasatch Mountains in northern Utah. On horseback was 35-year-old Orson Pratt, an apostle of the Church of Jesus Christ of Latter-day Saints, commonly called Mormon, and the young faith's leading intellectual. His companion was Erastus Snow, a dark youth only 28, who was already a veteran of a dozen years of conflict suffered by the new American religious movement in Missouri and Illinois.

As they neared the summit,[1] there suddenly appeared before them "a broad open valley about twenty miles wide and thirty long, at the north end of which the waters of the Great Salt Lake glistened in the sunbeams."[2] The pair whooped with gladness, swung their hats, and shouted, "Hosannah!" More than thirty thousand other members of their faith, after a long journey from the Missouri River, were to know the thrill of that sight over the coming ten years.

The next day Pratt, with corpulent Apostle George A. Smith and seven others, rode down into the valley, followed by most of the wagons of the first company. There, swarming in the drier places, they found an

---

[1]The spot is now the location of high-rise condominiums on Donner Hill near the mouth of Emigration Canyon. A historical marker just east of This is the Place State Park shows where the pair left Emigration Creek to begin their climb.

[2]"Extracts from O. Pratt's Private Journal," *Latter-day Saints' Millennial Star*, June 15, 1850, 177–80.

ugly, new enemy, the so-called Mormon cricket, later described by settlers as a cross between a spider and a buffalo. Despite the timely arrival
of sea gulls in 1848, in subsequent years the voracious insect and its relatives would bring Mormon settlements to the edge of starvation.[3]

The first arrivals dedicated the place to God, plowed up five acres of
ground, and built an irrigation dam. Slowed by a severe attack of
"mountain fever," Brigham Young came up with the last of the Mormon
party on July 24, now celebrated in Utah each year as Pioneer Day, just
after the first potatoes had been planted.[4]

THE PIONEER COMPANY

Who were these people, the first permanent white settlers in Utah?
Much can be learned from the 143 men, three women, and two children
who came that summer from Mormon emigration camps on the banks
of the Missouri River, around and opposite Council Bluffs, Iowa.
Reflecting the growth of their movement in only seventeen years, the
hand-picked company numbered natives of at least twenty states and
seven foreign countries.

The most from any one state, nearly thirty, hailed from New York,
generally from the Lake Ontario region, boyhood home of Joseph
Smith, Mormonism's founding prophet. Nearly forty came from New
England, thirteen of these from Vermont, Smith's birthplace. Some two
dozen claimed Ohio and Pennsylvania as their birthplace. The remaining Americans numbered only seventeen southerners from seven states
below the Mason-Dixon line. Of these, three were black slaves. Among
the pioneer party were also seven Englishmen, five Canadians, three
Irishmen, and individual natives of Norway, Germany, Denmark, and
Scotland.

Like the tribes of ancient Israel, these sojourners traveled in companies of ten, fifty, and one hundred, with a captain over each, according

---

[3]The wingless "Mormon cricket" is actually a grasshopper. Its more common relative, the Rocky Mountain
locust, ranges throughout the American South and West and "caused most of the insect damage in pioneer
Utah." See Bitton and Wilcox, "Pestiferous Ironclads: The Grasshopper Problem in Pioneer Utah," 340.

[4]For two of the best accounts of this 1847 company, see Bagley, ed., *The Pioneer Camp of the Saints: The 1846
and 1847 Mormon Trail Journals of Thomas Bullock*; and Schindler, ed. and comp., *Crossing The Plains; New and fascinating
accounts of the hardships, controversies and the courage experienced and chronicled by the 1847 pioneers on the Mormon Trail.* Also see
Smith, ed., *An Intimate Chronicle: The Journals of William Clayton.*

to a revelation to their prophet, "Ye are the children of Israel, and of the seed of Abraham."[5] Taking this to be literally true, they named themselves the Children of Israel and called outsiders "gentiles," a term that conveyed both scorn and mistrust. Reflecting an established military tradition, the head of the entourage held the rank of lieutenant general, followed by a colonel, two majors, and a captain of artillery who commanded a single small cannon.

One of the most striking qualities of this company was the youth of those who comprised it. The average age of the eight Mormon general authorities, all apostles, was just under 39.[6] The two oldest, both 46, were Brigham Young, then president of the Quorum of the Twelve Apostles, and his loyal lieutenant, Heber C. Kimball, both born in Vermont only two weeks apart. The youngest apostle, at 30, George A. Smith, had already served eight years in this office. Of all adults in the party, the average age was barely 32.

The only women in the party were 23-year-old Ellen Sanders Kimball, polygamous wife of Apostle Kimball; Harriet Decker Young, 41, wife of Lorenzo D. Young; and Clarissa Decker Young, youngest of Brigham Young's wives, just turned 19. There were also two children, ages 6 and 7.

A closer look at this company reveals at least eighteen members of a covert body known as the Council of Fifty,[7] or "The Kingdom of God and his Laws, with the Keys and power thereof, and judgment in the hands of his servants, Ahman Christ,"[8] charged to establish the King-

---

[5]Smith, *History of the Church*, 2:36–39. According to a leading Mormon theologian, "By the law of adoption those who receive the gospel and obey its laws, no matter what their literal blood lineage may have been, are adopted into the lineage of Abraham. 'The effect of the Holy Ghost upon a Gentile,' the Prophet [Joseph Smith] says, 'is to purge out the old blood, and make him actually of the seed of Abraham.'" See McConkie, *Mormon Doctrine*, 23. Brigham Young also said, "Nine tenths of those who come into this Church are the pure blood of Israel, the greater portion being purely of the blood of Ephraim." See Collier, ed., *The Teachings of President Brigham Young*, Vol. 3, 191.

[6]They were E. T. Benson, 36; Heber C. Kimball, 46; Amasa Lyman, 34; Orson Pratt, 36; Willard Richards, 43; George A. Smith, 30; Wilford Woodruff, 40; and Brigham Young, 46.

[7]They were E. T. Benson, Thomas Bullock, Albert Carrington, William Clayton, Heber C. Kimball, Amasa Lyman, John Pack, Orson Pratt, Willard Richards, Orrin Porter Rockwell, Albert P. Rockwood, Shadrach Roundy, Charles Shumway, George A. Smith, Erastus Snow, Wilford Woodruff, Brigham Young, and Phinehas Young. For more on this mysterious body, see Hanson, *Quest for Empire: The Political Kingdom of God and the Council of Fifty in Mormon History*. Also see Quinn, *The Mormon Hierarchy: Origins of Power*, 521–31; Smith, ed., *An Intimate Chronicle*, 129–31; Quinn, "The Council of Fifty and Its Members, 1844 to 1945"; and Ehat, "'It Seems Like Heaven Began on Earth': Joseph Smith and the Constitution of the Kingdom of God."

[8]Smith, ed., *An Intimate Chronicle: The Journals of William Clayton*, 153.

dom of God on earth, prior to the second coming of Jesus Christ, and to rule the world afterward. So secret was its very existence that any breech was held to be a serious sin that could only be atoned by the blood of the offender.

At the head of this unusual party was a man born to lead, one incapable of self-doubt. Educated only eleven days in a classroom, Brigham Young was well schooled in practical leadership by fourteen years at or near the head of a controversial religious movement. A committed follower of the faith's founding prophet, Joseph Smith, he called himself an apostle of Smith, never his equal.

In 1847 Young was clean-shaven, built for the long pull, and his gray eyes had seldom, if ever, fallen before the stare of any man. His greatest gift was to seize visionary ideas and stamp them into hardrock facts. To him, right was whatever served the duty to build the Kingdom of God. Three years after Smith's death in June 1844 he still had made no claim fully to succeed the man who held his devotion. Only with the emigration successfully begun would he move to become the faith's second president in more than title only. He was sustained to this calling late in 1847 by the Quorum of the Twelve, albeit reluctantly by some members. But not for three more years would he allow himself to be proposed and sustained by the faithful as their new prophet, seer, and revelator.

WHERE DID THEY COME FROM?

Young and his pioneer company departed the Mormon emigration base at Winter Quarters on the Missouri River in present Florence, Nebraska, now part of Omaha, on April 5 that year and headed west over the Oregon Trail, establishing a distinct route on the north side of the Platte River,[9] historic avenue of America's western migration. The line they traveled is closely followed by today's I-80 across much of Nebraska. From the river forks at present North Platte, Nebraska, the trail took them up the North Platte along present U.S. Highway 26 to

---

[9]See Mattes, *The Great Platte River Road*. Other recommended readings include Kimball, *Historic Sites and Markers along the Mormon and Other Great Western Trails*; Kimball and Knight, *111 Days to Zion*; and Hill, *The Mormon Trail: Yesterday and Today*.

Fort Laramie, where they crossed the river to ascend the right bank. Here they were joined by several Mormon families who had wintered at Pueblo, near the present Colorado city of the same name, on the upper Arkansas River.

At present Casper, Wyoming, the pioneer party again crossed the river, leaving nine men to operate a toll ferry before continuing on the line of today's State Highway 220 to Independence Rock. Still on the Oregon Trail, they traveled up the Sweetwater River, crossed the Continental Divide at South Pass on today's State Highway 28, then moved down Big Sandy River from present Farson to Green River.

Here they were joined by an advance party from the Mormon Mexican War volunteers who due to sickness had been detached from their main command, the Mormon Battalion, and sent to winter at Pueblo.[10] A few miles more brought them to the historic trading post, now not far off I-80, built by James Bridger five years before at a sheltered place on Blacks Fork where the trail headed northwest to Fort Hall, near present Pocatello, Idaho.

At Fort Bridger the enlarged party for the first time left the Oregon Trail and headed west over the California Trail's Hastings Cutoff, opened the year before by Lansford W. Hastings.[11] Except for a short stretch from Bear River, some eight miles south of present Evanston, Wyoming, to the head of Echo Canyon, near Castle Rock, they followed the 1846 wagon tracks of the Donner-Reed party all the way to Salt Lake Valley.

Going west, this route is generally paralleled today by I-80 and I-84 from Fort Bridger to Henefer, Utah, where the pioneers crossed the Weber River and turned southwest on the line of today's State Highway

---

[10]In the belief the Mormons would migrate to California, President James Polk in 1846 approved the enlistment of some five hundred volunteers to serve in American occupation forces in California, responding to Brigham Young's appeal for government assistance in moving west. The infantry command was mustered in at Council Bluffs, Iowa, and armed at Fort Leavenworth before marching to New Mexico, where about 160 were detached for health reasons and sent with a number of wives and children to Pueblo, a little settlement of trappers on the Arkansas River. The rest marched to southern California, where they were mustered out at Los Angeles on July 16, 1847. For one of the best works on this unique command, see Ricketts, *The Mormon Battalion: U.S. Army of the West, 1846–1848*.

[11]See Korns and Morgan, eds., revised by Bagley and Schindler, *West from Fort Bridger: The Pioneering of the Immigrant Trails across Utah, 1846–1850*. Also see Topping, "Overland Emigration, the California Trail, and the Hastings Cutoff"; and Spedden, "Who Was T. H. Jefferson?"

65. The trail took them up East Canyon, across Big and Little mountains and down Emigration Canyon to reach Salt Lake Valley near today's This is the Place State Park.

In III days they had journeyed that summer from the Missouri River to Great Salt Lake Valley. But in a larger sense, they had traveled an even longer road. After seventeen years of continuous conflict, they had come out of Babylon, "determined to get out from this evil nation." With divine retribution "at the door,"[12] they had shaken the dust from their garments and left the gentile nation to "fall like a millstone cast into the sea."[13]

Founded in 1830 in upstate New York, the fervent millennial movement had known little peace since the heavens had opened after centuries of silence and God had once again spoken to humankind. Its prophet, Joseph Smith, Jr., launched the new religion on the belief the second coming of Jesus Christ was imminent. Primitive forms of democracy on America's frontier proved unable to protect believers who moved as one in all things, according to the dictates of heaven, or the people they encountered on their hard odyssey.

An early source of dissension had been the formation of an illegal bank at Kirtland, Ohio, which had flooded the area with worthless money. But that was hardly any trouble at all compared with the strife that came soon after God revealed in 1831 that Jackson County, Missouri, was the land of Zion, and that its frontier seat, Independence, was the place to build New Jerusalem, the City of Zion, for the gathering of His people in the Last Days.

"Behold, the place which is now called Independence is the center place," He said, "and the spot for the temple is lying westward, upon a lot which is not far from the court house."[14]

As believers gathered, conflict broke out in 1833 and flared over the next five years across seven counties of western Missouri. Fewer than three dozen were killed, most of them in the unprovoked massacre of eighteen Mormons at Haun's Mill in Caldwell County. But if small in scale, the fighting was bitter and uncompromising. It culminated in the

---

[12]Roberts, ed., *History of the Church*, 7:515–16.

[13]*Times and Seasons*, November 1, 1845, 1017.

[14]Smith, *History of the Church*, 1:189–90.

Mormon War of 1838 when Gov. Lilburn W. Boggs on October 27 issued to the commander of his state militia forces the order for which he would become forever infamous in the annals of an American religion: "The Mormons must be treated as enemies," he instructed, "and must be exterminated or driven from the State if necessary for the public peace."[15]

For those who went through the Mormon War and stuck with the faith, there would be conflicts to come in Illinois and Utah Territory. But it would always be Missouri they remembered with a will for vengeance in their hearts and a determination to return and recover Zion that would take two generations to soften.[16]

Beaten and outnumbered, the Mormons surrendered to their enemies and braced for the oncoming winter under an edict to get out of Missouri before grass grew. In this desperate hour they found a deliverer. With Smith and most of their leaders under arrest, many of the prophet's broken followers looked to a Puritan-minded apostle from Vermont for guidance.

The self-confidence and restless energy of Brigham Young precluded any need for revelation to organize the Mormon exodus from Missouri. Largely under his leadership, Smith's followers, badly hurt but with reviving spirits, pooled their resources and struggled eastward across Missouri into western Illinois, where they were received with kindness.

There on a quiet bend of the Mississippi River, some fifty miles north of Quincy, they created an exotic frontier metropolis they named Nauvoo, meaning "the beautiful." Touched by the finger of the prophet, it became by 1842 one of the largest urban centers in Illinois with a growing population of ten thousand. The sovereign city-state was a small working model of the theocratic institutions later established on a regional scale in Utah.

The city charter, won from state lawmakers on the promise of revelation-ordered votes, allowed Smith and his people to create at Nauvoo, according to Illinois Governor Thomas Ford, "a government within a government, a legislature with power to pass ordinances at war with the

---

[15]See *Document Containing The Correspondence, Orders, &c. In Relation To The Disturbances With The Mormons; And The Evidence Given Before The Hon. Austin A. King,* 61.

[16]For one of the best books on this conflict, see LeSueur, *The 1838 Mormon War in Missouri.*

laws of the State; courts to execute them with but little dependence upon the constitutional judiciary; and a military force at their own command."[17] Here, too, Smith introduced by revelation the doctrine of plural marriage, or polygamy, denied in public but practiced in secret by a select circle.

Meanwhile the truth of Governor Ford's description was shown in 1843 when the Nauvoo court on a writ of *habeas corpus* freed the Mormon prophet from arrest by outside authorities. He then told his followers that "the municipal court had more power" than higher jurisdictions and that "he restrained them no more" from using violence "in self defense."[18] The city became a sanctuary for counterfeiters and organized bands who preyed on nearby settlements with little fear of arrest.[19]

Most alarming to neighbors was the Nauvoo Legion, a semi-private army, that grew under compulsory military training to about four thousand men, roughly half the size of the regular U.S. Army at the time. This imposing force, finely uniformed and fully equipped, was commanded by the nation's highest ranking military officer, Lt. Gen. Joseph Smith. It stood at the "disposal of the mayor," also Joseph Smith, "in executing the laws and ordinances of the city" as interpreted by the Nauvoo Municipal Court under its chief justice, Joseph Smith.[20]

In 1839 western Illinois had given food and shelter to the suffering refugees who streamed across the Mississippi River from Missouri. But within four years, its citizens had begun to sleep with one eye open. As opposition grew, the spark that touched off Smith's murder and the last days of Nauvoo came from opposition within the movement.

On June 7, 1844, dissenters published the only issue of their newspaper, *Nauvoo Expositor*, rejecting among other things "every attempt to unite church and state," before the city council under Mayor Smith ordered the offending sheet destroyed.[21] This action ignited a series of

---

[17]Ford, *A History of Illinois from its Commencement as a State in 1818 to 1847*, 2:66.

[18]Smith, ed., *An Intimate Chronicle: The Journals of William Clayton*, 109.

[19]For an account of such alleged crimes by a non-Mormon Council of Fifty member who became a bounty hunter at Nauvoo, see Bonney, *The Banditti of the Prairies*.

[20]Smith, *History of the Church*, 4:239–49.

[21]"Resolutions," *Nauvoo Expositor*, June 7, 1844, 2.

events that culminated in the murder of the Mormon prophet and his brother, Hyrum, on June 27 in the jail at Carthage, Illinois. After that it was Missouri all over again.[22]

At this decisive moment, most of the faithful looked to a proven leader, Brigham Young, and the collective authority of the Quorum of the Twelve Apostles, who led the exodus from Illinois early in 1846. The first wagons crossed the Mississippi River in February and headed west across Iowa to establish an emigration base on the Missouri River for the move the following year to the Rocky Mountains.

Meanwhile, responding to Mormon appeals for relief, President James Polk in 1846 authorized the enlistment of some five hundred members of the faith during the War with Mexico. The Mormon Battalion served with American forces in the California occupation and several of its veterans were on hand when gold was discovered. The soldiers also helped finance the Mormon move west with part of their pay and allowances.[23]

By 1847 the Oregon Trail was already a wheel-worn highway, some two thousand miles long, from Council Bluffs to the Columbia River country. But up to then, the world's longest emigrant road had seen nothing like the traffic that now rolled over the prairie in long, double lines—six hundred or more prairie schooners that fall alone. The oncoming parade was a monument of wagons to the leadership of Brigham Young.

WHAT WAS THEIR DESTINATION?

The requirements for a new gathering place—seclusion and ample room to grow in—were abundantly provided by the location the Mormons had chosen before leaving Winter Quarters. This was the Great Basin of North America, a vast region of high-altitude deserts and

---

[22]The brief but remarkable story of Nauvoo has never been fully told. Until it is, two of the best accounts are Flanders, *Nauvoo: Kingdom on the Mississippi*, and Hallwas and Launius, *Cultures in Conflict: A Documentary History of the Mormon War in Illinois*.

[23]Young later claimed the call for volunteers was part of a plot hatched by U.S. Senator Thomas Benton of Missouri to exterminate members of the young faith as they ventured into the wilderness. Under this design, Mormon leaders were expected to reject such a "tyrannical requisition" at which President Polk would order troops to "march against us and massacre us all," according to Young. For a more likely story, see Luce, "The Mormon Battalion: A Historical Accident?" 27–38.

north-south running mountain ranges within the Republic of Mexico, from which no water flows to any ocean.

Encompassing parts of six western states,[24] the arid and empty basin covers an area large enough to hold all of New England, plus New York, Ohio, and Pennsylvania, with room to spare. Its irregular rim encloses nine major river systems—Bear, Weber, Humboldt, Truckee, Carson, Walker, Owens, Provo, and Sevier—all of which end in sinks or briny lakes without outlets. The Great Basin reaches more than five hundred miles across at its widest point from the Bear River Mountains in western Wyoming on the east to the crest of the Sierra Nevada in California. From southeastern Oregon it stretches some eight hundred miles to its southernmost limit in the Baja California peninsula of Mexico.

Within this vast region of interior drainage, the Mormon pioneers had landed on the ancient bed of Lake Bonneville,[25] largest of the Great Basin's prehistoric freshwater bodies, which once covered twenty thousand square miles, a surface area almost equal to Lake Michigan. They made their camp near the eastern shore of its remnant, the Great Salt Lake, shrunk to one-fourteenth the size of its mighty ancestor.

They had come to this remote location, Young said on arrival, "according to the direction" of Joseph Smith.[26] Since the Mormon prophet had been killed before the publication of John C. Frémont's report on his 1843–44 exploration, which first defined the Great Basin, it is probable that Young referred only to his predecessor's indefinite mention of the Rocky Mountains as a place to settle. Not until the summer of 1845 was the probable destination decided on, and even then Mormon leaders continued to consider other possible locations for their settlement.

NOT THE FIRST TO COME

According to plan, the children of Israel in the Last Days had left the

---

[24]They are Utah, Nevada, Wyoming, Idaho, Oregon, and California. See Houghton, *A Trace of Desert Waters: The Great Basin Story.*

[25]The prehistoric lake was named after Capt. Benjamin L. E. Bonneville, U.S. Army officer and fur trader, immortalized in 1837 by Washington Irving, who edited and published his journals as *The Adventures of Captain Bonneville, U.S.A., in the Rocky Mountains and the Far West.* Irving gave Bonneville's name to the present Great Salt Lake, which the egocentric captain approved of, but the title failed to stick.

[26]See Kenney, ed., *Wilford Woodruff's Journal,* 3:240.

nations of Babylon and gone forth into the wilderness to find a new home, but they were not the first people of their kind to come to what is now Utah. Nor were they the first to settle on the western flank of the Wasatch Mountains. They could not even claim to be the first members of their faith ever to see the valley of Great Salt Lake.

Seventy-one years before, in 1776, the year of American independence, two Spanish Franciscans came from Santa Fé looking for an overland route to six new missions in Alta California. Fathers Domínguez, the head of the expedition, and Escalante, who gave his name to a river, town, and mountain range, entered the Great Basin at the head of Strawberry River and followed Diamond Fork and Spanish Fork to the mouth of Spanish Fork Canyon. There on Domínguez Hill, seen from today's U.S. Highway 6, stands a slender cross where they first overlooked Utah Valley.[27]

The Franciscan friars made contact with the Utahs, natives who lived near the shores of fresh water Utah Lake, but never ventured far enough north to see the Great Salt Lake. Instead they headed south to pass near present Milford, crossed the Colorado near today's Glen Canyon Dam, and eventually returned to New Mexico without ever finding a way to Monterey. But their trail became a trade route from Santa Fé to Utah Valley.

If the Franciscans failed to link the northern outposts of their faith, early traders achieved greater, though short-lived, success. For eighteen years, starting in 1829, mounted caravans carried woolen blankets from Santa Fé over the Spanish Trail to Los Angeles and returned with much-prized California mules. Their twelve hundred-mile pack trail looped across southern Utah, fording the Colorado River and Green River at today's towns of Moab and Green River. Entering the Great Basin near the head of Salina Canyon, the route went south up the Sevier River, then west to pass just north of Cedar City, and on to Mountain Meadows and the Virgin River.[28]

For more than a quarter-century before the Mormons, men from the British Northwest, Missouri, and New Mexico had trapped beaver on

---

[27]For more on the Domínguez-Escalante expedition, see Bolton, ed., *Pageant in the Wilderness; the Story of the Escalante Expedition to the Interior Basin, 1776.*

[28]See Crampton and Madsen, *In Search of the Spanish Trail: Santa Fe to Los Angeles, 1829–1848*; and Hafen and Hafen, *Old Spanish Trail.*

Utah's streams and explored its mountains and canyons. When the great Hudson's Bay Company captain, Peter Skene Ogden, for whom one of the state's largest cities is named, entered northern Utah with his Snake Country Expedition in 1825, he found the land covered with destructive cricket-like grasshoppers and the sky filled with screaming California gulls, today's state bird.

The year before, James Bridger out of curiosity had traced the Bear River from Cache Valley, near present Logan, to its mouth at an inland sea, just west of Brigham City, tasted the salty water there, and concluded he had found an arm of the ocean. He is often credited as the earliest known discoverer of Great Salt Lake, but Etienne Provost, the French-Canadian trapper out of Taos, New Mexico, from whom another large Utah city takes its name, was probably the first to see the lake that same year.[29]

An almost comical face-off came in 1825 when beaver hunters from three nations ran into each other on Weber River in northern Utah. The combative Americans under one Gardner Johnson, "with colours flying," claimed the place belonged to the United States.[30] As the leader of a Hudson's Bay brigade, Ogden argued they were on lands jointly occupied by the U.S. and Great Britain. And Provost, who had come from the Rio Grande, might have countered they were near, but well within, the northern limits of Mexico. Luckily, no blood was shed at the spot, now named Mountain Green, located some ten miles east of Ogden on today's I-84.

New Yorker Jedediah Smith was indisputably outside his nation's borders when he mounted expeditions in 1826 and 1827 to California and Oregon from the Great Salt Lake Valley, which he called "my home in the wilderness."[31] The most renowned western explorer of them all left the mountains in 1830 and was killed a year later by Comanche Indians at a water hole, called Wagon Bed Springs, near the confluence of the Cimarron River forks, not far from present Ulysses, Kansas.

A decade later, the journey of thirty-two men and one woman who carried a baby in one arm and led a horse with the other hand announced that the days of the romantic figures known as the mountain

[29]For a biography of Etienne Provost and review of his standing as first to see the Great Salt Lake, see Tykal, *Etienne Provost: Man of the Mountains*.

[30]See Miller, ed., "Peter Skene Ogden's Journal of his Expedition to Utah, 1825," 159–86.

[31]Morgan, *The Great Salt Lake*, 88.

men were coming to an end. The Bidwell-Bartleson party in 1841 left the emerging trace of the Oregon Trail at Soda Springs and headed their nine wagons down Bear River, looking for a way to California. They had "no guide, no compass, nothing but the sun to guide them."[32]

Entering the state's northern border near Clarkston, these intrepid venturers were the first emigrants to cross Utah with wagons, going on firmer ground around the north end of Great Salt Lake, and the first to cross the Sierra Nevada to California. The lone woman in the company, Nancy Kelsey, barely 18, was remembered for her "cheerful nature and kind heart." She was the first white woman ever to see Great Salt Lake.

Following the tracks of these earliest emigrants, but too proud to admit it, "the Great Pathfinder," John C. Frémont, came from the big bend of Bear River in 1843 to explore Great Salt Lake. On the island later named after Frémont, the explorer's scout and loyal friend, Kit Carson, engraved on a sheltered ledge a cross that can still be seen today if one knows where to look.

A second trip to the Great Basin in 1845 saw Frémont lead a large mounted expedition past the south end of Great Salt Lake on the line of modern I-80 to the 10,700-foot mountain on today's Utah-Nevada border that he named Pilot Peak. Later, his report at Sutter's Fort on the feasibility of the Salt Desert trail probably fired an ambitious young lawyer, Lansford W. Hastings, to hurry back the following spring over the route as far east as South Pass to promote it as a shortcut to California.

The first of some three hundred who took the new cutoff in 1846 was an assembly of emigrants named after George Harlan and Samuel Young, the heads of its two largest family contingents. The Harlan-Young party followed Weber River to the vicinity of Ogden, passed the northern limits of present Salt Lake City and struggled across the Salt Desert to Donner Spring at the base of Pilot Peak, some fourteen miles north of Wendover.[33] Among its members were the first Mormons ever

---

[32]Extract from "A Visit to California in Early Times" by Col. Joseph B. Chiles, published in Kelly, "The Salt Desert Trails." Also see Tea, "The Bidwell-Bartleson Trail," in DeLafosse, ed., *Trailing the Pioneers: A Guide to Utah's Emigrant Trails, 1829–1869*, 33–53.

[33]For detailed directions on following this emigrant trail, see Spedden, "The Hastings Cutoff," in DeLafosse, ed., *Trailing the Pioneers*, 73–92. Also see Kelly, *Salt Desert Trails*, DeLafosse, ed. To visit Donner Spring, where the Utah Crossroads Chapter of the Oregon-California Trails Association in 1994 dedicated a historical marker, take I-80 Exit 4, east of Wendover, and go north about twenty-four miles over a gravel road to the Dean Stevens ranch at the foot of Pilot Peak. Keep left.

to see Salt Lake Valley, who included the large family of Thomas Rhoads.

The last of those who succumbed to the California promoter's salesmanship that year were the eighty-seven members and twenty-three wagons of the Donner-Reed party, who pioneered a new trail from Weber River at present Henefer to Salt Lake Valley on the line of today's State Highway 65. At the mouth of Emigration Canyon, where the narrows blocked passage, they struggled up from the creek bottom to the crest, now named Donner Hill, where they viewed Salt Lake Valley, as would Pratt and Snow the next year, from a point just east of today's Hogle Zoo. The eleven days it took them to cut a trail for wagons from Weber River to Salt Lake Valley would prove a few too many for the thirty-five party members who would die in the snow that winter near Donner Lake in the Sierra Nevada. But the route they made would become the Mormon Pioneer Trail to Salt Lake Valley, followed by Brigham Young's pioneer company and tens of thousands of Mormon immigrants from 1847 on.

The honor of being Utah's first non-Indian resident goes to a red-haired free spirit from Connecticut who had come west in 1836 with the Presbyterian missionary, Marcus Whitman, and stayed to take up the life of a trapper. In 1846 Miles Goodyear built his home, Fort Buenaventura, near the confluence of the Ogden and Weber rivers, within the limits of present Ogden. There he lived with his Utah Indian wife, Pamona, and their children, when the Mormons came in 1847 and bought him out a year later with the mustering-out pay of Mormon Battalion veterans.

Like Goodyear, the new colonists found in the Rocky Mountains the freedom from outside interference they sought after years of conflict in Ohio, Missouri, and Illinois. But the Great Basin also offered these latest arrivals another benefit vital to the mission they had been called by God to perform. Besides seclusion, it gave them the room they needed for expansion.

What Was Their Purpose?

As the seed of Abraham in the Last Days, the Mormons came to fulfill the prophecy of Nebuchadnezzar's dream as interpreted by the Prophet Daniel:

> And in the days of these kings shall the God of heaven set up a King-dom, which shall never be destroyed: and the kingdom shall not be left to other people, but it shall break in pieces and consume all these kingdoms, and it shall stand for ever.
>
> Forasmuch as thou sawest that the stone was cut out of the mountain without hands, and that it brake in pieces the iron, the brass, the clay, the sil-ver, and the gold; the great God hath made known to the king what shall come to pass hereafter; and the dream is certain, and the interpretation thereof sure.[34]

Less than two months before his death in 1844, Joseph Smith told his people, "I calculate to be one of the instruments of setting up the Kingdom of Daniel by the word of the Lord, and I intend to lay a foun-dation that will revolutionize the whole world."[35] The musket balls that struck Smith down at Carthage Jail had failed to kill this vision. It was now carried forward by one of the Mormon prophet's most devoted and capable apostles.

Eight years after his arrival in Salt Lake Valley, Brigham Young told his people, "The Kingdom of God is actually organized and the inhab-itants of the earth do not know it."[36] Already advanced by then was the establishment of the Kingdom of God as a theocratic state that was des-tined to supersede the government of the United States and consume all of the nations of the earth before Christ's coming. How long would this take? Not long, said Apostle Parley P. Pratt, who imagined in 1845 that "One Hundred Years Hence," workmen on the foundation for a new temple in 1945, "near where it is supposed the City of New York once stood," would probably find "some coin of the old Government of the United States."[37]

This vaulting aspiration put the Mormon kingdom on a collision course with the most dynamic nation the world had ever witnessed, founded on concepts of religious and individual freedom unique in humankind's history. The confrontation between the Great Basin theoc-

---

[34]Dan. 2:44–45.

[35]Smith, *History of The Church,* 6:365.

[36]Brigham Young, July 1855, *Journal of Discourses,* 2:310.

[37]Crawley, *The Essential Parley P. Pratt,* 142.

racy and the American republic would go on for a half century and make Utah, one of the first places settled west of the Missouri River, among the last admitted to the Union.[38]

ENSIGN TO THE NATIONS

In the meantime, as the pioneer company neared Fort Laramie that summer, Young had severely reprimanded his followers for playing cards and checkers, using profane language, and indulging in loud laughter. Such conduct, he told them, ill suited those chosen to find the place "where the Standard of the Kingdom of God could be reared." For on this standard "would be a flag of ev[e]ry nation under heaven so their [sic] would be an invitation to all Nations under heaven to come unto Zion," he said.[39]

The day after Young's arrival in the valley, July 25, was Sunday, respected as a day of rest, when "many exhortations were given to the brethren to be faithful, obey the council of those in authority and we shall be blessed and prosperous."[40] Early the next day, though still unwell, the Mormon leader gathered a select company for a first order of business.

Together they climbed a steep knoll to the north of their newly plowed fields. Finding it an ideal place to proclaim the gathering, they gave it the name Ensign Peak.[41] Thus was fulfilled the prophecy: "And it

---

[38]One might ask how this confrontation can be squared with the often expressed Mormon belief that the American constitution is divinely inspired. The answer then was that God had inspired the constitution, with its guarantee of religious freedom, to provide a place to establish His Kingdom which would supersede its parent and prevail to universal dominion. The constitution was thus viewed as a stepping stone to a higher form of government, like *Magna Charta*, the Mayflower Compact, or the Northwest Ordinance, not an end in itself. Accordingly, Mormons considered themselves the true inheritors of the document because they were carrying out the divine purpose for which it was intended. Brigham Young expressed this belief in 1855 when he said, "When the day comes in which the Kingdom of God will bear rule, the flag of the United States will proudly flutter unsullied on the flag staff of liberty and equal rights, without a spot to sully its fair surface; the glorious flag our fathers have bequeathed to us will then be unfurled to the breeze by those who have power to hoist it aloft and defend its sanctity." For more on this question, see *Journal of Discourses*, 2:309–17 and 3:70–74.

[39]Kenney, ed., *Wilford Woodruff's Journal*, 3:187–89.

[40]Smith, ed., *An Intimate Chronicle: The Journals of William Clayton*, 365.

[41]The party included Apostles Heber C. Kimball, Wilford Woodruff, George A. Smith, Ezra T. Benson, and Willard Richards, plus fellow Council of Fifty members William Clayton and Albert Carrington. Ensign Peak is a knob-shaped hill about one mile north of today's State Capitol Building. It can be identified from some distance by a fifteen-foot stone pylon. For a spectacular view of the valley, the hill can be easily climbed from the parking lot of the LDS Ensign Peak Ward on North Sandrun Road (940 North). In 1996 the Ensign Peak Foundation dedicated a monument that included three flagpoles to fly the American, Utah State, and "other" flags, including the blue-and-white banner of the state of Deseret.

shall come to pass in that day, that the Lord shall set his hand again the second time to recover the remnant of his people . . . And he shall set up an ensign for the nations, and shall assemble the outcasts of Israel, and gather together the dispersed of Judah from the four corners of the earth."[42]

When the kingdom was established, "The Saints would have to keep the Celestial law," Young had also told his company on the journey west.[43] While never precisely defined, such higher codes of conduct would include plural marriage, or polygamy; revelations already received by Joseph Smith; rulings by the Council of Fifty, called by its members, "the living constitution of the Kingdom of God"; current directives from those in authority; and at least some Biblical ordinances, mainly from the Old Testament.[44]

CHIEF STAKE OF ZION

To the south of Ensign Peak, the first arrivals next laid out a new metropolis whose very design revealed collective purpose and millennial order. Surveyed one mile square, the city featured square, ten-acre blocks, each with eight lots, and main streets 132 feet wide that ran by the compass due east and west, north and south. Rows of houses were projected on two opposite sides of each block with trees in front, gardens in back, to create, Brigham Young said, "uniformity through out the City."[45] By alternating, block by block, the sides with dwellings, the design ensured that no one faced his neighbor across the street.

City planners often credit Young with the design, but the new Mor-

---

[42]Isa. 11:11–12. An interesting sidelight is that Matthias F. Cowley in his biography of Wilford Woodruff in 1907 said, "Here they unfurled the American flag, the Ensign of Liberty to the world. It will be remembered that the country then occupied by the Saints was Mexican soil, and was being taken possession of by the Mormon Battalion and pioneers as a future great commonwealth to the credit and honor of the United States." Aimed to promote faith, his version of the episode is purely fictional. See Cowley, *Wilford Woodruff, History of His Life and Labors, As Recorded in His Daily Journals*, 316.

[43]Kenney, ed., *Wilford Woodruff's Journal*, 3:188.

[44]A possible example of Old Testament law can be seen in the journal entry on May 7, 1853, of Andrew Love, a settler at Nephi: "Saw Brother Madison Hamilton [Hambleton] of Sanpete which it appears has forfeited his life & Priesthood by taking back his wife after killing Vaughn for seducing her." Hambleton apparently erred not for killing the seducer, which seems justified, but for taking his wife back after doing so. On whatever grounds, he was later cleared. See the Journal of Andrew Love.

[45]Kenney, ed., *Wilford Woodruff's Journal*, 3:239.

mon city was almost an exact copy of an earlier one, based on a square mile, conceived in 1833 by the faith's first prophet, Joseph Smith.[46] This urban center, still unbuilt, was New Jerusalem, where the Lord would come, in Jackson County, Missouri. "When this square is thus laid off and supplied," Smith had told his people, "lay off another in the same way and so fill up the world in these last days; and let every man live in the city for this is the city of Zion."[47]

The millennial community was designed to implement the Lord's will on consecration and stewardship. The faithful in 1831 had been told by revelation to consecrate their property to the church "with a covenant and a deed which cannot be broken." Every man would then be made "a steward over his own property," or at least as much as was "sufficient for himself and family."[48] But dire consequences, spiritual and temporal, would follow anyone "that sinneth and repenteth not," the Lord warned. He would be "cast out of the Church, and shall not receive again that which he has consecrated unto the poor and needy of my church, or in other words unto me."[49]

As laid out in the Great Basin, New Jerusalem's sister city featured a six-square-mile enclosure, called the Big Field, which was divided into ten, twenty, forty, and eighty-acre parcels for assignment to farmers together with lots in the city. Closer in to the center, five-acre lots were marked off for allocation to "the mechanics and artisans."[50]

Every man "should [have] his land measured of[f] to him for City & farming purposes what He could till," Young said, but he must "be industrious & take care of it."[51] Each steward must also "keep his lot whole for the Lord has given it to us without price," he continued. Since the Lord owned the land, it could not be sold or privately held. "No man will be suffered to cut up his lot and sell a part to speculate out of his brethren," the Mormon leader instructed.[52]

---

[46]A common story by Salt Lake City tour guides is that Brigham Young designed the streets 132 feet wide in order to allow enough room for a double ox team and wagon to make a U-turn without having to back up.

[47]Smith, *History of The Church*, 1:357–59. For more on the plat of New Jerusalem, see Schuster, "The Evolution of Mormon City Planning and Salt Lake City, Utah, 1833–1877."

[48]Ibid., 148–54.

[49]Ibid.

[50]Ibid., 60.

[51]Kenney, ed., *Wilford Woodruff's Journal*, 3:236.

[52]Smith, ed., *An Intimate Chronicle: The Journals of William Clayton*, 369.

"One thing wonderful for all you Englishmen to know, is, you have no land to buy nor sell; no lawyers waiting to make out titles, conveyances, stamps, or parchment," Young's clerk, Thomas Bullock, wrote to his friends in Great Britain. "We have found a place where the land is acknowledged to belong to the Lord, and the Saints, being His people, are entitled to as much as they can plant, take care of, and will sustain their families with food."[53]

Thus was founded the communitarian design represented by the beehive symbol on today's state flag and seal. Under this agrarian system, communal food gatherers, or farmer bees, were to live in the city, or hive, and harvest food from assigned plots in nearby fields for central storage from which all would share, according to their needs. As Joseph Smith charged, the "Zion square mile" would become the basic pattern, with many variations, for all Mormon settlements in the western United States.

The first of these new locations was given the name, "Great Salt Lake City of the Great Basin, North America."[54] Consistent with the economic concepts inherent in its design were other views Young expressed during his brief 1847 stay in the valley. Mormon colonists would spurn trade with the outside world, he said. "The Kingdom of God cannot rise independent of the gentile nations until we produce, manufacture and make every article of use, convenience or necessity among our own people."[55]

Afterward, like Joshua at Shechem,[56] Young called on his people to renew their covenants in a new land. First, the Mormon leader baptized other members of the Quorum of the Twelve, then all gathered at a mountain stream, probably today's City Creek, "to Baptize the Camp of Israel for the remission of our sins & to renew our covenants before the Lord."[57] All told, 288 were rebaptized over a three-day period.

Then all went to work to build before the onset of winter a stockade one block square, enclosing ten acres. Walls nine feet high were constructed of logs on the east and adobe on the other sides. The backs of

[53]Bullock to William, January 4, 1848, *Latter-day Saints' Millennial Star*, April 15, 1848, 118.
[54]The "Great" persisted until 1868 when it was dropped from the name.
[55]Journal of Norton Jacob, quoted in Morgan, *The Great Salt Lake*, 202.
[56]Jos. 24:1–27.
[57]Kenney, ed., *Wilford Woodruff's Journal*, 3:250.

the cabins, which faced inward, formed a portion of the wall. Main gates were constructed on the east and west sides.[58] The new settlers also dug irrigation ditches, built a bowery for meetings, and planted about one hundred acres of corn, potatoes, buckwheat, turnips, and other vegetables.

GENTILES, INDIANS, AND VENGEANCE

In addition to hard work, there was a lot of exhortation and preaching in the remote wilderness, unrestrained by any awareness outsiders might be listening. In the thirty-four days he spent in Great Salt Lake Valley during 1847, Brigham Young treated a number of subjects, as recorded by Apostle Wilford Woodruff and others, in words that foretold events to come in Utah.

Among them was a note of caution to gentiles: "All men or religions may dwell with us in peace, if they will keep the outward laws of the Kingdom of [God] so as to acknowledge his name & his right to reign."[59] But an outsider must leave his neighbors alone and "not blaspheme the God of Israel or damn old Jo Smith or his religion, for we will salt him down in the lake," Young warned.[60]

On the other hand, bonds of brotherhood would be forged with the natives, who, like Mormons, were considered descendants of Jacob from the lineage of Joseph. Young told his followers they would be "connected with every tribe of Indians throughout America & our people would yet take their squaws wash & dress them up teach them our language & learn them to labor & learn them the gospel of their forefathers." They would "raise up children by them," he went on, and "they will become A white & delightsome people," to fulfill *Book of Mormon* prophecy.[61]

When it came to past wrongs, real and imagined, Young said he knew many in government had "a hand in the death of Joseph & Hyram [Smith] & that they should be damned for these things & if they ever

---

[58]Called the "Old Fort," the stockade was located on the site of today's Pioneer Park at 400 South and 300 West in Salt Lake City.

[59]Kenney, ed., *Wilford Woodruff's Journal*, 3:189.

[60]Morgan, *The Great Salt Lake*, 202.

[61]Kenney, ed., *Wilford Woodruff's Journal*, 3:241.

sent any men to interfere with us here they shall have there [*sic*] throats cut & sent to hell." With "uplifted hand to Heaven," he swore "while he lived to make every preperation [*sic*] & avenge the blood of the Prophets & Saints."[62]

A final portent of things to come was the establishment of a theocratic body, called the Municipal High Council, to rule until Young's return in 1848. Chosen president of the first government in Salt Lake Valley was John Smith, an uncle of the faith's first prophet. He and other members, nominated by Young and unanimously received by the people, belonged to the Council of Fifty.

With work begun, the leaders of the pioneer company hurried back over the Oregon Trail to meet their followers—some sixteen hundred that fall alone—in double lines of wagons near South Pass and wave them on to their new home in the mountains. The newcomers had plowed and planted—and they had sowed the seeds of conflicts to come.

[62]Ibid.

Chapter 2

FOUNDING THE KINGDOM

And it shall come to pass in the last days, that the
mountain of the Lord's house shall be established in the
tops of the mountains, and shall be exalted above the
hills; and all nations shall flow unto it.
—Isaiah 2:2

The daughter of Zion had spurned her father's house and hid herself up in the Rocky Mountains to fulfill the words of an Old Testament prophet. In the Great Basin of North America she would establish a theocratic foundation for the role she was destined to carry out as a condition of Christ's coming again to inaugurate His millennial reign.

"We will roll on the Kingdom of our God, gather out the seed of Abraham, build the cities and temples of Zion, and establish the Kingdom of God to bear rule over all the earth," Brigham Young promised.[1] It was a revolutionary purpose, one for which God had safeguarded religious freedom in the New World under the inspired constitution of the United States.

Unlike any other emigrants in America's move west were the people who shared Young's vision. The first arrivals in Utah in 1847, and those who came after them, were ardent millennialists, acutely aware of their role at the culmination of human history. The children of Israel in the latter days bore a deep sense of destiny and self-consciously felt the eyes of humankind on them.

Yet even as they laid out their new city at the foot of the Wasatch Mountains, momentous events were taking place elsewhere that would change everlastingly their design to build the Kingdom of God as an earthly state in the mountain West. Among the most decisive in American history, these developments would also shape the destiny of the republic itself.

[1]Brigham Young, July 8, 1855, *Journal of Discourses*, 2:317.

In Mexico that summer an American army under Gen. Winfield Scott, outnumbered but highly aggressive, was closing in on Mexico City. And in Alta California, a Swiss entrepreneur named John Augustus Sutter, who never refused anyone a job who needed one, and his moody partner from New Jersey, James Marshall, decided to build a saw mill on the South Fork of the American River at a site located a few miles north of present Placerville.

Their project at Coloma went forward as planned until January 24, 1848, when workmen turned the river into the new mill race to test the flow of water on the wheel. That night, 32-year-old Henry W. Bigler, one of six Mormon Battalion veterans hired to build the mill, wrote in his journal words that would signal a massive population shift west: "This day some kind of mettle was found in the tail race that looks like goald."[2]

A few days later Bigler's companion, New Yorker Azariah Smith, 19, confirmed the find: "This week Mon. the 24th. Mr. Marshall found some pieces of (as we all suppose) Gold, and he has gone to the [Sutter's] Fort, for the Purpose of finding out."[3]

Even more pivotal than the discovery of gold at Sutter's Mill was the event that came less than two weeks later. On February 2 Mexico ceded to the United States virtually the entire Pacific Southwest, almost all of the territory now included in the states of Utah, Nevada, California, Arizona, Colorado, and New Mexico. It was the second largest land acquisition in American history.

So it came about that only six months after Young's pioneer company landed in Salt Lake Valley, the daughter of Zion was back under her father's roof, again a member of the American family, but now about to be exposed to the eyes of curious outsiders who would crowd the trails west to the gold fields. The disorganized flood of bickering fortune seekers, hell-bent to "see the elephant,"[4] would bring needed economic

---

[2]Paul, *The California Gold Discovery: Sources, Documents, Accounts and Memoirs Relating to the Discovery of Gold at Sutter's Mill*, 62.

[3]Bigler, ed. *The Gold Discovery Journal of Azariah Smith*, 108.

[4]An expression commonly used by gold rushers which had no exact meaning other than "to see it all." Most of the California-bound emigration bypassed Utah on the north, via Fort Hall, to avoid the Great Salt Lake and Wasatch Mountains, but significant numbers followed the Mormon Trail from Fort Bridger to Salt Lake Valley. From there, most west-bound parties headed north to cross Bear River north of Brigham City and join the California Trail at the Silent City of Rocks, near present Almo, Idaho. Others took the Hastings Cutoff west across the Salt Desert, followed by the Donner-Reed party, or the southern route through Mormon settlements to join the Spanish Trail, near Cedar City. For a guide to these routes, see DeLafosse, ed., *Trailing the Pioneers*.

renewal to threadbare settlements but would hardly enhance Mormon respect for the moral fiber of the nation.

The Treaty of Guadalupe Hidalgo settled one conflict, the War with Mexico, but it introduced another—nearly fifty years of cold war between the Kingdom of God and an American republic that never quite figured out how to handle the challenge. For the Great Basin theocracy, the gold discovery and the nation's expansion to the Pacific Ocean were like the fingers that wrote on the wall for Belshazzar, king of Babylon. They promised an end to isolation and change to come.

STATE OF DESERET

Meanwhile if Mormon leaders anticipated an early return to the country they had just left, their response to this unwanted development gave little sign of it. Their aim was independence, not affiliation with either the United States or Mexico. For this reason, they probably would have preferred to remain within the territory of America's weaker neighbor to the south. Either way, they expected a flood of emigrants to produce within ten years a population large enough to sustain a sovereign position against any outside power. Faced with the need to reach an accommodation with the United States, their actions demonstrated indecision and uncertainty over the form it should take.

At first Brigham Young seemed to favor territorial status, possibly in the belief it would be easier to throw off when the time came for the kingdom to stand on its own feet. In December 1848, Young and Council of Fifty members approved a memorial to Congress for a territorial government on the condition they would choose its officers. Fully consistent with theocratic procedure, the collecting of signatures began before the petition was finished or approved.

The following spring council member John M. Bernhisel, an able diplomat, headed for the nation's capital with the request for a territorial government "of the most liberal construction" allowed by the federal constitution. The proposed territory was "to be known by the name of Deseret."[5] The petition was twenty-two feet long and bore 2,270 signatures.

---

[5]Morgan, *The State of Deseret*, 27. This study is still the best on Mormon efforts to reach an accommodation with the United States on an early form of government in Utah. The word, Deseret, comes from *The Book of Mormon* and means "honey bee."

In the meantime, however, Mormon leaders apparently became fearful that this approach might lead to the appointment of carpetbaggers to territorial positions rather than the officers they had proposed. To head off this possibility, they decided to go ahead and create a new nation-state of their own without the approval of Congress. Their apparent purpose was to present national lawmakers with a fait accompli, a functioning government with officers in place that would require only ratification.

In keeping with this plan, they established in March 1849 "a free and independent government,"[6] called the State of Deseret, to stand until Congress should admit the new Mormon entity into the Union. As later events would show, Deseret was simply another name for the Kingdom of God.

Its constitution, patterned after similar American documents, specified that "it is a fundamental principle in all Republican Governments, that all political power is inherent in the People; and Governments instituted for their protection, security and benefit, should emanate from the same."[7] But this charter was in fact intended as a cover for the theocratic apparatus behind it that truly governed.

For example, the constitution of Deseret provided that elections for a legislative body and other officers would be held on May 7, 1849, but this election had been mapped out and officers chosen even before the constitutional convention met. In an open election held on March 12 in the bowery, Brigham Young was approved without opposition as governor and other officers were unanimously elected by 675 votes.

A new nation about twice the size of Texas with a seaport at San Diego was modestly staked out by fewer than ten thousand settlers. The limits of Deseret from east to west reached from the Rocky Mountain divide, west of present Denver, to the crest of the Sierra Nevada in California. From north to south, they extended from the Wind River Mountains of Wyoming to the Gila River in southern Arizona. And they encompassed all or parts of the future states of Utah, Nevada, Colorado, New Mexico, Arizona, California, Oregon, Idaho, and Wyoming.

At Washington, John Bernhisel admitted the claim looked a bit vast but pointed out "if land susceptible of cultivation, that will admit of a

---

[6]Ibid., 125.   [7]Ibid., 121.

dense population is taken into consideration,"[8] it was not as large as it seemed. The size by itself exposed Mormon designs for future expansion as missionaries went out to gather a rapid and growing inflow of Israel's children from the nations of the world, seen as Babylon.

On July 2 the General Assembly of Deseret, consisting of a Senate and House of Representatives, convened for the first time. No one knows for sure how its members were chosen since no record of an election on the date designated by the constitution, May 7, or any another day, has ever been found. The next day the House resolved to "memorialize the Congress of the United States, for a State or Territorial Government." This soon became a petition for admission "into the Union on an equal footing with other States; or such other form of civil government as your wisdom may award." Finally, Brigham Young advised Apostle Orson Hyde at Kanesville, Iowa, now Council Bluffs, "we have continued to agitate this question" until it became a memorial for "admission as a sovereign and Independent state into the Union upon an equal footing with the original States."[9]

Elected delegate to Congress by Deseret lawmakers was Council of Fifty member Almon W. Babbit, who left Great Salt Lake City late in July to present to Congress the newest petition, now a request for full statehood. The original bid for a territorial government was quietly shelved and never introduced.

No sooner had U.S. Senator Stephen A. Douglas of Illinois introduced the latest memorial than unexpected opposition appeared in the form of William Smith, brother of the faith's slain prophet, who introduced a counter memorial to oppose Deseret's bid. Smith alleged that Young's followers, before leaving Nauvoo, had taken an oath to "avenge the blood of Joseph Smith upon this nation, and so teach your children; and that you will from this day henceforth and forever begin and carry out hostility against this nation, and keep the same a profound secret now and ever."[10]

---

[8]Ibid., 85.

[9]Ibid., 30–39.

[10]"Remonstrance of William Smith, et al., of Covington, Kentucky, against the admission of Deseret into the Union," House Misc. Doc. 43 (31–1), 1850, Serial 581. Smith's charge appeared to fulfill a prediction by Apostle Kimball at Nauvoo that "a charge of treason would be brought against [the Twelve] for swearing us to avenge the blood of the anointed ones, and some one would reveal it." See Smith, ed., *An Intimate Chronicle: The Journals of William Clayton*, 223.

This sensational charge, like all of the indecision and maneuvering, had little bearing on the outcome. Preoccupied by the issue of slavery, Congress under Henry Clay's Compromise of 1850 reduced sharply Deseret's land area and created in September that year a new territory, named after its native American inhabitants.[11] U.S. Senator Thomas Benton of Missouri said he thought the name Deseret, so dear to the builders of Zion, sounded to him a little too much like "desert."

UTAH TERRITORY

Even after being cut back, the new territory still covered more than 220,000 square miles, which made it some two and a half times larger than the state of Utah today. Its original borders encompassed today's state of Nevada, except the southern tip, all of present Utah, the western slope of Colorado, and southwestern Wyoming, including Fort Bridger and today's Evanston.

Formation of Utah Territory ended the visible existence of one of the most unusual governments ever created within the United States, although its founders would try for years to resurrect it. When the corner stones of the Salt Lake Temple were laid in 1853, the "Deseret National Flag," a blue-and-white banner with stripes and twelve stars encircling a single large star, "was unfurled to the breeze."[12] And Deseret would reappear during the Civil War in the form of a ghost government. But its brief life span, 1849–50, would be the closest Mormon leaders ever came to realizing the dream of empire and independence under the universal kingdom of heaven.

An observer who lived in Deseret during this period said its people called their form of government a "Theo-Democracy," seeing no conflict between rule by God, from the top down, and government of the people, from the bottom up. Instead, he said, "they stand as the Israelites of old under Moses."[13] On hearing the word of the Lord from

---

[11]To avoid civil war, Congress in 1850 agreed to admit California into the Union as a free state, create Utah and New Mexico as territories without mention of slavery and, among other terms of the compromise, assume the debt incurred by Texas during the time it stood as a republic.

[12]"Minutes of the General Conference," *Deseret News*, April 16, 1853, 2.

[13]Gunnison, *The Mormons, or Latter-day Saints, in the valley of the Great Salt Lake*, 23.

their prophet, "all the people shall say, Amen."[14] The system would continue under a different name.

In a welcome sign that divine providence still watched over Zion, Brigham Young in 1850 was named to a four-year term as the first governor and superintendent of Indian affairs of Utah Territory.[15] Returning the favor, the territorial legislature the following year gave the last name of the president who made this appointment to Utah's first capital, Fillmore, a city then unbuilt, and went a step further to bestow his first name, Millard, on the county.[16]

Mormon lawmakers also declared "legal and in full force and virtue" earlier ordinances they had already enacted while serving as the General Assembly of Deseret, and passed some new ones. For a better understanding of early Utah society, a number of these merit a closer look, including a few that might appear worthy of consideration in the present day. For example, physicians were ordered not to administer any "drugs, medicines, and other preparations," without explaining their treatment in "plain, simple, English language" to "the patient, and surrounding friends and relatives, such as father, mother, husband, wife, children, guardian, or others as the case may be," or suffer the consequences. Any physician who violated this law could go to jail for "not less than one year" and pay a fine of $1,000.[17]

If this penalty seemed harsh treatment, equally strong was Mormon distrust of doctors who prescribed gentile medicines. At that time, customary therapies were quinine for fever, laudanum for pain and loose bowels, and the "cure-all" of the day, calomel, a mercurial purgative, for just about everything else. Perhaps at least as effective were the mild herbs and the gift of healing, as bestowed by the laying on of hands, on which the Mormons relied to cure whatever ailed them.

---

[14]Dt. 27:15–25.

[15]Other appointees were Broughton D. Harris of Vermont, secretary; Joseph Buffington of Pennsylvania, chief justice (who did not take office); Perry C. Brocchus of Alabama and Zerubbabel Snow of Ohio, a Mormon, associate justices; Seth M. Blair of Utah, U.S. attorney; and Joseph L. Heywood of Utah, a Council of Fifty member, U.S. marshal. Of the seven, four were Mormons.

[16]Settlers in 1855 finished the south wing of the statehouse and lawmakers that December convened for the only session held in the building, which was never completed. A year later, Great Salt Lake City became territorial capital. The wing of the original capitol can be seen at Fillmore where it serves as a museum.

[17]See Morgan, *The State of Deseret*, 175–80.

In a society where perfect justice was divinely revealed, an even higher level of suspicion, if not outright contempt, was held for lawyers and manmade ordinances of any kind. The Legislative Assembly in 1854 ruled that no laws not approved by themselves and the governor could be "read, argued, cited, or adopted" in any court. It also enacted that "no report, decision, or doings of any court" could be "read, argued, cited, or adopted as precedent in any other trial."[18] This eliminated the two standard foundations of American justice—legal precedence and English common law.

Further ensuring peace in the courtroom was an act which specified that "no person employing counsel in any court of the Territory shall be compelled by process of law to pay the counsel so employed for any services rendered." Moreover, a lawyer was obliged by law to tell everything he knew, "whether it helps his client, or not," or pay a fine of $100, or be clapped in jail at the whim of the judge for the term of the court, however long that might be.[19]

ELECTION LAW

Fundamental to the operation of the theocratic government that existed in Utah was the election law, which remained in force in the territory for more than a quarter-century. Section 5 set forth the following procedure:

"Each elector shall provide himself with a vote containing the names of the persons he wishes elected, and the offices he would have them fill, and present it neatly folded to the judge of election, who shall number and deposit it in the ballot box; the clerk shall then write the name of the elector, and opposite it the number of his vote."[20]

Hardly any wonder was it that John Bernhisel, candidate for delegate to Congress, won every one of the 1,259 votes cast in the first territor-

---

[18]*Acts, Resolutions and Memorials, Passed at the Several Annual Sessions of the Legislative Assembly of The Territory of Utah, from 1851 to 1870 Inclusive*, 32.

[19]Consistent with his religious beliefs was the disdain Brigham Young held for lawyers. In 1865 he said: "When a lawyer comes into the church, if he happens to have a little common sense left, and will take to plough-ing and cultivating the soil, there is a chance for him to make a man of himself; but if he follows his former customs and habits, the chances are against him, he may ruin himself, lose the Spirit of the Lord, if he ever possessed it, and go back into midnight darkness." See Brigham Young, June 18, 1865, *Journal of Discourses*, 11:125.

[20]*Acts, Resolutions and Memorials, Passed at the Several Annual Sessions of the Legislative Assembly of the Territory of Utah*, 89, 90.

ial election on August 4, 1851, as did the favored aspirants for other offices. Two years later, Dr. Bernhisel was opposed by a single vote from an uninformed resident who cast his ballot for Jedediah M. Grant, then mayor of Great Salt Lake City.

If a few always failed to get the word, even in a theocracy, there would not be enough of them to make any difference. A study of eighteen elections from 1852 to 1870 found that 96 percent of the 96,107 votes cast during this period went to the church ticket, a percentage that goes up to 97.4 when known non-Mormon ballots are discounted.[21] And from 1847 to 1874, not one candidate chosen in advance by Mormon leaders failed to win election.[22]

The absence of a secret ballot, a carry-over from Missouri and Nauvoo, safeguarded revealed truth and the destiny of the kingdom against human selfishness or folly. But as in the faith's earlier history, it was to prove a source of discontent among the faithful and of continuing conflict with non-Mormons who did not share the majority's confidence in the political rulings of inspired men who professed to speak for God.

To ensure legal supremacy, territorial lawmakers created probate courts on the county level whose judges were appointed by the governor and themselves, later vesting them with both civil and criminal jurisdiction. Average citizens were told to stay away from district courts, created by the territory's federal organic act, which dispensed traditional justice under appointed judges, usually outsiders.

Mormon bishops, unanimously elected justices of the peace early in 1849, soon found themselves adjudicating without benefit of custom or precedent the disputes of the flood of quarrelsome gold seekers who later that year began to pour through Salt Lake Valley. They usually did so with common sense and good judgment, but not all litigants were pleased with the treatment they received under a system that dispensed justice by inspiration.

Some 115 emigrants, forced by the lateness of the season or lack of resources to stay in Utah over the winter of 1849–50, later charged that Mormon legal proceedings were "informal, illegal, and unjust." Alleging that California-bound emigrants were put away "by shooting, strangling, beheading, drowning," under an "unfair and loaded court system,"

---

[21]Ivins, The Moses Thatcher Case, 3.
[22]Jack, "Utah Territorial Politics: 1847–1876."

they petitioned Congress to abolish the territorial government and replace it with military rule.[23]

The peculiar nature of Mormon justice was further pointed up by Utah's first capital punishment law under which the condemned enjoyed a choice among three methods of execution—shooting, hanging, or beheading. The latter option apparently related to the doctrine of blood atonement which held that some sins, not covered by Christ's sacrifice, could only be atoned by the shedding of the offender's own blood.[24]

PERPETUAL IMMIGRATION

To create a large and growing population, Mormon lawmakers established the Perpetual Emigrating Fund to "promote, facilitate and accomplish the emigration of the poor."[25] As missionaries called Israel's children out of the nations, the revolving fund advanced the money or resources they needed to gather to Zion. Within ten years, foreign-born newcomers, mainly from Great Britain and northern European countries, would make up about one third of Utah's population.

As companies arrived over the Mormon Trail from the east, other wagon trains rolled out from Salt Lake Valley to plant new colonies to the north, west, and south. Like Great Salt Lake City, each was a rough copy of Joseph Smith's mile-square plan for the City of Zion and carried out the prophet's dictum to "lay off another [Zion square] and so fill up the world in these last days."[26] The communal beehive design became the pattern for Bountiful and Farmington, established in 1848, Kaysville in 1849, Brigham City in 1850, and other northern cities and towns. To the west, Tooele and Grantsville were founded in 1849. In Sanpete Valley, the towns of Manti, Spring City (now a historic district), Mt. Pleasant, and Ephraim were settled from 1849 to 1852.

A string of settlements sprang up along the route to southern California, including Provo in 1849; Lehi, Pleasant Grove, American Fork, Springville, Payson, and Spanish Fork, all in 1850; and Nephi, Fillmore, Parowan, and Cedar City in 1851. More distant colonies included Mor-

---

[23]Slater, *Fruits of Mormonism or A Fair and Candid Statement of Facts Illustrative of Mormon Principles, Mormon Policy and Mormon Character, by More Than Forty Eye-Witnesses.* Slater's was the first book copyrighted in California.

[24]*Acts, Resolutions and Memorials, Passed at the Several Annual Sessions, of the legislative Assembly of the Territory of Utah,* 61.
[25]Ibid., 111–12.   [26]Smith, *History of the Church,* I:356–57.

mon Station on the Carson River, now Genoa, the oldest settlement in Nevada, founded in 1850, and San Bernardino, California, established a year later.

At each location, male settlers between ages 18 and 45 were enrolled for compulsory training in the theocracy's military arm, known as the Nauvoo Legion or the Militia of Utah Territory. Patterned after the earlier command in Illinois and drilled regularly, this force grew by 1857 to some 7,500 men, far more than required for defense against Great Basin tribes. Its top officer, like Joseph Smith, held the rank of lieutenant general.[27]

LAND OWNERSHIP

Since the lands of the kingdom belonged to God, none of the vast domain protected by this growing military power was considered privately or publicly owned. But even the most devoted believers at times found it hard to keep in mind that the land they tilled and built their houses on was not really their own.

"How long have we got to live before we find out . . . that all belongs to the Father in heaven," Brigham Young reminded them, "that these mountains are his; the valleys, the timber, the water, the soil."[28] Parcels were assigned to settlers as inheritances, which they could keep as long as they were good stewards and were faithful to the church.

However strongly held, this communal doctrine ran squarely counter to the policies of a nation that would sell off at bargain prices some two-thirds of its public domain during the nineteenth century. All it took for any citizen to acquire 160 acres was clearance of Indian rights and an official survey to establish a base line and meridian and divide the land into thirty-six-square-mile townships, one mile-square (640-acre) sections, and quarter-section homesteads as allowed by federal land laws. The process suggested that federal surveyors would not be welcome in Zion.

The first to find this out was Capt. Howard Stansbury of the U.S. Topographical Engineers. The 43-year-old civil engineer came to Utah with an expedition in 1849 to survey the valleys of Great Salt Lake and

---

[27]Ibid., 4; 293-95.
[28]Brigham Young, "Consecration," *Journal of Discourses*, 2:298–308.

Utah Lake as ordered by Col. John J. Abert, chief of the Corps of Topographical Engineers. Congress wanted to learn more about the region recently acquired from Mexico.

On his approach Stansbury heard rumors that the Mormons feared his survey "of their country" was to be made "in the same manner that other public lands are surveyed, for the purpose of dividing it into townships and sections." He was further advised "they would never permit any survey of their country to be made" and, if he pushed ahead, "my life would scarce be safe."[29]

Though he shrugged off such threats, the U.S. Army officer wisely called at once on Brigham Young to outline the purpose of his mission and explain how his survey of the region would benefit Mormon colonizers. A mollified Young gave his support to the project, but sent Council of Fifty member Albert Carrington, a graduate of Dartmouth College, to go as a member of Stansbury's staff, probably to keep an eye on the federal mapmakers.

Among other observers to note that "nobody but Mormons can hold property in Salt Lake City" was Solomon Carvalho, a Jewish artist who came to Utah in 1854 with John C. Frémont. "The moment they leave or apostatize," he said, "they are obliged to abandon their property, and are precluded from selling it."[30]

Methods used to keep gentiles or dissenters from owning land in the kingdom were both ingenious and effective. Control of creeks and canyons was given by law to trusted leaders, usually Council of Fifty members, who presided as stewards over these resources. To Brigham Young went all of City Creek Canyon with its water and timber. In an agricultural economy and desert climate, the availability of water decided what land was valuable and what was not worth having.

Another device took advantage of a provision in federal land laws that excluded any claim on land within the limits of a city or town. Territorial lawmakers made the corporate limits of their settlements large enough to enclose water resources and encompass all of the arable land

[29]Stansbury, *Exploration and Survey of the Valley of the Great Salt Lake of Utah, including a Reconnaissance of a New Route through the Rocky Mountains*, 84–86. For the definitive work on this important chapter in Utah history, see Madsen, ed., *Exploring The Great Salt Lake: The Stansbury Expedition of 1849–50*.

[30]Carvalho, *Incidents of Travel and Adventure in the Far West; with Col. Fremont's Last Expedition*, 142–43.

[31]*Acts, Resolutions and Memorials, Passed at the Several Annual Sessions of the Legislative Assembly of the Territory of Utah*, 138–41.

in the area. The city limits of Fillmore in 1852, as one illustration, encompassed thirty-six square miles, or nearly one square mile for each of its original colonizers.[31]

Control over property within a municipality was exercised under a law which required county surveyors to issue as "title of possession" a certificate of survey "countersigned by one or more of the Selectmen."[32] According to one early resident, unwanted persons, non-Mormons or dissenters, found it virtually impossible to meet these conditions and downright dangerous to try.[33]

If such ordinances kept outsiders out, equally effective were measures to keep the faithful at home in Zion. In 1854 Brigham Young reinstituted the law of consecration, given by revelation to Joseph Smith in 1831, which instructed church members to consecrate their properties "by a deed which cannot be broken" to the trustee-in-trust of the church, Young himself. And, continued the Lord, "he that sinneth and repenteth not shall be cast out of the church, and shall not receive again that which he has consecrated."[34]

The law of consecration was no more popular in Utah than it had been in Missouri, but those tempted to ignore it or take flight to the California gold fields could have their faith strengthened by an even sterner measure. An act of the territorial legislature "for the management of certain property," empowered probate judges to seize all property "left by any deceased or abscondent person" and turn it over to the Perpetual Emigrating Fund.[35]

Considering these laws, human and divine, the newly appointed territorial surveyor general who came to Utah in 1855 to survey the public lands before they were put on the open market was sure to find life in the Mormon kingdom exciting. David Burr's reports on what happened to him and his surveying crews were among the reasons later cited by President James Buchanan for dispatching a military expedition to Utah to enforce federal law.

[32]Ibid., 81, 82.

[33]See Baskin, *Reminiscences of Early Utah*, 164–72.

[34]Smith, *History of the Church*, 1:148–54. For the territorial law to implement consecration, see "An ACT concerning transfer of land claims and other property," *Acts, Resolutions and Memorials, Passed at the Several Annual Sessions, of the Legislative Assembly*, 92, 93.

[35]*Acts, Resolutions and Memorials, Passed at the Several Annual Sessions, of the Legislative Assembly*, 50.

THE DESERET ALPHABET

Old Testament ideas on land ownership and marked ballots were not the only indications that Utah's earliest settlers were bent on creating a society altogether unlike the rest of the country. Soon after arriving in the Great Basin they even undertook to create a new method to write the English language.

In 1854 the University of Deseret, predecessor of the University of Utah, introduced the Deseret Alphabet, consisting of thirty-eight characters to conform with the basic number of sounds in the English language. The curious set of symbols was created by 39-year-old George D. Watt, an expert in Pitman shorthand and the faith's first English convert.

Aimed to reform the representation of the English language, not the language itself, the new phonetic system offered a number of advantages. First, it demonstrated cultural exclusivism, an important consideration. It also kept secrets from curious non-Mormons, controlled what children would be allowed to read, and in a largely unlettered society that included non-English speaking converts, eliminated the awkward problem of phonetic spelling. For such reasons, for nearly two decades Brigham Young pushed the new alphabet on reluctant followers. The church-owned *Deseret News* at Great Salt Lake City, Utah's first newspaper, published portions of its 1859 editions in the distinctive system. And the University of Deseret's board of regents at one time voted $10,000 to print text books in the alphabet for students in classrooms across the territory.[36]

Like the law of consecration, however, the Deseret Alphabet never achieved widespread acceptance, despite repeated attempts by Young to promote the system. On some things, the people of Utah quietly overruled their strong-minded leader.

EARLY CONFRONTATIONS

On most fronts, however, this new territory of the United States appeared obstinately out of step with the rest of the nation. So it was

---

[36]See Brooks, "The Deseret Alphabet," 99–102.

ᏝᎫᏕᏤ LIII.

ᎵᏘᎴᏁᎪᏘᏁᎬ.

Ꮑ ᎤᎤᎪ ᎫᏄᎪ ᎩᎧ ᎳᏘᏝ Ꮑ ᏡᎫᏘᏘ.
ᏁᎫᏕ ᏕᎤᏄᎫᏘ ᎧᏘ ᏝᎬᏇᎫᏘ ᏁᏘᏅᎬ ᎧᏘᏇᎫᏘᏘ.
ᏣᎫᎪᎫᏕᎫᏘ ᏘᏇ ᎳᏝᎪᏇ ᎫᏁ Ꮏ ᏇᎧᏝ ᎧᏘᏄᎫᎫᏄᏘᏕ ᎫᏁ ᎩᎧᏞ.
ᏇᏝᎫᏘᏇᏁᏘ Ꮝ ᏝᏝᏇ ᎫᏁ ᎫᏘᎧᏞ.
ᏄᏝᏇᏝᎫᎧᏘ ᏄᎧ ᏇᏁᏘᏕ ᎫᏁ ᏁᎧᎳᏘ ᏁᎤᎪ.
ᏛᏁᏝᎪᏘᏕ ᏘᏇ Ꮝ ᎹᏇᎪᏝᎳᎪ ᎫᏁ ᏁᎫᏕ ᏥᎪᏘ ᎧᏘᏇᎫᏘᏘ.
Ꮝ ᏘᎤᏅᏝ ᎳᎧᎪᎪᏕ ᎫᏁ ᎺᏇᎦᏞᎧᏘ ᎤᏘ ᏕᎧᏘ ᏕᏥᎪᏘᏕᏝᎪᏁ.
Ꮑ ᎧᏘᎲᎫᎫᎲᎫᎪ ᎧᎫᎪᎪ ᏘᏇ Ꮏ ᏁᏛᏝᎵᏘᎧᏛᏝ ᎤᏘᎫᏕᎧᏘ.
ᏇᏘᎲᏇᏘᎦᎫᏘ ᎺᎫᏝ ᏁᎪᏂᎧᏘ ᎩᎧ ᎵᏘᎫᎧᏘᏕ.
ᏁᎧᏕᎠ ᏄᏄᎪ ᎫᏁ Ꮝ ᏈᏇᏁᏘᏇᏇ ᎩᎧ ᏁᎪᏁᎠᎧ.
ᏇᎫᏄᏈᏘᎪᏝᏄᏕ ᎧᏛᏄᎫᎪ Ꮑ ᎦᏝᏝᏕᎠᎪ ᏘᏄ ᎩᎧᏇ ᎩᎧ ᏁᏘ ᏘᏄ
Ꮝ ᏡᏝᎫᏘᎪ ᎫᏁ ᏝᎪᏘᎴᎪ.
ᏇᎫᎤᎫᏝᏘᏄᎪᏕ ᎵᏘᎧᏇᎧᎤᏕ ᏡᎫᏝᏝ ᎫᏁ ᎦᎳᎫᏘ ᎫᏄᎪ
ᏕᎤᏘᎫᏘᏝ ᎫᏁ ᎧᎫᏄᎪ.

Deseret Alphabet, *Second Book*, 1868.

hardly surprising that federal officers, named by various presidents, would find themselves either in confrontations with local authorities or simply ignored with nothing to do.

When 27-year-old Broughton D. Harris, one of three non-Mormons appointed to territorial offices, arrived from Vermont in 1851, he brought with him the territorial seal and $24,000 in federal gold to pay the expenses of the legislature. The first secretary of Utah expected to oversee the census, required by law to apportion representatives, and certify the elections that year, among other responsibilities. Harris found that Governor Young had already apportioned the number of representatives by a census taken when Deseret had applied for statehood. The new secretary viewed the earlier count "so false and exaggerated that a correct census would have betrayed the fraud." And he considered the 1851 elections,[37] carried out under "the provisional laws of the State of Deseret," nothing more than "a burlesque upon the order and decorum required by the organic act."[38]

Newly appointed district judges found equally irregular the manner in which Young had been sworn in as territorial governor. Expecting to administer the oath of office himself, Chief Justice Lemuel G. Brandebury, also a non-Mormon, arrived in June that year to discover that a Council of Fifty member had beaten him to it. Daniel H. Wells, chief justice of the state of Deseret, had done the honors months before when news of Young's appointment had first reached Utah in an eastern newspaper by way of Los Angeles.

Controversy was further fueled on the fourth anniversary of the Mormon entry into Salt Lake Valley, July 24, 1851, when Wells censured the national government for requiring the enlistment of the Mormon Battalion in 1846 during the War with Mexico. To impose such a levy, he reportedly said, "could have no other object in view than to finish by utter extermination the work they had so ruthlessly begun."[39] It was an old charge and outrageously untrue.

Not to be outdone, Young scorned President Zachary Taylor, who had died in office a year before. According to Associate Justice Perry Brocchus, a third outside appointee, the Mormon chief said the nation's twelfth president was "dead, and in Hell, and I am glad of it."[40] Such gusts typically expressed hostility toward the federal government and its

---

[37]In the first territorial elections on August 7, 1851, 1,259 votes were cast and all candidates were elected unanimously. See Jack, "Utah Territorial Politics: 1847–1876."

[38]"Report of Messrs. Brandebury, Brocchus, and Harris, to the President of the United States," House Exec. Doc. 25 (32–1), 1852, Serial 640, 8–22. One of the most important but neglected sources in Utah history, this report illustrates the causes of conflict on many fronts between the American republic and the Mormon theocracy during this early period.

[39]Ibid., 11. Wells simply repeated an earlier charge by Brigham Young that the enlistment of five hundred Mormons to serve in the Mexican War was part of a conspiracy by President Polk and U.S. Senator Thomas Hart Benton to exterminate the young faith as its members headed west into the wilderness. In fact, the president authorized the enlistment in response to Mormon appeals for aid "to conciliate them, and prevent them from assuming a hostile attitude toward the U.S." See Kenney, ed., *Wilford Woodruff's Journal*, 3:240–41; Tyler, *A Concise History of the Mormon Battalion in the Mexican War, 1846–1847*, 351–55; and Quaife, ed., *The Diary of James K. Polk during His Presidency, 1845 to 1849*, 1:446.

[40]"Utah Officials' Report to President Fillmore," *Congressional Globe*, new series, 25:87, as quoted in Roberts, *Comprehensive History*, 3:520.

officers, on one hand, and devotion to the constitution of the United States on the other.

Speaking at his own request before an audience of some three thousand, Justice Brocchus a few weeks later attempted to reply and "correct erroneous opinions in regard to the Government," but only appeared to impugn the patriotism of his Mormon listeners. The reaction was explosive. Brigham Young rose to his feet and called the offending magistrate "profoundly ignorant, or wilfully wicked." He went on to refer darkly to the "cutting of throats."[41]

While the judge was undergoing this baptism, Secretary Harris, having concluded the elections that year were illegal, refused to hand over some of the $24,000 in his custody to pay the expenses of the legislature. At this, Governor Young called a special session of that body, which unanimously ordered the territorial marshal to seize the money. Harris blocked that move with an injunction from the territory's only arm that was not controlled by the governor, the Utah Supreme Court, made up of the three district judges.

Increasingly fearful but still defiant, according to his wife Sarah the young secretary told Young that he was leaving the territory, "taking the money with him—and that he should if need be, defend it with his life."[42] Joining him in flight were Chief Justice Brandebury, Associate Justice Brocchus, and U.S. Indian Agent Henry Day. They were the first of at least sixteen federal officers who would abandon their posts in Utah out of frustration, fright, or both, over the next dozen years.[43]

Harris returned the government gold to the assistant U.S. Treasurer at St. Louis and went on to Washington, D.C., where he and the two justices reported to President Fillmore on conditions in the Great Basin theocracy. They said they found Mormon leaders disloyal to the national government and in complete control of the "opinions, the actions, the property, and even the lives" of the people.

---

[41]House Exec. Doc. 25, 15.

[42]Harris, *An Unwritten Chapter of Salt Lake, 1851–1901.*

[43]In addition to Harris, Brandebury, Brocchus, and Day in 1851, they included Indian Agent Stephen B. Rose, also 1851; Secretary Benjamin G. Ferris and Indian Agent Jacob Holeman, 1853; Surveyor General David H. Burr, Indian Agent Garland Hurt, and Associate Justices George P. Stiles and W. W. Drummond, 1857; Chief Justice Delano R. Eckles, 1858; Governor John W. Dawson, 1861; associate justices H. R. Crosby and R. P. Flenniken and Indian Agent Henry Martin, 1862. Three others, Chief Justice Lazarus Reid, Associate Justice Leonidas Shaver, and Indian Agent Edward A. Bedell, died in office during this period.

"Their conduct shows that they either disregard, or cannot appreciate, the blessings of the present form of government established for them by the United States," they told President Fillmore. Avoiding offense, they said, they had stayed on the job "until the conviction was forced upon us, that to remain longer would be to forfeit not only our own self-respect, but all claim to the approbation of the Government that had honored us with its confidence."[44] Hardly novices themselves when it came to public quarrels, their Mormon adversaries fired back with professions of innocence and accusations of their own. The absentee officials were branded as "run-a-ways" and worse. If they had tried to be active "in the discharge of their duties," Governor Young notified the president, "all would have been well."[45]

Amid the charges and counter-charges, Fillmore or any other impartial observer would find it difficult to figure out where to put the blame. But there was very little new about the argument itself. If the faces and some of the issues were different, it appeared to be almost a replay of earlier quarrels between the Mormons and their neighbors in Missouri and Illinois.

POLYGAMY

An echo of such earlier conflicts was the charge, leveled by the runaway officials, that "polygamy, or 'plurality of wives,' is openly avowed and practiced in the Territory." The custom, in fact, was so universal, they reported, that "few if any leading men in that community can be found who have not more than one wife each." Nor was it uncommon, they went on, "to find two or more sisters married to the same man."[46]

Their report corresponded with the appearance of a new book on society in Salt Lake Valley by an even more respected authority. Lt. John W. Gunnison had lived in Utah while serving as second in command of the Stansbury Expedition in 1849-50 during the survey of Great Salt Lake. That many had a large number of wives in Deseret, the young officer wrote, "is perfectly manifest to any one residing long among them."[47]

---

[44]House Exec. Doc. 25.   [45]Ibid., 31.   [46]Ibid., 19.

[47]Gunnison, *The Mormons, or, Latter-day Saints, in The Valley of The Great Salt Lake*, 67–73. Gunnison's account of the faith's earlier history, drawn mainly from hostile sources, is of little value, but his personal observations of early Mormon society in Utah are perceptive and significant.

The authoritative tenet, known as celestial or patriarchal marriage, or plurality of wives, often had been denied in the past.[48] But it was becoming increasingly clear that the practice could no longer be covered up. Accepting the inevitable, Brigham Young called a conference of his followers at Great Salt Lake in August 1852, when the faith's leading theologian, Apostle Orson Pratt, publicly acknowledged the dogma and defended it on biblical grounds. Young himself then took the stand to explain how the revelation on marriage came about and "deliver a prophecy upon it." Said he: "It will be fostered and believed by the more intelligent portions of the world, as one of the best doctrines ever proclaimed to any people."[49] Few predictions have ever undergone a more severe or prolonged test.

The immediate effect of the announcement on polygamy was to reduce sharply church membership in Great Britain and other northern European countries by 1860. This in turn would check the flow of foreign converts necessary to build up the population of the Great Basin theocracy and sustain its claim of sovereignty.[50] In America the practice was widely regarded as a brazen affront to morality and a threat to public order. Over the longer pull the marriage doctrine, by whatever name it was called, would lead to the downfall of the political Kingdom of God as conceived by the first prophet of the faith and planted in the American West by his strong-minded successor.

---

[48]As recently as a year before the Harris-Brocchus-Brandebury blow up, Apostle John Taylor in a public debate in France had vigorously denied, possibly on semantic grounds, the practice of polygamy. At the time, he had at least six wives.

[49]See *Deseret News*, September 14, 1852, which includes the full text of the revelation to Joseph Smith on July 12, 1843. For one of the best works on this topic, see Van Wagoner, *Mormon Polygamy: A History*.

[50]See Smith, ed., *An Intimate Chronicle: The Journals of William Clayton*, L.

GEN. DANIEL H. WELLS.
Wells commanded Nauvoo Legion forces during Utah's
Indian wars and other military operations.
Courtesy, LDS Archives.

Chapter 3

EARLY INDIAN WARS

If we have to fight huraw for the fight
If it can be all good peace *amen.*
—Andrew Love

With a thrill of discovery, Brigham Young and his 1847 pioneer company pitched the tents of latter-day Israel on lands long claimed by someone else. The valley of the Great Salt Lake was then part of Mexican territory, but it also formed a no-man's land between two peoples who predated the Spanish in the New World and claimed the place as their own.

On the north as far as the Wind River Mountains of present Wyoming and along the Snake River of Idaho ranged mounted bands of the Shoshoni Indians, commonly called Snakes or Snake-diggers. South of the Great Salt Lake, stretching into western Colorado and northern New Mexico, was the territory controlled by the native groups collectively known as the Utahs, or Utes.[1] From their earliest memory, these tribes had waged sporadic warfare at their disputed boundary in Salt Lake Valley. Now there settled between them an American millennial movement that had never lived anywhere with its neighbors in peace.

How the controversial newcomers got along with the longtime inhabitants of the region is often summarized under the professed policy of Brigham Young that it was better, or cheaper, to feed the Indians than to

---

[1]Early Indian agents Henry R. Day, Garland Hurt, and Jacob Forney divided the bands within Utah Territory, known as Utahs, into the Timpanogos, or Lake Utes, who inhabited Utah Valley; Uinta Utes, found in northeastern Utah; the San-Pitches, centered in Sanpete Valley and points east; the Pahvants, based on Corn Creek, near present Fillmore; and Che-ver-ets, or Cheveriches, a widely ranging body of horse Indians, known as Walker's Band. Among the Utah bands, the agents included the Py-edes, or Piedes, who lived south of the Pahvants; and the Pah-Utahs, or Paiutes, scattered across wide areas of southern Utah and Nevada, but these groups were actually part of a separate Indian people called today the Southern Paiutes. In total, these natives probably numbered fewer than 12,000.

fight them. But early Mormon religious beliefs, pertaining to the natives of the New World, made relations between the older inhabitants of Utah and the white newcomers more complex and, at times, contradictory than this seemingly sensible dictum would suggest.

THE REMNANT OF JACOB

An essential Mormon scripture, *The Book of Mormon*, is the professed record of the family of a God-fearing man, named Lehi, who was led by God in about 600 B.C. from Jerusalem to the New World, just before the fall of the city to the Babylonians. In America, these Israelites of the tribe of Manasseh became divided into two groups, the Nephites, named after Lehi's righteous son, Nephi, and the Lamanites, descendants of his sons Laman and Lemuel, whom God cursed with a dark skin because of their wickedness.

The history of these two great peoples, prior to about 421 A.D., was allegedly preserved on gold plates that were delivered by a resurrected Nephite prophet, Moroni, to Joseph Smith. With the aid of the urim and thummim, Smith said he translated this ancient record, which was published in 1830. It tells how the Lamanites eventually destroyed their white cousins and went on to become the American Indians, a "remnant of Jacob" in the New World. Thus the natives of the Americas, including those in the Great Basin, and the early settlers of that region shared an important bond. Under Mormon belief, they were both descendants of Abraham through Isaac, Jacob, and Joseph and were brothers by blood.

Book of Mormon prophets foretold that Jacob's native seed in the western hemisphere would one day return to the faith of their fathers, build New Jerusalem, and become, once again, "a white and delightsome people."[2] To fulfill this condition of Christ's return, Mormon missionaries within months of the church's founding in 1830 had gone out to show the natives "what great things the Lord hath done for their fathers . . . that they might know the covenants of the Lord."[3]

All of which seemed innocent enough, as far as it went, but there was

---

[2] *The Book of Mormon*, 2 Nephi 30:6. In recent years, the phrase "white and delightsome" has been changed to "pure and delightsome."

[3] Ibid., title page.

an aggressive, and potentially explosive, corollary to this doctrine. For in the Last Days when Israel was gathered and Zion redeemed, foretold the prophet Micah, "the remnant of Jacob shall be among the Gentiles in the midst of many people as a lion among the beasts of the forest, as a young lion among the flocks of sheep; who, if he go through, both treadeth down and teareth in pieces." His warning, early Mormons believed, referred to their time. Moreover, it was repeated by Nephi, a *Book of Mormon* prophet, with the caveat "if the Gentiles do not repent."[4]

An 1846 patriarchal blessing to John Borrowman even included the promise that "when the remnants of Jacob [the Indians] go through the Gentiles like a lion among the beasts of the forest, as the prophets have spoken, thou shalt be in their midst and shall be a captain of hundreds."[5] Such promises hardly enhanced the comfort level of settlers who lived in lonely cabins on the Indian frontier when Mormon missionaries called on nearby tribes. Mormon contacts with Indians had been a source of trouble in Missouri and Illinois.

On the other hand, Utah's millennial-minded early settlers were driven by a burning sense of urgency to prepare the way for the Lord to come again in their own day. They had little time to waste on recalcitrant Lamanites who did not wish to give up their wild ways and be reformed into proper Old Testament figures. This opposing side of the picture was given by Brigham Young, who told Utah Valley settlers in 1849 that the older natives could never be saved, "but they will die and be damned."[6]

So the choice between "feed" or "fight," in fact reflected the opposite extremes of a policy that failed to admit a moderate or middle ground. As a result, Mormon treatment of the natives in Utah vacillated unpredictably between generosity so open-handed it imposed on white settlers a "most oppressive burden," according to one early Indian agent, and extermination campaigns that sometimes failed to discriminate between hostile and friendly.[7]

---

[4]See Mic. 5:8, and *The Book of Mormon*, 3 Nephi 20:15, 16. Also see Crawley, ed. *The Essential Parley P. Pratt*, 23, 24.

[5]Journal of John Borrowman, 1846–1860.

[6]Journal History, May 7, 1849.

[7]See Hurt to Manypenny, November 20, 1856, "The Utah Expedition," House Exec. Doc. 71 (35–1), 1858, Serial 956, 183. Also see Christy, "Open Hand and Mailed Fist: Mormon-Indian Relations in Utah, 1847–52."

THE UTAHS

Most affected by this policy were the peoples who inhabited Utah and Sanpete valleys and the Uinta Basin and from whom the state takes its name. For centuries, the Utahs had lived in scattered bands close to the fresh waters of Utah Lake, then one of the most productive fisheries in western America, whose waters yielded an abundance of cutthroat trout, suckers, chub, and whitefish.[8]

The earliest European explorers in 1776 had marveled as they watched natives catch fish in thousands by hand. The stable food source had enabled the tribe to employ horses, acquired from the Spanish, for purposes other than simply eating them. They used this new technology to become the haughty overlords of the Great Basin and to oppress lesser tribes.

Before Brigham Young's followers reached the Salt Lake Valley, the renowned mountain man, James Bridger, had warned them that the "Utah tribe of Indians are a bad people; if they catch a man alone they are sure to rob and abuse him, if they don't kill him."[9] A later U.S. Indian agent, a friend of the Utahs but a realist when it came to these natives, said there was "not a braver tribe to be found among the aborigines of America than the Utahs, none warmer in their attachments, less relenting in their hatred, or more capable of treachery."[10]

Especially abhorrent to settlers was the practice of Utah Chief Walkara, commonly called "Walker," and his mounted band of raiding their poorer Great Basin relatives to steal their children and trade them to Mexican slavers from New Mexico for horses. This destructive custom had driven desert natives along the Virgin River and its tributaries in today's southwestern Utah into such decline that they faced extinction.

Though baptized himself in 1850, Walker had been infuriated when Young as governor interfered with this slave trade. But this was not the main source of trouble. The southward thrust of Mormon colonization onto the historic hunting and fishing grounds of the Utahs made conflict inevitable.

---

[8]For more on this important, but neglected subject, see Janetski, "Utah Lake: Its Role in the Prehistory of Utah Valley," and Carter, "A History of Commercial Fishing on Utah Lake."

[9]Journal History, June 28, 1847.

[10]Hurt to Simpson, May 2, 1860, published in Simpson, *Report of Explorations across the Great Basin of the Territory of Utah for a direct wagon-route from Camp Floyd to Genoa, in Carson Valley in 1859*, 459–64.

FIRST FIGHTS

The first armed showdown came early in 1849, even before the white newcomers had pushed settlements into the tribe's Utah Valley home ground. On February 28 word reached Great Salt Lake City that a party of Utah warriors had struck Mormon herds along Willow Creek in present Draper. Following a little-known Indian trail over the low divide between today's Alpine and the southeast corner of Salt Lake Valley, the raiders made off with horses reportedly belonging to Young himself and some cattle. What happened next set a pattern for conflicts to come.

The following day a company of fifty, short nineteen due to cold weather and sickness, mustered at Great Salt Lake under Nauvoo Legion Col. John Scott and rode south to punish the offenders. As it went, the force picked up five volunteers on the road and heard word that Young's horses had not been stolen, after all, but to go ahead anyway.[11]

Nightfall on March 2 found the company at the Jordan narrows between Salt Lake and Utah valleys where they camped under lowering skies. The next morning in intermittent snowfall they divided into two groups, one to scour the Jordan River to Utah Lake, the other to search the upper reaches of Dry Creek Valley, near present Lehi, before moving on to follow American Fork to the mouth of the canyon, where they camped for the night.

The next day, March 4, they awoke under two inches of snow. Taking an early start, they continued south across Provo Bench to Provo River, where they met their interpreter, Dimick Huntington, and Mormon trader, Barney Ward, who had gone ahead to keep the Utah camps along the stream from taking alarm. The natives were fearful at the large armed party, but friendly. Little Chief, one of their leaders, identified the guilty natives and sent his own son to lead the Mormon soldiers to their camp.

After nightfall the pursuit began. The command moved up the river to the mouth of Provo Canyon, then north along the foot of the mountains to Dry Canyon, where they left their horses and sent scouts ahead on foot. They discovered the camp fires of their quarry in the willows along the river bottom at the mouth of Battle Creek Canyon, just below the present reservoir. As they called up the rest of the command, their

---

[11]For an eyewitness account of this expedition, see Brooks, ed., *On the Mormon Frontier: The Diary of Hosea Stout*, 2:344–47. Also see Huntington, Statement on Battle Creek Fight, January 1, 1862, MS 4085, LDS Archives.

young Indian guide lost heart and cried he did not want to see his friends die.

At first light, the two lodges of Utahs, some seventeen in number, found themselves surrounded by soldiers on high ground on three sides while a fourth party blocked any escape down the creek bed. Refusing bids to surrender, the Indians fought back with guns and arrows while other Utahs gathered on the mountain side and shouted encouragement to their besieged tribesmen.

Women and children, discovered hiding in the water under heavy brush, gave themselves up, including a youth of about 16. But Blue Shirt and Kone, also known as Roman Nose, the two leaders of the party, and two other males were killed in a fire fight that lasted some two hours. None of the soldiers was hurt.

The episode would be repeated in several noteworthy later encounters. Whether or not they had given up or chosen to fight to the death, as reported, the adult males in the party were doomed. At the same time, women and children were treated with utmost kindness and usually placed for upbringing in Mormon homes, where they sometimes stayed but more often ran away and rejoined their own people.

Years later some said the native youth who survived the fight on Battle Creek was Black Hawk, the Utah war chief who scourged central Utah settlements in the 1860s, but others denied this.[12] But it was certain that the first encounter between the military arm of the Mormon kingdom and the native inhabitants of Utah Valley gave the latter something to think about when it came to their new neighbors.

PROVO RIVER FIGHT

The memory of the confrontation at Battle Creek was fresh a month later when a mission sent to colonize the valley, some forty-six miles south of Great Salt Lake, was stopped by an excited Utah warrior several miles before it reached the Provo River. The party of thirty men under John S. Higbee had been sent to fish, farm, and teach the Indians. The warrior, Angatewats, blocked the trail with his horse and would not let them pass. Only after interpreter Dimick Huntington vowed by

---

[12]See Driggs, *Timpanogos Town: Story of Old Battle Creek and Pleasant Grove, Utah*, 19, 20.

uplifted hand that the whites would not try to drive the Indians from
their lands did the young warrior allow the party to go on.

The newcomers built Fort Utah on the Provo River's south bank,
measuring some 330 feet by 660 feet, on or near the site of the present
replica on Center Street and the Geneva Road about two miles west of
downtown Provo. The fort featured a log stockade fourteen feet high
with log houses on the inside perimeter and an elevated platform in the
center where an iron cannon was perched to command the surrounding
countryside. That it was made for defense was obvious to the natives
who watched with growing alarm the intruders plow the land and seine
fish by barrelsful in organized companies.

A nervous calm was broken by Mormon Battalion veterans Richard
Ivie, Jerome Zabriskie, and John Rufus Stoddard, all in their twenties,
who quarreled with a native called "Old Bishop." The trio blamed the
Indian for wearing a shirt belonging to Ivie while he accused them of
poaching deer on Utah hunting ground.[13] They shot Old Bishop dead
to settle the argument. To cover up the crime, they eviscerated his body,
filled its abdominal cavity with rocks, and sank his remains in the Provo
River. But the stream was shallow, the current strong, and Old Bishop
refused to stay down.[14]

After his body was found, any hope of accommodation with the
Utah tribe was gone. Angry natives shot Mormon cattle with arrows,
stole horses with impunity, and threatened anyone who wandered
much beyond rifle range from the stockade. Almost as menacing was
an outbreak of measles in the tribe that made its members unwelcome
at the fort. Increasingly fearful, settlers by early 1850 appealed to
Brigham Young for military measures to rid them of the troublesome
Utahs.

Reluctant at first, Young called on Capt. Howard Stansbury, Corps of
Topographical Engineers, commander of the expedition to survey Great
Salt Lake, for advice. The U.S. Army officer did better than simply
endorse the action Mormon leaders had already decided to take. He also
supplied arms and ammunition and sent Lt. George Howland and Dr.
James Blake of his command to serve as military adviser and physician

[13]See Thomas Orr's story of this episode in Bagley, ed., *Frontiersman: Abner Blackburn's Narrative*, 153.

[14]A legend grew among the tribe that the spirit of Old Bishop arose from the river each year on the anniversary of his death and took out one of the rocks from his abdomen and dropped it into the water.

to Mormon forces.[15] The pendulum of Young's Indian policy was about to swing from the one extreme of feeding to the other of fighting.

On January 31, 1850, the top Mormon military officer, Maj. Gen. Daniel Wells, issued orders to Nauvoo Legion Capt. George Grant to march against the Utah tribe, "exterminating such, as do not separate themselves from their hostile clans, and sue for peace."[16] In sub-freezing weather, Grant's mounted force from Great Salt Lake, about one hundred strong, arrived on February 8 to join local troops at Fort Utah commanded by Capt. Peter W. Conover.

Moving out next day, the united force advanced less than two miles up Provo River before it ran into strong opposition from about seventy warriors under six-foot-plus Chief Big Elk, not far from today's Utah Valley Medical Center in Provo. The Indians made their stand behind a cutbank and log bulwark at a bend in the river and in a nearby abandoned log house built by settler James Bean. Heavy firing that day produced several wounded on both sides but no decision.

Again repulsed the next morning, the attackers took more aggressive action after young Joseph Higbee, son of one of the louder advocates of military action, Isaac Higbee, raised up for a better look and was killed by a shot through the head by a native marksman. A flying charge by fifteen picked horsemen, led by Lot Smith, William Kimball, and Robert Burton, followed by an infantry assault, finally dislodged the natives from the log house after a desperate fight. Wounded in his most prominent anatomical feature, as predicted, was 28-year-old Jabez Nowlan, whose wife had said if he was shot it would surely be in the nose.

Native defenders were further shaken by the appearance of a large brush-covered object that came slowly over the snow toward their position on the river. Built at the suggestion of Lieutenant Howland, the V-shaped barricade slid on runners and was hung inside with buffalo robes to slow any balls which penetrated its planks. Whether it protected anyone behind it or not, the apparition seemed to unnerve native warriors, who decided after dark on February 9 to abandon the field.

In two days of fighting, the Utahs had suffered only two or three warriors and one woman killed. But the body count for the tribe would go up sharply as the pitched battle quickly became a rout. Some of the fugi-

---

[15]See Madsen, ed., *Exploring The Great Salt Lake, The Stansbury Expedition of 1849–50*, 257–65.
[16]Wells to Grant, January 31, 1850, Utah Militia Records.

tives, including women and children, followed Big Elk across today's Brigham Young University campus toward Rock Canyon, pursued by Legion forces under Maj. Andrew Lytle, a former Mormon Battalion officer. At the mouth of the canyon the soldiers found Big Elk dead of gunshot wounds or measles or both.[17] The chief's wife, a handsome young woman, climbed the canyon wall to escape, but fell to her death, thereby giving Squaw Mountain its present name, according to legend. A few of Big Elk's band, not many more than a dozen, escaped to the Weber River.

Most of those who fled sought refuge in the Indian camps along Spanish Fork River, but they were closely pursued by mounted militiamen. Now under the direct command of General Wells, Mormon troopers on February 13 scoured the wickiups along the stream to Table Mountain at the south end of Utah Lake, where they caught up with the fugitives, killing five. That night, they put under guard fifteen or twenty warriors who surrendered with their families, but it appeared to Wells "they came rather through fear than otherwise and seemed not to give up."

"We shall deal with them in the most summary manner as soon as another day favors us with its light," the Legion commander told Brigham Young. What happened next is suggested by an addendum to his report, dated February 15: "Please to make some suggestion in relation to the disposal of some 15 or 20 squaws and children who probably belonged to some 11 warriors who met their fate in a small skirmish this morning."[18]

According to other reports, some of the natives tried to escape on foot across the frozen end of the lake, but were ridden down and killed, one by one, leaving a grisly trail of blood and bodies on the ice. Not to waste such a valuable resource, the Stansbury Expedition's British surgeon, Dr. James Blake, hired two militiamen, Abner Blackburn and James Orr, to cut off the dead natives' heads for research purposes. Reported

---

[17]The Utah tribe at this time was being decimated by an epidemic of measles acquired by Walker's band from the Navahos who caught the disease, in turn, at Mexican settlements. During his early exploration of southern Utah, on December 8, 1849 Apostle Parley P. Pratt met Walker and his camp "consisting of Men Women and Children, Cattle Horses and dogs" on the Sevier River. "Many of them and of the Indians South are Sick and dying of Measles," Pratt reported. "We visited Several Lodges this morn, and Laid hands on them after kneeling down with them and praying." Pratt to "Mrs. P. P. Pratt's," December 8, 1849, Family Correspondence, MS 14392, LDS Archives.

[18]Wells to Young, February 13–14, 1850, Utah Militia Records.

Blackburn, the job was not as distasteful as it might seem. The heads "were frozen and come off easy," he said.[19]

Unaware of this unpleasant episode, Brigham Young on February 15 welcomed as "cheering and gratifying" the news of the Legion's success "over your enemies yesterday morning, in which the courage and valor of the boys, as heretofore was manifested."[20] It would not be the last "skirmish" of its kind as settlements of the white newcomers took root in growing numbers in Utah and Sanpete valleys and along the southern route to California as far as the Colorado River.

Over five days, as many as forty Indians were killed or died from exposure, with an undetermined number wounded. Nauvoo Legion casualties came to one killed and several dozen listed as hurt in various degrees of seriousness. Notably absent from the fighting was the tribe's main war chief, Walker, who appeared at this point to prefer the benefits of peace with the newcomers.

The charismatic chief may not have known it at the time, but his choices had become strictly limited. This was laid down by Brigham Young, who approved the overall conduct of the campaign and added in final orders to General Wells: "If the Indians sue for peace, grant it to them, according to your discretionary judgment in the case. If they continue hostile pursue them until you use them up. *Let it be peace with them or extermination.*"[21]

As threatening to native inhabitants as this uncompromising directive was the appearance over the next twenty months of the new Mormon towns of Lehi, American Fork, Pleasant Grove, Springville, Payson, Spanish Fork, and Santaquin in Utah Valley; Allred's Settlement (Spring City) and other places in Sanpete Valley; Clover Creek (Mona) and Salt Creek (Nephi), some eighty miles south of Salt Lake; and Fillmore in central Utah. To these and other new locations came a steady flow of settlers.

Meanwhile Young's order included a curious directive:

> We will not suffer Indians, who are known to be hostile, and have come into your possession, because they were sick and could not fight, to want for any thing, neither suffer them to go free until they are cured. Your Surgeon,

---

[19]For the best account of this episode, see Bagley, ed., *Frontiersman: Abner Blackburn's Narrative,* 170.
[20]Young to Wells, February 14–15, 1850, Utah Militia Records.
[21]Ibid. Emphasis in the original.

Mr. Blake, is no doubt well provided with medicine, and will be ready to prescribe that which will effect that most desirable of all objects, *perfect health*.[22]

What the governor meant by this is not entirely plain, but Great Salt Lake blacksmith, William McBride, who played a leading role in the Provo River campaign, in 1851 suggested at least one explanation. As captain of a mounted company, McBride in June of that year caught up with native cattle rustlers in Tooele Valley, wounding two in a long range exchange and finding some fifteen freshly butchered cattle hidden in the cedars. In reporting the action, the captain concluded with this forth-right demand: "We wish you without a moment's hesitation to send us about a pound of arsenic. We want to give the Indians' well a flavour. Also a spade to dig for water. A little strickenine would be of fine service, and serve instead of salt for their too-fresh meat." He added an urgent reminder not to forget "the spade, strickenine and arsenic!"[23]

Whether his request was filled or not made little difference to the nine Indians killed next day by McBride's and other forces. It was neither the first nor the last time that the "better to feed than fight" policy really seemed to mean peace or extermination.

Earlier that year, a company under Orrin Porter Rockwell arrested some thirty warriors from an Indian camp in Tooele Valley for allegedly stealing horses. According to the Mormon lawman, most of the natives escaped after killing a non-Mormon member of his party, Ohioan Lorenzo D. Custer. But four who failed to make it "were sacrificed to the natural instincts of self-defense."[24] Peaceful relations were marred by similar isolated incidents, but no widespread fighting until 1853.

THE WALKER WAR

That year Brigham Young put a stop to the commerce in Indian children between the Utahs and slave traders from Santa Fé and Taos, but he won no thanks from Walker. On the contrary, the action infuriated the

---

[22]Ibid. Emphasis in the original. For other accounts of this campaign, see Bagley, ed., *Frontiersman: Abner Blackburn's Narrative*, 153–57, 169–71; Jensen, *History of Provo, Utah*, 45–60; *Provo, Pioneer Mormon City*, 54–61; and Christy, "Open Hand and Mailed Fist: Mormon-Indian Relations in Utah, 1847–52," 216–35.

[23]McBride Report, June 24, 1851, Utah Militia Records.

[24]See Tullidge, *Histories of Utah Volume 2: Northern Utah and Southern Idaho Counties*, 84. For the best account of this action see Schindler, *Orrin Porter Rockwell: Man of God, Son of Thunder*, 193–96.

unpredictable chief and thereby precipitated the so-called Walker War of 1853–54. The conflict was less a war in the customary sense than a series of atrocities by both sides, ambushes and mutilations by one and outright executions, sometimes billed as "skirmishes," by the other.

It began in April 1853 when Young, at the start of his annual tour of the southern settlements, was accosted at Provo by a heavily armed American from New Mexico dressed in buckskin. The stranger defied the territorial law, enacted in 1852, which restricted the right to acquire and rear Indian children to Mormons.[25] He menaced the governor and boasted that he had four hundred Mexicans and many more Indians at his command to back up the right to trade in Indian children. But he tried to bluff the wrong man.[26]

Within hours Governor Young announced on April 23 that Utah had been invaded by a "horde of Mexicans" who were "stirring up the Indians" and giving them "guns and powder" in violation of the law. His proclamation directed 31-year-old Capt. William M. Wall and a force of thirty men from Utah County to ride south to the southern settlements and hold "suspicious persons or parties." All Mexicans were told not to leave the territory until so directed.[27] Young then cut short his trip after visiting the new Mormon colonies in Sanpete Valley.

Aware these actions would enrage Walker, he sent 22-year-old George W. Bean off on one of the many hazardous missions performed by the Mormon Indian interpreter to find and placate the volatile Utah war chief. At the same time, General Wells alerted militia commanders in Sanpete and Utah Valleys "to keep a vigilant look out" and arrest any New Mexican traders who unlawfully furnished guns and ammunition

---

[25]See *Acts, Resolutions and Memorials, Passed at the Several Annual Sessions of the Legislative Assembly of the Territory of Utah*, March 7, 1852. The act specified that any white person within an organized county of the territory could acquire by indenture for a period of twenty years any Indian prisoner, child, or woman, provided "the master to whom the indenture is made" was found to be "a suitable person, and properly qualified to raise and educate" such natives.

[26]Mormon interpreter George W. Bean said the slave trader was named Bowman and that he was later "waylaid and killed by some Indians in Salt Creek Canyon." Mary Ettie V. Smith, then in good standing with Mormon leaders, identified the young American as New Yorker Wallace Alonzo Clark Bowman, with whom she became acquainted after he had been arrested and held in Great Salt Lake. She said the six-foot-plus Bowman was ambushed in Salt Creek Canyon by John Norton and James Ferguson who brought his body back to the capital in a wagon, where she saw his remains and cut off a lock of his hair, which she later gave to Indian Agent Garland Hurt. See Bean, *Autobiography of George Washington Bean*, 88, 89; and Green, *Fifteen Years among the Mormons: Being the Narrative of Mrs. Mary Ettie V. Smith*, 252–77.

[27]Young, Proclamation by the Governor, Territory of Utah, April 23, 1853.

to the Indians in exchange for "their children, to sell into Mexican bondage, for horses."[28]

For a time, the show of force, plus conciliation, seemed the right combination, and the peace held. Captain Wall arrested three Mexican traders at Payson, but elsewhere found little cause for alarm. The Pahvant tribe under Chief Kanosh, near Fillmore, was peaceful. At Fort Harmony, south of Cedar City, he found the Piedes "perfectly under the control" of Council of Fifty member John D. Lee, an adopted son of Brigham Young.[29]

But a nervous peace with Walker and his Utahs would be broken by one of the same family whose members managed to start two Indian wars and thereby earn a singular, if unwanted, distinction in the annals of the territory. Three years before, 25-year-old Richard Ivie had been one of the trio that killed Old Bishop and ignited the bloody Provo River conflict.

In July 1853 the wife of Ivie's younger brother traded some flour for fish with a wife of Shower-o-sho-a-kats, one of Walker's band, while Mrs. Ivie's husband, James, dug a well in the yard at their cabin near Springville, some fifty miles south of Great Salt Lake. When the male native disapproved the exchange and began beating his spouse in Ivie's dooryard, the settler intervened and a free-for-all ensued. With one blow, Ivie cracked the warrior's skull with the barrel of the man's own gun, then floored the Utah woman after she expressed her gratitude for his efforts on her behalf by hitting him in the face with a stock of wood.

The Utah warrior lingered in agony several days and then died. Even then the incident might still have been resolved peacefully if Ivie had agreed, as he was urged to do by the settlement head, Aaron Johnson, to compensate the tribe to the tune of an ox. But the stubborn settler, not one to take the blame for an act he felt was justifiable, stoutly stood his ground and refused. His pride would prove costly for both settlers and Indians.

On July 18 Capt. Stephen Perry, Lt. James Guyman, Sgt. Abraham Durfee, and William Hatch of the Springville militia rode out to find the Indians and negotiate a settlement. At Payson, they were joined by James McClellan, William Head, Nathaniel Hawes, and James Mangram, "all unarmed," and that afternoon the little party headed cautiously up Payson Canyon.

---

[28]Wells to Conover and Higgins, April 23, 1853, Utah Militia Records.
[29]Wall to Adjutant General, May 11, 1853, Utah Militia Records.

They found the Indian camp only two or three miles up the defile at a place known as "little Juab Valley." When the Mormon peacemakers came in sight, "the Indians raised the war whoop and the air rung with their horrid yells which would have appal[l]ed the stoutest heart."[30] Unable to retreat, the men swallowed their fear and rode straight into the heaviest crowd of natives, who had begun to argue over whether to kill them or not. As the excitement subsided, the Mormon emissaries talked with Walker and his brothers, Arapene and Tabby, who appeared to accept a proposal to allow Brigham Young to settle the dispute. But many of their warriors were dissatisfied and threatening, if they understood the agreement at all.

Later that day at Payson, 31-year-old Alexander Keele, whose family had come to Utah only weeks before, took over the watch at the gate on the southeast corner of the "fort," an enclosure of cabins facing inward. Just before dark, two Utahs mounted on one horse approached, the rear rider holding a rifle across his lap. Considered friendly, the pair was allowed to enter. Slowly they circled the inside of the stockade, and as they passed the gate to go out, the Indian with the rifle held it close to the guard and fired. With a cry, "Aleck" Keele fell, mortally wounded. It was an execution, a life for a life.

To the warlike Utahs, the killing of Keele may have satisfied tribal justice and settled the score, but to their white neighbors it was a declaration of war and a treacherous act that called for punishment. Express riders sounded the alarm to new settlements along the corridor from Salt Lake Valley to the rim of the Great Basin in southwestern Utah. Everywhere they found inhabitants complacent and unprepared to fight an Indian war.

At Provo, Col. George A. Smith, Nauvoo Legion commander for the Southern District, reported there were no more than fifty firearms in the entire town and "two men to each gun."[31] Nearly a hundred miles farther south, at Fillmore, "it took a day and a night," expressman Edson Whipple reported, to wake the inhabitants up to their danger. Ironically, the town was "in a defenceless condition,"[32] he said, from trading its ammunition to the Indians for buckskins.

---

[30]Perry to Ferguson, September 12, 1853, Utah Militia Records.

[31]Smith to Young, July 22, 1853, Utah Militia Records.

[32]Whipple to Young, July 23, 1853, Utah Militia Records.

In greatest immediate peril were the settlements in Sanpete Valley at Manti and Allred's Settlement, which were approached by a wagon road through rugged Salt Creek Canyon, a likely place for an ambush. Fearing the warriors in Payson Canyon would attack these locations by taking the Indian trail on the east side of Mt. Nebo, followed today by a Utah Scenic Byway between Payson and Salt Creek Canyon, Col. Peter Conover, commanding the military district at Provo, moved fast to raise a mounted force large enough to push through Salt Creek Canyon and head them off.

Without waiting for orders, the 45-year-old Kentuckian called out companies from Provo, Springville, and Payson and with 150 men covered the eighty miles to Manti in less than a day. He found conditions generally quiet in the valley, but a detachment from his command quickly changed all that when it attacked an Indian camp on Pleasant Creek, near today's Mt. Pleasant, killing six or seven natives who were probably not hostile. Unfortunately, the action came only hours before Brigham Young addressed a conciliatory note to Chief Walker.

"I send you some tobacco for you to smoke in the mountains when you get lonesome," Young said. Calling the Mormons "the only friends that you have in the world," he invited the unhappy chief to "send for some beef cattle and flour." Then he added a curious note: "If you are afraid of the tobacco which I send you, you can let some of your prisoners try it first and then you will know that it is good."[33]

As they tried to pacify Walker, Mormon leaders mustered all of their authority to shake their followers out of their complacency. As "First Presidency . . . Governor [and] Superintendent of Indian Affairs of Utah Territory and Commander in Chief of the Militia and Lieutenant Gen of the Nauvoo Legion," they told settlers on July 30 to "fort up" and protect their families and property. In ordering surplus livestock to Salt Lake Valley herd grounds, they said any who refused would be treated "as aliens and not Brethern as enemies and not friends."[34]

For settlers in Sanpete Valley, where Conover's force had been

---

[33]Young to Wacher, July 25, 1853, Utah Militia Records. This often-quoted note is in the almost-illegible hand of Daniel Wells.

[34]Young, Kimball, and Richards to Smith, July 29, 1853, Utah Militia Records. Since militia records during this period identify Wells as a major general, he apparently held the rank of lieutenant general under the State of Deseret. Brigham Young commissioned him a lieutenant general of the territory in 1855 and he was elected to this higher rank in April 1857 under a new militia law enacted that year.

unwisely withdrawn less than a week before, the advice was good but one day late. On July 29 as many as one hundred warriors swooped down on the herd at Allred's Settlement, seventeen miles north of Manti. They rode off with about two hundred head of cattle and horses, reported Maj. Nelson Higgins, Sanpete Military District commander, "nearly all the stock the post owned."[35]

Utah warriors on August 11 struck Mormon herds again, this time at Clover Creek, but were driven off after suffering several losses and wounding one militiaman. Four days later, they ambushed a party of four hauling wood at Parley's Park, present Park City, killing Englishman John Dixon, 35, an original 1847 pioneer, and 20-year-old John Quayle, Jr., from the Isle of Man.

Raid on Fort Bridger

When Brigham Young's 1847 company had met Jim Bridger on the Oregon Trail and asked about the suitability of Salt Lake Valley as a gathering place, "Old Gabe" had tried to discourage the people of the beehive from swarming in his backyard. He reportedly told Young he would give $1,000 for a bushel of corn grown in the Great Basin valley. He also apparently proposed the desert country along the Gila River in present southern Arizona as a good place for the religionists to settle. "If there is a promised land," said he, "that's it."[36]

While the Mormons ignored his advice, friction still continued between the unlikely neighbors. For one thing, Bridger's post on Blacks Fork took California Trail trade away from Mormon settlers. For another, Fort Bridger was the center of an unholy collection of mountain men who disputed the right of Mormons to operate the Green River ferries on the Oregon Trail.[37] These leftovers from the fur trade unwisely continued to intimidate Mormon ferrymen even after the Utah legislature gave exclusive rights to operate the ferries to Gen. Daniel H. Wells.

---

[35]Higgins to Adjutant General, July 29, 1853, Utah Militia Records.

[36]Bagley, ed., *The Pioneer Camp of the Saints: The 1846 and 1847 Mormon Trail Journals of Thomas Bullock*, 209–13.

[37]The main crossings were located at the mouth of Big Sandy River in today's Seedskadee National Wildlife Refuge, about thirty miles north of Green River, Wyoming, and on the Oregon Trail's Sublette Cutoff, near La Barge, Wyoming.

With the Walker War came an opportunity to resolve these differences with one stroke. At reports Bridger was supplying arms, ammunition, and whiskey to the hostiles, a warrant was issued on August 17 to seize the mountain man. Named "sheriff" to make the arrest was James Ferguson, the Nauvoo Legion's Irish adjutant general, reporting directly to General Wells. Making it all even more respectable, Young as governor issued a proclamation on August 19 forbidding any trade with the Indians without the permission of the superintendent of Indian affairs, himself.

That same day, Sheriff Ferguson and his "posse," three full legion companies, some 150 men in all, rode hard over the 110 miles to Fort Bridger to make the capture before Bridger and his friends found out they were coming. With Ferguson's command rode William A. Hickman, a reputed killer, whose very name struck fear in the hearts of the enemies of Zion. The force closed in but found its game flown. Jim Bridger had eluded too many Blackfeet war parties to be caught by a herd of militiamen thundering over the trail from Salt Lake Valley.

After seizing Bridger's trading goods, Hickman and the "posse" rode on to Green River where they finished their work by "shooting two or three mountaineers" at the ferries and confiscating several hundred cattle and other property.[38] Two years later, Mormon agent Lewis Robison would purchase the Blacks Fork trading post through Bridger's partner, Louis Vasquez, to settle the dispute, although Bridger to the end of his days claimed the Mormons stole his property.[39]

If the raid on Fort Bridger ended the confrontation on Green River, it did little to restore peace elsewhere in Utah, especially at Manti, where Maj. Nelson Higgins had always taken a hard line toward the destitute band known as the Sanpitches, led by Chief Arapene, Walker's half-brother. When a starving native was found guilty of killing three cattle during the hard winter of 1851-52, soldiers under the former Mormon Battalion captain "took him out a little north and shot him."[40]

The outbreak of hostilities in 1853 saw a replay of the New Yorker's uncompromising attitude when nine adult Indians, four men and five

---

[38]See Hickman, *Brigham's Destroying Angel; Being the Life, Confession, and Startling Disclosures of the Notorious Bill Hickman, the Danite Chief of Utah,* 91–93.

[39]See Gowans and Campbell, *Fort Bridger: Island in the Wilderness.*

[40]Journal of Azariah Smith, January 28, 1852.

women, and some children, came to the fort on September 13 asking for peace. Higgins ordered 42-year-old Capt. Gardner "Duff" Potter of his command to backtrack the natives and check their camp in the nearby mountains for stolen property. Potter's findings and his own interrogation soon convinced the major the Indians "were our most bitter enemies."[41]

Even so, he still tried to talk with them, he reported more than two weeks later, but one of the natives without warning turned on the settlement head, Isaac Morley, upon which "two of the guard immediately shot him down." When the other three males tried to escape, the major said, Potter's men opened fire and "brought them all to the ground."[42] But the truth was "the Indians were taken down the street and shot," said Manti settler, Azariah Smith.[43] "It was a sad afare [sic]," said Smith's father, Albert, "as the sequel will show."[44]

In unrelated incidents, normally friendly Pahvant Indians early on September 13 sneaked up on the corral at Fort Fillmore and shot William Hatton, 37, dead as he stood watch. Less than two weeks later a militia force under Maj. Stephen Markham, an original Utah pioneer who bore the scars of bayonet thrusts by mobs in Illinois, surrounded a small camp of Utah Indians south of Utah Lake and killed four or five.

Meanwhile one who would pay the price for the brutal conduct of Higgins and Potter at Manti was a 52-year-old Englishman who had more important things on his mind that fall than watching out for Indians. William Luke was expecting his three sons, Charles, 34, William, Jr., 19, and Henry, 17, to arrive in Utah from Manchester, England. And he could not wait to see them.

That was probably why he went with three others by ox team to deliver two wagon loads of wheat to the tithing house in Great Salt Lake. The party left Manti on September 30, expecting to camp at a safe place on San Pitch River, near present Moroni, and wait for a larger company with a militia escort, bound for church conference at Salt Lake, to catch up with them before attempting to pass Salt Creek Canyon. But they foolishly went too far and made camp at the likeliest spot for an ambush on the entire trail, Uinta Springs, at today's Fountain Green.

---

[41]Higgins to Ferguson, September 29, 1853, Utah Militia Records.
[42]Ibid.
[43]Journal of Azariah Smith, September 14, 1853.
[44]Journal of Albert Smith, October 1853.

At this scenic place, surrounded by willows and trees, the next day the main company came upon the overturned wagons, spilled wheat, and mutilated bodies of Luke, 60-year-old James Nelson, and William Reed, 47. Luke had been struck twice in the head with an ax, Nelson had his throat cut, and Reed had tried to run and been shot with his own gun. Maj. James Guyman and a militia company from Springville found the remains of 18-year-old Thomas Clark, a Canadian, buried under the wheat.

Burning with outrage, the larger party loaded the bodies in a wagon and proceeded to Nephi, where the venerable "Father" Morley, Anson Call from Fillmore (a former "Danite"),[45] and others plotted that night to take vengeance. They decided to kill the next day, Sunday, "all of the Indians that came to town."[46] Maj. George W. Bradley, Nephi militia commander, reported it as a skirmish, but a local settler from England, Martha Spence Heywood, told what really happened: "Nine Indians coming into our Camp looking for protection and bread with us, because we promised it to them and without knowing they did the first evil act in that affair or any other, were shot down without one minute's notice."[47] Nor was that the end of it.

Two days later, 39-year-old New Englander John Warner, part owner of the grist mill at Manti, headed up the canyon with young William Mills to get some wood when Indians "shot them boath dead on the spot."[48] When two warriors came to Warner's house, not long after, sporting the dead man's necktie and pen knife, his widow, Eunice, flew at them with a butcher knife but was restrained by her father.

In October, 25-year-old Ferney Fold Tindrell was surprised by Indians near the abandoned settlement of Summit, now Santaquin, while digging potatoes. So frightened was he that he ran seventy-five yards or so after being shot through or near the heart. His friends watched in horror as the natives waved his bloody scalp at them. In four months, his wife, Polly Lucina, would give birth to a baby daughter. Tindrell would not be the last to die before that bloody month came to a close.

---

[45]Bound by secret oaths, the paramilitary Danites were organized in 1838 to execute judgment on "apostates" and take vengeance on enemies of the Mormon movement in Missouri.

[46]Journal of Albert Smith, October 1853.

[47]Brooks, ed., *Not by Bread Alone: The Journal of Martha Spence Heywood, 1850–1856*, 97.

[48]Higgins to Wells, October 5, 1853, Utah Militia Records.

GUNNISON MASSACRE

John Williams Gunnison at age 40 was one of the U.S. Army's brightest ornaments. A devout Christian, he had taught school in New Hampshire before graduating second in a class at West Point whose thirty-seven surviving members at the start of the Civil War produced twenty-three general officers, both Union and Confederate. After serving in the Seminole War, he was assigned to the elite Corps of Topographical Engineers and named at age 37 second in command of the 1849–50 Stansbury Expedition to map the Great Salt Lake.[49]

Gunnison's work during these years had produced the first engineered map of Great Salt Lake and Utah valleys, which still offers the only source for the Indian names of watercourses in the region. He had also taken notes for a book about the Mormons in Utah, published in 1852, by far the best by an outside observer written during this early period.[50] While the young officer generally was considered a friend, Mormon leaders could hardly have applauded his book's revelations about the practice of polygamy, hitherto denied.

Now a captain, Gunnison returned to Utah in 1853 at the head of the Central Route Railway Survey after being chosen for the coveted appointment over John C. Frémont. Following the Spanish Trail, his expedition, including scientists, an escort of thirty Mounted Riflemen, teamsters, and others, crossed Green River on the line of today's I-70 and camped that October on the Sevier River at present Gunnison. At Manti, he hired as guides "Duff" Potter, the local militia captain, and his younger brother, William, before going on to Cedar Springs, now Holden, on present I-15.

After visiting nearby Fillmore, the new territorial capital, the captain on October 24 moved the expedition northwest to the Sevier River, near present Deseret, where he divided his command. Anson Call, head of the Fillmore settlement, later said he warned Gunnison about the Indian hostilities, although the Pahvant tribe in that area under Mormon chief Kanosh was considered friendly. The mapmaker also apparently feared no danger because he was a known friend of the natives in the region.

Taking a small party, including the expedition's botanist, F.

---

[49]See Madsen, ed., *Exploring The Great Salt Lake: The Stansbury Expedition of 1849–50.*

[50]See Gunnison, *The Mormons or Latter-Day Saints, in the Valley of the Great Salt Lake.*

Kreutzfeldt; Richard Kern, artist; Gunnison's black servant, John Bellows; William Potter, the Mormon guide; and eight enlisted men, Gunnison set out to trace the Sevier River to its mouth at Sevier Lake, some sixteen miles away. Before water was withdrawn upstream for farming and towns, the river wound through wetlands lined with willows and alive with waterfowl. Expecting no trouble, they made camp on October 25 in a low, exposed place on a loop of the stream.

That night a Pahvant hunting party moved into ambush position in the surrounding willows to take revenge for a crime earlier that month that Gunnison had nothing to do with, the killing of the war chief's father by the members of an emigrant train on the southern trail to California. At first light the next morning, just after Bellows had started the campfire, they opened fire.

First to fall in the volley as they stood warming their hands by the blaze were the cook, Kern, and Kreutzfeldt. Potter, 34, was killed soon after. At the first shot, the military escort jumped on their horses and took off. Even then, three soldiers died in the attack.

There are several versions of how Gunnison was killed, the most credible given years later by Mareer, one of the natives who took part in the ambush.[51] The captain was shot, he said, as he knelt by the river to wash his hands and face. When found, his mutilated body had fifteen arrow wounds. Indian stories said his heart was so full of blood and life when it was torn from his chest that it bounded on the ground.

John Gunnison was a national figure, engaged in a project of national interest, and the reaction to his death was immediate and strong. Many charged the Mormons were behind the massacre, an accusation that continues still today, but there is no convincing evidence or motive for such involvement.[52]

The captain's memory lives on in the names of cities and a county in Utah and Colorado, the Gunnison River (a main tributary of the Colorado River), Gunnison Island in Great Salt Lake, Gunnison National Forest, and more than a dozen other places. A vandalized marker on the

[51]Gibbs, "Gunnison Massacre, Indian Mareer's Version of the Tragedy," 66–75.

[52]The latest to imply Mormon involvement, although the author denies any such intent, is Fielding, *The Unsolicited Chronicler: An Account of the Gunnison Massacre, its causes and consequences, Utah Territory, 1847–1859: A narrative history,* the most detailed study. A more balanced, if less complete work, is Mumey, *John Williams Gunnison, 1812–1853, the Last of the Western Explorers: A History of the Survey through Colorado and Utah with a Biography and Details of His Massacre.*

river bend, five and a half miles west of Hinckley, Utah, on U.S. Highway 6, identifies the massacre site.[53] An attractive headstone stands over the only part of his body recovered, a single bone, in the Fillmore cemetery.[54]

INDIAN GRIEVANCES CONTINUE

Even before the topographical engineer fell, Chief Walker and his followers had driven the Mormon cattle they had stolen south to spend the winter on the Colorado River. The war chief's absence and the coming of the hunger season meant the only Indians abroad for a time would be hungry ones begging in the snow for food. As settlers built walls around their towns, the cycle of ambush and execution slowly came to close.

The following spring, Brigham Young on his annual trip to the southern settlements and Walker, returning to tribal homelands from the south, met in May at Chicken Creek, near present Levan, to make peace. The unpredictable chief agreed to accompany Young's party of 101 followers and thirty-four wagons to the southernmost colony of New Harmony, but resentment still burned deep in his heart.

A month later, Walker raged at Nephi whites and demanded they stop building an adobe wall around the settlement as Brigham Young had ordered. "We cant shake hands across a wall," he said.[55] He had given the newcomers "the privilege of settling on these lands . . . using land, water, grass, timber together as brothers," the chief ranted, but if they "fenced off their settlements, they would have to stay inside and the Indians outside."[56]

About that time, war was barely averted when one of Walker's war-

---

[53]Byron Warner, a member of the party from Fillmore that buried the remains, in 1888 guided Andrew Jenson, Dr. John R. Park, and David Allen, all of Salt Lake City, and LDS Bishop Joseph Black of Deseret to the massacre site where they planted a large cedar post. Thirty-four years later, Jenson led another party there and proposed erection of a permanent monument that was dedicated in 1927 by Fillmore affiliates of the Daughters of Utah Pioneers, American Legion, and Boy Scouts of America. It was unveiled by Edwin Stott, then 91, last survivor of the burial party. Defaced and broken down, this monument still marks the spot.

[54]For a century the bone of John Gunnison lay in an unmarked grave until the spot was identified by the Millard chapters of the Daughters of Utah Pioneers, who placed over it the memorial: "John Williams Gunnison, 1812–1853, Topographical Engineer, Explorer and Pioneer Martyr."

[55]Journal of Andrew Love, June 10, 1854.

[56]Bean, *Autobiography*, 96.

riors suffered the indignity of having "his weapons of death wrestled out of his hands & broke over his head" by 45-year-old Andrew Love at Nephi. "[Walker] feels to trample under foot the authority of Brigham," the Carolinian prophesied, "so Brother Walkers End is fast approaching."[57]

---

[57]Journal of Andrew Love, June 16, 1854.

U.S. Indian Agent Garland Hurt, known as
"the American" to the Utah tribe, escaped from
the Spanish Fork Indian farm and in 1874
became president of the St. Louis
Medical Society as shown here.
Courtesy, St. Louis Metropolitan Medical Society.

Chapter 4

THE KINGDOM SOVEREIGN

> Though I may not be Governor here, my power will not be
> diminished. No man they can send here will have much influ-
> ence with this community, unless he be the man of their choice.
> Let them send whom they will, and it does not diminish my
> influence one particle.
>
> —Brigham Young

To the Utah tribe he was known as "the American," a title that set
him apart in native minds from the white settlers of Utah, but his real
name was Garland Hurt, a 35-year-old devout Methodist and self-
taught physician, who came as U.S. Indian agent in 1855. His service
over the next five years would point up the importance of Indian relations in the early years of the territory and throw needed light on the
real causes of conflict between the Great Basin theocracy and the American republic.[1]

Born on a frontier farm in Virginia, Hurt attended Emory and Henry
College before studying medicine as an apprentice to a local physician.
He later moved to Kentucky where he practiced medicine and served in
the legislature. In what he called one of his life's greatest achievements,
he once amputated a man's gangrenous foot, having never witnessed the
procedure, using only a honed butcher knife and small carpenter saw.
Perhaps an even greater challenge came in September 1854 when President Franklin Pierce, a fellow Democrat, named him U.S. Indian Agent
in Utah Territory.

Characteristically, Hurt determined to "reach the field of my official
duties before winter sets in," but he underestimated the distance.[2] On

---

[1]For more on Hurt, see Bigler, "Garland Hurt, the American Friend of the Utahs," 149–70.

[2]Hurt to Mix, September 7, 1854, Letters Received by the Office of Indian Affairs, Utah Superintendency.

gaining the head of the Oregon-California trails at Independence, Missouri, he wrote to his new superior, Governor Brigham Young, the ex-officio superintendent of Indian affairs for Utah Territory, that he had been delayed by bad weather, but would come as soon as he could.[3]

When he finally arrived on February 5, he came with four mountaineers who carried the first mail of 1855 from the east. It included news that caused a "good deal of excitement through the City"[4]—President Franklin Pierce had named a U.S. Army officer, brevet Lt. Col. Edward J. Steptoe of Virginia, commander of a force then wintering in Utah, as the governor of the territory to replace Brigham Young, whose term had just expired.[5] Nor was this the only development that would affect Hurt's new assignment.

DEATH OF WALKER

Within weeks of his arrival, Walker, the troublesome war chief of the Utahs, died suddenly on January 28, 1855, at his camp on Meadow Creek, near the present town of Meadow, south of Fillmore. His death came just one day after a visit from Mormon Indian missionary David Lewis, who had given Walker a note and presents from Brigham Young. Lewis said the chief was seriously ill when he called on him.

Although Walker had been baptized a Mormon, he was buried according to the customs of his people for a noted leader. Two Indian women and as many as twenty horses were killed and placed beside the corpse in a burial pit at the base of a rock slide in the mountains to accompany his spirit to its new home. Two Piede children were tied alive next to the body to act as guides. After the corpse began to stink, the youths pleaded piteously to be let go, but passing natives refused.[6]

Lewis reported Walker's followers were "mad" and threatening to take Mormon lives and livestock at Fillmore as retribution for the chief's death, but he did not say why the tribe blamed white settlers for the loss

---

[3]Hurt to Young, December 1, 1854, Brigham Young Collection, MS 1234, LDS Archives.

[4]Kenney, ed., *Wilford Woodruff's Journal*, 4:304.

[5]Steptoe held the regular rank of major. He won brevet promotion to lieutenant colonel in 1847 for "gallant and meritorious conduct" in the battle of Chapultepec during the Mexican War. In September 1850 President Fillmore named Brigham Young to a four-year term as governor of the territory "unless sooner removed" by the president.

[6]For the possible location of Walker's burial place, see Kelly, "We Found the Grave of Chief Walker," 17–19; and Kelly, "Charles Kelly Discovers Chief Walker's Grave," 197–98.

of their charismatic chief.[7] The first task of Garland Hurt on his arrival was to placate the angry Utahs. At the same time, he was called on to assist Colonel Steptoe, who kept President Pierce's commission as governor in his pocket without accepting or rejecting it.

In April 1854 Steptoe had been ordered to deliver horses, mules, and replacement troops overland to army units being sent by sea, via Panama, to the West Coast. As he prepared to leave Fort Leavenworth, he received a further directive to stop in Utah and punish the Indians who had massacred Capt. John W. Gunnison and seven others the year before. The second order required Steptoe's expedition of some 175 officers and men, 130 civilian employees, and 750 horses and mules to winter in the Great Basin.[8] Otherwise the mission looked routine enough.

But on arriving that summer in Great Salt Lake, the colonel discovered the task he had been given was not only difficult but downright puzzling. Months after the massacre of his 1837 West Point classmate, the Pahvant perpetrators of the outrage had lived undisturbed under their Mormon chief, Kanosh, as if nothing had happened. The normally peaceful band of about five hundred, with a hundred or so warriors, was usually located in full view at Corn Creek, near Fillmore, right on the southern trail to California.

No steps had been taken by anyone in the territory, starting with the governor and superintendent of Indian affairs, to bring to justice the killers of Gunnison and his party. This inaction was especially striking because the colonel was invited, shortly after his arrival, to witness the prompt hanging after a short trial of two Goshute warriors who had been found guilty of murdering two Mormon youths, William and Warren Weeks, in Cedar Valley.

Steptoe that summer may have felt some interest in succeeding Brigham Young. If so, by the time his commission came with Indian Agent Garland Hurt, events had produced second thoughts about such a political career. By then, all he wanted to do was settle the Gunnison affair as best he could and leave the place where Brigham Young ruled, no matter who held the title of governor, and the exercise of justice appeared to discriminate between Mormons and other Americans.

Nor did his hosts want him to stay, as pointed up by brawls over the

---

[7]For this report, see Brooks, ed., *Journal of the Southern Indian Mission, Diary of Thomas D. Brown*, 162–63.
[8]For a facsimile of Steptoe's orders to punish Gunnison's killers, see Fielding, *The Unsolicited Chronicler*, 212.

winter of 1854-55 between as many as a hundred soldiers and Mormon youths on a side. A source of trouble, too, was the affair between Lt. Sylvester Mowry of Steptoe's command, an ardent womanizer, and Mary Ann Young, Brigham Young's daughter-in-law. So smitten was the 27-year-old officer by the pretty wife of Young's son Joseph, then on a mission, that he considered eloping with her until Young reportedly cooled his ardor by sending word he would have him killed if he tried it.[9]

Faced with a choice between using military force against the peaceful tribe or taking Governor Young's advice to parley for the surrender of the guilty natives, Steptoe to his later regret opted for the latter. George Bean, Young's trusted Indian interpreter, conducted the parley with Kanosh, a likely participant in the deed, while Agent Hurt provided presents as an inducement for the Pahvant chief to cooperate.

By the time Bean finished his work, the colonel had come to believe the Mormons were actively conspiring to protect the tribe rather than punish the guilty. Especially suspect had been the chief's offer to surrender one tribesman for each murdered member of Gunnison's party, minus one for the Pahvant killed earlier by passing emigrants, a total of seven. This proposed settlement reflected the tribal concept of a life for a life, not the purpose to identify and punish those who had actually committed the crime.

When Kanosh finally surrendered the allegedly guilty natives, now reduced in number to six for reasons known only to the chief, even Bean had to admit their appearance "shocked us all."[10] Two of the natives were so old they were blind, one was a woman, and three were apparently chosen because they were not in the Pahvant chief's favor. The colonel now knew for sure he had been fooled, but it was too late for him to start over.

THE GUNNISON TRIAL

The charade continued in March 1855 when U.S. Army troops, federal prosecutors, Indian chiefs and their followers, witnesses, and assorted observers poured into the little town of Nephi, some eighty miles south of Great Salt Lake, for the trial. Reflecting the gathering of foreign-born to Zion, some jurors had to come from other places

---

[9]For Mowry's boastful account of this affair, see Mulder and Mortensen, eds., *Among the Mormons*, 272–78.
[10]Journal History, February 21, 1855.

because Nephi could not provide the required number of naturalized citizens. "We have a real gentile crowd in our Midst," said local settler, Andrew Love, "& the Spirit appears to be spreading."[11]

But the "gentile" spirit did not spread to Mormon grand jurors under Jacob G. Bigler, the 41-year-old bishop of Nephi. When U.S. Attorney Joseph Hollman demanded indictments, Bigler's panel threw out charges against three of the Indians and drew up an indictment instead against Hollman himself for being drunk and abusive. Chastened, the federal prosecutor apologized, and the trial before the new territorial chief justice, John F. Kinney, 38, an eloquent but opportunistic politician, proceeded to explore new worlds of farce. Even federal visitors laughed when Chief Kanosh testified that he had not told the defendants to confess but just "threw them away" because George Bean told him to.[12] Several key witnesses were not even called.[13]

Watching the show was Agent Hurt, who acted as a physician in treating "a violent epidemic" among the Utah tribesmen gathered on the outskirts of the settlement to follow the court proceedings. He reported that several natives had died of the disease, possibly measles, including Chief Walker himself some weeks before.[14]

At the trial the most astonishing development came after the judge instructed jurors to choose between only two verdicts, first degree murder or acquittal. Ignoring his order, the panel found the remaining three Indians guilty of manslaughter, an offense only punishable by a three-year term in Utah's new prison. Kinney was outraged, but in a portent of his later career in Utah, he decided after thinking it over to go along.

"Our streets are once more Clear of gentiles & Thank the Lord," said Andrew Love, "beware of the leven of the gentiles, their atmosphere is poisenous to Mormonism." He reported some town gossip that U.S. Attorney Hollman and Judge Kinney's clerk had "visited [Chief] Ammon's Camp lay with his squaws & Caught the Clap & Then were not willing to pay their fare to friend Ammon. This is Gentile ism."[15]

If Love was glad the outsiders had left, he could have been no happier at the parting than the colonel from Virginia who had tried to bring the

[11]Journal of Andrew Love, March 19, 1855.

[12]Miller, "The Impact of the Gunnison Massacre on Mormon-Federal Relations: Colonel Edward Jenner Steptoe's Command in Utah Territory, 1854–1855," 182.

[13]Such as Anson Call, then bishop at Fillmore, and Mormon Indian interpreter Dimick B. Huntington, as pointed out by Fielding, *The Unsolicited Chronicler*, 257.

guilty Pahvants to justice. The duty had been "one of excessive embarrassment and annoyance to me," Steptoe reported. He called the jury's work "lamentable" but proposed no further action on the case. But he did recommend that a military force be located in the territory.

Later, in reporting that the convicted trio had walked away from the territorial penitentiary, he gave his opinion that Brigham Young had told the tribe "whatever number should be surrendered for trial would escape any serious penalty." He expressed regret that there were "citizens of our country so disregardful of their high obligations to the laws as many connected with this affair have shown themselves to be."[16]

Prior to his coming, Steptoe said, the Indians "had been taught to believe that the Americans were feeble in comparison with the 'Mormons,'" but had "learned from me for the first time, what position the latter hold in our great national family."[17] If this was some consolation, the colonel could have little doubt as to who was sovereign in the part of the republic known as Utah Territory. He departed without accepting his appointment as governor and left that office to its true holder, Brigham Young.[18]

THE INDIAN MISSIONS

On his first visit to Utah's native inhabitants, Garland Hurt found them "exceedingly destitute . . . and turned upon the white settlers to beg for their subsistence."[19] Bloodied by the Mormon militia, threatened by more advanced fishing methods, and displaced from the land around their Utah Lake food source, the once dominant Utahs were growing increasingly desperate and full of resentment.

To help the suffering tribe, Hurt charted a course between the extremes of feeding or fighting reflected in Brigham Young's policy

---

[14]Hurt to Manypenny, April 2, 1855, Letters Received by the Office of Indian Affairs, Utah Superintendency.

[15]Journal of Andrew Love, March 24, 1855.

[16]Steptoe to Cooper, March 26 and April 15, 1855, Selected Letters from Col. E. J. Steptoe, 1854–55.

[17]Ibid.

[18]Brigham Young was not reappointed as governor after his four-year term expired in 1854. He simply continued to serve in a kind of acting capacity under a provision of the 1850 organic act that allowed a governor to serve "until his successor shall be appointed and qualified," and President Pierce, for whatever reason, did not reappoint him or name a successor.

[19]Hurt to Young, March 1855, Letters Received by the Office of Indian Affairs, Utah Superintendency.

toward the natives. The agent undertook to teach the Utahs the arts of agriculture so they could feed themselves and come to rely on the produce of their own hands rather than the charity of white settlers. In return, he consciously determined, too, to win their loyalty for the United States. But before he got started, Hurt was surprised by a development among the millennial-minded settlers of Utah that directly affected his work and demanded his attention. The man to whom he reported as governor and superintendent of Indian affairs observed the twenty-fifth birthday of the territory's dominant faith by making a momentous announcement:

"Pres[ident] Young said the day has come to turn the key of the Gospel against the Gentiles, and open it to the remnants of Israel," reported one; "the people shouted, Amen, and the feeling was such that most present could realize, but few describe."[20] The moment had arrived for the "remnant of Jacob," believed by Mormons to be the American Indians, to hear the gospel of their fathers and return as foretold by Old Testament and *Book of Mormon* prophets to build up Zion before Christ came again.

To gather the native Americans known as Lamanites, some 160 missionaries were called at the April 1855 general conference of the church at Great Salt Lake. They were the first of many who would be sent to the Crows, Cherokees, Choctaws, Delawares, Hopis, Piedes, Shoshonis, Goshutes, Navahos, Bannocks, Paiutes, Utahs, Nez Perces, and many other north American tribes. This important millennial overture followed the work of some twenty-one Mormon missionaries who had gone the year before to the Piedes, or Southern Paiutes, on Virgin River and its tributaries in southwestern Utah. South of Cedar City, on the Colorado River side of the Great Basin's rim, they had built a fort and settlement named New Harmony. There they had gone out to protect the desert natives from the raids of their predatory kinsmen to the north and teach them to farm. In return, the Piedes had gone down to the waters of baptism by the hundreds.

For those called, the life of an Indian missionary was hard and at times dangerous, but it held out the hope of a great reward, said Apostle Orson Pratt, who reminded them of an earlier promise. According to prophecy, when the time came to gather the remnants of Israel, "then the lord should appear unto them" and to them "the face of the Lord

[20]Brooks, ed., *Journal of the Southern Indian Mission*, April 21, 1855.

will be unveiled."[21] One of the newly called missionaries summed it all up in fewer words. Said Lorenzo Brown before going to preach to the natives at Las Vegas Springs in the present Nevada city: "The Gentiles have rejected the truth & lo we turn to Israel."[22]

At all this, the newly arrived U.S. Indian agent was not favorably impressed. Firing off a confidential report to the head of Indian affairs, Garland Hurt said he believed the Mormons were encouraging among the natives a distinction between themselves and other Americans, "prejudicial to the interests of the latter." He urged that agencies be alerted nationwide to ensure enforcement of laws "to preserve peace on the frontiers."[23] His warning touched off a spate of reports over the next few years of Mormon tampering with the Indians.[24]

ELK MOUNTAIN MISSION

For those called, it was the worst of times to leave their families and go on an Indian mission. Plain for all to see was the specter of famine that lay that spring across Utah fields ravaged by drought and the voracious Mormon cricket. In 1848 flocks of California gulls had come just in time to save the crops from the destructive grasshopper. But in 1855 the black-shelled creature with an insatiable appetite had overwhelmed today's state bird and pioneer efforts to stop it.

Perhaps for this reason, not more than three dozen of the forty or more chosen turned out to establish a mission to the Utah Indians at the Spanish Trail crossing of the Colorado River, near Elk Mountain, now the La Sal Mountains, at present Moab. At Manti they assembled and voted to accept 29-year-old Alfred Billings from northeastern Ohio as mission president. The party that headed out on May 21 included fifteen wagons and enough seed grain, livestock, and equipment to plant a self-sufficient colony.

Over the next three weeks, they traveled some two hundred miles "over a barren wilderness and desert,"[25] following the Spanish Trail. From

[21]See Orson Pratt, *Deseret News*, May 16, 1855.
[22]Journal of Lorenzo Brown, April 6, 1855.
[23]Hurt to Manypenny, May 2, 1855, Letters Received by the Office of Indian Affairs, Utah Superintendency.
[24]For examples, see Bigler, "Garland Hurt, the American Friend of the Utahs," 156, n28.
[25]McEwan to McEwan, June 24, 1855, Journal History.

today's Salina, Utah, this historic route took them on the line of I-70 to Fremont Junction, then looped to the north of the modern highway to cross Green River near the present town of that name. It then paralleled U.S. 91 to the crossing of the Colorado River at present Moab.

In mid-June they traveled between walls of deep red stone, past today's entrance to Arches National Park, to reach the silt-laden Colorado River less than a mile downstream from the modern highway bridge. Crossing the river, they beheld a valley about two miles wide almost hemmed in by red rock cliffs as high as 1,500 feet but opening to the east to frame the white peaks of Elk Mountain, some fifteen miles away. It was a wondrous land they had come to "with high rocky bluffs, the soil is a fine red sand," said Mission President Billings.[26]

But little time was wasted admiring the scenery. They were rebaptized in the river and went to work with a will, making so much dust and smoke that a local Utah chief saw the "great smokes (from the boys burning sage)" in the north end of the valley and came down from the mountains to investigate, said William Pace.[27] Through their interpreters, Clark Huntington and John Lowry, Jr., the newcomers told Chief Quit-Sub-Socketts, also called St. John, why they had come, and he seemed satisfied.

It is unclear today why such early acceptance turned so soon to hostility. A sign of trouble came when the Indians expressed "some little feelings," similar to Walker's anger at Nephi, over construction of a stone fort.[28] Another common source of misunderstanding was that Mormons regarded all Indians simply as Lamanites and failed to understand that friendship with one tribe required sharing ancient enmities against another, in this case, the Utahs versus the Navahos.

Moreover, the missionaries had been ordered to take Indian wives, a practice made possible by polygamy, as a practical means to fulfill *The Book of Mormon* prophecy that the remnants of Israel would become, once again, "white and delightsome." But this was one instruction they usually failed to carry out, which only tended to emphasize the cultural differences between them and the natives they professed to serve.

---

[26]Diary of Alfred Nelson Billings, September 6, 1855.

[27]Diary of William B. Pace, June 30, 1855.

[28]Ibid., July 10, 1855. The stone fort was sixty-four feet square with walls some fourteen feet high and a base about four feet thick. It was located not far from a Daughters of Utah Pioneers monument on the north end of Moab that now marks the site.

If all of these factors to some degree applied, the most likely source of conflict were the reports, possibly spread by Chief Arapene, Walker's successor, who visited the mission, about fighting between other members of the tribe and Mormon settlers in Utah and Sanpete valleys. A half-brother of the dead war chief, Arapene professed conversion and friendship, but wherever he went, Indian trouble seemed to follow. Whatever the cause, certain it was that by late summer the Indians' mood had turned from friendly to "saucy and impudent." The missionaries saw the fruits of a summer's labor disappear as the natives began carrying off melons and squashes, digging up turnips and potatoes, and "Stealing ev[e]ry chance they get," said Billings.[29] When the newcomers tried to prevent such theft, the Indians only became more resentful.

Resentment turned to open hostility on September 23 when the missionaries in a protective measure moved their livestock closer to the fort. As three Indians moved threateningly toward the herd, James Hunt from American Fork ran out with a lariat to get his horse. He was followed by a mounted Indian, "Charles," who taunted him to stay in front and asked what he was afraid of when he looked back. A mile from the fort, Charles yelled to the missionary to see the herd. When Hunt lifted up on his toes to look, the Indian shot him in the back.

His friends carried their wounded companion back to the fort in a blanket and tried to round up some livestock while "the balls whistled very briskly all around." After that came a fierce fire fight in which "every Man was engaged."[30] The Indians set fire to the haystack and corral while defenders for a time managed to save most of the animals. But they could do little to help William Moroni Behunin from Manti and 21-year-old Edward Edwards, who were killed on the mountain as they tried to get back to the fort.

That night James Hunt begged his companions to "exercise their priesthood" and save him by the gift of healing. "Take me out of here and baptize me," he pleaded. Then in a few minutes he said, "Boys, I am dying."[31] As they gave him a final blessing, the young missionary breathed his last.

Early the next morning, after talking to interpreter Clark Hunting-

---

[29]Diary of Alfred Nelson Billings, September 23, 1855.
[30]Ibid.
[31]Ibid., September 24, 1855. A common practice at this time was baptism for healing.

ton, the mission president decided it was best to get out while they had a chance. Without eating breakfast, they gathered up what they could, a few horses and some food, and abandoned the ill-fated undertaking. They left behind most of their animals and equipment and the bodies of their three companions, whose remains have never been found.

An express from Springville a week later carried news of the disaster to Great Salt Lake. The missionaries "had not time to get even a single horse but just took what provisions they could carry along" with them and left, the messenger said. "It took a week for the brethren to walk to Manti and they were nearly starved to death when they arrived."[32] On empty stomachs, they had still averaged more than twenty-seven miles a day.

SALMON RIVER MISSION

More successful for a time were the twenty-seven who headed north from Utah settlements in May 1855 to gather the Bannocks, Shoshonis, Flatheads, and Nez Perce tribes who then lived in Oregon Territory. Typical of those called, they ranged in age from the youngest at 19, Ira Ames, Jr., and Abraham Zundel, to the oldest, Francillo Durfey and Thomas Butterfield, both 43. At least twenty left wives behind, including William Batchelor, who said farewell to a new bride of less than a week, now single in name only.

Led by New Yorker Thomas S. Smith, 37, the party with eleven wagons crossed Bear River at the ferry near present Honeyville, then followed the trail to Fort Hall explored in 1849 for a wagon road by Captain Stansbury.[33] This took them along today's I-15 to Malad City, Idaho, then up the Little Malad River to intersect on Wright Creek the California Trail's Hudspeth's Cutoff. Crossing the divide between the Great Basin and Columbia River waters, they came down Rattlesnake and Bannock creeks to reach the Portneuf River within five miles of Fort Hall, near present Pocatello.[34]

---

[32]Journal History, October 2, 1855.

[33]For Capt. Howard Stansbury's report of his 1849 reconnaissance of this route to Fort Hall, see Madsen, ed., *Exploring the Great Salt Lake*, 157–88. Stansbury's report was also published as "The Bannock Mountain Road" in *Idaho Yesterdays*, 18:1, 1964, 10–15.

[34]Historic Fort Hall was established in 1834 by Nathaniel G. Wyeth as a trading post on Snake River. The New Englander sold the fort three years later to Hudson's Bay Company. See Robertson, *Fort Hall, Gateway to the Oregon Country*.

Before them spread Snake River valley, "a vast green plain interspersed with groves of timber and patches of shrubery," said B. F. Cummings, orderly sergeant.[35] Here they met two mountain men, Neil McArthur, fur trader for Hudson's Bay Company, and his partner from Bitterroot Valley, Louis Maillet, who had constructed a crude bridge across the Portneuf to exact a toll from occasional travelers. The pair allowed the Mormons to cross for only a third of the usual rate, one dollar per wagon and loose cattle free.

Mission clerk David Moore described Fort Hall as built "on a square of about 100 feet" and "kept very neat and clean." He said the Mormon visitors were treated with "the greatest of courtesy" by Hudson's Bay clerk James Sinclair, whose opportunities to be kind to strangers would run out in ten months when he was killed by Indians near the Upper Cascades of Oregon.[36] Several miles upstream, the missionaries ferried Snake River and traveled on the line of today's I-15 over a sagebrush plain to Market Lake, a game-rich prairie basin flooded each year by Snake River, near its big bend, some eighteen miles north of Idaho Falls. Here they left the Flathead Trail to Bitterroot Valley and struck out in a northwest direction. They traveled up Birch Creek on the line of present Idaho highway 28 and over a low divide to pick up and follow the headwaters of Salmon River's east fork, now Lemhi River, to the strategic location chosen for their new settlement.

At this spot, just west of the pass where Lewis and Clark crossed the Continental Divide with Sacajawea in 1805, some seventeen miles south of present Salmon, they established Idaho's first white settlement and named it after a *Book of Mormon* king, Limhi. Here horse trails from north and south funneled hunting parties of potential converts, Shoshonis, Bannocks, Flatheads, and Nez Perces, eastward over the divide to the buffalo grounds along Horse Prairie Creek and other headwaters of the Missouri River. This northernmost outreach of Mormon settlement, some 380 miles north of Great Salt Lake, would for nearly two years fulfill with some success its mission to the Indians. Then, for a few shining months, Fort Limhi would rise from being an obscure Indian mission to become a location of historic importance in Utah's early history and a place of destiny in the Mormon theocracy's push for independence.

---

[35]Biography and Journals of Benjamin Franklin Cummings, May 27, 1855.
[36]Journal of Salmon River Mission, May 28, 1855.

A third company of thirty missionaries in June 1855 established a new mission to the desert tribes at Las Vegas Springs on the Spanish Trail, now within the limits of Las Vegas, Nevada. For the next two years they labored without reward to protect the impoverished desert natives from raids by the warlike Utahs, teach them farming, and win their friendship.

HURT'S INDIAN FARMS

There was at least one tribe that had little love for the people who had taken over its lands and fishing grounds. "Almost all of our canyons, north and south, have been burned," reported Apostle Heber C. Kimball in 1855.[37] And Andrew Love at Nephi that summer said, "a destructive fire in our pinerry has been burning for several days." According to the Utahs who set the fires, "the Mormons cut their timber & use it & pay them nothing for it, & they prefer burning it up."[38]

In undertaking to help the tribe, Garland Hurt first informed Brigham Young of his plan to establish farms for the natives "whose lands the whites have occupied" and requested the governor's advice as to suitable locations.[39] Young promptly approved the idea and suggested sites in Utah, Sanpete, Juab, Millard, and Iron counties. Given such support, Hurt moved in November 1855 with a zeal that bordered on recklessness. In three weeks he laid out a full township, thirty-six square miles, for an Indian farm at Corn Creek, where he found good soil and enough water to farm up to a thousand acres. In Sanpete County he quadrupled this spread, marking off four townships, 144 square miles, encompassing the tribal hunting grounds in Twelvemile Canyon and the present towns of Gunnison, Mayfield, Centerville, and Redmond. On the Spanish Fork River in Utah Valley he blocked off 12,380 acres between the town of Spanish Fork and Utah Lake, where he established his headquarters.[40]

The magnitude of these plans revealed that Hurt had more in mind than just establishing training farms for the natives under his care. His

---

[37] *Latter-day Saints' Millennial Star*, 17:46, November 17, 1855.

[38] Journal of Andrew Love, July 26, 1855.

[39] Hurt to Young, November 20, 1855, Brigham Young Collection, MS 1234, LDS Archives.

[40] The Spanish Fork farm extended from a point about two miles south of Spanish Fork to West Mountain and Utah Lake and took in today's town of Lake Shore. See David A. Burr, "Map of a Survey of the Indian Reservation on Spanish Fork Cr., Utah Territory, Showing its Connection with the U. S. Survey of the Territory."

larger purpose, actively supported by David H. Burr, the territory's new surveyor general, was to establish reservations for the tribe, an essential step in extinguishing the Indian land claim. Then all it would take for the lands of Deseret to go on sale to any and all comers would be for Burr to finish his survey to divide the territory into townships and sections as commissioned by Congress. It was an audacious, backdoor attempt to break Mormon economic control.

To carry it out, the agent advised the governor of his plans to purchase livestock and farming equipment "to carry on a vigorous system of agriculture" at these locations. Moreover, he asked Young to have Congress pass a law "confirming these reservations as the future home of these bands" and demanded that farming instruction be extended to other tribes before they were forced to "starve, or subsist by rapine and murder."[41] To pay for these grandiose plans he called for an appropriation of $75,000 to $100,000, plus $30,000 to cover his commitments to neighboring tribes.

Without doubt all of this was more than Brigham Young had in mind when he approved the farming scheme in the first place and beyond his power to deliver even if he wanted to, which he surely did not. Not only did he refuse to endorse these proposals for new legislation and funding, he also failed to curb Hurt's reckless spending, made by personal drafts against the credit of the Office of Indian Affairs, from existing appropriations. As a result, the agent would soon find himself on the edge of financial disaster.

Another sign of the governor's disapproval was the opposition encountered by Burr's surveying crews. Despite Hurt's efforts to reassure the natives, one deputy surveyor reported the Indians were being told by Young's agents that "we were measuring out the land in order to take possession of it, and would drive away the Mormons and kill the Indians." He also said the mayor of Payson City had issued a writ against him "to answer a charge for damages incurred by running a line across their fields."[42]

If the surveyors were a threat, even more serious was the challenge Garland Hurt mounted as the Mormon theocracy moved to establish its

---

[41]Hurt to Young, December 31, 1855, Letters Received by the Office of Indian Affairs, Utah Superintendency.

[42]Craig to Burr, August 1, 1856, House Exec. Doc. 71, 1858, 117–18.

independence from federal control. At a time when missionaries from Utah were fanning out across the west to gather the "Lamanites," the agent with growing success was busily winning the friendship and loyalty of the main tribe in their own backyard. So it was that the man called "the American" by the Utahs and a people who considered themselves chosen by God moved toward an inevitable showdown.

1856 STATEHOOD CONVENTION

Before it came, Hurt tried to improve understanding between the fledgling territory and the national government. Invited to speak before the 1855 Independence Day observances, he extolled the American constitution, sure to please Mormon audience members who believed, then as today, that the republic's founding document was divinely inspired.[43] And he pointed to persecution as a cause of the "delicate relations that exist between the United States and the little colony of Utah."[44] He would go even further.

After asking Congress three times from 1852 to 1854 to authorize a constitutional convention and being ignored each time, Utah lawmakers on December 10, 1855, went ahead and took this step on their own. In the last session ever held in the first capital at Fillmore, they authorized an election of delegates from every county to a constitutional convention at Great Salt Lake in 1856 to draw up a state constitution and memorialize Congress for admission to the American Union.

As customary, there was "not much stir or excitement" when the election was held on February 18 because none of the delegates was opposed.[45] Among the sixteen delegates chosen from Salt Lake County were two non-Mormons, including U.S. Indian Agent Garland Hurt. A month later, the American flag flew from "nearly all the stores" and public buildings and "the day was celebrated by the firing of cannon" when the delegates assembled at Great Salt Lake City, about to become the new capital. Over the next eleven days, they approved a constitution

---

[43]In establishing their theocracy within the bounds of the United States, Mormons believed that they were fulfilling the true purpose of the constitution, while federal officials were subverting it by trying to make the document an end in itself.

[44]Remarks by Hurt, July 4, 1855, as reported by J. V. Long and revised in Hurt's own handwriting, Brigham Young Collection, MS 1234, LDS Archives.

[45]Brooks, ed., *On the Mormon Frontier*, 2:592.

for the "free & independent State" of Deseret,[46] which differed little from the first founding document of Deseret, patterned, in turn, after the charters of other states.

Chosen to present to Congress the memorial for admission into the Union were apostles and Council of Fifty members John Taylor and George A. Smith. In keeping with the functioning of the theo-democracy, an election on April 7, in conjunction with the dominant faith's general conference, approved unanimously the new founding document and those chosen to carry it to the nation's capital.

It was the wrong time to ask for equal "constitutional rights enjoyed by the states in their internal regulation, election of officers and representation."[47] For that year a rising political movement, the Republican Party, was demanding an end to "those twin relics of barbarism—polygamy and slavery" in the territories, the only political entities over which Congress at that time held unquestioned control.[48] After meeting with John Bernhisel, Utah's delegate, Taylor and Smith decided not to present the statehood memorial.

Brigham Young later complained that a constitution had been adopted, a census taken, and delegates chosen "to present our application to Congress for admission into the Union as a sovereign and independent state." Moreover, he said, a census had been taken which showed Utah's population to be 77,000 in 1856 with 20,000 added by the end of the year.[49] Such totals, he said, exceeded the ratio of representation for congressmen, which removed any possible objection on the ground of insufficient population.

His conclusion: "Our application has not been presented, owing to the intolerance evinced by the predominant party in the house of representatives."[50] The time was at hand for the state of Deseret, another name for the political Kingdom of God, to rise up and stand on its own feet.

---

[46]Ibid., 2:595.

[47]Message by Governor Brigham Young, December 11, 1855, published in Roberts, *Comprehensive History*, 4:226.

[48]Wills, "The Twin Relics of Barbarism," 41.

[49]Governor Brigham Young, "Annual Message," *Deseret News*, December 24, 1856, 333. Young's numbers were highly exaggerated. The 1860 federal census showed Utah's population to be 40,273, of whom 12,754 were foreign-born. See Neff, *History of Utah*, 204; and Powell, *Utah History Encyclopedia*, 431. Garland Hurt in 1859 estimated the population by county and came up with a total of 41,400. See Simpson, *Report of Explorations across the Great Basin*, 451–55.

[50]Ibid.

Chapter 5

THE HANDCART DISASTER

Since Brigham has the way laid out that's best for us, we'll try,
Stand off you sympathetic fools, the hand carts now or die,
Then Cheer up ye Elders, you to the world will show
That Israel must be gathered soon and oxen are too slow.
—Missionary's Handcart Song

In the earliest days of the territory, the settlers of Utah were "satis-fied to abide their time, in accession of strength by numbers, when they may be deemed fit to take a sovereign position," said the perceptive observer, John W. Gunnison.[1] But faced with growing outside pressure, a lower than expected flow of emigrants (due at least in part to the 1852 polygamy announcement), and a lack of funds, Mormon leaders in 1855 moved more aggressively to promote a population buildup.

On October 19 settlers at Manti heard instructions given earlier that month at their faith's general conference in Great Salt Lake City. One had to do with polygamy, "telling the young men to get married at six-teen, and take two wives and a dozen if they wished," while girls were told "they were old enough to get married at fourteen," said Azariah Smith.[2]

Lorenzo Brown liked the "humorous" touch that Apostle Heber C. Kimball put on the teaching at the fall meeting. Brigham Young's first counselor "wanted all the girls 14 & boys 16 to go to it and get married or rather get married and go to it," the 33-year-old New Yorker said. Brown also noted that Brigham Young said "there were spirits of a nobler class waiting to take bodies & it was the duty of every man to be taking to himself more wives."[3]

---

[1]Gunnison, *The Mormons or Latter-day Saints, in the Valley of the Great Salt Lake*, 23.
[2]Journal of Azariah Smith, October, 19, 1855.   [3]Journal of Lorenzo Brown, October 8, 1855.

New Emigration Plan

That same month Brigham Young announced a new plan under the Perpetual Emigrating Fund to hurry up at the lowest possible cost the gathering of Israel from overseas. To collect those who could not afford otherwise to emigrate, he said, "let them come on foot, with handcarts or wheelbarrows; let them gird up their loins and walk through, and nothing shall hinder or stay them." In no other way could the "honest poor" be brought to Zion, he said.[4]

Thus was introduced the most unusual chapter in the story of America's move west during the nineteenth century. To look for gold along the west slope of the Sierra Nevada, men had walked to California with packs on their backs or pushed wheelbarrows across plains and mountains. But never before had a planned effort been made to move large numbers west in organized parties in which the people themselves took the place of draft animals, motivated not by the appetite for gold or the dream of land, but by religious faith. Not until 1856.

That year the children of Israel began to gather out of the European nations of Babylon to build up Zion in western America by walking across the heart of the continent, pulling a few belongings in handcarts behind them. If heroic, the handcart emigration also produced the greatest, if least known, disaster in the story of the nation's western migration, exceeding in lives lost the more famous Donner party tragedy of 1846–47 by some seven times. Before that happened, the new method of emigration was met with enthusiasm, high hopes, and initial success. There was even a new song to lift the spirits of emigrants as they struggled along the way to their new home in the American West:

Ye Saints that dwell on Europe's shore
Prepare yourselves with many more
To leave behind your native land
For sure God's Judgments are at hand.
Prepare to cross the stormy main
Before you do the Valley gain,
And with the faithful make a start
To cross the plains with your handcart.

Chorus

Some must push and some must pull
As we go marching up the hill,
As merrily on the way we go
Until we reach the Valley, oh![5]

[4]Thirteenth General Epistle, Church of Jesus Christ of Latter-day Saints, October 29, 1855, *Deseret News*, October 31, 1855.

[5]Hafen and Hafen, *Handcarts to Zion, the Story of a Unique Western Migration, 1856–1860, with contemporary journals, accounts, reports; and rosters of members of the ten Handcart Companies*, 66.

Oversight of the new emigration scheme fell to one of the faith's newest apostles, 35-year-old Franklin D. Richards, who had proved himself able to carry such responsibility. Ordained in 1849 at age 28, the Massachusetts native in 1854 had been named to head the important British and European missions. After seeing the last shipload of converts off in late May, weeks behind schedule, the apostle himself sailed two full months after that, expecting to overtake the emigrants on the trail during his own return to Utah.

For the slower handcart emigrants, the trip to Salt Lake Valley would take as long as six months and cover more than five thousand miles, the last thirteen hundred of which would be the hardest. It started at Liverpool, England, where the first wave, more than eight hundred strong, boarded ships in March and April 1856 and set sail for America. Landing at Boston, they traveled by rail to New York, then due west to Iowa City, Iowa, the termination of the railroad and the designated emigration base. At this jumping off place they camped for about four weeks building carts and getting ready for the final leg of their trip.

As described by handcart historian Lyndia Carter, design of the carts was ruled by two imperatives—lightest possible weight and lowest possible cost.[6] Vehicles at first were built entirely of wood, usually hickory or oak but often unseasoned, which led to frequent breakdowns, and weighed as little as fifteen pounds. The application of light iron tires and fittings raised the weight of later models up to fifty pounds or more. To roll easily over the existing wagon road, the cart measured the same width as a wagon. The wheels were four and a half to five feet in diameter, lifting the axle some two and a half feet above the ground. The open bed, or box, was three to four feet long with sides about eight inches high. Extending about three feet in front was the bar, "or singletree for the lead horse or lead man, woman or boy of the team" to push against to pull the cart.[7]

Companies were tightly organized and closely ordered. Four or five persons, usually a family, were assigned to each cart, with each member allowed to carry seventeen pounds of baggage, including clothing, bedding, and utensils. A wagon and ox team loaded with tents and supplies

---

[6]Carter, "The Mormon Handcart Companies," 2–18. Also see Lyndia McDowell Carter's forthcoming *Tongue nor Pen Can Never Tell the Sorrow: A Documentary History of the Mormon Handcart Experiment.*

[7]Josiah Rogerson as quoted in Hafen and Hafen, *Handcarts to Zion,* 53–55.

went with every twenty carts or one hundred emigrants. For every twenty persons a large tent was provided, and one of its occupants was named tent captain. The captains of five tents reported to a captain who reported, in turn, to the company captain.

FIRST COMPANIES ROLL

From Iowa City in early June the first two companies jumped off two days apart on the first leg of their journey, a 280-mile run to the Winter Quarters emigration base at Florence, Nebraska, now in Omaha. Leading the first company with 274 pioneers was Edmund Ellsworth, Brigham Young's son-in-law, about to turn 37. Right behind came 36-year-old Daniel McArthur, also a returning missionary, with 221 emigrants under his charge. They arrived at the established emigration base on the Missouri River five weeks later, averaging less than ten miles a day.

Exulted one who saw them roll in, "One would not think that they had come from Iowa City, a long and rough journey of from 275 to 300 miles, except by their dust-stained garments and sunburned faces."[8] Even so, the short "warm up" over a relatively smooth, well-traveled road was enough to convince some families that the handcart method of travel was not for them. They decided they had suffered enough sun, dust, and hard labor and dropped out to await easier forms of transportation.

The more intrepid rested a week or two, repaired their carts, and took off in late July in two companies, four days apart, for the greatest ordeal of their entire journey, the one thousand-mile stretch to Great Salt Lake Valley. By 1856 the Oregon-California-Mormon Trail was a well-worn highway from the Missouri River to Utah and beyond. But never had these great emigrant routes seen anything like the long lines of handcarts, pulled by two in front, usually a wife and husband, with children pushing from the rear, that now rolled over the prairie.

At first a great adventure, the journey soon turned into a monotonous routine. A typical day began about 5 A.M. when the sound of a bugle awakened the closely regulated pioneers and set everyone to work mak-

---

[8]Latey to Taylor, August 14, 1856, *Latter-day Saints' Millennial Star*, 18:40, October 4, 1856, 637–38.

ing fires, cooking breakfast, and packing for the day's travel. After prayers about seven, the parade of carts rolled out to cover from ten to twelve miles before stopping during the heat of the day to rest. A few miles more in late afternoon ended the day's travel and the bugle blew lights out at ten.

Arrival in Valley

Except for some two dozen deaths, mainly from disease, so it went for more than two months until the first two companies reached their destination on the very same day, September 26, after rolling over the miles at an average rate of about fifteen a day. Proudly pulling the first vehicle was Captain Ellsworth himself. The only complaint of those who followed was that "they had been detained by the ox teams . . . the oxen not being able to keep up with them."[9] They were met at the foot of Little Mountain in Emigration Canyon by Brigham Young, a company of mounted lancers, the Nauvoo Brass Band, and other Mormon luminaries who formed an escort for the ninety-six handcarts, eight wagons, and more than four hundred pioneers. The grand procession marched into the city with lancers, officials, and bands in front, followed by the hardy marchers who had made it all the way, with more Nauvoo Legion horsemen bringing up the rear. Apostle Woodruff described the emotional scene:

"The people of the city gathered on each side of the road . . . & it was an effecting sight," he said. "Women Children & old men had drawn their bedding clothing & food the whole distance & this company of poor people from England had travelled this whole distance in about 9 weeks. They were covered with dust & some worn down but cheerful. They had beat any horse or ox team during the time."[10] Down today's South Temple Street, the emigrants pulled their handcarts past Brigham Young's house and formed in two lines at the public square, Woodruff said, where they set up camp for the night. "No tongue can tel[l] No pen Can write, the sensation it created in the reflecting mind to behold the scene."[11]

[9]Ibid., Woodruff to Pratt, September 30, 1856, 18:50, December 13, 1856, 794–96.
[10]Kenney, ed., *Wilford Woodruff's Journal*, 4:452–53.
[11]Ibid.

THE WELSH COMPANY

Much of the excitement and novelty had worn off by the time the third handcart company, some three hundred strong, rolled into the valley a week later. The party under Mormon Battalion veteran Edward Bunker, 34, was made up almost entirely of emigrants from Wales who spoke little English, which made the New Englander's "burden very heavy."[12] Even so, the Welsh Company completed the journey from the Missouri River in only sixty-five days, averaging an impressive sixteen miles a day.

So far, the handcart experiment had been a shining success. Over eight hundred men, women and children of all ages, mainly from Great Britain, had made the long journey to Zion. The loss of life on the trail had not been excessive. Most had died from disease or exhaustion, although one had been unlucky enough to be struck by lightning. From the tightly regulated companies, only one person had turned up missing. Exulted Samuel W. Richards on October 7 to members of the faith still in England:

"One fact is established—that the Saints can cross the Plains almost without means, and only for the mighty waters that intervene, Israel would indeed come 'like doves to their windows, and like clouds before a storm.'"[13] But he rejoiced too soon. A thousand or more men, women, and children from Great Britain and northern Europe were still out on the plains. Not prepared for winter and short of food, they had begun a struggle for survival, hundreds of miles from Salt Lake Valley.

THE LAST COMPANIES

The last wave of Zion-bound emigrants, larger than the first, had sailed in two ships from Liverpool on May 4 and May 25, much later than any prudent margin of safety allowed for the overland journey to Utah, even by wagon. Learning on July 31 of the late departure, Brigham Young had expressed his concern. The emigrants should be shipped "earlier in the season," he instructed. "They should be landed early in May, and not much, if any after the first of that month, in Boston or New York."[14]

---

[12]Autobiography of Edward Bunker, 1856.

[13]Richards to Turnbull, October 7, 1856, *Latter-day Saints' Millennial Star*, 19:3, January 17, 1857, 41, 42.

[14]Ibid., Young to Pratt, July 19, 1856, 18:41, October 11, 1856, 651.

Main cause of the delay had been an unexpectedly enthusiastic response to the opportunity to go to Zion by the low-cost method of travel. Full of zeal but uninformed about the American West and its geography and climate, foreign Mormons had been all too willing to put their trust in the missionaries assigned to tell them what to do. Further delays had resulted from a shortage of ships bound for northern American ports and, perhaps most telling, conflicting lines of authority among church leaders planning the move.

But why they came so late made little difference to workers at the Iowa City outfitting camp who found themselves overwhelmed when some sixteen hundred emigrants landed there in late June and early July, some to travel by wagon, but most by handcart. Shortages of skilled workers and construction materials handicapped a crash effort to build 250 handcarts. The quality of the light vehicles suffered accordingly, with deadly consequences.

After losing three weeks, on July 15 some five hundred emigrants, 120 handcarts, and five wagons rolled out from Iowa City in the fourth handcart company under 41-year-old Englishman James Willie. The fifth and last company, some six hundred strong, left the camp two weeks later under Captain Edward Martin, 37, also from England, for the relatively short pull to Florence, Nebraska. The names Willie and Martin would become forever engraved in the annals of Utah.

Their companies arrived a full month later at Florence, the point of no return. The relatively easy haul over a good road had already proved too much for many of the hastily built carts, which took extensive repair before going on. More precious days were lost. To any but the most zealous, it was evident that the season for overland travel was over.

ONE SPEAKS OUT

Among the returning missionaries that summer was one who had marched two thousand miles in 1846 from Council Bluffs, Iowa, to southern California with the Mormon Battalion during the War with Mexico. Thirty-six-year-old Levi Savage, Jr., had already proved he was a man of faith, and the Ohioan would now show he was also no fool. He spoke out against "taking women & children through destitute of clothing, when we all know that we are bound to be caught in the snow, and severe cold weather, long before we reach the valley."[15] He was opposed as preparations continued by James Willie who urged the emigrants to go forward. Willie said the God "he served was a god that was able to save to the ut[t]ermost, that was the *God* that *He served,*" and he called those who opposed him "Job's comforters." Savage replied "warmly" that he had "spoken nothing but the *truth,*" and stood his ground. But in the end, he said, most of the handcart emigrants "determined to go forward if the Authorities say so."[16]

Trusting in the arm of the Almighty to hold back the oncoming winter, on August 18 Willie's handcart company pulled out from the emigration base on the Missouri River. Full of the same innocent faith, the even larger party under Martin headed slowly toward the Platte River over a week later. With the first company, hoping for the best, fearing the worst, but determined to do what he could to help the trusting souls who were heading into a probable disaster, went Levi Savage.

On Loup Fork of the Platte River, Franklin D. Richards in a comfortable mule-drawn carriage overtook the Willie Company on August 26. His heart had been warmed a few days before by Martin Company members who had given him "cordial shakes of the hand, with a fervent 'God bless you,'" as he passed.[17] Hearing of Savage's opposition to the late start, the apostle now called a meeting of the Willie Company and "reprimanded me sharply," the Ohioan said. He was compelled to ask forgiveness "for all that I had said and done wrong."[18]

Having corrected Savage's lack of faith, Richards hurried on to the territorial capital where he delivered the first news that a thousand or more handcart pioneers were still out on the plains. Arriving just in time for fall general conference, Richards told the assembled faithful on October 5 that the emigrants under his charge "feel that it is late in the season," and they "expect to get cold fingers and toes."[19]

"But they have this faith and confidence towards God, that he will overrule the storms . . . and turn them away," he said, "that their path may be freed from suffering more than they can bear." When he had

[15]Journal of Levi Savage, Jr., August 12, 1856.
[16]Ibid., August 13, 1856.
[17]Richards to Little, September 3, 1856, *Latter-day Saints' Millennial Star,* 18:43, October 25, 1856, 682.
[18]Journal of Levi Savage, Jr., August 26, 1856.
[19]Franklin D. Richards, October 5, 1856, *Journal of Discourses,* 4:114–18.

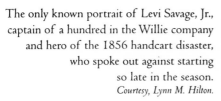

The only known portrait of Levi Savage, Jr.,
captain of a hundred in the Willie company
and hero of the 1856 handcart disaster,
who spoke out against starting
so late in the season.
Courtesy, Lynn M. Hilton.

talked with the emigrants about the handcarts, he went on, he had "felt
to prophesy good about them."[20] The apostle still did not grasp the seriousness of the situation. Fortunately for those in the wilderness, however, there was one who did understand this reality and had the power to
do something about it.

"Many of our brethren and sisters are on the plains with hand carts,
and probably many are now 700 miles from this place, and they must be
brought here, we must send assistance to them. The text [of my sermon]
will be to get them here," said Brigham Young. "That is my religion; that
is the dictation of the Holy Ghost that I possess, it is to save the people."

"I shall call upon the Bishops this day, I shall not wait until to-morrow, nor until next day, for 60 good mule teams and 12 or 15 wagons. I
do not want to send oxen, I want good horses and mules. They are in this
Territory, and we must have them; also 12 tons of flour and 40 good
teamsters, besides those that drive the wagons."[21]

His words launched the most desperate rescue operation in western
history, a two-month struggle against winter, hundreds of miles from
the nearest settlement, that saw heroism and heartbreak almost beyond
human capacity to perform or endure. For contrary to the promise by

---

[20]Ibid.

[21]"Remarks by President Brigham Young," *Deseret News*, October 15, 1856, 252.

Apostle Richards that the Almighty would hold back the storms, veteran plainsmen would later say they had never seen so much snow or colder temperatures so early in the season on the high plains of present Wyoming.

THE WILLIE COMPANY

At first Willie Company spirits were high, despite the need to haul a ninety-eight-pound bag of flour on each handcart to make up for the lack of oxen to pull accompanying supply wagons. "Brother Savage's warning was forgotten in the mirthful ease of the hour," later said one member of the company.[22] But the added load more than doubled the weight allowed for personal belongings which wore down the emigrants and caused constant breakdowns and delays to repair the hastily constructed vehicles.

The shortage of livestock grew more critical on the Platte River near Grand Island when the party's cattle stampeded after being spooked by vast herds of buffalo. Some animals were found, but most ran off to join their Pleistocene cousins on the plains. With hardly a murmur, the tiring emigrants loaded another bag of flour on their carts.

Even so, Captain Willie realized at Fort Laramie that at the company's rate of travel food supplies would run out some 350 miles from the valley. He reduced the daily food allotment. Rations were further cut after promised relief wagons from the west failed to show up. Unknown to the pioneers, a provisions train from the Mormon settlement at Fort Supply, near Fort Bridger, had traveled east for some distance on the trail, but failing to meet anyone, it had too soon decided the emigration was over and turned back.

As the Willie Company moved painfully up the Sweetwater River, temperatures in October plummeted and the skies lowered. Seventeen pounds of bedding and clothing proved inadequate to keep exhausted emigrants warm. First to droop and die were the old and infirm. Soon the burial ritual each morning began to include the bodies of younger members, mainly men. "Life went out as smoothly as a lamp ceases to burn when the oil is gone," John Chislett said. "Many a father pulled his

---

[22]John Chislett, "Chislett's Narrative," published in Stenhouse, *The Rocky Mountain Saints*, 314–32.

cart, with his little children on it, until the day preceding his death. I have seen some pull their carts in the morning, give out during the day, and die before next morning."[23]

At the sixth crossing of the Sweetwater, some 270 miles from their destination, on October 20 the suffering company could go no farther. "This morning when we arose we found several inches of snow on the ground; and is yet snowing," Levi Savage said. The emigrants and cattle were so much reduced from the lack of food and hard labor that unless help came, he said, "we surely can not move far in this snow."[24] Captain Willie and a companion rode out to look for supply wagons and quickly disappeared in the storm. That day was issued the last bread.

THE MARTIN COMPANY

The Martin Company suffered even greater hardship because it numbered among nearly six hundred members a higher proportion of women and children and was a month or more behind the Willie party by the time it reached Fort Laramie. From that point, said Samuel Jones, it was one long funeral march.[25] At the last North Platte River crossing at present Casper, Wyoming, more people died fording the river than at any other point in the entire journey, according to Josiah Rogerson. Dodging blocks of ice, he said, "more than a score or two of the young female members waded the stream that in places was waste deep."[26] After the crossing, Rogerson was assigned to wheel "Aaron [Jackson] on an empty cart with his feet dangling over the end bar, to camp." He put up the tent and helped Jackson's wife make the man as comfortable as possible under his blankets. Later that night, he accidentally bumped Jackson's feet and discovered they were stiff. "Reaching my hand to his face," he said, "I found that he was dead with his exhausted wife and little ones at his side all sound asleep."[27]

Among the Martin Company was 13-year-old Heber McBride, oldest son of five children, who told a few years later how his father's strength daily ebbed away as he gave his own meager rations to his children. The elder McBride would get up each day before the rest and

---

[23]Ibid.   [24]Journal of Levi Savage, Jr., October 20, 1856.

[25]Whitney, *History of Utah*, 4:297.

[26]Josiah Rogerson, "Martin's Handcart Company, 1856."   [27]Ibid.

struggle ahead until he sank exhausted. When the rest of the family later found him lying on the trail, they loaded him on the cart and hauled him as far as they could. Then they left him to struggle in on his own after dark. At last came the inevitable night when father McBride failed to come into camp at all. His son, Heber, looked for him the next morning in new snow eighteen inches deep. He found him, he said, "under a wagon with snow all over him and he was stiff and dead."

"I felt as though my heart would burst," the boy said. "I sat down beside him on the snow and took hold of one of his hands and cried Oh Father Father."[28] Then the oldest man in the family at age 13 took up the burden his father had laid down.

About forty miles west of the North Platte River crossing, nearly four hundred miles from Salt Lake Valley, a heavy blizzard struck and Martin's suffering party came to a dead stop. Snowed in, exhausted, and starving, the emigrants waited for relief or death to arrive, whichever came first. Days passed, and when even hope was gone, three men—22-year-old Joseph A. Young, son of Brigham Young; Missourian Daniel Jones, 26; and Abel Garr—rode into camp. The emigrants cried and cheered at the sight of these deliverers from the west and fell to their knees in the snow. But the agony of the fourth and fifth companies had only begun.

THE RESCUE

Less than forty-eight hours after Young's call for action, men and wagons moved out from the assembly point near today's Mountain Dell Reservoir, east of Salt Lake City, and headed back over the trail. Leading the first parties were two Nauvoo Legion officers, George D. Grant, 40, a veteran Indian campaigner after whom present Grantsville is named, and Maj. Robert T. Burton, then 36.[29] Some of the territory's most experienced plainsmen went with them, including Charles Decker; James Ferguson and John R. Murdock, Mormon Battalion veterans; William H. Kimball, son of Apostle Heber C. Kimball; Abel Garr; Daniel Jones; and Stephen W. Taylor. Among younger rescuers were two 17-year-olds, George Grant, son of the company's captain, and Ira

[28]Autobiography of Heber R. McBride.
[29]For an account of the rescue, see Bartholomew and Arrington, *Rescue of the 1856 Handcart Companies.*

Nebeker. David Patton Kimball, also a son of Apostle Kimball, was 18. Benjamin Hampton was 19, and Cyrus Wheelock, Brigham Young, Jr., and Harvey Cluff were 20.

Amid falling temperatures and intermittent snow, the rescue companies passed Fort Bridger and moved on to the Green River, but found no emigrants there as expected. With growing fears, they pushed over the Continental Divide to the Sweetwater River where they met a severe blizzard and sought shelter. Here they were discovered almost by accident in the snowstorm by James Willie, who was just trying to stay on the trail.

The English captain returned to his company next day with the first of many supply wagons from Salt Lake Valley. The relief they provided was only temporary, just enough to get the company moving again, but inadequate to stop its suffering. While Grant with some of the supply wagons headed east to find the Martin Company, William Kimball led the Willie party in a blinding snowstorm over the five-mile ascent known as Rocky Ridge, the worst ordeal of the journey.

In charge of the teams, Levi Savage drove wagons so full of the sick and children he feared many would smother. When the last wagons reached camp on Rock Creek, about eight miles southeast of today's South Pass City, Wyoming, some of the emigrants were badly frozen, "some dying and some dead," he said. "It was heartrending to hear children crying for mothers, and mothers crying for children."[30]

All that night he worked to make them as comfortable as he could. Morning on October 24 found the Ohioan too exhausted to help bury in a common grave the thirteen company members who had died during the night.[31] He was also too tired to keep making daily entries in his journal.

The next day the Willie Company approached South Pass where they met Reddick Allred with fresh teams and wagons loaded with provisions. After leaving the last of their carts on November 2 at Fort Bridger, most of the survivors arrived in Salt Lake Valley a week later in bright sunshine. For them, the terrible ordeal was over. Not so for the Martin Company.

---

[30]Journal of Levi Savage, Jr., October 23, 1856.

[31]A monument at the Rock Creek camp site can be seen today by taking a gravel road from South Pass City.

THE MARTIN COMPANY RESCUE

After meeting Willie's company, George Grant pushed on with part of his party to save the last handcart pioneers. Hoping to find them at Devil's Gate, rescuers covered the distance of sixty miles through snow eight to twelve inches deep, but found not a sign of the party on arrival. At the historic Oregon Trail location, Grant made a base camp in the old mail stockade and sent Joseph Young, Daniel Jones, and Abel Garr out on the best horses with orders to keep going until they found the Martin handcarts. For some twenty miles, the three rode east at a gallop whenever the snow was light enough on the trail for them to go that fast.

On Horse Creek, near today's Pathfinder Reservoir, about a dozen miles east of Independence Rock, they found the Martin party and nearby stranded wagon trains. There was a rush to shake their hands. "Many declared we were angels from heaven," said Jones.[32] Fifty-six had already died, mostly older members, but many others were failing fast; increasingly these were middle-aged husbands and fathers who had borne the heaviest load. Many of the European emigrants were disoriented and demoralized.

The three express riders carried little to eat, but brought a load of life-renewing hope that relief was coming. After issuing most of the remaining supplies, they soon had the handcart marchers moving west again. Young rode ahead to carry the news to the base camp, where rescuers hurried to cut wood and prepare shelter. Having a new lease on life, the Martin Company covered the distance to the Devil's Gate base camp in two days.

As it neared this destination, a new blizzard struck with torturing winds and sub-zero temperatures. The renewed onslaught of winter and declining food supplies now served notice that not only the handcart emigrants but their rescuers, too, faced death on the trail unless relief came soon. On November 3 Grant sent two dependable expressmen, Joseph Young and Abel Garr, each with a spare horse, on a mid-winter ride all the way to Great Salt Lake City to report on their condition. Averaging nearly thirty miles a day, they arrived at 4 A.M. on November 13.

In his written report to Brigham Young, Grant said "you can imagine

---

[32]Jones, *Forty Years among the Indians*, 65.

between five and six hundred men, women and children, worn down by drawing hand carts through snow and mud, fainting by the wayside; falling, chilled by the cold; children crying, their limbs stiff[e]ned by cold, their feet bleeding and some of them bare to snow and frost. The sight is almost too much for the stoutest of us; but we go on doing all we can, not doubting nor despairing."

"Our company is too small to help much, it is only a drop to a bucket, as it were, in comparison to what is needed. I think that not over one-third of br. Martin's company is able to walk. This you may think is extravagant, but it is nevertheless true. Some of them have good courage and are in good spirits; but a great many are like children and do not help themselves much more, nor realize what is before them . . . Br. Charles Decker has now traveled this road the 49th time, and he says he has never before seen so much snow on the Sweet Water at any season of the year." Grant concluded: "We will move every day toward the valley, if we shovel snow to do it, the Lord helping us."[33]

At Devil's Gate on November 4 Grant decided to move the Martin Company about three miles to a more sheltered location, now known as Martin's Cove, where nature had shaped a circular wall of granite along the north side of the Sweetwater River.[34] To get there, emigrants had to pull their carts across the ice-clogged Sweetwater River. The stream was only two feet deep and a hundred feet or so wide, but to the weakened travelers it seemed an impossible ordeal. Three of the rescue party's youngest members waded into the icy stream and worked throughout the day, pulling carts and carrying people across. When he learned of their heroism, Brigham Young reportedly said, "that act alone will ensure C. Allen Huntington, George W. Grant, and David P. Kimball an everlasting salvation in the Celestial Kingdom of God, worlds without end."[35]

For the next five days the company waited in the cove, slightly sheltered from the deadly winds but still suffering from the lack of food and temperatures as low as eighteen degrees below zero. Still no further help

---

[33]Grant's November 2 report to Brigham Young from Devil's Gate is published in *Deseret News*, November 19, 1856, 293.

[34]A monument today identifies Martin's Cove about three miles west of Devil's Gate on Wyoming Highway 220.

[35]This quote by Young, if true to character, may be apocryphal. It was published in 1914 in Solomon F. Kimball, "Belated Emigrants of 1856," 288, and repeated in Hafen and Hafen, *Handcarts to Zion*, but handcart historian Lyndia Carter has found no earlier mention of it.

came. Finally, with warming skies, Grant got the emigrants moving again to shorten the distance between the company and the relief wagons he knew were coming.

The first they met was a solitary but heavily loaded wagon driven by frontiersman Ephraim Hanks, then 29. This legendary loner had pushed ahead on his own, killing a buffalo along the way and loading strips of the meat on his horses. When he met the handcart pioneers on the Sweetwater River and entered their camp, what he saw could "never be erased from my memory," he said. "Many of the immigrants whose extremities were frozen, lost their limbs, either whole or in part. Many such I washed with water and castile soap, until the frozen parts would fall off, after which I would sever the shreds of flesh from the remaining portions of the limbs with scissors. Some of the emigrants lost toes, others fingers, and again others whole hands and feet."[36]

Even so, the worst was over for the survivors of Martin's company. The arrival of Hanks was followed by a parade of wagons in which the suffering foreign faithful were loaded and carried in relative comfort to Salt Lake Valley. They arrived on November 30 in front of the tithing offices located on the site now occupied by the Joseph Smith Memorial Building, the former Hotel Utah. They had gathered at last to their Zion, but this time there was no celebration. Instead the homes of settlers were opened to receive the suffering newcomers, some with frozen hands and feet requiring amputation, others near death.

An accurate count of the number who died will probably never be known because the authorities tried to keep the full horror of the disaster from becoming public, especially in England. But it would be safe to estimate the total at well over two hundred, or at least one in five of the last two companies, with many others maimed for life.[37] Like the Donner party, most of those who died from hunger, exhaustion, the cold, or a combination of the three were men or the elderly. One thing is certain—the handcart disaster of 1856 was the greatest single tragedy in the history of the nation's move west in the nineteenth century.

In view of this, it is ironic that the handcart emigration that year actually proved the feasibility of moving large numbers of people over-

---

[36]Hanks and Hanks, *Scouting for the Mormons on the Great Frontier*, 136–42.

[37]John Chislett estimated about one-fourth or the Martin Company perished, or about 150, and Captain James Willie reported seventy-seven deaths in his company.

land by this new travel method, provided they started early enough and were suitably equipped. This was pointed up by Brigham Young who said, "if even a bird had chirped it in the ears" of Apostle Richards and his first counselor, Daniel Spencer, "they would have known better than to rush men, women and children on to the prairie in the autumn months, on the 3d of September, to travel over a thousand miles."

"I repeat that if a bird had chirped the inconsistency of such a course in their ears, they would have thought and considered for one moment," he said, "and would have stopped those men, women and children there until another year." He then pronounced a bone-rattling curse on anyone who had the temerity to blame him or his counselors for the lateness of the last handcart companies.[38]

A determined effort would be made over the next four years to revive the handcart method of travel. To prove its feasibility, a company of missionaries going east in 1857 would pull handcarts from Utah to Florence. That same year, the sixth and seventh westbound companies, a total of 479 people, would travel by cart to Utah, leaving the Missouri River early in June and arriving in early September. The last handcart company made the trip in 1860.

Over four years, 1856, 1857, 1859 and 1860, nearly three thousand emigrants made the journey in ten companies. Of these, more than twenty-six hundred arrived safely. Despite this record, the fear of death on the plains dampened the zeal of emigrants to come to Zion pulling a handcart across the heart of the continent. Although feasible, the low-cost method of emigration never overcame the disaster of 1856.

Meanwhile, still recovering from his ordeal, Levi Savage on April 7, 1857, attended his faith's general conference at Great Salt Lake City and heard Brigham Young give "a severe chastisement" to Apostle Richards and Daniel Spencer "for starting the handcart Companies so late to cross the plains last Season." So sharp was the tongue-lashing Young publicly administered that others at the meeting would describe it as a whipping.

Said Savage: "It has been the best conference that I have ever attended."[39]

---

[38]"If any man, or woman, complains of me or of my Counselors, in regard to the lateness of some of this season's immigration, let the curse of God be on them and blast their substance with mildew and destruction, until their names are forgotten from the earth." See *Deseret News*, November 12, 1856, 283.

[39]Journal of Levi Savage, Jr., April 7, 1857.

JEDEDIAH MORGAN GRANT
Grant, "the sledgehammer of Brigham," preached
blood atonement during the Reformation of 1856
and made sinners afraid.
Courtesy, LDS Archives.

Chapter 6

THE GREAT REFORMATION

The fire of God is burning here and I command you and your
quorums to scour up your armor both temporally &
Spiritua[l]ly. Prepare yourselves to stand by me when Israel is to
be cleansed for this has got to be done that the Gentile bands
may be broken.

—Bishop Jacob G. Bigler

On entering Salt Lake Valley in 1847, Brigham Young reportedly
served notice to the world: Leave us alone for ten years and we will stand
up to anyone. As the end of this time neared, he made clear the Kingdom of God was ready to take an independent position in the American
West. "As the Lord lives," he said in September 1856, "we are bound to
become a sovereign State in the Union, or an independent nation by
ourselves."[1]

The first course he mentioned, to become a sovereign state, reflected
the widely held view at that time that the primary power to govern rested
in the individual states rather than the federal government. By this
understanding, if a state chose to introduce slavery or even practice
polygamy, Young said, it would not be the business of the president "to
meddle with this matter." Congress would not be allowed, "according to
the Constitution, to legislate upon it."[2]

When Congress in 1856 failed even to consider their bid for entry
into the Union as the state of Deseret, territorial leaders took the preferred road to sovereignty and, in their own lifetimes, universal dominion. They launched a great reformation that year to cleanse the people of
sin and disobedience in order to merit divine favor in the inevitable confrontation with the American republic. Chosen to lead the spiritual cru-

---

[1]*Deseret News*, September 17, 1856, 220.   [2]Ibid.

sade was a man who called himself "Mormon Thunder," but was better
known to the faithful of his day as "the sledgehammer of Brigham." By
whatever name he was called, the puritanical reformer and favored associate of Brigham Young was an awesome and at times a frightening figure.

Jedediah Morgan Grant in appearance was not unlike a young Abraham Lincoln. He stood over six feet tall, his build was lanky, his eyes
deep-set, complexion swarthy, jaw square, and face long. Perhaps to a
combative nature may be attributed his crooked nose which bent somewhat to his left from an old break near the bridge. But his smile was natural and his face not at all unpleasant. Behind the smile was an enigmatic
figure, one untroubled by doubt, driven to enforce righteousness, yet a
man who was deeply attached to his home, devoted to his wives (of
whom he had six) and children, and intensely loyal to his faith's leaders.
In 1847, to keep a promise to his dying first wife, he had driven a wagon
non-stop for a hundred miles to take her body from the crossing of Bear
River, near present Evanston, Wyoming, to Salt Lake Valley, where she
became the first woman buried in the new Mormon settlement.[3]

What made Grant truly exceptional, however, was the fire that burned
in his belly at the sight of so much filth and imperfection among the
chosen people of God. Calling on forensic skills honed by a dozen years
of verbal combat with ministers of other faiths, he was driven like an
Old Testament prophet to cry repentance and compel cleanliness and
obedience. Born in upstate New York, Grant traced his family roots, like
many religious zealots of his day, to New England. At age 17 he followed the Mormon prophet, Joseph Smith, and never looked back. At
28 he became a member of the Council of Fifty, governing body of the
earthly Kingdom of God. Elected unanimously, he became in 1851 the
first mayor of Great Salt Lake. On the death of Willard Richards in
1854, he was chosen to replace the beloved herb doctor as second counselor to Brigham Young only weeks after delivering a scorching sermon
on the need to shed the blood of some sinners as the only hope to save
them.

Now, at age 40, "Brother Jeddy" in 1856 was called to his greatest
mission. This was to lead a great reformation to qualify his people in the

---

[3]For the best work to date on this important early Utah figure, see Sessions, *Mormon Thunder: A Documentary History of Jedediah Morgan Grant*.

eyes of the Almighty for divine intervention in the forthcoming quarrel between the Great Basin theocracy and the United States. To cleanse Israel spiritually before the impending showdown, the choice fell to the man ideally suited for the task.

The great reformation of 1856 was no spur of the moment or spontaneous revival. It was launched on the same weekend in mid-September by Brigham Young and his loyal subordinate at different points in the territory. In Great Salt Lake on September 14, Young "spoke in the power of God & the demonstration of the Holy Ghost & his voice & words were like the thunderings of Mount Sina[i]," said Apostle Woodruff. That Sunday the people were "justly, Strictly & strongly chastized & rebuked," he said, "for lying, stealing, swareing, commiting Adultery, quarelling with Husbands wives & children & many other evils."[4] At the same time, Jedediah Grant and Joseph Young, Brigham Young's older brother, ignited the spiritual conflagration in Davis County, north of the capital. In Kaysville and Farmington, the fiery New Yorker "worked up the people with his tongue," as he would say, and demanded that they "repent and be baptized for the remission of their sins."[5] So overpowering was he that as many as a thousand confessed and went down to the water to be cleansed and begin anew. Grant personally baptized and confirmed hundreds over six days as new members of the faith.

BLOOD ATONEMENT

A week later, Grant and Brigham Young jointly introduced in the bowery at Great Salt Lake City a doctrine that would loose a torrent of confession, repentance, and rebaptism throughout Zion. After Young had "rebuked the sins of the people," wrote Woodruff. "He said that the blood of Heifers lambs Doves &c would again be offered for certain sins but for some sins no blood would be acceptable except the life & blood of the individual." No doubt understating the congregation's reaction, the apostle added, "He made the H[e]arts of many tremble."[6]

There had been indirect references before, but this was the first pub-

[4]Kenney, ed., *Wilford Woodruff's Journal*, 4:448.
[5]*Deseret News*, September 24, 1856, 228.
[6]Kenney, ed., *Wilford Woodruff's Journal*, 4:451.

lic pronouncement of blood atonement, a doctrine founded on the belief some sins were so serious they could not be cleansed by the blood of animals or even Christ's sacrifice.[7] First taught to a few in leadership circles, this doctrine was revealed not to punish sinners, but to ensure their exaltation and to save them. "Let these principles be known by an individual, and he would be glad to have his blood shed," Brigham Young explained. "Will you love your brothers or sisters likewise, when they have committed a sin that cannot be atoned for without the she[d]ding of their blood? Will you love that man or woman well enough to shed their blood? That is what Jesus Christ meant."[8]

Lest anyone in the audience got the idea that Young meant someone else might have to take this hard road to glory, but not I, Grant took pains to make clear who the Mormon president was talking about. "If the arrows of the Almighty ought to be thrown at you we want to do it, and to make you feel and realize that we mean you," he said. His advice to some sinners was to go to Young "and ask him to appoint a committee to attend to their case; and then let a place be selected, and let that committee shed their blood."[9]

As his listeners trembled, the fiery herald of truth laid it squarely on the line: "Brethren and sisters, we want you to repent and forsake your sins," he said. "And you who have committed sins that cannot be forgiven through baptism, let your blood be shed and let the smoke ascend, that the incense thereof may come up before God as an atonement for your sins, and that the sinners in Zion may be afraid."[10]

Lesser offenders whose shortcomings were treatable by baptism were cut off from the faith until they had confessed their faults publicly, undergone rebaptism for remission, and been reconfirmed as members of the church. After that, they were to be held to a higher moral code.

---

[7]Mormon theologian Bruce R. McConkie denied that "there has been one event or occurrence whatever, of any nature, from which the slightest inference arises that any such practice existed or was taught." At the same time, he wrote, "under certain circumstances there are some sins for which the cleansing of Christ does not operate, and the law of God is that men must then have their own blood shed to atone for their sins." However, he went on, "this doctrine can only be practiced in its fullness in a day when the civil and ecclesiastical laws are administered in the same hands." The purpose of the reformation was to usher in that very day. See McConkie, *Mormon Doctrine*, 92, 93.

[8]Brigham Young, February 25, 1857, *Journal of Discourses*, 4:219–20.

[9]Jedediah Grant, *Deseret News*, October 1, 1856, 235.

[10]Ibid.

As Lorenzo Brown explained: "The Saints have the privilege of their sins being forgiven by making restitution to those we have injured & then renew our Covenants before God." But after that, he said ominously, "all sins must be atoned."[11]

If atonement by blood made the wicked shake, other themes of the reformation would have dreadful consequences before many months passed. Among these was a warning to complacent leaders to wake up spiritually and compel righteousness and obedience among the people or lose their places. Some of them, charged Grant, were "as dry and dead as an old chip and . . . as tight as the bark of a tree." They were asleep, he said, and "if they do not wake up they should be cut off."[12]

Bishops were told to "repent and wash themselves, cleanse their premises, their Houses, back houses, and everything else about them, and then get the Holy Ghost and go from house to house and purify the whole city." If they do not do this, "the Marshal shall receive orders to send Policemen round to wash the Bishops and people and cleanse every house," Grant warned, "for the wrath of God burns against us, owing to the filth and abomination that exists here."[13]

Closely related to the call for local leaders to get their houses in order was the demand for the unquestioning obedience of the people to those placed in authority over them. None can "treat with impunity the authority of God, and the light of God, the chain that the Almighty has let down from heaven to earth, which we call the Priesthood," Grant made clear.[14]

His associate Heber C. Kimball used a favorite metaphor to call on the faithful "to be like clay in the hands of the potter." He said that Brigham Young was their head potter and Young's word was the "word of God to this people, and to those he has called to assist him in this great work," referring to local authorities.[15] Over and over, the word from the pulpit was hammered home into the consciousness of listeners—repent your sins and obey your file leader.

Singled out for special "working up" during the reformation were the

[11]Journal of Lorenzo Brown, April 1, 1857.

[12]Kenney, ed., *Wilford Woodruff's Journal*, 4:468–69.

[13]Bishops' Meetings, September 30, 1856, LDS Archives, as quoted by Sessions, *Mormon Thunder*, 219.

[14]Jedediah M. Grant, October 26, 1856, *Journal of Discourses*, 4:122–29.

[15]*Deseret News*, October 1, 1856, 234.

many Utah women who were desperately unhappy about sharing their husbands with other wives and yearned for normal marriages. In a direct reference to polygamy, Jedediah Grant said, "We have women here who like anything but the celestial law of God; and if they could break asunder the cable of the Church of Christ, there is scarcely a mother in Israel but would do it this day."[16]

"They say they have not seen a week's happiness since they became acquainted with that law or since their husbands took a second wife," he railed, admitting the doctrine's unpopularity. "They want to break up the church of God, and to break it from their husbands and from their family connections."[17] His calling polygamy "the cable of the church" and "the celestial law of God" pointed up the importance of the revealed doctrine in Utah's early religious culture.

To silence such complainers once and for all, Brigham Young on September 21 announced he would give Mormon women two weeks "to make up their minds whether they would stay with their Husbands or be liberated at the General Conference." After that period, "if they decided to stay with their husbands," Young said, "they should keep the law of God & not murmur or Complain." Otherwise, "I will set all at liberty," he vowed.[18]

How many took him up on this offer is not known, but enough apparently considered it that Young at the end of the two weeks felt it necessary to qualify his promise. On October 6, he set "certain conditions" before he would release women from unwanted marriages. They must first "appear forthwith at my office & give good & sufficient reasons" for him to grant divorces from their husbands. After that, he said, they must "marry men that will not have but one wife."[19]

CATECHISM

The most intrusive feature of the 1856 spiritual cleansing was the catechism. This was a list of questions, drawn up by Jedediah Grant himself, to probe the lives of Utah settlers for violations of cleanliness

---

[16]Jedediah M. Grant, September 21, 1856, *Journal of Discourses*, 4:49–51.

[17]Ibid.

[18]*Deseret News*, October 1, 1856, 235. Also see Kenney, ed., *Wilford Woodruff's Journal*, 4:451.

[19]Kenney, ed., *Wilford Woodruff's Journal*, 4:464.

and moral conduct. Using this device, bishops and teachers were told to go into every home and "find out those who are not disposed to do right." Said Grant, "let their names be written down and let the offence and place of residence be written against the name, that we may know who are living in sin, where they live and what their offences are."[20]

One who underwent this trial and intensely disapproved of it was an educated, 49-year-old Englishwoman who had "stepped out of my beautiful, happy home" in the university town of Cambridge "for the Gospel's sake." Hannah Tapfield King, one of many remarkable women in Utah history, told how the bishop and two or more teachers "catechised the people in every house," using a list of questions "over a foot in length."[21]

"It was a fearful ordeal," she said, then passed her own moral judgment, "and fear is a slavish passion and is not begotten by the spirit of God."[22]

Among the questions addressed by local leaders to the members under their authority were these:

> Have you ever committed adultery?
> Have you ever spoken evil of Authorities or anointed of the Lord?
> Have you ever betrayed your brethren?
> Have you ever stolen or taken anything that was not your own?
> Have you ever took [sic] the name of God in vain?
> Have you ever been drunk?
> Have you ever taken any poles from the big field or fences or taken your brothers hay?
> Have you ever picked up anything that did not belong to you and kept it without seeking to find out the owner?
> Have you made promises and not performed them?
> Do you pay all your Tithing?
> Do you labor Faithfully and diligently for your employer?
> Do you preside over your Family as a servant of God or are they subject to you?
> Do you teach your children the gospel?
> Do you attend your Ward meetings?
> Do you pray in your families night and morning?
> Do you pray in Secret?
> Do you wash your bodies once a week?

[20]Jedediah M. Grant, November 2, 1856, *Journal of Discourses*, 4:83–87.

[21]Journals of Hannah Tapfield King, October 8, 1856, MS 628, LDS Archives. Hannah King came to Utah in 1853 and died at Salt Lake City in 1886. Her journals are among the most important, if often overlooked, sources on Utah society and events during this period.   [22]Ibid.

Poet Hannah Tapfield King
left her "happy home" in Cambridge,
England, "for the Gospel's sake," but
deeply disapproved of the fearful
ordeal known as the Reformation.
Courtesy, Utah State Historical Society.

Brigham Young himself encountered difficulties on the last of the
above questions. In a meeting of church officers, he confessed "he did
not," although "he had tried it." The Mormon leader said he was "well
aware that this was not for everybody."[23]

Meanwhile, as his people squirmed under intense interrogation,
Young and other Utah leaders turned their attention that fall to a more
immediate crisis—the plight of the handcart companies. Left to carry
forward the work of reform on his own was "Jeddy" Grant, who threw
himself into his last great calling—to fan the spirit of confession,
repentance, and rebaptism throughout the territory. For the people of
Utah, it was an unhappy time. Said Hannah Tapfield King: "Every
Bishop had the 'cue' given to him and he rose up and lashed the people
as with a cat-o-nine tails. The people shrunk, shivered, wept, groaned
like whipped children. They were told to get up in meeting and confess
their sins. They did so 'till it was sickening, and brought disease."[24]

---

[23]Catechism questions and quotes are from the Diary of John Moon Clements, November 4, 1856, as
quoted in Sessions, *Mormon Thunder*, 220–21.

[24]Journals of Hannah Tapfield King, October 8, 1856.

Then without notice, suddenly and unexpectedly, the voice of the obsessed reformer was stilled. Working too many hours on not enough rest, exhorting and baptizing in cold mountain waters as winter came on, the man who called himself "Mormon Thunder" was struck down by typhoid and pneumonia. The fearsome reformer died on December 1, just after the last wagon load of handcart survivors rolled in. "A mighty man in Zion is laid low; a valiant man in Israel has fallen," lamented Apostle Woodruff.[25]

Certain it is that Jedediah Morgan Grant was one of the most influential, if least known, figures in early Utah, one who would have an important impact on the history of the territory during the nineteenth century and the state's culture thereafter. Born nine days before his death was a son, Heber Jeddy, who would become the gentle future president of the church his father served.

In the meantime, Grant's death and the rescue of the handcart pioneers were only interruptions in the great revival for which the alarming preacher is best known. Allowing an interval of two weeks for mourning, other Mormon leaders put their full weight behind the crusade for reform and the spiritual flames leaped even higher in Utah settlements.

In Great Salt Lake City, newly named seat of government for the territory,[26] the Social Hall on December 23 became "filled as with consumeing fire" during a meeting of the Legislative Assembly. Representatives spoke until sundown and "the House was filled with the spirit of God almost to the Consuming of our flesh," recorded Wilford Woodruff. That night he attended the bishops meeting and "the fire of God still burned in us."[27]

Attending these meetings at the capital was Jacob Bigler, the bishop of Nephi, who alerted priesthood leaders of his town, some eighty miles to the south. "The fire of God is burning here and I command you and your quorums to scour up your armor both temporally & spiritual[l]y," he wrote. "Prepare your selves to stand by me when Israel is to be cleansed for this has got to be done that the Gentile bands may be broken."[28] He then revealed that the time to sever ties with the American

---

[25]Kenney, ed., *Wilford Woodruff's Journal*, 4:498.

[26]By resolution of the governor and Legislative Assembly on December 15, the capital of Utah Territory was moved from Fillmore to Great Salt Lake City. See *Deseret News*, December 24, 1856, 336.

[27]Kenney, ed., *Wilford Woodruff's Journal*, 4:520.

[28]Bigler to Presidents of Seventies Quorums, Nephi Mass Quorum of Seventies, December 22, 24, 1856.

republic was at hand: "The Saints in Carson & Sanbernidino [sic] are called to Come Home Come Home Come Home."[29] The callback as early as December 1856 of exposed settlements at San Bernardino in southern California and Carson Valley at present Genoa, near Carson City, Nevada, indicated that the move to independence anticipated a possible armed confrontation with the United States.

As the excitement grew, a purposeful mob on December 29 broke into the law offices of Associate Supreme Court Justice George P. Stiles and looted the federal appointee's papers and library. The raiders pretended to dump his books and court records into a nearby privy and set them on fire.[30] An outspoken defender of the primacy of the district courts, Stiles was so upset by the apparent burning of government property and so fearful for his own safety that he soon after fled the territory.[31]

The next day both houses of the Legislative Assembly, the Council and House of Representatives, met in joint session to take up the state of the reformation. There was such an outpouring of the spirit of God, said Hosea Stout, that the members unanimously voted "to repent and forsake our sins and be rebaptized for their Remission."[32] After dinner they filled up the baptistery and all thirty-nine lawmakers and some others went under the water. Said Apostle Woodruff: "This was a New feature in Legislation."[33]

Before the reformation, said Indian Agent Garland Hurt, "all was peace, sobriety and good order." Then the word had come down from "the Lord's anointed," commanding the people "to bow at the Confessional, and repair to the streams of the mountains and be rebaptized forth with." He had seen men and women, "weeping in the utterest ago-

[29]Ibid.

[30]Books the mob pretended to destroy apparently included some 109 volumes of U.S. House and Senate executive documents and journals delivered a month before by O. P. Rockwell under contract with Almon W. Babbit, territorial secretary, who was killed apparently by Indians shortly after, near Fort Kearny, Nebraska.

[31]A native of New York, Stiles had served as city councilor at Nauvoo, Illinois, where he was said to have advised Joseph Smith in 1844 to destroy the dissident newspaper, Nauvoo Expositor. Named associate justice of the Utah Supreme Court in 1854, he had made himself unwelcome by defending the primacy of the district courts against the competing Mormon probate court system. A week before his offices were looted, Stiles had been "cut off from the Church root and Branch" for alleged adultery. Said Hosea Stout: "Amen to the damnation of that wicked & corrupt Judge." See Brooks, On The Mormon Frontier, 2:611.

[32]Ibid., 2:613.

[33]Kenney, ed., Wilford Woodruff's Journal, 4:524.

nies of soul," Hurt said, "and when I attempted to console them would say, they abhorred the idea of being forced into a confessional but dare not refuse."[34]

PARRISH-POTTER MURDERS

If emotionally over-stressed, most people in Utah dampened the spiritual conflagration with common sense, but here and there the flames of reform appeared to flare out of control. On Christmas day 1856 a fine snow fell all day and city streets were "filled with sleighs," said Hosea Stout. "This evening a young woman by the name of Williams committed suicide by cutting her throat."[35]

In Springville, where 49-year-old Aaron Johnson was bishop, Alvira Parrish had heard it preached that if apostates tried to leave, "hogholes would be stopped up with them." Even so, she said, her husband, William, did not believe in "killing to 'save,' as taught by the teachers," and decided to get away with his two sons, William Beason, 22, and Orrin, 18. The three Parrish men mistakenly put their trust in two "friends" who offered to assist their escape.

Shortly after nightfall on March 14, 1857, the elder Parrish and his guide slipped out of the west gate and walked a little way to the south where they waited in a lane for Orrin and "Beason" with their own guide to meet them. But before they came, muskets flashed in the dark and Parrish's guide was hit. Then a man sprang out of the night and grappled with Parrish. He stabbed the escapee with a knife and, after he went down, cut his throat.

The first to fall, shot and killed by mistake, was Gardner "Duff" Potter, who had led Parrish into the ambush. He was the same man who in 1853 had ordered the execution of five Sanpitch Indians in the street at Manti. Ironically, his younger brother, William, had been killed that same year in an oddly similar ambush of Captain Gunnison and his

---

[34]Hurt to Cumming, December 17, 1857, Territorial Papers, Utah Series.

[35]Brooks, *On The Mormon Frontier*, 2:611. According to Garland Hurt, a woman who had come with the handcart companies committed suicide on the night of December 24, 1856, in the eastern suburbs of Great Salt Lake City rather than become a polygamous wife of the man with whose family she was living. Hurt said she was told she would be denied subsistence and denounced as a prostitute if she did not comply, "and the fatal razor was brought to its relief." See Hurt to Cumming, December 17, 1857, Territorial Papers, Utah Series.

party on the Sevier River while acting as a guide for the topographical engineer.

Near the southwest corner of the fort, Orrin Parrish heard the gunfire, but hardly had time to wonder what it meant before shots banged close at hand and his brother fell, mortally wounded. Their guide, one Abraham Durfee, then pointed a revolver at the youth and pulled the trigger, but the gun misfired. The surviving Parrish jumped over the wall and ran to his uncle's house for safety. He saved himself by pretending he did not know what had happened, why, or who was involved.[36]

That same winter, young Thomas Lewis from Manti was being escorted one night to the territorial prison at Great Salt Lake for alleged sexual misconduct. At Willow Creek, near Ephraim, he was seized by a party of men under 38-year-old Warren Snow, the bishop of Manti, who "took him into the willows" and castrated him "in a brutal manner Tearing the chords right out." They left the youth lying in the snow, bleeding and senseless on "a bitter cold night." He was found two days later, crazed and nearly dead.[37]

Brigham Young's brother, Joseph, himself one of the Mormon hierarchy, disapproved this act and told his younger sibling that "he would rather die than to be made a Eunuch." To this, Brigham Young replied the day was coming when thousands would be made eunuchs "in order for them to be saved in the kingdom of God."[38] Moreover, he said, apparently referring to Snow, "when a man is trying to do right & do[es] some thing that is not exactly in order I feel to sustain him & we all should."[39]

Young's tolerance for the misdeeds of loyal subordinates meant that justice would be delayed for the victim of the crime on Willow Creek, but some twenty-six years later, retribution apparently did come to the perpetrator. After several unsuccessful attempts by persons unknown to return to Snow the favor he paid to young Lewis, the following notice

[36]The above quotes are from the testimony of Alvira L. Parrish and Orrin E. Parrish and confession of Abraham Durfee, *Kirk Anderson's Valley Tan*, 1:25, April 19, 1859. Also see Cradlebaugh, *Utah and the Mormons*, 43–60.

[37]Diary of Samuel Pitchforth, May 31, 1857. Also see Peterson, "Warren Stone Snow, a Man in Between: The Biography of a Mormon Defender." For a colored account, see Lee, *Mormonism Unveiled; or The Life and Confessions of the late Mormon bishop, John D. Lee; Written by Himself*, 285–86. Lee said Lewis was castrated because he refused to give up a young woman Snow wanted to make one of his polygamous wives.

[38]An apparent reference to Mt. 19:12.

[39]Kenney, ed., *Wilford Woodruff's Journal*, 5:55.

appeared on October 10, 1883, in *The Salt Lake Tribune* under the head-line, "Retributive Justice": "Bishop Warren Snow couldn't attend Con-ference by reason of sickness, which was brought on by a band of men, who served him as he served a young man several years since. The Bishop is no longer a man. 'Vengeance is mine,' saith the Lord."[40]

It is significant that none of these and possibly other crimes during the reformation period was ever reported in the territory's only newspa-per of record, *Deseret News* at Great Salt Lake City. Nor were the perpe-trators ever punished, although what they had done was common knowledge in their settlements. To the contrary, Aaron Johnson and Warren Snow soon after received new honors.

Eventually, the great spiritual conflagration known as the reformation ran its course in 1857 as even Brigham Young tired of trying to sustain the emotional outburst. One Sunday, said Hannah Tapfield King, Young rose up in the stand, "peaceful and benign," and told the people to go to anyone they had wronged and confess it to him alone, "but stop this confessing in public." "He would have no more of it," she said. His words "fell like balm on the spirits of the people."[41]

Even so, the cleansing of Israel to prepare for independence from the American republic would influence the culture of Utah and events in the territory for years to come.[42] More immediate was the impact on rela-tions with officials of the national government as local leaders dropped what little pretense they may have shown in the past of respecting the work or authority of federal judges, surveyors, Indian agents, and other outside appointees.

FLIGHT OF THE FEDERAL OFFICIALS

Even before the reformation began, two of Utah's three supreme court judges had already fled. Especially controversial had been William Drummond, who had lasted on scene less than a year. Named to replace Justice Leonidas Shaver, who died suddenly just before he arrived in 1855, Drummond had affronted the moral sensibilities of a religious

---

[40]"Retributive Justice," *The Salt Lake Tribune*, October 10, 1883. The author is indebted to historian Harold Schindler for this item.

[41]Journals of Hannah Tapfield King, 142.

[42]For one evaluation of the reformation's cultural impact, see Peterson, "The Mormon Reformation."

people who practiced polygamy, but damned adultery, by bringing as his companion a prostitute from the East instead of his own wife from Illinois. That was bad enough, but when he had challenged the sweeping powers of the probate courts, granted by Utah lawmakers but never intended by Congress under the act establishing the territory, the new judge found himself under arrest by the territory's marshal on charges of attempted murder. Drummond took to his heels in June 1856 but would be heard from loudly again.

More circumspect but no more successful had been John F. Kinney, named in 1853 at age 37 to become chief justice of the Utah Supreme Court at an annual salary of $2,500. Kinney brought his family to Utah the following year and rented a house "for which the Mormons charged me $2,000 dollars a year," he complained. Other costs were equally high, but he managed to stick it out for nearly two years.[43]

During that time, Kinney presided over the trial of Captain Gunnison's killers in 1855 and in private reports often protested Mormon control of the judicial system. "The avowed doctrine of the 'great Apostle' is, that the authority of the Priesthood is and shall be the law of the land," he once told the U.S. attorney general.[44] The judge came to grief by ruling unconstitutional an act of the Territorial Assembly that attempted to curtail his authority to exercise common law jurisdiction. For this, Utah lawmakers simply put him out of a job. Acting under powers granted by the organic act, they created a new district for him to preside over, five hundred miles from Great Salt Lake City, in a region, now in western Nevada, "sparsely inhabited except by Indians, & destitute of the necessary comforts."[45]

Having been "legislated out of office," the troublesome magistrate had taken offense at the "insult to me and my family" and in July 1856 returned to his home in West Point, Iowa, where he came down with bilious fever.[46] Kinney would return to Utah in 1860, again as supreme court chief justice, but this time he would show that he had learned well

---

[43]Kinney to Cushing to Black, undated, U.S. Attorney General, "Records relating to the appointment of Federal judges, attorneys, and marshals for the Territory and State of Utah."

[44]Ibid., Kinney to Cushing, March 1, 1855.

[45]Ibid., Kinney to Black, undated.

[46]Ibid. Also see Julia Kinney to Cushing, September 3, 1856.

from his earlier experience in the territory. Never again would he step
out of line and question the authority of Brigham Young.

In the meantime the reformation made Utah's climate even more hostile for remaining federal appointees who soon decided to follow the
first two federal justices. In February 1857 Surveyor General David Burr
was handed a copy of a letter he had sent through the local post office
months before to the General Land Office in Washington, D.C., accus-
ing Brigham Young of trespass on federal lands. Territorial Marshal
Alexander McRae and Hosea Stout demanded to know if he had written it. When the surprised surveyor admitted he had, they told him "the
country was theirs, that they would not permit this interference with
their rights." Further, they warned, "this writing letters about them
would be put a stop to."[47]

Several weeks later, Wilford Woodruff reported what happened when
the surveyor general and Indian Agent Hurt demanded a ruling from
Associate Justice Stiles, upholding the supremacy of federal law in the
district court at Great Salt Lake. The pair of federal officials "went out
of the house in the form of a sled, using the seat of their honor for runners," the apostle said.[48] At this, the last member of the territory's highest court, Judge Stiles, decided it was time to go.

As relations collapsed altogether, Burr in a privately mailed letter told
the General Land Office commissioner that the "United States courts
have been broken up and driven from the Territory." The plain fact was,
he said, *these people repudiate the authority of the United States in this country, and
are in open rebellion against the general government.*"[49] The surveyor general further reported that Brigham Young had announced that federal surveyors
"shall not be suffered to trespass on *their* lands as they did the last season." He also believed his life was in danger, especially after the Parrish-
Potter murders at Springville, and said that unless federal protection was
provided, every official of the national government in the territory
would have to leave.[50]

Perhaps the greatest indignity of all was suffered by one of Burr's

[47]Burr to Hendricks, February 4, 1857, House Exec. Doc. 71, 118.
[48]Woodruff to Smith, Journal History, April 1, 1857.
[49]Burr to Hendricks, March 28, 1857, House Exec. Doc. 71, 118–20. Emphasis in the original.
[50]Ibid.

clerks after he had gone. C. G. Landon on July 25 was first knocked senseless, then heard pounding that night on the surveyor's office doors. The back entry was forced and voices ordered him to come down. He jumped out of the second story window, dressed only in his pants and a stocking, and ran for his life. In a remarkable demonstration of the will to survive, he turned up two months later at Placerville, California, where he found work in a stone quarry, "having walked nearly all the way from Salt Lake City barefooted and nearly naked."[51]

By May 1857 all of the federal appointees in Utah except one had fled to report in person at the nation's capital on conditions in an American territory, now considered to be in a state of open rebellion. The last to remain, either braver or more foolish than the rest, was Garland Hurt. Putting his trust in the Utah tribe to protect him, the Virginian moved to the Spanish Fork Indian farm to reside with the Indians he had befriended.

Meanwhile, to prepare for a military confrontation, Lt. Gen. Daniel H. Wells on April 1, 1857, announced a reorganization of the territorial militia, or Nauvoo Legion. All able-bodied white males in the territory between 18 and 45 were told to enroll for military duty in units patterned after the hosts of ancient Israel.

In the new organization, a division consisted of two brigades under a major general, a brigade numbered one thousand men in two regiments under a brigadier general, a regiment comprised five hundred rank and file in five battalions under a colonel, each battalion numbered one hundred rank and file in two companies of fifty under a major, companies of fifty counted five platoons of ten under a captain, and platoons were commanded by lieutenants.[52] According to its new judge advocate, Hosea Stout, the military arm of the kingdom was patterned after "the good old Bible rule of Captains of 10's 100's &c."[53]

At the same time, General Wells under General Order No. 1 divided Utah into thirteen military districts under designated leaders who were to enroll settlers liable for military service in platoons and companies. Named to high ranks in command of the San Pete and Peteetneet

[51]Landon to Burr, September 18, 1857, House Exec. Doc. 71, 122–23.
[52]*Deseret News*, April 1, 1857, 28.
[53]Brooks, *On The Mormon Frontier*, 2:623.

(southern Utah County) districts, were Warren Snow and Aaron Johnson, respectively.[54]

YOUNG LOOKS NORTH

As the territory prepared for defense, four exhausted riders whose "trail could be followed by the blood from our horses legs," arrived at Utah settlements on February 16, 1857, after a 380-mile midwinter ride from Fort Limhi, near present Salmon, Idaho.[55] They carried to Brigham Young a report of an exploration of Bitterroot Valley, now in southwestern Montana, by Mormon Indian missionaries under 35-year-old Benjamin Franklin Cummings. On orders from Young, in November 1856 Cummings had led 29-year-old Pleasant Green Taylor and Ebenezer Robinson, 21, on the Lewis and Clark trail over the Continental Divide to Horse Prairie Creek on the upper Missouri River. Riding past the future site of Bannack City, Montana, the trio then followed the Flathead Trail north along the Big Hole River to recross the Continental Divide and enter Bitterroot Valley from the south. They saw "little in the way to obstruct the passage of wagons," Cummings recorded.[56]

The three explorers from the arid Great Basin gazed in wonder upon the valley of the Bitterroot River, defended by the Flathead Indians against their more numerous foe, the Blackfeet. The fertile valley stretched northward as far as they could see, spread by "groves of pine interspersed with beautiful prairies and threaded across with numerous streams of pure water," Cummings said. "The scenery was grand and sublime in the highest degree."[57] Cummings and his companions then rode "over a prairie of rich soil" to Cantonment Stevens, a few log cabins and corrals about four miles north of present Hamilton, Montana.[58] There they found Neil McArthur, Hudson's Bay agent, and carried out one purpose of their journey—to make an offer to buy Fort Hall.

---

[54]*Deseret News*, April 22, 1857, 48.

[55]Shurtliff, "Life and Travels of Lewis Warren Shurtliff."

[56]Autobiography and Journals of Benjamin Franklin Cummings, November 16, 1856.

[57]Ibid., November 18, 1856.

[58]Ibid., November 19, 1856. The abandoned Cantonment Stevens on the Bitterroot River, some twelve miles south of Fort Owen, had been built by Lt. John Mullan in 1853 as a base camp for the Northern Pacific Railroad Survey and named after Isaac I. Stevens, first governor of Washington Territory.

McArthur allowed he was "not prepared to make the sale," but would let the Mormons know in the spring "what he could do."

While Taylor occupied McArthur, the most experienced member of the Mormon party devoted himself to the main reason for riding 160 miles north into Washington Territory. B. F. Cummings gathered all the information he could about the region. Obvious at once to the trained eye of the Nauvoo Legion officer was the defensive potential of the Flathead tribe's homeland. The great valley of the Bitterroot was a natural fortress girdled on three sides, east, west and south, by high mountains that allowed entry only by a handful of narrow trails. The region also appeared large enough to sustain an extensive agricultural economy. At McArthur's camp the valley was about ten miles wide, Cummings noted, and it "extended about 40 miles" from there "to the junction of Bitter-Root and Hells Gate river." At its northern end, location of present Missoula, the valley opened upon other fertile regions that offered natural approaches to the Canadian border, less than two hundred miles away.

Cummings also learned that "the northern railroad survey passed over the divide of the Rocky Mountains from Fort Benton on the Missouri down Hells Gate river across the north end of the valley west." This distance, he saw, was only two hundred miles. In addition, he recorded, it was only two hundred miles from Fort Benton "to Fort Union the present head of navigation."

"From Surveyors reports which I saw, the Missouri could be navigated 30 miles from Fort Benton by steam boats of the lightest draught," he noted. Before construction of a railroad, "there was a good rout[e] for a waggon road" to carry goods and emigrants that had been transported by steamboat to Fort Benton over the remaining distance to the Flathead country.[59] All of this, "when considered with Mormonism," struck Cummings as "very interesting." In fact, the New Englander said: "We could not help thinking that some day Bitter-Root

---

[59]Ibid. That this was certain to interest Mormon leaders is pointed up by Brigham Young's open letter "To Those Who Are Engaged in Freighting on The Western Waters," published in *Deseret News* on November 21, 1855. Young said "steamboats of heavy burden and deep draft have made annual trips for the fur companies far up the Missouri." He called for "a new field of enterprise" to transport goods by that route to the nearest point from Mormon settlements "by boats of the lightest draft." He then proposed to build a fort at the head of navigation to receive and ship goods the rest of the way by wagon.

valley as well as other portions of the country over east of the mountains would become the abode of the saints." He concluded his work by
making a map of the route they had taken from Fort Limhi on today's
Lemhi River, near Tendoy, Idaho, to Bitterroot Valley.[60]

After their return, the Salmon River Mission head, Thomas S. Smith,
called for volunteers to "inform President Brigham Young of brother
Taylor's and company's doing in regard to Fort Hall and the prospects
of the Flat Head country."[61] He chose four men, Pleasant Green Taylor,
Laconias Barnard, Lewis Shurtliff, and himself, to make the hazardous
winter ride and named Cummings to preside over the Fort Limhi Indian
mission in his absence. They made it, but just barely.

For four weeks the messengers struggled south through deep snow,
fog, and freezing winds at an average rate of only three or four miles a
day. Worn out and half starved, the riders from Fort Limhi at last
reached Great Salt Lake in mid-February and reported in person to
Brigham Young and other leaders. If they wondered at the keen interest
bestowed upon them that day, they certainly had reason to marvel when
an unusual honor soon after fell suddenly on their modest outpost in the
northwest.

On February 22, less than a week after the interview, Brigham Young
announced before the congregation in the tabernacle that he would go
north to Fort Limhi as soon as the weather allowed. That Sunday, "a
large number" of Utah's leaders, including many from the southern settlements, was called "to accompany prest B. Young to Salmon River in
Oregon."[62] When it came to moving large numbers of people over long
distances, Young never looked to the Almighty to point the way or drop
manna from the sky. Instead he put his trust in wheat, cached or planted,
along a good trail with water and grass for livestock. Nor was he one to
delegate to another the responsibility to decide the feasibility of such an
undertaking.

Brigham Young would go north and see for himself.

---

[60]Ibid., November 19, 1856.
[61]Salmon River Mission Journal, January 18, 1857.
[62]Brooks, *On The Mormon Frontier*, 2:623.

COL. ALBERT SIDNEY JOHNSTON, SECOND U.S. CAVALRY
Johnston replaced Gen. William Harney as
commander of the Utah Expedition.
Courtesy, Utah State Historical Society.

Chapter 7

Utah in Rebellion

President B. Young . . . declared that the thre[a]d was cut between
us and the U.S. and that the Almighty recognised us as a free and
independent people and that no officer ap[p]ointed by government should come and rule over us from this time forth.

—Hosea Stout

In its short history, the controversial faith of Utah's first settlers had
excited violent opposition from neighbors in New York, Ohio, Missouri, and Illinois. Its foes had come in many shapes—state militias,
sheriffs' posses, bounty hunters, and even militant rabble best described
as mobs in the customary meaning of the word. Now, in 1857, there
came a regular army of the United States sent by an American president.

On May 28 the aging Mexican War hero, Gen. Winfield Scott, ordered
that year "not less than 2,500 men," about one sixth of the U.S. Army at
the time, to march to Utah.[1] The force included all or major parts of three
regiments, the Second Dragoons, Fifth Infantry, and Tenth Infantry;
Phelps' and Reno's batteries of the Fourth Artillery; supply trains, transportation, and staff. The expedition's commander, Brig. Gen. William
Harney, was told his army was to serve as a *posse comitatus*[2] in aiding a new
governor and federal officers to keep the peace and enforce the law in the
territory the president considered to be in a state of rebellion. Harney was
ordered to provide troops for this purpose when called on, but was not to
attack any "body of citizens," except in self-defense. Somewhat ambigu-
ously, he was told he would not be subject to the orders of the new governor, but should "conform your action to his requests."[3]

---

[1]Scott to Adjutant General, et al, May 28, 1857, House Exec. Doc. 71, 4.

[2]A force representative of all citizens called by the legitimate authority of a political jurisdiction to enforce
the law.

[3]Lay to Harney, June 29, 1857, House Exec. Doc. 71, 8, 9.

To justify his decision to send an American army to Utah, President James Buchanan later submitted to Congress nearly five dozen letters and reports written over a six-year period, alleging treason, disloyalty, or other serious offenses.[4] Pointing up the importance of Indian relations in Utah's early years, forty-six of this number came from the Office of Indian Affairs, six written by Garland Hurt.

Especially inflammatory was the list of charges leveled in the fiery resignation on March 30, 1857, of Associate Justice William Drummond. Among other things, Drummond said there were men "set apart" by the Mormon church to "take both the lives and property" of dissenters, that American citizens were illegally imprisoned, and that Brigham Young told grand juries "whom to indict and whom not." Highly inciting was his unsupported allegation that Capt. John Gunnison had been murdered in 1853 "under the orders, advice, and direction of the Mormons."[5]

Why the president failed to include in his justification a number of other charges is not known. These included the detailed report to President Fillmore by Utah's first "run-away" officials, Harris, Brandebury and Brocchus; Major Steptoe's charges of Mormon tampering with the Indians; and John Kinney's numerous complaints to the U.S. Attorney General over Mormon control of the courts during his first term as chief justice. Also unmentioned were complaints by private citizens.

JOURNEY TO FORT LIMHI

The president's decision to act on these charges came while the governor of the allegedly mutinous region was off on a journey that would have an important bearing on the course of events over the coming year. Brigham Young said the 141 people who made the trip went to Fort Limhi "to rest their minds, to invigorate their bodies," and to examine the country.[6] But the make-up of the company that headed north from Great Salt Lake on April 24 revealed there was more to the junket than Young's known fondness for travel.

---

[4]Despite various theories, there is no real evidence that Buchanan ordered the U.S. Army expedition to Utah for any reason other than the reports of federal officials over a six-year period. See MacKinnon, "125 Years of Conspiracy Theories: Origins of the Utah Expediton." Of these, "The Utah Expedition," House Exec. Doc. 71 (35–1), 1858, Serial 956, offers an adequate, if incomplete, listing.

[5]Ibid., Drummond to Black, March 30, 1857, 212–14.   [6]*Deseret News*, June 10, 1857, 107–09.

The cavalcade was led by all three members of the Mormon triumvirate, or First Presidency, Young, Heber C. Kimball, his first counselor, and Second Counselor Daniel Wells, who also held the lofty title of lieutenant general of the Nauvoo Legion.[7] In addition, it listed three of the four Quorum of Twelve members not outside the territory on other duties, apostles Orson Hyde, Lorenzo Snow, and Franklin Richards. Only Wilford Woodruff was left behind to steer the ship of Zion into darkening skies ahead.[8]

Representing the Great Basin kingdom's military arm were at least seven generals,[9] as many as eight colonels, and a flock of lesser field officers, including such gifted young commanders as Maj. John D. T. McAllister, Col. Robert T. Burton, and Maj. Lot Smith. Among others, the party also included the commandants of the Weber, Salt Lake, Lehi, Peteetneet, San Pete, and Iron military districts.

Significantly the Fort Limhi company numbered officials of most Mormon settlements from the direction opposite to Young's line of march. To make the round trip, leaders from Parowan and Cedar City, nearly three hundred miles south of the territorial capital, had to go roughly as far as the distance from Nauvoo on the Mississippi River to Great Salt Lake Valley. Outweighing the inconvenience, however, was the opportunity to see the landscape and trails to the northern Mormon outpost.

Related to this interest was the task of two members of the party, former school teacher Jesse Fox, and the territory's road commissioner, Thomas Brown, who brought "the necessary instruments for taking observations in the mountains."[10] They mapped and measured the entire route to Fort Limhi and the Lewis and Clark Pass over the Continental Divide to an accuracy of one-thousandth of a mile. Published on June 10, the potential way-bill for emigrants was the equivalent of a modern road map.

---

[7]Wells was sustained to the First Presidency on April 7, 1857, to replace Jedediah Grant, firebrand of the reformation, who died in December 1856.

[8]The whereabouts of other apostles at this time: Parley P. Pratt was on his way to Arkansas where he was killed three weeks later; Orson Pratt and Ezra T. Benson were presiding over the European Mission in England; John Taylor was editor of the newspaper, *The Mormon*, in New York City; George A. Smith was enroute to Utah from Washington, D.C.; Charles C. Rich and Amasa Lyman were enroute to Utah from San Bernardino in southern California; and Erastus Snow was on a special mission in the eastern states.

[9]This number included Daniel Wells, James Ferguson, George D. Grant, H. B. Clawson, William H. Kimball, Aaron Johnson, and Franklin D. Richards.

[10]*Deseret News*, June 10, 1857.

Among the members of Young's company was a noted leader of the Great Basin tribes who came to represent his hosts favorably to his counterparts in Oregon Territory. Chief Arapene of the Utahs could be expected to perform this role convincingly, especially if such service would clear the way for white settlers to leave his own tribal homeland. Young, superintendent of Indian affairs for Utah Territory, held powwows with the Indians of Oregon Territory, clearly outside his jurisdiction, in which Arapene took part. The governor further presented "many presents of blankets"[11] and other gifts to the Shoshoni and Bannock chiefs that later appear incorrectly charged to the Office of Indian Affairs for other alleged purposes.[12]

Over the next thirty-three days, Young and his companions inspected the Lewis and Clark trail over the Continental Divide "from the fort to Horse Prairie and the waters of the Missouri River" and saw it was steep and narrow, but extended only "some 10 or 15 miles."[13] And they "traveled over the surrounding country," selecting a location to the north, "some two miles down the river," for a second fort and settlement.[14]

What they talked about with the Indians went officially unreported, but stories the natives told about the meetings spread rapidly in the Northwest and struck alarm on the eve of major Indian uprisings there. Among the least fearful of such accounts was a report that "Choosuklee, (Jesus Christ,) had recently appeared on the other side of the mountains; that he was after awhile coming here, when the whites would be sent out of the country."[15] Such rumors persisted until the commanding general of the Department of the Pacific at San Francisco in early 1858 alerted U.S. Army units at Fort Walla Walla:

> Information from various sources and points on the frontier leads to the conclusion that through the Mormons the Indians are being inclined to

---

[11]Ibid. A number of participants reported on the meetings and giving of presents, including Lewis Shurtliff, John D. T. McAllister, and John Brown. For the account of the latter, see Brown, *Autobiography of Pioneer John Brown,* May 1 to May 27, 1857.

[12]For evidence of this, a careful study of "Accounts of Brigham Young, Superintendent of Indian Affairs in Utah Territory," House Exec. Doc. 29 (37–2), 1862, Serial 1128, is recommended.

[13]Ibid.

[14]Salmon River Mission Journal, May 11, 12, 31, 1857.

[15]Clarke to Thomas, January 1, 1858, Sen. Exec. Doc. 1 (35–2), 1858, 335–36. This may have been an early version of the Ghost Dance religion that swept the western tribes years later.

hostility, and that a conflict in Utah may be the signal for trouble on the frontier, and it is not improbable that the Mormons may move north.[16]

Unaware his visit had stirred up so much interest, Young on his return had little good to say in public about the region he had seen. "When people are obliged to live in the north country, that will be high time for them to go there," he told a gathering of his followers on May 31.[17] Later in 1857, aware that an American army was marching to Utah, he gave a completely different opinion, according to Wilford Woodruff. "He said the North is the place for us not the South" and that none "but the Saints would want the cold North country." Moreover, Young said the region near the upper Missouri River was "the key of this continent," the apostle recorded, and he proposed to send a company to build a new settlement as a way station on Snake River, near Fort Hall. Said Young, "we want to send them this fall so that we can put in grain this season."[18]

The news that gave urgency to this move was known to Utah leaders for at least a month before it was made public on July 24, the tenth anniversary of the arrival of Young's pioneer company in Salt Lake Valley.[19] That day, Porter Rockwell, Judson Stoddard, and A. O. Smoot interrupted festivities at present Brighton in Big Cottonwood Canyon with tidings that U.S. troops and a new governor were coming. The trio's dramatic arrival apparently was staged to fulfill to the day Young's alleged prophecy, ten years before, "If the people of the United States will let us alone for ten years, we will ask no odds of them."[20]

At this anticipated turn of events, the man known to his followers as "the Lion of the Lord," left little doubt as to where he stood. "As for any nation's coming to destroy this people, God Almighty being my helper, they cannot come here," Young roared.[21] "Good God!" added Heber C. Kimball, his first counselor, "I have wives enough to whip out the

---

[16]Ibid., Mackall to Steptoe, January 12, 1858, 336–37.

[17]Brigham Young, May 31, 1857, *Journal of Discourses*, 4:323–27.

[18]Report of meeting with Brigham Young, September 6, 1857, Wilford Woodruff Collection, MS 5506, LDS Archives.

[19]Frederick H. Burr, a trader from Bitterroot Valley, one month earlier noted at the Oregon Trail crossing of Thomas Fork of Bear River, just north of present Cokeville, Wyoming: "News of troops coming to Salt Lake." The news could not have reached this point without having arrived even sooner in Salt Lake Valley. See the Journal of Frederick H. Burr, June 24, 1857. For other evidence the July 24 announcement was staged, see Cooley, ed., *Diary of Brigham Young 1857*, n.52, 49–53.

[20]Brigham Young, September 13, 1857, *Journal of Discourses*, 4:226.   [21]Ibid.

United States."[22] But this was not the only thing that stirred the will to take up arms in the summer of 1857, Utah's most eventful year.

On May 13 the popular, 50-year-old apostle, Parley P. Pratt, was brutally murdered in northwestern Arkansas. The gifted writer, theologian, and missionary was slain as he attempted to escape from one Hector McLean, the angry husband of a woman Pratt had taken as his tenth wife. But to overheated emotions in Utah, the apostle was killed for his religious beliefs. Like Joseph and Hyrum Smith, he was a martyr whose blood cried for vengeance.

So it came to pass that an American territory of fewer than forty thousand threw down the gauntlet to a nation of more than thirty million, and even felt a little sorry for the other side. If forced to fight, they would do so "in the strength of Israel's God," Young told his people, when "one will chase a thousand, and two will put ten thousand to flight."[23] At reports Harney had sworn to winter in Utah or in hell, a settler at Nephi retorted, "May God grant in the latter place."[24] He almost got his wish.

As the weeks of spring and summer slowly slipped away, the hastily called military expedition was stalled by one delay after another. Its commander had been told no expense would be spared to prepare his force, but it took time to line up on short notice the contractors, teamsters, and supplies he needed. Weeks were spent at Fort Leavenworth concentrating the regiments whose companies were scattered from Minnesota to Florida. Then General Harney and the Second Dragoons were detached and sent to Kansas to quell civil unrest. This stripped the expedition of its commander and only cavalry support.

Although ordered to escort a new governor to Utah, the force was further held up when the president found it difficult to find a willing successor to Brigham Young. Also scarce were qualified candidates for the three seats on Utah's highest court, vacated in haste by the last to warm them. Appointed at last to the unwanted office of governor was Alfred Cumming, 54, former mayor of Augusta, Georgia, then serving as superintendent of Indian affairs for the Upper Missouri Agency at St. Louis.

[22]*Deseret News*, August 12, 1857, 172. Kimball married forty-three wives and had sixty-five children.

[23]Brigham Young, September 13, 1857, *Journal of Discourses*, 4:229. Compare with Dt. 32:30.

[24]Diary of Samuel Pitchforth, August 24, 1857.

Secretary of State Lewis Cass told the rotund bureaucrat to "take care that the laws are faithfully executed, and to maintain the peace and good order of the Territory." The president hoped the employment of military force would not be necessary to carry out this duty, Cass went on, but should resistance occur, "it must be met with firmness." With any "peculiar opinions" of the people in Utah, an apparent reference to polygamy, "however deplorable in themselves or revolting to the public sentiment of the country," Cumming was not to interfere.[25]

Van Vliet's Mission

When the Tenth Infantry on July 18 at last marched from Fort Leavenworth, it was already dangerously late in the season to make the 1,200-mile journey overland to Salt Lake Valley, much less to undertake a military campaign on the high plains. By then it was only prudent for the War Department to send ahead an officer with known diplomatic skills to arrange a camping place and supplies for the expedition in or near Utah's capital.

Chosen for this task was Quartermaster Capt. Stewart Van Vliet, who left his military escort behind on Hams Fork as a sign of peaceful intentions and rode alone into the Mormon stronghold. There he was treated courteously but was told the expedition would not be allowed to enter unopposed and, in any event, should expect no supplies or a place to camp. Invited to sit on the stand in the bowery on Sunday, September 13, the officer was also treated to the customary display of Mormon unity in support of their leaders. The sea of uplifted hands never failed to impress the uninitiated. Van Vliet afterward reported that "Governor Young and the people of Utah will prevent, if possible, the army for Utah from entering their Territory this season." The officer thought it would not be difficult to stop this entry, given "the lateness of the season, the smallness of our force, and the defences that nature has thrown around the valley of the Great Salt Lake."[26]

Having apparently planned to proclaim martial law a month earlier,

---

[25]Cass to Cumming, July 30, 1857, Territorial Papers, Utah Series.

[26]Van Vliet to Pleasanton, September 16, 1857, House Exec. Doc. 2 (35–1), Serial 943, 24–27, also published in Hafen and Hafen, eds., *The Utah Expedition, 1857–1858, A Documentary Account of the United States Military Movement under Colonel Albert Sidney Johnston, and The Resistance by Brigham Young and the Mormon Nauvoo Legion*, 50–55.

Brigham Young waited until Van Vliet had left the city, then on September 15 issued his broadside.[27] "CITIZENS OF UTAH," he announced, "We
are invaded by a hostile force." Standing on the constitution, Young
branded the American army "an armed, mercenary mob," forbade armed
forces of any kind from entering the territory, and ordered the Nauvoo
Legion to repel the "threatened invasion." He also declared that no one
could enter or leave the territory without a permit.[28]

The next day, September 16, Young and his top officer, Lt. Gen.
Daniel Wells, outlined to local military district heads the scorched earth
tactics they would employ to resist the intruders. "We intend to deso-
late the Territory, and conceal our families, stock and all our effects in
the fastnesses of the mountains, where they will be safe," they said,
"while the men waylay our enemies, attack them from ambush, stampede
their animals, take the supply trains, cut off detachments, and parties
sent to canyons for wood, or on other service."[29]

Young justified such actions on the narrow ground that he had not
been properly notified of his removal from office under the 1850 act
creating Utah Territory. The governor was to serve four years, "and until
his successor shall be appointed and qualified."[30] Since no one had been
named to take his place, Young had continued to serve under this provision after his appointment expired in 1854. This gave him the power, he
held, to resist by armed force an order by an American president to move
U.S. troops within the country.

ESCAPE OF GARLAND HURT

On the Spanish Fork Indian farm, the last remaining federal official
watched with growing concern as militia companies in Utah Valley
mobilized for war. Garland Hurt now wanted to get out, but as an
American citizen he refused to ask Brigham Young for a permit to come
or go on American soil. From this sanctuary, he urged the Utahs to reject

---

[27]Two copies of the proclamation, one dated August 5, the other September 15, are located in Special Collections, Marriott Library, University of Utah. Also see Cooley, *Diary of Brigham Young*, 82, 83.

[28]"Proclamation by the Governor," September 15, 1857, House Exec. Doc. 71, 34, 35.

[29]Young and Wells to Evans, September 16, 1857, David Evans Papers.

[30]See "An Act to Establish Territorial Government for Utah," Sec. 2, *Acts, Resolutions and Memorials Passed at the
Several Annual Sessions of the Legislative Assembly of the Territory of Utah from 1851 to 1870*, 25.

Mormon overtures to form an alliance against U.S. forces, offering himself "as a hostage for the peaceful intentions of the troops."[31]

Hurt's decision to escape came soon after he heard that a party of
California-bound emigrants had been attacked in southern Utah by
Piede Indians, but the natives themselves had "insisted that Mormons,
and not Indians, had killed the Americans." The agent sent a native
youth off by a secret trail to discover the truth of what had happened.
The warrior returned on September 23 with an awful tale of blood.

Hurt now made up his mind to take off, but the local militia moved
first. On September 27 natives rushed into the two-story adobe building where he made his office crying, "Friend! Friend! the Mormons will
kill you." Hurt looked from his window. He saw about one hundred
armed horsemen guarding the Spanish Fork Canyon escape route on the
east. More Indians rushed in to report that bodies of armed men were
coming from Springville and Payson. Then his interpreter came in and
said, "Doctor, you're done in!" The Virginian vowed to escape or "die in
the attempt."[32]

The troops Hurt saw had been ordered to arrest him by over-anxious
Nauvoo Legion officers who feared he might get away before Gen.
Aaron Johnson, head of the military district, returned with orders from
Brigham Young on how to handle the troublesome agent. Expecting the
natives to fight for their agent "at the drop of a hat," they had raised
some three hundred men "to awe them into submission" and make Hurt
"a prisoner *this day.*"

But within eighty rods of the Indian farm the militiamen ran into a
growing swarm of Utah warriors, "armed and much excited." Two other
companies of ten each, ordered to block the mouth of Spanish Fork

---

[31]See Hurt's biography in Reavis, *Saint Louis: The Future Great City of the World*, 781–89. For reports of Mormon
overtures to the Indians at this time, see Dimick Huntington Journal, September and October, 1857, MS 1419
2, LDS Archives. On September 1, 1857, Huntington said he told Chief Ammon and other Utahs that "they
[the soldiers] have come to fight us & you for when they kill us they will kill you and they sayd the[y] was afraid
to fight the Americans." He also said some Indians feared taking the food he offered because they were "afraid
of being Poisend [sic]." Also, Gen. Wells told Lehi Maj. David Evans to inform the Indians "that our enemies
are also their enemies and how they are continually fighting against them somewhere and that it will come upon
them as well as the Sioux and Cheyennes in due time, that they must be our friends and stick to us, for if our
enemies kill us off, they will surely be cut off by the same parties." See Wells to Evans, August 13, 1857, David
Evans Papers.

[32]Quotes are from Hurt to Forney, December 4, 1857, House Exec. Doc. 71, 199–205.

Canyon, rode into more angry Utahs "who would not let them pass." Meanwhile an Indian boy saddled Hurt's horse and off the agent rode with three warriors, heading first to West Mountain on Utah Lake to confuse his pursuers, then back that night to ride up Spanish Fork Canyon. Too late, General Johnson arrived on September 28 with orders from Brigham Young to "convey the Indian Agent Dr. Garland Hurt to this place." Finding the Indian farm a "perfect scene of waste and confusion," Johnson regretfully reported that "the bush had been shook and the bird flown."[33]

From Hurt's later report, it is likely that his Indian escort took him up Diamond Fork on the 1776 Escalante Trail and into the Uinta Basin, where he holed up in the Indian camps near present Vernal, Utah, until the route ahead was clear. He then rode over Diamond Mountain into Brown's Hole on the Indian trail later known as the Outlaw Trail, then up Green River to the Oregon Trail, which he followed east to meet oncoming U.S. Army units on the Sweetwater River near present South Pass City, Wyoming.

MILITARY OPERATIONS

In the so-called "Utah War," the geography of the approaches to Salt Lake Valley governed the strategy of both sides. For a large expedition moving west on the Oregon-California Trail, one that required passable roads for its supply trains, the Wasatch Mountains offered only two feasible entry points. The most direct was at Echo Canyon, a red-rock defile on the Mormon Trail from Fort Bridger, followed today by I-80. The other was at Soda Springs, where the Bear River breaks through the mountains and turns almost due south to provide an avenue toward the heart of northern Utah. Both routes were highly defensible.

As it developed, the Nauvoo Legion's near-term objective was to hold the U.S. Army out until snows filled up the canyons and blocked any passage. "The Government of our country will go by the board through its own corruptions, and no power can save it," said Brigham Young. "If

---

[33]Quotes are from "Report of Genl. A. Johnson to Lt. Genl. D. H. Wells in regard to the flight of Dr. Garland Hurt, U.S. Indian Agent, Oct. 1857," undated, Utah Militia Records. This document complements Hurt's own account and raises questions about Young's truthfulness in reporting the episode. Also see Autobiography of John Butler.

we can avert the blow for another season," he predicted, "it is probable that our enemies will have enough to attend to at home."[34]

Accordingly, small, fast-moving companies on strong horses would use increasingly aggressive guerrilla tactics as the U.S. Army neared. They would hover on its flanks to create alarm, burn grass to destroy livestock feed, capture stray animals, and employ other tactics to delay the command's progress but avoid outright combat. In the meantime, larger bodies of the estimated seven thousand-man Nauvoo Legion would fortify Echo Canyon, while scouting parties at the head of Salina Canyon kept watch for any enemy incursions in force over the Spanish Trail from Fort Union, near Santa Fé.

Mormon leaders were prepared to abandon Fort Bridger, but there the line would be drawn. If American troops moved west of the trading post, said General Wells, he would "take it as a sure indication that the Lord wants them used up."[35] Any attempt by the U.S. Army to pass Echo Canyon or move south from Soda Springs would be met by armed force. Utah soldiers would go on the attack and spill the blood of their former countrymen, if necessary, to keep them out.

FORT LIMHI STRENGTHENED

Above all, the coming forth that fall of the Kingdom of God, known by the name of Deseret, ruled out the possibility of further compromise or co-existence with the United States. In the event all else failed, Young ordered Col. Andrew Cunningham, a 40-year-old Virginian, to take a company of fifty and establish a new settlement on the Blackfoot River, near today's Idaho city of the same name. Significantly, the location was midway between Utah settlements and Fort Limhi.

To convert the Indian mission into a supply station on the route to Bitterroot Valley, a new company of more than sixty men, women, and children, with wagons and livestock, crossed Bear River on October 6 and moved north to expand the Salmon River settlement. As companies from San Bernardino to the south and Carson Valley on the west

---

[34]Brigham Young, *Journal of Discourses*, September 13, 1857, 4:229.

[35]Wells to Young, November 16 and 20, 1857, Nauvoo Legion Correspondence, Brigham Young Collection, as quoted in Peterson, "Warren Stone Snow, A Man in Between: the Biography of a Mormon Defender."

returned to defend Zion, the only direction new outbound colonists moved that fall was north.[36]

Less complicated were the considerations dictating the U.S. Army advance from the east. Its commanders had been ordered by the president of the United States to escort a new governor to Utah and enforce the law in the territory. Moreover, the force was in no condition to spend the winter in the open on the high plains of present western Wyoming. It desperately needed to reach Salt Lake Valley or some other sheltered place where it could be supplied, peacefully if possible, but by force if not, before winter set in.

LOT SMITH'S RAID

General Harney had been ordered to keep the troops "well massed and in hand,"[37] but Harney soon after had been reassigned. By early October, the expedition was scattered across present Wyoming from Fort Laramie to Hams Fork, a dozen miles or so north of Granger, without a permanent commander and entirely out of the grip of its senior officer, Col. Edmund Alexander of the Tenth Infantry. As Alexander dithered, hoping Harney's replacement would soon come, the force's supply trains, unguarded by cavalry, offered a tempting target.

So thought the black-bearded Mormon officer who eyed from a nearby hill the supply wagons of the army contractor, Russell, Majors & Waddell, lined up on Green River near the Oregon-California Trail crossing. With his boots on, he stood over six feet and weighed some two hundred pounds. At age 27, he never drank, swore, or used tobacco, but he was one of an unusual breed. For Maj. Lot Smith of the Nauvoo Legion was a born cavalry soldier.

Patiently Smith and his little mounted company waited until federal infantry had marched a few miles beyond support distance from two supply trains near present Seedskedee Wildlife Refuge, then early the next morning, he struck. While the American soldiers helplessly watched the smoke, the Mormon major burned their bacon, more than

---

[36]Salmon River Mission Journal, October 27, 1857. Also see Journal of Charles Franklin Middleton, October 5, 1857.

[37]Lay to Harney, June 29, 1857, House Exec. Doc. 71, 7–9.

forty-five tons of it, and much more. He next captured another unprotected train on Big Sandy River, a few miles west of present Farson, and
destroyed it as well. In a busy day, Smith and some two dozen men or so
torched enough provisions to feed the federal expedition at least two
months. Later that month, he teamed up with a company under noted
plainsman Porter Rockwell to rustle more than a thousand head of cattle from government herds feeding along the valley of Hams Fork.[38]

These attacks and early signs of winter at last spurred the federal
army's bemused senior officer to assume command and take some
action, however ill-considered. With Echo Canyon fortified, Alexander
in desperation decided to attempt an invasion of the territory from the
north. On October 7 he ordered his troops to march up Hams Fork to
Sublette's Cutoff, north of today's Kemmerer. He then planned to take
this road over the rim of the Great Basin to Bear River, then follow the
main Oregon-California Trail north to Soda Springs where he could
turn south into Utah or continue harmlessly on to Fort Hall on Snake
River.

To counter this move, General Wells on October 17 ordered Lot
Smith's company to join the command of Maj. John D. T. McAllister
"near the junction of the Sublet Cut Off, where it comes to Bear River,"
at present Cokeville. "If the enemy continue on the road to Fort Hall,
let them go unmolested," he said. But "if they leave the Oregon road,
pitch into their picket guards and sentinels, and among them all you
can."[39]

Wells also instructed his willing subordinate "to burn no more trains."
His intent was to delay the approaching army and force it to winter at
Fort Bridger or Fort Hall, not to destroy it entirely. At the same time,
Wells ordered Nauvoo Legion infantry forces to move north from Utah
settlements to stop the army from entering the territory by the Bear River
Valley. On October 20, Maj. B. F. Cummings at Ogden received orders
to march his command against the approaching army that "designed to
try to come in by way of Soda Springs on the north."[40]

[38]For a good account of Rockwell's activities and other guerrilla operations during this time, see Schindler,
Orrin Porter Rockwell, Man of God, Son of Thunder, 250–67.

[39]Wells to Smith, October 17, 1857, Lot Smith Collection.

[40]Biography and Journals of Benjamin Franklin Cummings, October 20, 1857, 49, 50, 58.

In a blessing for both sides, on the day Wells dictated his attack order to Lot Smith, Colonel Alexander was seized by another fit of indecision. That very day, he halted the northward movement of his command; then he turned it around and marched back down the valley of Hams Fork toward the stream's mouth at Granger.

JOHNSTON TAKES COMMAND

To the disgust of his young subordinates, the "old woman,"[41] as they called Alexander, was being completely out-generaled by his Nauvoo Legion counterpart, Daniel Wells, who made his headquarters at Cache Cave in Echo Canyon. As a consequence, the expedition so thoughtlessly ordered west so late in the season now faced disaster as temperatures fell and darkening skies threatened early winter. But riding hard to take command was an energetic officer who never knew the meaning of indecision.

Named to replace the reassigned Harney, Col. Albert Sidney Johnston of the Second U.S. Cavalry was a native of Kentucky, a West Point graduate, and former secretary of war for the Republic of Texas, his adopted state. With Jack Hays, the renowned Texas Ranger captain, he had commanded one of the two Texas regiments in the War with Mexico, winning praise for his coolness under fire. At age 54, he was over six feet tall, athletic in build, temperate in habit, grave and dignified in manner.

In less than five years, this gifted American officer would hurl forty thousand untried Confederates soldiers against a Union army under U. S. Grant on the Tennessee River, near Shiloh Church, and die from an untended wound with victory at his finger tips.[42] Ironically, his death would come while leading an army against the very government whose laws he now, in 1857, undertook to uphold.

Assuming command, Johnston reported the Mormons "have placed themselves in rebellion against the Union, and entertain the insane design of establishing a form of government thoroughly despotic, and

---

[41]Hammond, ed., *The Utah Expedition, 1857–1858, Letters of Capt. Jesse A. Gove, 10th Inf., U. S. A., of Concord, N. H., to Mrs. Gove, and special correspondence of the New York Herald,* 66.

[42]Johnston fell on the thirty-second anniversary of the founding of the Mormon church, April 6, 1862. Some in Utah took this as a sign of God's displeasure for the role he played in the so-called Utah War.

utterly repugnant to our institutions." Accordingly, he said, "I have ordered that wherever they are met in arms, that they be treated as enemies."[43] The next day, he moved to concentrate his scattered army at Fort Bridger as blizzards swept the high plains and temperatures fell to thirty degrees or more below zero.

The march from Hams Fork to the shelter of the trading post on Blacks Fork, a distance of only about thirty-five miles, took fifteen days and cost the lives of at least three thousand cattle, horses, and mules. Even then it was a close call. The expedition "took the last possible step forward at Bridger, in the condition of the animals then alive," Colonel Johnston later reported.[44] He was not one to embellish the truth.

Even closer was the margin for Lt. Col. Philip St. George Cooke and six companies of the Second Dragoons, finally released from duty in Kansas and assigned to escort the new governor and his wife to Utah. Rather than spend the winter at Fort Laramie, the former Mormon Battalion commander had driven his command across South Pass, arriving at Bridger's trading post only two days after Johnston. The horse soldiers at last were up, now mainly on foot, having killed most of their horses in Cooke's determination to provide cavalry support.

Two weeks before, as U.S. troops began their tortured march up Blacks Fork to Fort Bridger, they were watched by Andrew Love, at age 48 one of the older members of Maj. Warren Snow's Nauvoo Legion company, who "had a fair view of the enemy." In a heavy snowfall, he and his companions from Nephi, David and Samuel Cazier, Charles Cummings, Edsel Elmer, and Morton Rollins, fell back slowly before the advancing column. The next day, they warmed their hands on the fires of the "remaining portion of houses" as Mormon forces burned the trading post to the ground.[45]

The Nauvoo Legion surrendered the ashes without firing a shot, but there the line was drawn. In a meeting with three of his most aggressive officers, majors Snow and McAllister and Capt. Ephraim Hanks, General Wells on November 7 ordered them to watch but not molest the

[43]Johnston to McDowell, November 5, 1857, House Exec. Doc. 71, 46, 47.

[44]Johnston, *The Life of Albert Sidney Johnston, Embracing His Services in the Armies of the United States, the Republic of Texas, and the Confederate States*, 214. Also see Furniss, *The Mormon Conflict, 1850–1859*, 95–118.

[45]Journal of Andrew Love, November 6, 7, 1857. On November 8, Love and advance Mormon units camped "in the Cedar (Verry Cold)" at the Mormon Trail crossing of Muddy Creek, visible today from I-80, about ten miles west of Fort Bridger.

army, unless the enemy "demonstrated their intentions of pushing on to Salt Lake by moving west of the fort." In that case, he instructed, "Pitch into them in every possible way." They were to "make the first attack as soon as the army passed the fort."[46]

In no shape to make such a move, the American army was glad just to reach Blacks Fork without losses other than from desertion. Along the waterway, near the remains of Fort Bridger, Johnston made his winter camp, a sprawl of tents and crude houses, and named it Camp Scott after the nation's highest general. Casting a baleful eye to the west, the colonel then moved to preserve his command and its dependents, including the new governor and his wife, over the winter and prepare for a frontal assault on the Mormon stronghold in the spring.

At about this time, there occurred a curious incident, one that tells much about the quality of Mormon intelligence and may suggest even more. It began on November 13 when Johnston, moving from Hams Fork to Fort Bridger, dispatched an express ordering the commander of Fort Laramie to push forward "as soon as practicable" a train of thirty pack mules loaded with salt. "There is no salt with this Army," he said.[47]

Less than three weeks later, three Mormon riders arrived at Camp Scott during one of the heaviest snowstorms of the season with pack mules loaded with salt and a letter to Johnston and Colonel Alexander from Brigham Young.[48] Being informed the army was much in need of salt, the note began, "I have taken the liberty to at once forward you a load (some eight hundred pounds) by Messrs. Henry Woodard and Jesse J. Earl." Young went on to make a bizarre assurance, much like his July 1853 note to Utah Chief Walker:

"Should any in your command be suspicious that the salt now forwarded contains any deleterious ingredients other than those combined in its natural disposition of the shore of Great Salt Lake," Young said,

[46]Wells, Grant, and Rich to Young, November 15, 1857, Brigham Young Collection MS 1234, LDS Archives.

[47]Johnston to Hoffman, November 13, 1857, Army of Utah, Letters Sent, also published in Hafen and Hafen, *The Utah Expedition, 1857–58*, 165–66.

[48]Brigham Young was told the army needed salt by Ben Simonds, chief of a mixed band of northern Utah Bannocks and Shoshonis, who freely visited both sides and played one against the other to the benefit of his followers. According to Wilford Woodruff, the wily Simonds was a Cherokee, but most who knew him said he was a Delaware. See Kenney, ed., *Wilford Woodruff's Journal*, 5:125; and Hammond, *The Utah Expedition*, 133–34.

his messengers, Woodard and Earl, would "freely partake of it to dispel any groundless suspicions, or your doctors may be able to test it to their satisfaction."[49]

Johnston refused to honor the offer with a written reply, but his adjutant, Fitz-John Porter, said the colonel told the pair he rejected it, "not for the reason hinted at," but because he would accept nothing from his Mormon adversaries as long as they "took a hostile position to my government." He further informed them that he regretted Young had suggested the possibility the salt would be refused out of fear it might be poisoned. "There is no portion of the American people who would be guilty of so base an act, and none to suspect it," he wrote."[50]

Young's letter conveying the salt also carried an open taunt to the former acting commander of the expedition who must have read it with a crimson face. Addressing himself to Colonel Alexander, Young noted that a number of army mules had happened to "come into our settlements," including a small white one, "belonging to you." He said he had placed it in his personal stables where it would be cared for and ready "for your use upon your return to the east in the spring."[51]

To replace animals lost to winter and Mormon raiders, Johnston ordered Fifth Infantry Capt. Randolph Marcy to lead a hazardous winter expedition across the Rocky Mountains to get horses, mules, and beef cattle at Fort Union, near Las Vegas, New Mexico.[52] In a heroic exploit, the captain and his forty enlisted volunteers and twenty-four civilian guides ate their mules and broke trail through the snow at one point on their hands and knees but carried out the task and returned in the spring, losing only one man.

Johnston also sent one of the more adventurous figures in western annals, Benjamin Ficklin, an employee of Russell, Majors & Waddell, north to buy animals from mountaineers known to winter in Bitterroot Valley and on the headwaters of the Missouri River. Described as a "restless man, ruthless to outlaws and other evil-doers," the Virginian marked his thirtieth birthday struggling north through the snow along

---

[49]Young to Johnston and Alexander, November 26, 1857, House Exec. Doc. 71, 110–11.

[50]Johnston, *The Life of Gen. Albert Sidney Johnston,* 218–19.

[51]Young to Johnston and Alexander, November 26, 1857, House Exec. Doc. 71, 111.

[52]For the story of this expedition, see Marcy, *Thirty Years of Army Life on the Border,* 198–243.

Bear River with a ten-man pack party and four gallons of whiskey, allegedly for trading purposes.[53] Ficklin and his civilian volunteers passed within a few miles of the Mormon mission at Fort Limhi as they journeyed north on the east side of the Continental Divide. Intentionally or not, they would also touch off events that would affect the course of Utah history.

Meanwhile Captain Marcy's mission to Fort Union opened to Garland Hurt, now at Camp Scott, a new opportunity for service. At reports the Mormons had organized a mounted force of three hundred to intercept Marcy at Green River on his return, Hurt volunteered to become a scout in the region he now knew. In January 1858 the agent and five Utah warriors rode back into Uinta Basin to live at times "upon roots alone" before returning in April to find that Marcy had come back by a different route.[54]

Before leaving on this dangerous mission, the agent reported to Utah's new superintendent of Indian affairs, Jacob Forney, on his escape from the Spanish Fork Indian farm and what he had heard about a massacre of emigrants on the southern trail to California. According to the report, Hurt said, the Piedes had attacked a train "about one hundred in number" after Mormon settlers in southern Utah had assured the natives that "if they were not strong enough," they would help "whip them."[55]

Hurt went on to report the first essentially accurate account of the massacre by Mormons and Indians of some 120 emigrants from Arkansas, men, women, and children, at a quiet resting place on the Spanish Trail, known as Mountain Meadows.

---

[53]See Porter to Clark, December 4, 1857, Army of Utah, Letters Sent. A native of Virginia, Benjamin Franklin Ficklin attended V.M.I. and suffered serious wounds in the Mexican War. Later he was associated with Russell, Majors & Waddell, when he perhaps originated the idea of the Pony Express. He was a Confederate blockade runner during the Civil War and afterward operated the dangerous San Antonio–San Diego mail route through Comanche and Apache country. His name is on a plaque in front of the Salt Lake Tribune Building as superintendent of the stage station there. For more, see Thrapp, *Encyclopedia of Frontier Biography*, 1:489.

[54]Reavis, "Hurt Biography," 786–87.

[55]Hurt to Forney, December 4, 1857, House Exec. Doc. 71, 199–205.

Chapter 8

An Awful Tale of Blood

The scene of the massacre, even at this late day, was horrible to look upon. Women's hair, in detached locks and in masses, hung to the sage bushes and was strewn over the ground in many places. Parts of little children's dresses . . . dangled from the shrubbery or lay scattered about.

—Maj. James Carleton

There were no survivors old enough to remember, so the exact make up of the company that gathered in mid-April 1857 at the place now known as Caravan Spring, in Boone County, Arkansas, near Harrison, will probably never be known.[1] But it did present a striking contrast to the smaller, usually undisciplined parties of adventurous young men who passed through Utah during the days of the Gold Rush, eager to reach the California diggings and "see the elephant."[2]

Led by 52-year-old John T. Baker and Alexander Fancher, 45, the company was made up mainly of farm families from northwest Arkansas moving west to make new homes in California. Among an estimated 135 members, it numbered at least fifteen women, most young mothers. Dependent children made up the largest age group, more than sixty, or roughly half the total. Of these, more than twenty were girls between the ages of seven and eighteen. The rest were adult males,

---

[1] For the definitive account of this crime, see the forthcoming *An Awful Tale of Blood: A Documentary History of the Mountain Meadows Massacre* by Will Bagley, to whom the author is indebted for information in this chapter. The classic documentary account is Juanita Brooks' *The Mountain Meadows Massacre*.

[2] Caravan Spring is identified today by an Arkansas State historic marker which reads: "Near this spring in September 1857 gathered a caravan of 150 men, women and children who here began the ill-fated journey to California. The entire party with the exception of seventeen small children was massacred at Mountain Meadows Utah by a body of Mormons disguised as Indians." The month the company assembled was April, not September.

mostly heads of families, but they also included some teamsters and other hired hands.[3]

The Arkansas company was relatively affluent. Most of its wealth took the form of a large herd of cattle, estimated by various observers to number from three hundred to a thousand head, not including other animals, work oxen, horses, or mules. Whatever the exact count, the cattle would slow the party's progress from the average rate for an ox train of about fifteen miles a day to ten or twelve miles daily over a long distance.

Since they were moving permanently, Baker-Fancher train members were also better off in other worldly possessions than typical emigrant parties on the California Trail. John W. Baker later placed the value of property his father took on the journey at "the full sum of ten thousand dollars." Besides animals, some thirty or forty wagons and equipment, members also carried varying amounts of cash to cover unforeseen costs on the journey. "Jack" Baker's oldest son, George, for example, carried "in cash in hand about [$]500," no small sum at that time.[4]

At the head of this distinctive caravan were experienced plainsmen making their third overland journey. Both George Baker and Fancher had gone to California in 1849 or 1850, locating first in San Diego County. Apparently deciding there was more to gain from raising cattle than washing for gold, they had returned to Arkansas to bring families and livestock back to their new home; they planned to settle in California's central valley, near Visalia in Tulare County.[5] Their route to Utah was the Cherokee Trail, opened in 1849 by members of the Cherokee Nation and a party of whites from northwest Arkansas, possibly including Baker himself. By 1857 this was an established wagon road, one especially suited for cattle because it was less traveled and offered abundant grass early in the season for parties with herds coming from the south.

[3]Judge Roger V. Logan, Jr., of Harrison, Arkansas, has assembled the most complete known roster of the company. For the names and ages, see the monument about eight miles south of Enterprise, Utah, on State Highway 18. Also see the program, "Mountain Meadows Memorial Dedication Ceremonies," September 15, 1990, Southern Utah State College, now Southern Utah University, Cedar City, Utah.

[4]Logan, "New Light on the Mountain Meadows Caravan," 224–37.

[5]For evidence the Fanchers went to California as early as 1850, see William Bedford Temple to "Wife and Littleones," June 2, 1850, Mss 1508, Oregon Hist. Soc. Also see Loving, ed., Mountain Meadows Newsletter.

At Caravan Spring, where the Baker-Fancher train began its
tragic journey in April, not September, 1857,
Arkansas remembers the Mountain Meadows Massacre.
Courtesy, Roger V. Logan, Jr.

From near Fayetteville, Arkansas, the route ran north to meet the
Santa Fé Trail near present McPherson, Kansas, then followed this route
and its northern branch on the line of today's U.S. Highway 50 along
the Arkansas River to Pueblo, Colorado. It then went north along the
front of the Rocky Mountains on a line paralleled today by I-25 to Fort
Collins, then northwest to the Laramie Plain and west between I-80 and
the Colorado-Wyoming border to meet the Oregon-California-Mormon trail at Fort Bridger. From this point, it took the latter road into
Salt Lake Valley.[6]

Following this established route, the Baker-Fancher train arrived in
the capital of Utah Territory that year on August 3. The date was fixed
on December 19, 1877, by the sworn testimony of Malinda Cameron
Thurston, daughter of William and Martha Cameron, who with their

[6]See Fletcher and Fletcher, "The Cherokee Trail," 21–33, and a forthcoming book by the Fletchers, *Cherokee
Trail(s): Routes to the California Gold Rush.* Also see Berry, ed., *Western Emigrant Trails, 1830–1870, Major Trails, Cutoffs,
and Alternates.* Evidence suggests that in 1857 some of the Arkansans left the Cherokee Trail near today's Rawlins,
Wyoming, to join the main overland trail on the Sweetwater River, due to dry conditions on the Cherokee route.

other six children, ranging in age from 8 to 24, also belonged to the company.[7] From that day, the first Monday of the month, the Arkansas party appeared to be a marked train. It had come to the wrong place at the wrong time, too soon after President Buchanan had ordered an army to Utah and Apostle Parley Pratt had been brutally murdered in Arkansas. Most of its members came from the wrong section of that state, only one county removed from the place in northwest Arkansas where Hector McLean had struck down the popular apostle.[8]

At daybreak that same day, Apostle George A. Smith, then 40, took off from Great Salt Lake City in a horse-drawn carriage and headed south. Known as the father of Utah's southern settlements, Smith had led the first party of colonists to that region in 1850, had personally organized Iron County, and was known and trusted by local leaders there. St. George, today one of the state's fastest growing population centers, was named after him.

Traveling fast, Smith averaged nearly forty miles a day over the 250 miles or so from the territorial capital to Iron County. Even so, he found time at each settlement along the southern trail to California to instruct local leaders to sell no grain or other supplies to "gentile" emigrants, to harvest and hide up their wheat early, and to drill and outfit their military forces for active operations to repel the approaching U.S. Army expedition. Wherever he went, the apostle fanned the militant spirit of the reformation. According to legend, Smith told Parowan settlers that bones make a good fertilizer for fruit trees. As for American soldiers coming to Utah, he went on, he could "think of nothing better that they could do than to feed a fruit tree in Zion."[9] He later said, "in spite of all I could do, I found myself preaching a military discourse."[10] At Harmony, a few miles south of Cedar City, Rachel Lee said Smith "delivered a discourse on the spirit that actuated the United States toward this people—full of hostility and virulence."[11]

[7]Wise, *Massacre at Mountain Meadows, An American Legend and a Monumental Crime*, 186–87. Also see Brooks, *The Mountain Meadows Massacre*, xv, xvi.

[8]A violent man, McLean soon after boasted to a San Francisco relative that the brutal deed, perpetrated as his friends looked on, was the best act of his life. Said he: "My duty to myself, demanded it; my duty to my children, demanded it; my duty to my relations, demanded it; and my duty to society, demanded it. And the people of West Arkansas agree with me in this view of the commission of the deed." His letter, published on July 9, 1857, may have sealed the fate of the Baker-Fancher Train. See *Daily Alta California*, 2.

[9]Brooks, *The Mountain Meadows Massacre*, 35.

[10]George A. Smith, *Deseret News*, September 23, 1857, 226–27.

Settlers in the south hardly needed one more firebrand to kindle resentment over past wrongs. Their spiritual head, Elisha Groves of the Cedar Stake of Zion at Cedar City, gave patriarchal blessings, similar to those Isaac bestowed on Jacob and Esau, that breathed vengeance for the blood of slain prophets. Col. William H. Dame, 38, was commander of the ninth military district, which included Beaver, Iron, and Washington counties. Patriarch Groves, a 59-year-old Kentuckian, gave the colonel a prophetic blessing that even specified how such retaliation was to be carried out: "Thou shalt be called to act at the head of a portion of thy brethren and of the Lamanites [Indians] in the redemption of Zion and the avenging of the blood of the prophets upon them that dwell on the earth   the angel of vengeance shall be with thee."[12]

Nor was Groves alone in seeing the Indians as the instrument of such retaliation. David Lewis, called to serve in the Southern Indian Mission, remembered in 1854 how his brother, Benjamin, had been killed nineteen years before at Haun's Mill in Missouri and exulted that he was alive "to avenge his blood when the Lord will." Referring to the natives as "the battle axe of the Lord," he asked fellow missionaries, "May we not have been sent to learn and know how to *use* this axe, with skill?"[13]

At Cedar City, the offices of mayor, president of Zion's Cedar Stake, and commander of the Nauvoo Legion battalion were all held by 44-year-old Isaac C. Haight, a former member of the Nauvoo "Old Police." Fanning the reformation, he had warned that year "the pruning time has come" and spoken of the day "when the servants of God will come forth to slay the wicked." Not to be outdone in zeal was Haight's counselor, 30-year-old John M. Higbee, who ordered the people to prepare themselves "for every thing, and to every thing required at our hands."[14]

At Harmony Apostle Smith stayed overnight at the home of one of the faith's most capable members and at the same time one of its most powerful and disliked leaders in southern Utah. John D. Lee, a native of Illinois, then 44, was an adopted son of Brigham Young under a doctrine introduced at Nauvoo by Joseph Smith and since discontinued, relating to the Mormon tenet of eternal progression. It stressed unques-

[11]Diary of Rachel Lee, August 17, 1857, quoted in Brooks, *The Mountain Meadows Massacre*, 37.

[12]William H. Dame Papers, February 20, 1854, MS 2041, LDS Archives.

[13]Brooks, ed., *Journal of the Southern Indian Mission*, May 14, 1854.

[14]Cedar Stake Journal, January 29 and March 29, 1857, Palmer Collection.

tioning obedience to one's adopted parent.[15] From his relationship with Young, Lee had great influence, which he wielded like a blunt instrument over others, yet he was a man of high ability in his own right. That he was favored by his father by adoption was testified by the sixteen wives he had been given over the years. That he could be trusted to perform with discretion any assignment, however difficult, he had often proved since joining the new religious movement in 1838.

Ostensibly a government agent, holding the post of "Indian farmer," Lee had been chosen in 1851 to locate at Harmony and serve as Young's personal ambassador to the Piede, or Southern Paiute, Indians on the Santa Clara and Virgin rivers. Within two years, he had so mastered this duty that the commander of a scouting party to the south in 1853 reported the natives in the area were "perfectly under the control of Major J D Lee." Elevating Lee a grade or two, he said, "They reverence Colonel J D Lee as the Mormon Chief & are willing to obey him."[16]

What Lee and Smith discussed at Harmony is not known, but it can be noted that the two men had several things in common beyond their long-standing friendship. Both men were tried and trusted; both were zealots, dedicated to establish the Kingdom of God as a condition of Christ's millennial reign; and both were members of the ultra-secret Council of Fifty.

During his visit south, Apostle Smith also delivered a letter, dated August 4, to Indian missionary Jacob Hamblin, 38, signed by Brigham Young, not as Utah superintendent of Indian affairs, but as a "Fellow Laborer in the Gospel of Salvation." The church leader appointed Hamblin to succeed Rufus Allen as president of the Santa Clara (Southern) Indian Mission and instructed him "to enter upon the duties of your calling immediately."[17] Young told his Indian agent to continue "the

---

[15]Under this ordinance, Joseph Smith adopted as sons certain male subordinates with their families, such as Young, who in turn adopted others, such as Lee, who adopted others, and so it went, in concert with related doctrines of polygamy and baptism for the dead, until all Israel was joined in one great family with Smith at the head. Lee himself said, "In the Winter of 1845 meetings were held all over the city of Nauvoo, and the spirit of Elijah was taught in the different families as a foundation to the order of celestial marriage [polygamy], as well as the law of adoption." He went on: "All persons are required to be adopted to some of the leading men of the Church. In this, however, they have the right of choice, thus forming the links of the chain of priesthood back to the father, Adam, and so on to the second coming of the Messiah." See Lee, *Mormonism Unveiled*, 165.

[16]Report of Capt. William Wall, April 24 to May 11, 1853, Utah Militia Records.

[17]Young to Hamblin, August 4, 1857, MS 1234, LDS Archives, quoted in Brooks, *The Mountain Meadows Massacre*, 34, 35.

conciliatory policy towards the Indians, which I have ever recommended, and seek by works of righteousness to obtain their love and confidence, *for they must learn that they have either got to help us or the United States will kill us both.*"[18] The appointment of Hamblin, who had his summer quarters on the edge of a grassy valley known as Mountain Meadows near the head-waters of the Santa Clara River, to direct the Piede mission made him a key player in the fate of the Baker-Fancher train.

BAKER-FANCHER TRAIN GOES SOUTH

Unaware of these events and attitudes, the Arkansas party began its journey along the corridor of settlements, now followed by I-15, to meet the Spanish Trail near present Parowan, apparently the first train that summer to take the southern route. Apostle Charles C. Rich, a Council of Fifty member, reportedly recommended that they go north to Bear River and take Hensley's Salt Lake Cutoff, which meets the northern California Trail in Silent City of Rocks, near present Almo, Idaho, but this is not at all likely.[19] If Rich so advised, it is hard to understand why the apostle, who had just come over the southern trail and knew every foot of it, would suggest that they go to the north. He was aware the way to southern California would be free of ice and snow all winter. He knew, too, the southern desert natives would pose no threat by themselves to such a large train, while Indians on the northern route, who often molested trains with livestock along the Humboldt, were on a rampage. Brigham Young had warned George Q. Cannon on August 4, "The Saints who come through the north route had better supply themselves with efficient arms and keep strong guards, as the Indians on that route are said to be exceedingly hostile."[20] Much more likely is it that Rich, for whatever reasons, advised the Arkansans to go south.

---

[18]Ibid. Italics added. As Mrs. Brooks pointed out, this phrase was not included in the manuscript record, "Annals of the Southern Utah Mission, Book A" and other accounts.

[19]In an interview with a *New York Herald* reporter in the wake of the Lee trials, Brigham Young claimed that Rich had told him that he advised the train to go by the northern trail and believed they had gone "as far north as Bear River." See "Interview with Brigham Young," *Deseret News*, May 12, 1877. This highly improbable account was later repeated in Bancroft, *History of Utah*, 547. Rich himself never confirmed or commented on the story.

[20]Young to Cannon, August 4, 1857, MS 1234, LDS Archives.

This is how Malinda Cameron Thurston recalled it twenty years later when she reported that her father, William Cameron, told her on August 5 the Mormons had recommended the southern trail because there was better grazing on that route. William and Martha Cameron decided to go with their five children and most of the train that way. But Henry Scott, Malinda's husband, and his brother, Richard, decided to take their families to the north instead. Malinda never saw her parents or brothers and sisters again.

As the caravan moved south, it struck sparks at settlements along the way. A constant source of friction was the refusal of settlers to sell at any price the flour or other provisions the Arkansas emigrants badly needed. With few exceptions, settlement leaders carried out Brigham Young's order on August 2 not to sell "one kernal" of grain to "our enemies" and to keep a record of those who did.[21] In a region where the land was possessed under the law of stewardship, not by federal code, an even greater cause of trouble was the train's large herd. Grazing as they went, the cattle trampled cultivated fields and invaded common feeding grounds.

Near Provo, according to one report, the company and its herd, "near 400 head of livestock," camped in a hay meadow that was being reserved for winter use. When an acting city marshal, Simon Wood, advised the intruders of the need to save the grass for winter feed and ordered them to move on, he was told "with some feeling" by the emigrants, "This is Uncle Sam's grass." When they refused to go, the marshal gave them an hour "to decide whether you want to fight or pull up stakes."[22] They pulled up stakes.

"There is a company of Gentiles at Millers Springs who have 300 head of cattle," reported Samuel Pitchforth on August 15 at Nephi.[23] "The Bishop sent out to them requesting them to move for they were distroying our Winter feed. they answered that they where [sic] American Citizens and should not move." Two days later, Pitchforth said, "The company of Gentiles passed through this morning—they wanted to purchase Flour." He spent the next day, "Fixing my Gun."[24]

[21]Young to Bronson and Haight, August 2, 1857, MS 1234, LDS Archives.

[22]Anonymous undated statement, possibly by John G. McQuarrie, Collected statements on Mountain Meadows Massacre, MS 2674, LDS Archives.

[23]Miller's Spring was located on the southern trail near Mona, a few miles north of Nephi.

[24]Diary of Samuel Pitchforth, August 15 and August 17, 1857.

Twenty-one days after leaving Great Salt Lake, the Arkansans on August 25 camped on Corn Creek, home of the Pahvant tribe under Chief Kanosh whose members in 1853 had massacred Captain Gunnison. That night Apostle George A. Smith pulled up to camp "within forty yards of them." Smith was on his way back to the capital from his trip south. With him were Jacob Hamblin, the newly appointed Santa Clara Indian Mission president, and a number of Indian chiefs from southern Utah on their way north to meet with Brigham Young. According to the apostle, the Arkansans became excited at seeing the Indians and doubled their guard. Three of them visited Smith's camp, including the "Captain of the company," probably Jack Baker, and asked if there was "any danger from the Indians who were encamped near us," the apostle later claimed. "I replied that if their party had not committed any outrage upon the Indians there would be no danger."[25]

Smith's alleged answer apparently did little to settle the Arkansans' fears. They had journeyed from Great Salt Lake to Corn Creek, about mid-way to their final resting place, at the leisurely pace of about seven miles a day, allowing the cattle to graze along the way. After the encounter at Corn Creek, however, they stepped up their rate of travel to more than twelve miles a day, about as fast as an ox train with a large herd could go after more than four months on the trail.

As they hurried to get away, Hamblin and some twelve Indian chiefs on September first met with Brigham Young and his most trusted interpreter, 49-year-old Dimick B. Huntington, at Great Salt Lake. Taking part in this pow-wow were Kanosh, the Mormon chief of the Pahvants; Ammon, half-brother of Walker; Tutsegabit, head chief of the Piedes; Youngwuds, another Piede chieftain, and other leaders of desert bands along the Santa Clara and Virgin rivers.

Little was known of what they talked about until recently when it came to light that Huntington (apparently speaking for Young) told the chiefs that he "gave them all the cattle that had gone to Cal[ifornia by] the south rout[e]." The gift "made them open their eyes," he said. But "you have told us not to steal," the Indians replied. "So I have," Hunt-

---

[25]Smith to St. Clair, November 25, 1869, George A. Smith Typescript Collection, MS 2737, 941–49, LDS Archives. This letter must be treated skeptically since much of the information it offers is now known to be false. But it is known that Smith, Hamblin, and the chiefs did camp that night near the emigrants and the apostle's description of the encounter carries a ring of truth, if little else in the letter does.

ington said, "but now they have come to fight us & you for when they kill us they will kill you."[26] The chiefs knew what cattle he was giving them. They belonged to the Baker-Fancher train.

Two days before, Huntington and Bishop Chauncey West of Ogden had met on the Weber River with a large gathering of Shoshoni Indians under their leader, Ben Simonds. "I told them that the Lord had come out of his Hiding place & they had to commence their work," Huntington said. "I gave them all the Beef Cattle & horses that was on the Road to California the North rout[e]."[27] There would be reports of Indian attacks on wagon trains along the California Trail and its cutoffs to the north, some allegedly led by whites, over the next five years.[28]

Meanwhile, still moving fast, the Arkansas train on about Thursday, September 3, reached the outskirts of Cedar City, where settlers again refused to sell them food. From later accounts, some tempers apparently flared, but it is unlikely the emigrants gratuitously provoked confrontation. Two or three days later, they passed Hamblin's crude ranch house on the north edge of the grassy valley on the rim of the Great Basin, a few miles south of present Newcastle on today's Utah Highway 18, now appropriately named the Legacy Loop Highway.

Crossing the gradual swell that marked the divide, they moved another four miles and stopped by a spring that fed Magotsu Creek and the Santa Clara River, tributaries of the Virgin. The place they came to was known as Mountain Meadows because it was more than a mile above sea level and offered plenty of water and grass for travelers on the Spanish Trail. Here, some thirty-five miles beyond the nearest settlement, they apparently felt safe to rest and recruit their livestock after driving them hard for nearly two weeks. For them, however, it was the most perilous spot on the trail.

On Sunday, September 6, the Arkansans camped in the narrow southern end of the valley, "shut in by smooth, rounded hills," according to Maj. Henry Prince, who mapped the area in May 1859.[29] The

---

[26]Journal of Dimick Baker Huntington, September 1, 1857, MS 1419 2, LDS Archives.

[27]Ibid., August 30, 1857. While Huntington has dated this entry September 30, it is obviously the month before. For confirmation of this meeting by Chief Ben Simonds, see Hurt to Forney, December 4, 1857, House Exec. Doc. 71 (35–1), 1858, Serial 956, 204.

[28]For examples, see the report "in relation to the Mountain Meadow and other massacres in Utah Territory," Sen. Exec. Doc. 42 (36–1), 1860, Serial 1033, 104–39.

[29]Prince, Ground of the Mountain Meadow Massacre, May 17, 1859. The quotes are from this map.

location was barely defensible for a limited time, exposed on most sides to fire from concealment, and impossible to escape from if surrounded. If an enemy were to select a secluded place on the entire route between Fort Bridger and Las Vegas Springs to ambush and destroy an emigrant train, this would be it.

That same day at Cedar City, Stake President Isaac Haight was still in a militant mood when it came to the emigrants. "They come among us asking us to trade with them, and in the name of humanity to feed them," he said. But he was ready to "feed to the Gentiles the same bread they fed to us."[30] Haight and other local leaders met to figure out what to do, fearful their quarry would get away before some action was taken. Unable to agree, they sent James Haslam, a 32-year-old Englishman, to ride more than five hundred miles to Great Salt Lake and back to find out from Brigham Young what they should do about the intruders from Arkansas.

THE MASSACRE

Haslam had not left Cedar City when Indians quietly surrounded the emigrant camp and before daybreak on Monday, September 7, opened a deadly fire that killed or wounded as many as ten men as they stood by the camp fire. Most of the attackers were Piedes, three hundred or so in number, whose chiefs had met with Brigham Young the week before. Since these natives were known to possess few firearms and little skill at using them, the impact of the initial volley suggests the involvement of Indian missionaries. On his crude map, Major Prince marked the location "where the Mormons painted and disguised themselves as Indians."[31]

The surprise attack, destructive though it was, did not break the Arkansans' ability to resist. John D. Lee later described them as "brave men and very resolute and determined," mostly armed with muzzle-loading Kentucky rifles, a deadly instrument in the hands of experienced marksmen.[32] The emigrants chained the wheels of their wagons together, dug rifle pits, and fought back, reportedly killing and wounding several natives. The one-sided battle was on.

On Wednesday night, September 9, two young volunteers, noted for

[30]Cedar City Ward Records, September 6, 1857, quoted by Brooks, *The Mountain Meadows Massacre*, 52.

[31]Prince, Ground of the Mountain Meadow Massacre.

[32]Lee, *Mormonism Unveiled*, 240.

their courage and lack of family obligations, tried to escape and go back to Cedar City for help. One of them, William Aden, reportedly had joined the train at Provo in an attempt to leave the territory. According to Lee, Aden was shot and killed at a nearby spring by William Stewart. As he fell from his horse, Joel White, another Mormon outrider, wounded his companion. Lee said the man managed to get back to the emigrant camp, but this is unlikely.[33]

That same night, 30-year-old Maj. John M. Higbee arrived at Mountain Meadows with selected Nauvoo Legion soldiers from Cedar City as reinforcements. He found a stand-off which could not be allowed to continue. Surrounded and under fire, their animals killed or run off, the emigrants were unable to move, but were now aware that at least some white men were acting in concert with the Indians. A plan had to be worked out to decoy them into the open where they could be killed at minimum risk to local Mormons as well as their native allies.

At sunrise Thursday, September 10, Haslam, the express rider from Cedar City, arrived at Brigham Young's office. After resting, he took off on a fresh horse about 1 P.M. with Young's alleged reply.[34] It said, among other things: "In regard to the emigration trains passing through our settlements, we must not interfere with them until they are first notified to keep away. You must not meddle with them. The Indians we expect will do as they please but you should try and preserve good feelings with them."[35] This seemed to say that white settlers should mind their own business and not interfere but maintain good relations with the Indians while they took care of the emigrants. If so, that was all very well on paper, but on the ground, there was the problem of the resolute Arkansans and their Kentucky rifles. As Lee put it: "We knew that the original plan was for the Indians to do all the work, and the whites to do nothing, only stay back and plan for them, and encourage them." But it turned out "the Indians could not do the work, and we were in a sad fix," he said.[36]

---

[33]Ibid., 234. Also see Brooks, *Mountain Meadows Massacre,* 70–72.

[34]Penrose, "Testimony of James Holt Haslam," in *Supplement to the Lecture on the Mountain Meadows Massacre,* 91–94.

[35]Young to Haight, September 10, 1857, Church Letter Book, No. 3, 827–28, LDS Archives, quoted in Brooks, *Mountain Meadows Massacre,* 63.

[36]Lee, *Mormonism Unveiled,* 228.

The ones in the saddest fix, however, were the frightened men and women inside the crude barricade. On the day Haslam left Great Salt Lake, the train's three best scouts, possibly Abel Baker, Joseph Miller, and John Milum Jones, slipped out after dark in a desperate effort to reach California on foot. They reportedly carried an account of what had happened, a list of the emigrants' names, and a plea for help.

Today little is known for certain of their fate. But accounts from several sources, including the report of Maj. James Carleton, who investigated the massacre site in 1859, indicate they were tracked by Indians led by Ira Hatch, then 22, a member of the Southern Indian Mission who spoke Paiute like a native, and killed, one by one. The most successful of the three apparently got as far as Las Vegas Springs before he was stripped and his throat cut as he struggled in the sand.[37]

On Friday, September 11, Lee and William Bateman drove two wagons under a white flag into the emigrants' fortified encampment. According to Lee, they found those inside almost out of ammunition and increasingly desperate.[38] "If the emigrants had a good supply of ammunition they never would have surrendered," he said, "and I do not think we could have captured them without great loss." The pair told the Arkansans that their only hope was to give up their arms, "so as not to arouse the animosity of the Indians," and put their lives under the protection of the Mormon militia.[39]

Soon after, there emerged from the camp the most melancholy parade ever staged on Utah soil. Leading it was a wagon loaded with children under six years of age driven by one Samuel McMurdy from Cedar City. Behind it on foot came Lee, followed by a second wagon driven by Samuel Knight, carrying two or three wounded men and one woman. Some distance behind walked the women and older children. After them, a quarter mile or so to the rear, marched in single file the disarmed men of the Arkansas train, each escorted by an armed Mormon guard.

---

[37]"Special Report of the Mountain Meadow Massacre, by J. H. Carleton, Brevet Major, United States Army, Captain, First Dragoons," House Doc. 605 (57–1), 1902, Serial 4377, 8–12, 13. The value of this report cannot be overstated. Also see Lee, *Mormonism Unveiled*, 244; Brooks, *The Mountain Meadows Massacre*, 97–100; and Lyford, *The Mormon Problem, An Appeal to the American People*, 271–323.

[38]Only two weeks before, the Cedar Stake congregation had voted to restore Bateman to membership after he had confessed his error in going to California and had promised "to do better." The 33-year-old Englishman was apparently now undergoing a loyalty check. See Cedar Stake Journal, August 30, 1857.

[39]Lee, *Mormonism Unveiled*, 240.

As the women and older children walked into a narrower place between the hills, heavy with brush, Nauvoo Legion Maj. John Higbee, who flanked the rear of the procession on horseback, gave the order: "Halt. Do your duty." Each white Mormon was to shoot and kill the man at his side, which most did but some did not. At the firing, the Indians swarmed out of the brush to kill the women and children with hatchets, knives, and rocks.[40]

It was horrific. One can only imagine the men, not killed outright, running to their wives and children before being cut down and the valley filled with the screams of women and children under murderous attack. One native later told the story about two girls who "hid in some bushes" until they were discovered and how they "were crying out loud" as they were dragged away by their dresses to be killed.[41] It was all over in a few minutes.

How Many Killed?

Pending an archaeological survey, an accurate estimate of the number slain cannot be determined because no one knows for sure how many were in the emigrant camp that day. Judge Roger V. Logan from Boone County, Arkansas, where the train assembled, has said he is hard pressed to account for more than eighty, plus about a dozen packers. The late Juanita Brooks figured about 110 before it left Great Salt Lake. And up to now, no one has even tried to determine how many Mormons may have joined the caravan as it passed through the settlements, but it is probable there were some, especially in the wake of the reformation.

All things considered, a reasonable estimate would put the number of dead at 120, including about fifty men, twenty women, and fifty or so children between the ages of seven and eighteen. Measured in lives lost, the massacre at Mountain Meadows was the second worst tragedy during America's westward migration during the nineteenth century, exceeded only by the Mormon handcart disaster the year before. It was also about three times the number who died in the Donner party.

---

[40]John D. Lee claimed that Mormon interpreters led the attack on the women and children. See Ibid., 237, 243. Lt. Nephi Johnson later admitted, "white men did most of the killing." See Quinn, *The Mormon Hierarchy: Extensions of Power*, 252.

[41]Carleton, House Doc. 605, 6.

How Many Survived?

Surviving the massacre were seventeen children under six years of age who were spared, not so much because they were too young to talk, but because they came under a theological exemption known as "innocent blood."[42] John D. Lee and others killed that day without guilt or compassion, but to shed innocent blood would have been in their eyes a horrendous sin.[43] There were no other survivors.

Immediately after the massacre, Cedar City Bishop Philip Klingensmith left the bloody field and took over the care of the surviving children, several badly hurt, who were placed in Mormon homes.[44] Sarah Dunlap, hardly more than a toddler, had been shot in the arm, the ball severing both bones. In 1859, all seventeen children were reclaimed, for a price, by U.S. Indian agent Jacob Forney and returned to family members in Arkansas.

Jacob Hamblin, who helped Forney round up the children, billed the government $2,643.76 for board, clothing, and schooling for the several children under his care from the date of the massacre to April 18, 1859. John D. Lee had the temerity to claim that he bought one of the Fancher children from the Indians for one horse saddle, bridle, and blanket, valued at $150. He charged this amount, plus board, clothing, and schooling, when he gave the lad up to Forney.

How Many Whites Took Part?

Not counting Lee and the Indian missionaries who were involved from the outset, more than fifty members of the Nauvoo Legion from Iron and Washington counties took part in the killings. Why they did this may have been best expressed by Samuel McMurdy. As he pointed

---

[42]There is no real evidence that more than seventeen survived, although a story persists that an unidentified eighteenth child was never found but was reared as a member of a Mormon family. At that time, innocent blood would include children under eight years of age and, therefore, too young to have consciously sinned, and Mormons who had confessed their sins and been rebaptized during the reformation.

[43]Lee was among those whose "Second Anointing" at Nauvoo sealed them up unconditionally to eternal life against all crimes except the shedding of innocent blood and apostasy. It is noteworthy that dissenters at Nauvoo in 1844 named "the unconditional sealing up to eternal life, against all crimes except that of shedding innocent blood" among the secret doctrines, since discontinued, which they considered "contrary to the laws of God." See *Nauvoo Expositor*, June 7, 1844, 2.

[44]For Klingensmith's story, see Backus, *Mountain Meadows Witness: The life and times of Bishop Philip Klingensmith*.

his rifle at the wounded men in Knight's wagon, according to Lee, he cried: "O lord, my God, receive their spirits, for it is for thy Kingdom that I do this." Then he killed two helpless men, one with his head on the other's breast, with a single shot.[45]

RECRIMINATIONS AND COVER-UP

John D. Lee slept soundly that night, and on the morning of Saturday, September 12, he with other local leaders rode out to the field of slaughter. There they beheld the scattered bodies in the oddly twisted postures of violent death. Little affected himself, Lee said that Colonel Dame from Parowan, military district commander, was overcome at the sight. "Horrible, horrible," he said over and over, and his mind seemed to reject any notion of his own involvement. I had no part in this, he said, I had nothing to do with it.[46]

At this, Isaac Haight, commander of the Cedar City forces who did the killing, whirled on him in fury. "It is too late in the day for you to order things done and then go back on it." he fired back. *I did not think there were so many of them,* Dame said again and again, *or I would not have had anything to do with it.* Haight was furious. "You cannot *sow pig* on me, and I will be damned if I will stand it," he swore. "Isaac, I did not know there were so many of them," Dame said.[47]

After the two stopped quarreling, the dead were thrown into ravines and covered with a light layer of dirt. All those who had taken part then gathered in a prayer circle. Their leaders first gave "thanks to God for delivering our enemies into our hands," Lee said. Then they vowed to keep their involvement in the massacre a secret and always to say "the Indians did it alone." Every man swore a solemn oath "to help kill all who proved to be traitors."[48] As if to anticipate their alibi, Brigham Young that same day at Great Salt Lake blamed the U.S. Army expedition to Utah for Indian attacks on emigrants. "The sound of war quickens the blood and nerves of an Indian," he told the Indian affairs commissioner. In some cases, he went on, "this was the reason assigned

---

[45]Lee, *Mormonism Unveiled,* 241.
[46]Ibid., 246–47.
[47]Ibid. Emphasis in original.
[48]Ibid.

why they made the attacks which they did upon some herds of cattle." Keep the troops away, he advised, and provide more money for presents. He himself had shown it was "cheaper to feed and clothe the Indians than to fight them."[49]

A day later, James Haslam reached Cedar City with Young's purported instructions to his southern Utah followers not to get involved in any attack on the Baker-Fancher train. After riding more than five hundred miles in less than seven days, he was about forty-eight hours too late. The coyotes had already begun to dig up and feed on the bodies.

John D. Lee personally reported the massacre to Young on September 28 and 29, less than three weeks after it happened. According to Apostle Woodruff, Lee said the emigrants had provoked the attack by poisoning the spring and an ox at Corn Creek, causing the death of four Pahvants and several Mormons.[50] Enraged, the Indians had killed the men, then "Cut the throats of their women and children," except for some eight or ten children who were sold to the white settlers, Woodruff wrote. "When Brother Lee found it out he took some men & went and buried their bodies."[51]

If Woodruff had stopped there, he may have provided evidence that Lee withheld from Young the truth about Mormon involvement. But the apostle went on to give Lee's assurance that there was no "innocent Blood in the Camp" because only one of the two children that he had recovered would "kneel down in prayer time" while the other one laughed at her for doing so and "they would sware like pirat[e]s."[52] If the Indians alone were guilty, there would have been no need for concern over the shedding of innocent blood.

An entirely different, and probably more accurate, version was later given by Lee who said he held nothing back, but gave Brigham Young "all the information there was to give." Young was upset, he said, and

---

[49]Young to Denver, September 12, 1857, House Exec. Doc. 71, 183–85.

[50]Some historians still malign the Arkansans with this highly implausible charge in an apparent attempt to justify the massacre. In refuting this story, U.S. Indian Agent Jacob Forney said: "Why an emigrant company, and especially farmers, would carry with them so much deadly poison is incomprehensible. I regard the poisoning affair as entitled to no consideration. *In my opinion, bad men*, for a bad purpose, have magnified a natural circumstance for the perpetration of a crime that has no parallel in American history for atrocity." See Forney to Greenwood, August 1859, Sen. Exec. Doc. 42, 75–80.

[51]Kenney, ed., *Wilford Woodruff's Journal*, 5:102–03.

[52]Ibid.

called it "the most unfortunate affair that ever befell the church." If only men had been slain, he reportedly said, he would not have minded so much, but "the killing of the women and children is the sin of it."[53] Lee said Young ordered him to tell no one and send him a letter as the Indian farmer, blaming the natives for the massacre.

Lee later entered a claim of $3,527.43 against the Office of Indian Affairs for goods provided "on superintendent's order" to the natives "near Mountain Meadows" less than three weeks after the massacre. Submitted to Brigham Young, superintendent of Indian affairs, the voucher was signed by Lee and Dimick Huntington who certified "on honor" they saw the listed articles distributed on September 30 to the very chiefs who took part.[54]

Not until November 20 did Lee dutifully put in writing the story that Indians alone had carried out the slaughter because the emigrants had poisoned the natives at Corn Creek, raising "the ire of the Indians which soon spread through the Southern Tribes." His tale and Woodruff's strikingly similar account became the accepted version.[55] With his report, Lee brazenly entered additional claims against the federal Indian agency for Jacob Hamblin, William Dame, Philip Klingen-smith, and himself for goods and services allegedly given to the chiefs involved in the massacre totaling $2,200. Quoting from Lee's letter, which dated the event eleven days after it happened, Brigham Young on January 6, 1858, finally got around to reporting the massacre to the commissioner of Indian affairs. The citizens of Utah had often "compromised their own safety and otherwise peaceful relations with the Indians," Young said, "by interposing in behalf of travellers." The Indians cannot "be expected to be otherwise than hostile," he added, if emigrants "persist in the practice of indiscriminately shooting and poisoning them as above set forth."[56]

The next day the Mormon leader favored his adopted son by presenting him a seventeenth wife, Emma Batchelor, a spirited 22-year-old English survivor of the Martin handcart company. Lee and his latest

---

[53]Lee, *Mormonism Unveiled*, 252–54.
[54]For this and similarly remarkable documents, see "Accounts of Brigham Young, Superintendent of Indian Affairs in Utah Territory," House Exec. Doc. 29 (37–2), 1862, Serial 1128, 100–02.
[55]For Lee's report, see Brooks, *The Mountain Meadows Massacre*, 151–53, and Lee, *Mormonism Unveiled*, 255–56.
[56]Young to Denver, January 6, 1858, Letters Received by the Office of Indian Affairs, Utah Territory.

bride were "sealed" together for time and eternity in Young's own seal-ing room.

It would not take that long, however, for the truth of the massacre at Mountain Meadows to begin to come out. In less than two years, Secre-tary of War John B. Floyd at the urging of family members in Arkansas ordered U.S. Army commanders in the West to investigate. At Los Ange-les, Maj. James H. Carleton of the First Dragoons in April 1859 was ordered to escort army paymaster Maj. Henry Prince and the payroll for Camp Floyd in Utah as far as the Santa Clara River. He was also ordered to bury the bones of the victims.

At Mountain Meadows Carleton's command met three companies from Camp Floyd, one of dragoons and two of infantry, under Capt. Reuben Campbell of the Second Dragoons, who had been sent to escort Prince from there back to the post at present Fairfield. Campbell also carried orders from Albert S. Johnston, now a general, to look into Indian depredations in southwestern Utah, which meant only the mas-sacre. In their reports, both officers opened a telling fire on Mormon settlers for committing the atrocity.[57]

Carleton was deeply outraged at what he beheld on the field. "Nearly every skull I saw had been shot through with rifle or revolver bullets," he said. "There has been a great and fearful crime perpetrated," the officer concluded, and "kept most artfully concealed." He said the "hellish atrocity has no parallel in our history" and called those who did it "these relentless, incarnate fiends." Said the major: "The Thugs of India were an inoffensive, moral, law-abiding people in comparison."[58]

Carleton and the men of Company K collected the bones of thirty-four emigrants and buried them in a common grave on the north side of the Arkansans' rude fortification. Over the remains, they erected a coni-cal monument twelve feet high, made of granite stones and surmounted by a twelve-foot cross, facing toward Great Salt Lake City, cut from cedar. On the cross was deeply carved: "Vengeance is mine: I will repay, saith the Lord."[59]

---

[57]For their reports, see Carleton, House Doc. 605; and Campbell to Porter, July 6, 1859, Sen. Ex. Doc. 42, 14–16.

[58]Carleton, House Doc. 605, 17.

[59]Ibid., 15. The scripture quoted is Romans 12:19. The next verse reads: "Therefore if your enemy hungers, feed him; if he thirsts, give him a drink; for in so doing you will heap coals of fire on his head."

The biblical warning struck no apparent fear in Brigham Young's heart when he read the inscription two years later during his first visit to southern Utah settlements after the massacre. Apostle Woodruff accompanied him to the site and reported that the Mormon leader read Carleton's epitaph, thought for a while, and then said: "It should be Vengeance is mine and I have taken a little."[60] One of Young's escort lassoed the cross with a rope, turned his horse, and pulled it down. Brigham Young "didn't say another word," recalled Dudley Leavitt. "He didn't give an order. He just lifted his right arm to the square, and in five minutes there wasn't one stone left upon another. He didn't have to tell us what he wanted done. We understood."[61]

But too many had been involved to cover up the atrocity by tearing down monuments, taking oaths of secrecy, or swearing to falsehoods, however artfully contrived. As more and more of the story was revealed, protests spread and outrage grew. Pressure for an investigation and punishment came from within the faith itself. The crime also threatened to stop indefinitely Utah's efforts to achieve statehood. So it came about that one man was chosen to pay the price for many.

The most likely candidate, John D. Lee, was excommunicated by his church in 1870 as a show of punishment and sent to operate a ferry at a remote location on the Colorado River to get him safely out of the way. Still known as Lee's Ferry, the site is located a few miles down river from present Glen Canyon Dam, just south of Page, Arizona. In November 1874 Lee was arrested. He was tried a year later at Beaver, Utah, for his part in the massacre, but the trial was abortive. Others included on the indictment could not be found. Missing, too, were key witnesses, and those who did appear suffered lapses in memory. Moreover, the outcome was foreordained because prosecutors tried to implicate Brigham Young. As a result, while all four non-Mormon jury members voted for conviction, eight Mormon jurors chose acquittal.

In a second trial, restricted by agreement to Lee's role, witnesses found their memories restored and an all-Mormon jury unanimously

---

[60]Kenney, ed., *Wilford Woodruff's Journal,* 5:577. Also see Brooks, *John Doyle Lee: Zealot, Pioneer Builder, Scapegoat,* 265–66. The monument was rebuilt in 1864 by the officers and men of Company M, Second California Volunteer Cavalry.

[61]Brooks, *The Mountain Meadows Massacre,* 183.

found him guilty. On March 23, 1877, he was taken to Mountain Meadows, the scene of the crime, where at age 64 he was perched on the edge of his coffin and shot to death by a firing squad. He died without fear. Five months later, Brigham Young, his father by adoption, went to his reward at age 76 in Salt Lake City. But Lee's execution did not end the story.

In a footnote, which seems only to raise more questions, the First Presidency and Quorum of the Twelve Apostles of the Church of Jesus Christ of Latter-day Saints in April 1961 met in a joint session to consider Lee's case. Afterward, "It was the action of the Council after considering all the facts available that authorization be given for the reinstatement to membership and former blessings to John D. Lee."[62] The necessary ordinances were performed the following month in the Salt Lake Temple.

The latest chapter in the Mountain Meadows story was written in 1990 when relatives of the emigrants and descendants of John D. Lee with the cooperation of the LDS church joined on September 15 at Southern Utah State College in Cedar City in public ceremonies to dedicate a new monument to the memory of those slain. Among those taking part in the program were Judge Logan, who had many relatives in the massacre; Clifford Jake, Paiute spiritual leader; President Gordon B. Hinckley, then first counselor, First Presidency, LDS church; and the four hundred-voice "Iron County Mountain Meadows Choir," made up of singers from many nearby Mormon churches.[63]

Dedicated the evening before in a private ceremony conducted by President Hinckley, the monument is inscribed: "In the valley below, between September 7 and 11, 1857, a company of more than 120 Arkansas emigrants led by Capt. John T. Baker and Capt. Alexander Fancher was attacked while en route to California. This event is known in history as the Mountain Meadows Massacre." Oddly failing to tell who did it, the historic marker is located on Utah Highway 18 about ten miles south of Enterprise.

The final resting place of John D. Lee, the only man to pay the price

---

[62]Ibid., 223.
[63]See program, "Mountain Meadows Memorial Dedication Ceremonies," September 15, 1990, Centrum, Southern Utah State College, Cedar City, Utah.

for the massacre at Mountain Meadows, can be seen today in the cemetery at Panguitch, Utah, where he lies beneath a cement blanket with an inscription that puts a final bizarre touch on the blackest chapter in the western theocracy's story:

"Know the Truth, and the Truth shall make you free."[64]

---

[64]John 8:32.

Chapter 9

PEACE BUT NO PEACE

Give way: Go on giving: be superior to all provocation this single summer through:—and I promise you as complete a triumph for the future, as the most hopeful among you ever
dreamed of.

—Thomas L. Kane

The early winter of 1857 closed down the heroic performances that
enlivened the bloodless confrontation known as the Utah War, bringing
both sides a time for cooling off. Almost silent by year's end was the
reformation rhetoric that had inflamed emotions in Utah. Also shaken
was the pride that led an American president to underestimate a theocratic territory and order an ill-prepared military expedition to march
west. Now came a time for reflection on past actions and their consequences.

In Washington President Buchanan in December asked Congress for
four new regiments to put down the rebellion and more money to meet
the unexpected cost of the expedition he had already put in the field. But
lawmakers put his request on hold and asked instead to know just "how
far said Brigham Young and his followers are in a state of rebellion or
resistance to the government of the United States."[1] Buchanan began to
think about finding a peaceful way out of the crisis he had precipitated.

No such indecision existed that winter in the mind of Albert Sidney
Johnston, the commander at Camp Scott, who was converting a demoralized collection of military units into a purposeful force. Having suffered embarrassment and near disaster on the plains, the American
troops now under his leadership on Blacks Fork were becoming an efficient, motivated command ready to mount a spring assault on the Echo

---

[1]House Exec. Doc. 71 (35–1), 1858, Serial 956, 1.

Canyon approaches to Salt Lake Valley. Should the Mormons "desire to join issue," Colonel Johnston said ominously, "I believe it is for the interest of the government that they should have the opportunity."[2]

If he was looking for a fight, the colonel had good reason to think he could win it whether Congress approved the establishment of four new regiments or not. Reinforcements were expected "as early in the spring as practicable."[3] Numbering nearly four thousand, they would include the crack First Cavalry, ten companies each from the Sixth and Seventh Infantry, the two remaining companies of the Second Dragoons, more artillery, and 850 recruits. In total, they would bring the forces under Johnston's command up to more than 5,600, or nearly one-third of the regular army.

Waiting at Fort Bridger for the troops to seat him, against the almost unanimous wishes of the people, was Utah's second governor, Alfred Cumming. That November the 250-pound Georgian had issued a proclamation to citizens of the territory that he would "enforce unconditional obedience to the Constitution, to the organic laws of the Territory, and to all the other laws of Congress applicable to you."[4] One of its addressees called it an "informal injust and illegal document."[5] Most in Utah just ignored or laughed at the lofty pronouncement.

At Great Salt Lake City, the man he hoped to succeed, surely the choice of virtually everyone who could vote under the existing election law, sounded less militant but still defiant and not yet willing to surrender his seat. No longer could Brigham Young rest his right to be governor on the claim that he had not been properly notified of his removal. So he now took a legalistic stand on the American constitution and adopted, in a possible reference to the Mountain Meadows Massacre, a defensive posture. Appearing before the Legislative Assembly on December 15, 1857, Young blamed the "passers-through," without mentioning by name the Baker-Fancher Train, "who have cheated, and then poisoned and wantonly slain untutored savages." He censured the "lying and corrupt presses throughout the Union" for "charging upon

[2]Johnston to McDowell, January 20, 1858, Sen. Exec. Doc. I (35–2), 1858, Serial 975, 44, 45.

[3]Ibid., 31.

[4]Hafen and Hafen, The Utah Expedition, 296–98.

[5]Brooks, On the Mormon Frontier, 2:646.

[6]Brigham Young, "Governor's Message to the Legislative Assembly, Territory of Utah," Journal History, December 15, 1857.

us all the murders and massacres" between the Missouri River and California. The sole intent of this "prolonged howl of base slander," said he, was "to excite to a frenzy a spirit for our extermination."[6]

From this polemic, he went on to stamp as unconstitutional any laws that allowed the president to appoint outsiders, like Cumming, to rule in a territory against the will of the people. "Congress has not one particle more constitutional power to legislate for and officer Americans in Territories than they have to legislate for and officer Americans in States," he said. To do so was "British colonial vassalage," he went on, "unconstitutionally perpetrated by tyranny and usurpation in the powers that be."[7]

Standing Army of Israel

Territorial lawmakers voiced "the feeling of this assembly" in support of his position.[8] His message also triggered orchestrated resolutions that no appointed official "shall exercise any dominion over us while their armies are menacing our Territory."[9] Assembly members also took up an act to repeal territorial taxes, apparently preferring to finance the theocratic entity through special levies, consecration, and tithing.[10] The same fiscal plan also was applied in the creation that winter of a full-time military force.

Patterned after the Continental Army, "the Standing Army of Deseret" was created to defend the right to autonomous rule voiced by Young. The one thousand-man brigade of mounted riflemen, or dragoons, was organized into two regiments of five hundred, ten battalions of one hundred, and twenty companies of fifty. It was to be supported by the subscription of the people, some pledging to outfit and support one soldier, others one-half or one-fourth of a man, while others gave what they could, a horse, rifles, revolvers, or even "5 bushels of potatoes."[11]

[7]Ibid.

[8]Brooks, On the Mormon Frontier, 2:649.

[9]"Resolution by Committee on behalf of Citizens," Great Salt Lake City, Journal History, January 16, 1858.

[10]Juanita Brooks believed this was to deprive federal appointees of the money they required to function as office holders, but this view assumes legislators knew at the time that federal authority would prevail in the showdown between theocratic and republican forms of government. See Brooks, On the Mormon Frontier, 2:651.

[11]A List of donations toward fitting out Soldiers for the Army of Israel 1st ward Ogden City, Weber Co., 1st February 1858, MS 9310, LDS Archives. Also see Harker, Bennion, Harris, Hickman, and Bennion to Young, January 15, 1858, Utah Militia Records.

To raise and outfit soldiers, a levy was imposed by decree, requiring
no legislative approval, on the northern Utah military districts. Great
Salt Lake and Tooele, the most populous, were assigned to raise 375
men; Davis, 150; Weber (Ogden) and Box Elder (Brigham City), 175;
and Lehi, Provo, Peteetneet (Payson), Juab, and Sanpete, 300. In meeting their quotas, military districts were warned against "rendering inef-
ficient" the other militia units in their area. But the new host of Israel
was to train and serve as a separate, professional force under Nauvoo
Legion General Daniel Wells.[12]

Named to command the new brigade of riflemen at the rank of
brigadier general was 31-year-old New Yorker William H. Kimball, son
of Brigham Young's first counselor, Heber C. Kimball. Chosen colonels
of the two regiments were George D. Grant, 45, also from New York,
and Virginian Andrew Cunningham. The ten majors chosen to head battalions and twenty captains of companies included many of the territory's most experienced military leaders and plainsmen. Officers below
the rank of colonel averaged 34 years in age and numbered natives of ten
states, Ireland, and England.[13] More than half came from New York and
New England, birthplace of the uniquely American millennial faith they
served. Eight were veterans of the Mormon Battalion during the Mexican War. Never fully activated, their command existed for only about
three months, but in that time it became one of a kind in American military history.

INTERCESSION OF THOMAS KANE

The mission of Utah's first and only regular army was brought to a
sudden end by two surprising events that happened on the same day,

---

[12]See General Orders No. 1, Nauvoo Legion, Great Salt Lake City, March 6, 1858, Nathaniel Vary Jones
Papers, MS 2628, LDS Archives. For other standing army references, see Brooks, *On the Mormon Frontier*, 2:649,
652; Kenney, ed., *Wilford Woodruff's Journal*, 5:156; and George A. Smith to John L. Smith, February 4, 1858, Journal History.

[13]Named majors over battalions (100) were Brigham Young, Jr., Thomas Callister, Lot Smith, Reddick N.
Allred, Marcellus Monroe, Howard Egan, Ephraim Hanks, Henson Walker, Madison D. Hamilton, and Warren
S. Snow. Chosen captains of companies (50) were Stephen Taylor, Charles Decker, Wilford Hudson, George
Knowlton, Horton D. Haight, John D. Parker, Charles Layton, Joseph Grover, Erastus Bingham, H. P. Kimball,
Daniel McArthur, Jacob Truman, William W. Casper, Samuel S. White, John R. Murdock, Abraham Conover,
Isaac Bullock, George P. Billings, and William Maxwell.

many miles apart.[14] That fateful Thursday, February 25, there landed in Great Salt Lake a self-appointed peacemaker, Thomas Kane, the psychosomatic son of a federal judge and influential Democrat in Philadelphia. An ardent defender of the oppressed, the 35-year-old Kane was a disciple of Auguste Comte, the French philosopher and father of "scientific socialism."[15]

The tireless humanitarian had helped the Mormons before. In 1846, at age 21, he had masterminded President James Polk's offer to enlist a battalion of five hundred Mormons to serve in the Mexican War, which largely financed the Mormon migration a year later. Kane stood only five feet six, weighed not more than 130 pounds, and suffered from bouts of "Bilious Fever; Connecting itself seriously with the Nervous System,"[16] but the Pennsylvanian was anything but timid or fearful. He was feisty, combative, and quixotically brave almost to the point of foolhardiness.[17]

Learning of the armed standoff in Utah, he had applied his uncommon political skills to win a verbal concession from President Buchanan that he would pardon Mormon leaders for rebellion if they would accept the new governor and let the army camp somewhere near the city, perhaps in Rush Valley on the other side of the Oquirrh Mountains. Carrying presidential letters of introduction, he had traveled by sea (sick all the way) under the pseudonym "A. Osborne" to the West Coast, then overland to Utah to mediate the dispute.

Over the next twelve days, Kane urged Brigham Young to accept Mr. Buchanan's unofficial offer and hold out an olive branch to his adversaries in the mountains. But on March 8, when he rode out for Camp Scott, escorted by Porter Rockwell and other officers, there was no sign Young was ready to make peace, despite his cordial reception of an old friend.

---

[14]In the event Mormon leaders decided to evacuate the Great Basin and move north, via Fort Limhi, the likely mission of the standing army would be to block at Soda Springs any attempt to intercept or prevent this migration.

[15]For an excellent account of Kane's mission and its aftermath, see Poll, "Quixotic Mediator: Thomas L. Kane and the Utah War."

[16]Winther, ed., *The Private Papers and Diary of Thomas Leiper Kane: A Friend of The Mormons*, 23.

[17]An early volunteer in the Civil War, Kane in 1861 was elected lieutenant colonel of the 13th Pennsylvania Regiment, known as the "Pennsylvania Bucktails." Just before the Battle of Sharpsburg (Antietam) in 1862, in which the regiment fought, he was promoted to brigadier general. In 1865 he received the rank of brevet major general of volunteers for "gallant and distinguished service" in the Battle of Gettysburg.

Earlier that day, however, two tired express riders arrived at the capital carrying a report that came like a sharp gale from the north. And the door to independence banged suddenly shut.

ATTACK ON FORT LIMHI

Stitched into the coat lining of the youngest messenger, 22-year-old Baldwin Watts, was a letter from Thomas Smith, head of the newly expanded settlement at Fort Limhi on the east fork of Salmon River. Watts and Ezra Barnard, 28, had slipped through the Indian camps around the main stockade after dark and ridden on the fort's best horses nearly four hundred miles in mid-winter to cover the distance in only eight days. Eclipsing this feat, one of the Utah War's most heroic, was the shocking news they bore.

On February 25, the same day Kane had arrived, more than two hundred Bannock and Shoshoni warriors attacked the settlement south of present Salmon, Idaho. Killed defending the herd were 31-year-old George McBride and James Thadeas Miller, 20, a recent arrival, both from Farmington. Five others, Andrew Quigley, Fountain Welch, Oliver Robinson, Haskell Shurtliff, and the mission head himself, were wounded. The raiders made off with more than two hundred head of cattle and some thirty horses and laid siege to the kingdom's northernmost colony.

Seen in the Indian camps before the raid had been John Powell, mountaineer husband of a Shoshoni woman. He and a partner, Craven Jackson, would be accused of provoking the raid to steal cattle for the army. Although they later hotly denied it, the pair showed up at Camp Scott at about the same time Benjamin Ficklin returned from his trip north to Beaverhead and beyond. Moreover Nauvoo Legion troopers sent to rescue the settlers reported seeing tracks of the Mormon cattle in the Portneuf River bottoms, near today's Portneuf Reservoir, heading toward Soda Springs and the army encampment.[18]

Above all the attack on Fort Limhi by the Indians Brigham Young had

---

[18] The accusation that agents from Camp Scott provoked the attack on Fort Limhi and other places was made in *Deseret News*, April 14, 1858, 35. For Ficklin's report and denials of the three men, see House Exec. Doc. 71, 68–71, 79–82. For the charge that most of the cattle were driven to Camp Scott, see Bluth, "The Salmon River Mission," 901–13. Powell's later claim that he tried to warn the settlers appears borne out in several accounts the day before the attack. See Salmon River Mission Journal and Journal of Charles F. Middleton, February 24, 1858.

courted the year before destroyed the option, if all else failed, to evacuate the Great Basin and move north. No longer was the settlement a place of rest and resupply at the north end of a protected corridor running between two mountain ranges from the bend of the Snake River to the Lewis and Clark Pass. Now it was a dangerous and costly liability.

The news that broke on March 8 as Thomas Kane left for Camp Scott marked the turning point in the conflict between the United States and a rebellious territory. Mormon leaders spent that day and the next organizing a 140-man force under Col. Andrew Cunningham to rescue settlers in peril to the north and deciding what to do. Then, on March 9, at 8 P.M., Brigham Young swallowed his pride and dispatched his son Joseph A. and George Stringham with a letter to Kane. They caught up to the self-appointed peacemaker before he reached Fort Bridger. Having just learned that "the troops are very destitute of provisions," the note began, Young had decided to send two hundred head of cattle and as much as twenty-thousand pounds of flour, to which his enemies were "perfectly welcome, or pay for, just as they choose."[19] Colonel Johnston stiffly refused the offer, preferring to go hungry rather than take food from rebels defying the federal government. But Alfred Cumming, to Johnston's disgust, saw the gesture for what it was, a peace overture, and he welcomed it.

Four weeks later the new governor entered Salt Lake Valley with Kane and a Mormon escort. He reported that he received the respect "due to the representative of the executive authority of the United States." Like others before, the Georgian was deeply impressed during his appearance before an assembly of thousands in the tabernacle on Sunday, April 25, when he was introduced as Utah governor by Young himself. Those gathered listened to what he had to say quietly, "approvingly even, I fancied," he said. Then he made the mistake of asking for comments from the congregation.[20]

At this invitation, "several powerful speakers" got up and whipped the assembly to near frenzy with a rehearsal of grievances. Forcefully they objected to his being governor "while backed up by an armed force." When one cried, "Send home your troops and then come among us as a friend," there was a standing ovation. Louder still were the cheers,

[19]Young to Kane, March 9, 1858, House Exec. Doc. 2, Vol. 2, Pt. II (35–2), 1858, Serial 998, 87, 88; also in Hafen and Hafen, The Utah Expedition, 269–70.
[20]Ibid., Cumming to Cass, May 2, 1858, 91–97.

when Cumming conceded "he would not hang as a rag on our garments against our will."[21] This pacifying stance would be the mark of his administration over the next three years.

THE MOVE SOUTH

Besides unwilling acceptance, Utah's second governor also found the citizens of his new jurisdiction abandoning their homes in the north and streaming south, away from an imagined invasion.[22] The move to "'Burn up' and flee" as a tactic to expose "the folly, and meanness of the President" had been proposed by Brigham Young on March 18 as an alternative to armed resistance.[23] The image of refugees fleeing before an advancing U.S. Army had an impact more powerful than all the muskets Zion could muster.

Even before he was faced with this disturbing picture, President Buchanan had decided to resolve the issue peacefully if he could. On April 7, he named two respected Americans, Lazarus W. Powell, former governor of Kentucky, and the famed Texas Ranger captain, Ben McCulloch, as peace commissioners. They were ordered not to negotiate, but to "bring these misguided people to their senses, to convert them into good citizens and to spare the effusion of human blood."[24] With them, Buchanan sent a proclamation offering to make peace, but only on his own terms.

In his message, the president neither took on himself any blame for what had happened nor made any concessions. Instead he charged Utah for years had shown "a spirit of insubordination to the Constitution and laws of the United States." This rebellion, he said, was "without just cause, without reason, without excuse." Even so, he offered "a free pardon for the seditions and treasons heretofore by them committed," to all willing to obey the laws, but no leniency to those who were not.[25]

---

[21]Brooks, *On the Mormon Frontier*, 2:657–58.

[22]In a desperation move, Brigham Young in March ordered companies to explore remote areas of the Great Basin in present Nevada in the hope of finding a location for followers rather than accept federal authority. For more on this abortive effort, see Stott, *Search for Sanctuary: Brigham Young and the White Mountain Expedition*.

[23]Brooks, *On the Mormon Frontier*, 2:654. Also see Young, A Series of Instructions and Remarks by President Brigham Young at a Special Council, Tabernacle, March 21, 1858.

[24]Floyd to Powell and McCulloch, April 12, 1858, House Exec. Doc. 2, Vol. 2, Pt. II, 160–62; also in Hafen and Hafen, *The Utah Expedition*, 329–32.

[25]Sen. Exec. Doc. I (35–2), 1858, Serial 974, 69–72; also in Hafen and Hafen, *The Utah Expedition*, 332–37.

After much speechmaking, when the "the voice & roar of the Lion," Brigham Young, was heard by all concerned, Mr. Buchanan's offer on June 13 was accepted unconditionally.[26] Only time would tell whether the acceptance reflected a real change of heart. In the meantime, it ended Utah's fourth bid for sovereign statehood or full independence as a separate nation.

Anxious to keep peace, Governor Cumming opposed any plan by Johnston to establish a post near the capital city or any other settlement, but the newly breveted brigadier general had no such intention. As a show of federal authority, however, he marched his army in perfect order through the almost deserted city. Then he made his permanent camp in Cedar Valley and named it after fellow southerner, John B. Floyd, then secretary of war.[27] With the troops out of the way, the people went back home.

THE ONE-EYED JUDGE

Not long after, a tall, lean lawyer from Circleville, Ohio, turned up on November 3, 1858, at the tavern between Big and Little mountains. To the inn's owner, Ephraim Hanks, he had the appearance of an ox driver. He was "very roughly dressed" and had "but one eye," Hanks said, "and that is a very good one." The newcomer gave up his carriage to a woman who wanted "to go to Zion" and proceeded on foot. When Hanks caught up with him later, he was riding into the city on a load of wood. He wanted no special treatment or "airs," the Ohioan said. "I have come here to do my duty."[28]

Appointed in June, 39-year-old John Cradlebaugh was the last of the territorial supreme court's latest judges to arrive. Unlike Delano R. Eckels, the new chief justice, his attitude had not been negatively frozen by a long winter in the snow at Camp Scott. At first, the Ohioan reportedly thought Eckels suffered from prejudice against Utah's people. But the judge soon saw things differently with his one good eye and launched an investigation that would turn the territory into an armed camp.

The trouble began right after territorial lawmakers in January 1859

---

[26]Kenney, *Wilford Woodruff's Journal*, 5:196.

[27]Camp Floyd, renamed Fort Crittenden at the start of the Civil War, is today Camp Floyd/Stagecoach Inn State Heritage Park at Fairfield on Utah Highway 73. For more on the post, see Moorman with Sessions, *Camp Floyd and The Mormons: The Utah War*.

[28]Report by Ephraim Hanks, Journal History, November 4, 1858.

JUDGE JOHN CRADLEBAUGH
When the one-eyed judge in 1859
investigated Mountain Meadows Massacre
and other crimes, many settlement
leaders headed for the hills.
Courtesy, Utah State Historical Society.

redrew at Governor Cumming's suggestion Utah's three judicial districts, effective May 1, to pack Cradlebaugh safely off to serve as judge over the most remote portion of the territory, now western Nevada.[29] In the meantime, the new law left open a three-month window for the new justice to look into some major recent crimes, including the massacre at Mountain Meadows, and to bring the wrongdoers to justice.

Cradlebaugh first told General Johnston that he would hold a term of his court at Provo on March 8 and requested troops to act as a *posse comitatus* in holding alleged criminals prior to trial. True to his orders, Johnston sent a company from Camp Floyd under Tenth Infantry Capt. Henry Heth to perform the task. Heth tried to bivouac outside the town, but found the city limits had been drawn from the base of the mountain to Utah Lake to keep outsiders from acquiring land. So he camped in a corral by the building used as a courthouse.[30]

Protected by the troops, Cradlebaugh and the judge who would shortly succeed him, Associate Justice Charles Sinclair, impaneled a

[29]Cumming explained that the district's remoteness "has had the effect of depriving its inhabitants of the advantages of district and other Courts—And that region has been in a state bordering upon anarchy. This condition of things will, I trust, be remedied by the establishment of the Hon. Judge Cradlebaugh in his new district." See Cumming to Cass, January 28, 1859, Alfred Cumming Papers.

[30]A Virginian, Heth as a major general would win a lasting place in American history when he marched his Confederate division to Gettysburg to find shoes for his men and in July 1863 touched off the most famous battle of the Civil War.

grand jury and took sworn testimony on a number of crimes. They included the Parrish-Potter murders at Springville and the execution-style killings of five out of six Californians, known as the Aiken party, in November 1857, among others.[31]

As the hearings began, protests broke out over the presence of soldiers in the town. Provo Mayor Benjamin Bullock, allegedly "to preserve the peace," demanded they be removed "beyond the limits of this city."[32] His request was all but impossible for Heth to grant without ending up in another town or in Utah Lake.

The growing clamor was joined by Governor Cumming himself, who visited the city and concluded "the presence of the military force in this vicinity is unnecessary." Curtly he asked Johnston to keep his soldiers outside the town wall and remove other troops Johnston had sent to Battle Creek, now Pleasant Grove, to prevent an attempt to rescue prisoners in military custody. Equally curt was the general's reply that he was "under no obligation whatever" to comply with the governor's wishes.[33]

One who did not share Cumming's confidence in the benign intentions of the populace was the judge who started the uproar. The protection of soldiers was necessary, Cradlebaugh held, because those who came forward to testify were "threatened and intimidated" and "compelled to fly from reasonably expected violence." Some of the witnesses were so afraid, he said, they would "burst into tears in open court" when they were "compelled to testify to the horrid crimes" they knew about.[34] When Mormon grand jurors refused to bring indictments, the undaunted magistrate handed U.S. Marshal Peter Dotson warrants for the arrest of a dozen or more alleged offenders. Unable to execute them, "with the means now at my command," Dotson took his turn in calling on Johnston for "at least two hundred troops" to make the arrests.[35]

---

[31]In a badly mishandled operation, two of the Californians were killed on the Sevier River, near today's I-15 crossing, two were killed at Willow Creek, north of Nephi and dumped in the spring at present Mona, and the fifth was later murdered north of Great Salt Lake. Of the five alleged assassins, including Porter Rockwell and William Hickman, only Sylvanus Collett was ever brought to trial, which is reported in Chapter 15. For the story of this party, see Schindler, *Orrin Porter Rockwell*, 268–80. Also see *San Francisco Daily Evening Bulletin*, January 18 and February 16, 1858, and Hickman, *Brigham's Destroying Angel*, 279–81.

[32]Bullock to Cradlebaugh, March 11, 1859, Sen. Exec. Doc. 2 (36–1), 1859, Serial 1024, 142.

[33]Ibid., Cumming to Johnston, March 20, 1859, and Johnston to Cumming, March 22, 1859, 149–52.

[34]Cradlebaugh and Sinclair to Buchanan, April 7, 1859, Sen. Exec. Doc. 32 (36–1), Serial 1031, 5–9.

[35]Sen. Exec. Doc. 2, 155.

So it happened that U.S. dragoons on the night of March 25 closed in on Bishop Aaron Johnson's house in Springville only to find their quarry flown. The soldiers now came under heavy verbal fire from some of Johnson's wives and replied with a war dance.[36]

As troops and deputies scoured three counties, local leaders fled to the mountains and companies sprang to arms to protect them. Favored retreats were those that afforded strong natural defenses and several avenues of escape. They included the canyons of Hobble and Peteetneet creeks in Utah County; a spot referred to as "an old ruined castle," named "Ballagarth" or "Balleguarde," in upper Salt Creek Canyon or in the mountains east of Levan in Juab County; and Maple Canyon in Sanpete.[37]

With the countryside in turmoil, Cradlebaugh closed his court and Marshal Dotson asked the military to escort the only prisoners he had managed to catch to the only jail in Utah County, the Camp Floyd guardhouse. There followed one of the most unusual parades staged in Utah, then or since. Nearly one thousand troops, about five percent of the U.S. Army "in regular order of infantry, artillery and dragoons," on April 4 marched five men accused of the Parrish-Potter murders through Utah Valley towns.

When the column passed American Fork, the fife and drums of the "old-fashioned" Seventh Infantry struck up and the dragoon guidons were "loosed to the breeze." This martial display brought "cat-calls, groans and whistles" from onlookers, while two youths wheeled a dummy cannon, made of a "beer cask mounted on a pair of cart wheels," on the parade's flanks. At the center one of the prisoners, six-foot-three Alexander F. McDonald, the 33-year-old former mayor of Springville, "towered above the guard" and strode with "an air of martyr-like defiance."[38]

With his territory nearing a state of rebellion, Utah's new governor gave in to growing pressure. On March 25 Cumming told his superior at Washington that the crusade of the judges would only "lead to much bloodshed" and recommended that requisitions for troops to enforce the law only be made with his approval. Two days later, he issued a

---

[36]For an account of this amusing episode, see Auerbach and Alter, eds., "The Journal of Albert Tracy," 64.

[37]See Diary of Samuel Pitchforth, April 5, 1859.

[38]Auerbach and Alder, "The Journal of Albert Tracy," 64, 65.

proclamation to protest military movements he believed violated "the letter and spirit" of his instructions.[39]

For a time the governor's actions to restore peace at any price did little to discourage the energetic justice who started the trouble. On April 21, Cradlebaugh went with three companies of troops from Camp Floyd to look into the Mountain Meadows Massacre. As southern Utah settlers took to nearby hills, he inspected the massacre ground, heard secret testimony at Cedar City, and issued arrest warrants for more than three dozen alleged participants in the affair, including John D. Lee, Isaac Haight, and John Higbee.[40]

Even as the judge undertook his latest crusade, orders came from Camp Floyd to Capt. Reuben Campbell, commander of his military escort, that put a stop to it. Acting on Cumming's recommendation, President Buchanan had changed Johnston's orders and limited the authority to requisition troops for a *posse comitatus* to only the governor. Since Campbell's force was recalled, Cradlebaugh had no choice but to break off his investigation and return north with the soldiers. On his arrival the judge found a sharp reprimand from U.S. Attorney General Jeremiah Black. The president had enough problems as the North and South headed into a civil war without having to worry about a couple of troublemaking judges who wanted to do more than "hear patiently the causes brought before them."[41] Buchanan's support for the governor's appeasement policy in Utah ended for a time efforts to punish perpetrators of major crimes.

Since Cumming had already refused to approve a requisition of troops, Marshal Dotson returned to the judges warrants for the arrest of a number of Utah leaders, "being fully satisfied that I could not execute the command of the writ by any civil posse."[42] The list of alleged offenders included more than three dozen from southern Utah; Bishop Jacob Bigler, Mayor Timothy B. Foote, Samuel Pitchforth, and John Wolf from

---

[39]Cumming to Cass, March 25, 1859, and Proclamation, March 27, 1859, Alfred Cumming Papers.

[40]John D. Lee and Bishop Philip Klingensmith hid out in the mountains near Cedar City, where they could watch the federal expedition, while other massacre participants, including Isaac Haight, William Stewart, and others, rode north to join alleged offenders at the place in Juab County identified only as "old Castle Ballagarth."

[41]Black to Cradlebaugh and Sinclair, May 17, 1859, "Correspondence between the judges of Utah and the Attorney General or President, with reference to the legal proceedings and conditions of affairs in that Territory," Sen. Exec. Doc. 32 (36–1), Serial 1031, 2–4.

[42]Dotson to Cradlebaugh, June 3, 1859, U.S. Attorney General, Records relating to the appointment of Federal judges, attorneys, and marshals for the Territory and State of Utah.

Nephi; George Hancock from Payson; Springville Bishop Aaron John-son; Porter Rockwell; and others. Not only did Mr. Buchanan's support for Cumming prevent the marshal from making these arrests, it also made it impossible for him to hold the alleged lawbreakers he already had in custody at Camp Floyd. On June 27 General Johnston told Dotson he regretted having to free men charged with "the most atrocious crimes," but under his present orders he could no longer hold prisoners awaiting trial. Since the territory would not keep them elsewhere, McDonald and four others were released to go back to Springville.

All this the general took in stride, but not so the marshal. In an angry resignation, Dotson on August 1 warned the president that his policy of appeasement would strengthen "the political and ecclesiastical power" of Brigham Young and his followers. No more would he try to serve while being "opposed and annoyed continually by those whose cordial support and co-operation" was necessary for him to do his job.[43] He seemed to include in that number Cumming and President Buchanan himself.

CREATION OF NEVADA TERRITORY

Less easily discouraged was the one-eyed judge who opened his court that summer in Carson County, which encompassed the present Nevada counties of Washoe, Douglas, Ormsby, Storey, and Lyon; and portions of Esmeralda, Churchill, and Humboldt. There he became a leader in a growing movement to break off from Utah and create a new territory. Complaints over theocratic rule had grown after the withdrawal in 1857 of Mormon settlers from the western reaches of the territory.

As early as 1856 some local residents had petitioned Congress to annex Carson Valley to California, listing as reasons that they suffered "gross persecutions" at the hands of the Mormon majority. The House Com-mittee on Territories turned down the request on the ground that stronger measures were needed "to effect a radical cure of the moral and political pestilence which makes Utah the scandal of the American people."[44]

Encouraged by this attitude, western Utah settlers in a convention at Genoa adopted on July 28, 1859, a new constitution and called on Con-

---

[43] *Utah and the Mormons. Speech of Hon. John Cradlebaugh, of Nevada, on the admission of Utah as a state. Delivered in the House of Representatives, February 7, 1863*, 25, 26.

[44] "Citizens of Carson Valley, Territory of Utah, for annexation to California," House Rep. 116 (34–3), 1856, Serial 912.

gress to form a separate territory named Nevada. Behind the move were dissenters and newcomers who had taken over the property of Mormons who had first colonized Carson Valley in 1850 when a party of six, including Abner Blackburn, had planted Mormon Station, later renamed Genoa, near present Carson City.[45] It was supported by California lawmakers who called on their own congressional delegation to work for creation of "a new Territory in Western Utah."[46]

In declaring the causes for separation, the petitioners listed eleven grievances against "the Mormons of eastern Utah," including several that showed Cradlebaugh's hand, such as, their compatriots had "conferred upon Probate Judges the sole right to select juries in civil and criminal cases."[47] Echoes of the massacre at Mountain Meadows and overtures to the tribes during the Utah War sounded in the charge that Mormon emissaries had "poisoned the minds of the Indians against us, forced us frequently to open war with them."[48]

To many in Congress, it was only the first step in reducing Utah to a governable size when on March 2, 1861, they created the Territory of Nevada. Revealing Cradlebaugh's influence, the new territory's organic act explicitly gave the supreme and district courts "authority for redress of all wrongs committed against the Constitution or laws of the United States, or of the Territory, affecting persons or property."[49] Not in Nevada would territorial legislators give probate courts final jurisdiction over civil and criminal cases.

The new territory took some 73,574 square miles away from Utah's domain, all west of the 116th degree west longitude, near today's Carlin. Elected as its first delegate to Congress was Cradlebaugh himself, who promptly sponsored the 1862 measure that cut Utah back still further to the 115th meridian, near present Wells.[50] In 1866 Nevada, now

---

[45]See Bagley, *Frontiersman: Abner Blackburn's Narrative,* 159–62.

[46]"Resolution of the Legislature of California in favor of the establishment of a new Territory in Western Utah," Sen. Misc. Doc. 17 (36–1), 1860, Serial 1038.

[47]*History of Nevada with Illustrations and Biographical Sketches of Its Prominent Men and Pioneers,* 63.

[48]Ibid.

[49]See "An Act to organize the Territory of Nevada," March 2, 1861, *Statutes at Large of the United States,* 12:212.

[50]Despite his sight disability and age, Cradlebaugh in 1863 left Congress and returned to his hometown to recruit the 114th Ohio Volunteer Infantry, which he headed as colonel. While leading his regiment that year in the first charge at Vicksburg, he was struck in the mouth by a minie ball that knocked out many of his teeth and shot away parts of his lip, palate, and tongue before emerging from his neck just below the ear lobe. He eventually recovered and went back to Nevada where he had difficulty in speaking, a sore handicap for a lawyer, until his death in 1872 at Eureka of pneumonia. His remains were later moved for final burial to Circleville, Ohio.

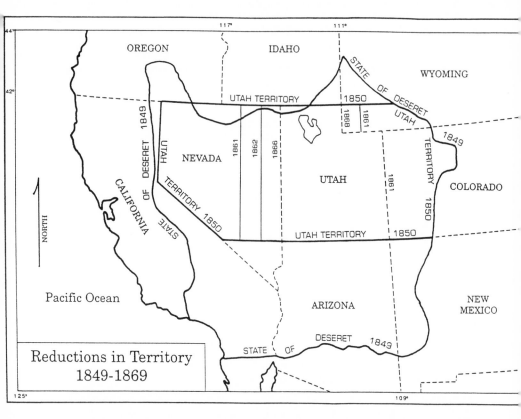

a state, took another bite to put the line at present Wendover. In deliberately punitive acts, Congress by 1870 reduced Utah from 220,196 square miles to approximately its present area of 84,899 square miles, giving the difference to neighbors.

OVERLAND STAGE, PONY EXPRESS

As the territory was reduced in size, the time it took to travel between its borders also shrank. Soon after Camp Floyd was established, Capt. James Simpson of the Corps of Topographical Engineers, one of West Point's youngest graduates, produced some of the Utah Expedition's most lasting benefits. The first was to open in 1858 a new wagon road up Provo Canyon to the Weber River, then up Chalk Creek from present Coalville to Fort Bridger.

A year later the New Jersey native led an expedition from Camp Floyd across the Great Basin to explore a more direct wagon road to Carson Valley. The route he opened ran well to the south of the trail across Salt Desert and the California Trail along the Humboldt River to cut some

250 miles from the distance between Camp Floyd and San Francisco. It followed a line of crude way stations, laid out the year before by mail contractor George Chorpenning, to Hastings Pass at the south end of the Ruby Range, where it left the Hastings Cutoff and headed south-west to Carson City and Genoa.[51]

As the nation looked for ways to shorten travel time and speed communications to the West Coast, Simpson's proposed wagon road won interest that reached well beyond emigrants. The central Great Basin crossing attracted the transportation pioneers who established the Pony Express, transcontinental telegraph, and the Overland Mail and stage line.[52] Portions of the route would later become part of America's first coast-to-coast thoroughfare, the Lincoln Highway, and of U.S. Highway 50.

First to use the trail was the famed Pony Express, created in April 1860 by Russell, Majors & Waddell to deliver mail from St. Joseph to Sacramento in ten days or less by relays of tough, young riders on fast horses. That month, 18-year-old Richard "Ras" Egan, son of Irish Mormon Battalion veteran Howard Egan, was first to ride the seventy-five-mile leg from Great Salt Lake to the Rush Valley station. Aboard his prized sorrel mare, "Miss Lightning," the teenager galloped over the first twenty-two miles in one hour and five minutes.

Lasting only eighteen months, the Pony Express covered more than 1,800 miles and everlastingly captured America's fascination. In one of their most historic achievements, Pony Express riders in March 1861 carried Abraham Lincoln's inaugural address from St. Joseph to Sacramento in seven days and seventeen hours. One of the loneliest and most haunting stretches of the Pony Express Trail can be followed by automobile today, preferably a light truck or sports utility vehicle, from present Fairfield to the Nevada border.

LAST DAYS OF CAMP FLOYD

When Sir Richard Burton came to Great Salt Lake in 1860, the English explorer and writer found Governor Cumming disheartened because his "scrupulous and conscientious impartiality" had served only to alienate other federal officials, who considered him to be a pacifist and

[51]See Simpson, *Report of Explorations across the Great Basin of the Territory of Utah.*
[52]For more on this route, see Townley, *The Overland Stage: A History and Guidebook.*

had won no acceptance of him from the people.[53] Still firmly in command was the territory's true governor, Brigham Young, while other federal officials, civil and military, had either quit in disgust or were getting ready to go.[54]

That year, Cumming reported Utah was "bordering on anarchy" with judges Cradlebaugh and Sinclair absent and Chief Justice Eckels about to leave. In a complete retreat, he proposed that probate courts be granted the jurisdiction they claimed, in effect, of equal standing with any court in the land, with only the possible exception of the U.S. Supreme Court. Recognizing that "public service in this Territory has been deemed undesirable," he urged appointment of a Mormon, Elias Smith, as district judge.[55]

Deeply disillusioned, the federal bureaucrat later reported his labors had been "onerous and embarrassing" and asked for a leave of absence until a new appointee "shall have arrived and qualified."[56] When asked how a successor would get along, he replied, "Get along? well enough, if he will do nothing. There is nothing to do. Alfred Cumming is Governor of the Territory, but Brigham Young is Governor *of the people*." Let his successor learn that, Utah's second governor said, "and he will get along, and the sooner he knows that the better."[57]

The well-intentioned Georgian stuck to his post until May 1861, when he advised William Seward, new secretary of state for the Lincoln administration, that he was going home. He followed Albert Sidney Johnston, who took leave early in 1860. The man who had upheld federal authority in Utah by military force would, on the secession of his adopted state, Texas, raise his sword against the United States as commander of Confederate forces in the western theater of the war.

Meanwhile the guns in Charleston Harbor that opened on Fort Sumter early on April 12, 1861, also sounded the last days of Camp Floyd, for a time the nation's largest military encampment. The greatest reduction in troop levels actually took place in 1860 when the garrison

---

[53]Burton, *The City of the Saints*, 216.

[54]In addition to judges Cradlebaugh and Sinclair and U.S. Marshal Dotson, Indian Agent Garland Hurt left at the end of 1859 to finish his medical education at St. Louis, where he became president of the St. Louis Medical Society.

[55]Cumming to Cass, March 1, 1860, Alfred Cumming Papers.

[56]Ibid., Cumming to Cass, July 19, 1860.

[57]Stenhouse, *The Rocky Mountain Saints*, 445.

was cut back from nearly 2,500 to about one fifth that number. At the same time, the army began the sale of surplus supplies and livestock at a fraction of their original price, which gave the territory an economic lift.

The last commanding officer to blow out the oil lamps at the post was Philip St. George Cooke, who had won the rank of lieutenant colonel in October 1846, when he was named to command the Mormon Battalion during the War with Mexico. Cooke renamed the post Fort Crittenden in honor of John Crittenden of Kentucky after its first namesake, John B. Floyd, secretary of war under President Buchanan, declared his allegiance to the South. Cooke then sold to the highest bidder the remaining supplies, valued at some $4 million, for less than three cents on the dollar. Wagons went for $14 each, horseshoes for a quarter-cent apiece, and flour sold for about fifty cents per hundred pounds. Of the about $100,000 taken in at the final auction, some $40,000 came from Brigham Young himself, probably acting as agent for his church. Everything not sold, including houses, buildings, and, to Young's hot indignation, ammunition, was destroyed.[58]

After the last soldier had marched off to take his stand with North or South, many to win fame during the Civil War, Cooke with his customary flair for the dramatic on July 27, 1861, presented the Camp Floyd flagpole to Brigham Young.[59] The Mormon leader likely received it with satisfaction, knowing it signified that he and his people in the end had prevailed over the military expedition that came in 1857 to enforce federal law in an allegedly rebellious territory.

With the closure of Fort Crittenden and onset of war on the eastern seaboard there would be no American military presence in Utah for a period of eighteen months. Some events would take place during that time that would make this period among the most significant and revealing in the history of Utah Territory.

[58]See Alexander and Arrington, "Camp in the Sagebrush: Camp Floyd, Utah, 1858–1861," 3–21.

[59]A number of the officers who served at Camp Floyd were killed during the war, including, but not limited to: Capt. Lewis A. Armistead, killed in Pickett's charge at Gettysburg in 1863 as brigadier general, CSA; Capt. George B. Anderson, 2nd Dragoons, fatally wounded in 1862 at Sharpsburg (Antietam) as brigadier general, CSA; Capt. Barnard E. Bee, 10th Infantry, killed in 1861 at Manassas (Bull Run) as brigadier general, CSA; Capt. Reuben Campbell, 2nd Dragoons, killed in 1862 at Gaines Mill as colonel, 7th North Carolina Infantry, CSA; Capt. Jesse A. Gove, 10th Infantry, killed at Gaines Mill as colonel, 22nd Massachusetts Volunteers, USA; Brig. Gen. Albert S. Johnston, killed in 1862 at Shiloh as general, CSA; 1st Lt. John Pegram, 2nd Dragoons, killed in 1865 as brigadier general, CSA; and Capt. Jesse L. Reno, 4th Artillery, after whom Reno, Nevada, is named, killed in 1862 at South Mountain as major general, USA.

JOHN W. DAWSON
Utah's third governor was Indiana editor
Dawson, who lasted just nineteen days on
the job after vetoing a statehood bill.
Courtesy, Utah State Historical Society.

Chapter 10

THE GHOST GOVERNMENT
OF DESERET

These are the kind of Rulers the Gentiles send to rule over Israel and Israel Begins to Feel that it is time to rise up and appoint her own Governors, Judges & Rulers & trust in God for the Result.

—Wilford Woodruff

By 1861 it had become customary for federal officers in Utah Territory to take off or die before their terms expired, but the record for holding the office of governor the shortest time belongs to John W. Dawson of Indiana, 41, editor of the *Fort Wayne Times*. Named by President Lincoln on October 3 to succeed Alfred Cumming, the dyspeptic lawyer, political activist, and newspaper editor fled that year under mysterious circumstances after spending fewer than nineteen days on the job.

Utah's third governor has been described as a man of "strong and well grounded" convictions for which he contended editorially with such vigor he often made enemies. If argumentative, he was known to be "scrupulously honest" and dedicated to the public good. He was an outspoken advocate of public education, then called "free schools," and a warm defender of all "eleemosynary institutions," those devoted to charity. Of him it was said that the "worthy needy were never turned from his door unrelieved."[1]

Although unconfirmed by the U.S. Senate, Dawson hurried to Utah to deliver the governor's message on December 10, 1861, before the opening of the Legislative Assembly, perhaps to make an appeal for loyalty to the Union. In a long-winded address with rhetorical flourishes, he displayed not only a lack of knowledge about the territory, including its

---

[1] *A Biographical History of Eminent and Self-Made Men of the State of Indiana*, 2:20. Also see McMullin and Walker, *Biographical Directory of American Territorial Governors*, 294–95.

theocratic form of government, but a misunderstanding of what proposals might be appropriate or acceptable to its people. His first offense was to ask lawmakers to levy an annual tax of $26,982 in compliance with a new federal law and thus vindicate themselves of the charge of disloyalty which, he said with feigned regret, "has obtained some credence in portions of the United States."[2] It was a gratuitous slight that overlooked the problem that a lack of cash in the territory, where most trade was carried out by barter, made it difficult to raise currency by any method.

This was bad enough, but in a place where land was dedicated to God and held under the law of stewardship, especially provoking was Dawson's call for a survey of the territory and sale to all comers of the public domain to allow "settlers to procure title." The new governor went on to propose the creation of common schools to replace existing ward schools of uneven quality. Every child should be educated, he said, "because they are the children of the Territory and the subject of its guardian care."[3]

To these proposals, Brigham Young expressed his views "vary plainly," said Apostle Woodruff. First, they will ask us to pay taxes, he said, and then "they will want us to send 1,000 men to the war." He would "see them in Hell before I will raise an army for them." As for education, Young's views perhaps reflected his own lack of it. "We should never Croud [sic] and force the minds of our children beyond what they are able to bear," he said. "If we do we ruin them for life."[4]

As Young instructed, Utah lawmakers ignored the governor's remarks. Instead they unanimously enacted a bill calling for an election of delegates to meet in convention, draw up a new state constitution, and form a state government. Governor Dawson forthrightly vetoed the measure. To justify his rejection, he said the bill did not allow enough time for Congress to consider the issue. But he later told President Lincoln that the real reason for his veto was that the act aimed to "put in operation a State Government & if not allowed into the Union, to completely oust federal authority in this Territory."[5]

For Governor Dawson, it was one transgression too many. Two days later, he was shocked when someone on East Temple, right in front of his room, fired a pistol five times at the new associate justice, H. R.

---

[2]"Governor's Message," *Deseret News*, December 18, 1861, 6.   [3]Ibid.

[4]Kenney, ed., *Wilford Woodruff's Journal*, 5:605, 536.

[5]Dawson to Lincoln, January 13, 1862, Robert T. Lincoln Collection.

Crosby, and nothing was done about it. Right after that, he was accused of making improper proposals to the widow of Thomas Williams, his seamstress, who reportedly "drove him out of her house with a fire Shovel because of his vulgar abuse to her."[6] The new governor began to fear for his life.

According to the *Deseret News*, Dawson on December 31 took off unexpectedly on the afternoon stage, escorted by noted ruffians Lot Huntington, Moroni Clawson, and Jason and Wilford Luce, to each of whom he allegedly paid $100 for protection. The following day, Judge Crosby and Henry Martin, "repudiated quasi ex-superintendent of Indian Affairs," also took the eastbound stage "for reasons best known to themselves."[7] In a familiar exodus, not far behind was the other associate justice, R. P. Flenniken.

Dawson left because he could not "look the people in the face because of his crimes," said Woodruff, but quite different was the governor's account of his departure.[8] It had been known "for some days," he said, that he intended to leave for home when he did. On the outskirts of town, Ephraim Hanks rode up and told him that some "desperate men" might "follow me for violence or plunder." Dawson asked Hanks to accompany him to his stage station at Mountain Dell, but the noted tavern owner said he could not but would send Moroni Clawson, "who would do just as well."[9]

"Clawson shortly after came up and introduced himself, and on the route I handed him five dollars for his trouble," Dawson said. Jason Luce soon appeared and allowed the governor to ride his mule. Another known desperado, Lot Huntington, joined the party and let Clawson ride his horse while he rode in the stagecoach. So it went until all had arrived at Hanks' stage station between Little and Big mountains.[10]

That night, New Year's Eve, the crowd at the place became "very drunk." When Dawson and a companion, Dr. Chambers, went out to see about their seats in the coach, they discovered that their blankets and "an elegant beaver robe" had been stolen. While he was sitting in the coach, Dawson was confronted by the driver, Wood Reynolds. The governor,

[6]Kenney, ed., *Wilford Woodruff's Journal*, 5:616. Thomas Stephen Williams was a Mormon Battalion veteran who left the church after an argument with Brigham Young. He was killed in 1860 on the Mohave Desert, apparently by Indians.   [7]*Deseret News*, January 1, 1862, 212.

[8]Kenney, ed., *Wilford Woodruff's Journal*, 5:616.

[9]"Dawson to Editor," *Deseret News*, January 22, 1862, 234.   [10]Ibid.

who was not robust, tried to get back to the station, but the driver knocked him down. Then Jason Luce and others joined Reynolds and beat and kicked him so severely that he never fully recovered from the injuries.[11]

President Lincoln reportedly forgot he had appointed Dawson in the first place, but what the runaway governor told him on January 13 would hardly enhance Utah's standing with the new administration or improve its chances to win sovereign statehood. District courts had been stripped of their powers, he said, disloyalty was preached from the pulpit, "horrid crimes," such as the massacre at Mountain Meadows, had gone unpunished, and federal officials were afraid "to represent the truth in writing."[12]

He called these things to Lincoln's attention, Dawson said, in the hope "an adequate army may be sent here—as the only conservator of public peace—& effectual advocate & maintainer of federal power."[13] Nor did he stop there. He later told William Dole, the new Indian affairs commissioner, that federal officials should be recalled, Utah's organic act repealed, and "an efficient armed expedition" ordered to march to Utah as early as May 1 in order to arrive by August 1. He seemed unaware that Buchanan had already tried the latter approach.[14]

ESTABLISHMENT OF DESERET

Meanwhile, with Dawson out of the way, formation of the new state of Deseret proceeded with the approval of Frank Fuller, the territorial secretary, acting as governor, and the repentant Chief Justice John F. Kinney.[15] As Dawson had predicted, this would be done whether Con-

---

[11]Ibid. Wood Reynolds, Isaac Neibaur, and Jason, John, and Wilford Luce were later arrested, and warrants were issued for Lot Huntington and Moroni Clawson. Dawson took some satisfaction that those who took part in the assault later suffered violent deaths. Huntington was shot dead on January 16, 1862, by Porter Rockwell at Faust's stage station west of Camp Floyd. At about the same time Moroni Clawson and John P. Smith, another supposed participant, were arrested and killed at Great Salt Lake while allegedly trying to escape. Reynolds had his head peeled by Indians who ambushed his stage coach on June 10, 1863, about two miles south of the Jordan River ford, near Lehi, and killed him and a companion. The natives soon after displayed without fear of retribution their bloody scalps at Nephi. Jason Luce was shot to death on January 12, 1864, by a firing squad for the murder of one Samuel Burton.

[12]Dawson to Lincoln, January 13, 1862, Robert T. Lincoln Collection. A common complaint of federal officials was that their mail was routinely opened and read at Utah post offices.

[13]Ibid.   [14]Ibid., Dawson to W. P. Dole, February 27, 1862.

[15]Without his "solicitation, (or knowledge until the fact was announced through the press)," in June 1860 John F. Kinney was again appointed by President Buchanan to the Utah supreme court as chief justice. Not again, however, would he oppose the territory's theocratic form of government or judicial system, as he had done during his

gress approved or not. "If the United States will admit us [—] well," Brigham Young said. If it does not, he went on, "better." The government would be established, "and what are they going to do about it?"[16]

In so doing, Young believed his followers would be the only ones actually true to the Constitution and its inspired purpose.[17] He argued that Congress had no authority to create Utah Territory in the first place since every power "not named in the Constitution for Congress to act upon is reserved to the people."[18] Since the territory was an illegal entity, in this view, the establishment of the state of Deseret simply restored the legitimate government that had been created in 1849.

On January 22 a convention at Great Salt Lake approved the constitution of Deseret, essentially a copy of the earlier version, nominated state officers, and called an election in March. At that time, William Clayton, convention secretary, reported the result to Brigham Young. The founding document was adopted and Young "duly elected to the office of Governor of the State of Deseret, by the unanimous vote of the people," he said. Also chosen were Heber C. Kimball as lieutenant governor and John Bernhisel, representative to Congress. The exact count was 9,880 to zero.[19]

Governor-elect Young called the first session of the Deseret General Assembly on April 14, when George Q. Cannon and William H. Hooper were elected U.S. senators. In a formal message, read by Clayton, Young said that they were not "aliens from our government, but we are tried and firm supporters of the Constitution, and every constitutional right."[20] Later, in personal remarks, he said, "We have got to frame our own Government and govern ourselves [for] we shall not be governed ownly by the devel [sic] & wicked men and go to Hell together."[21]

first term. Instead he would willingly do all that was expected of him. See biography of John F. Kinney. Also see Kinney address before the constitutional convention on January 23, 1862, *Deseret News*, February 5, 1862, 250.

[16]Kenney, ed., *Wilford Woodruff's Journal*, 6:10, 11.

[17]This belief was expressed by Apostle Woodruff: "Our Fathers who made the declaration of independence and formed the American Constitution was inspired to lay the foundation of a Free and independent Government and the Lord protected them in it. But they did not know that they were inspired to do it. There was a veil over them that they did not know what the purposes of the Lord were or that he was protecting them. It is not so with us. We know that God is leading us and is inspiring his people to Esstablish [sic] his Kingdom & governme[n]t upon the Earth & we know it." See Kenney, ed., *Wilford Woodruff's Journal*, 6:6.

[18]*Deseret News*, July 2, 1862, 1, 2   [19]Ibid., March 19, 1862, 300.   [20]Ibid., April 16, 1862, 330.

[21]Kenney, ed., *Wilford Woodruff's Journal*, 6:40.

SALT LAKE THEATRE OPENING

Such evil and its consequences, as well as good and its happy results, could best be portrayed upon the stage, Brigham Young told the hundreds who came from all parts of the territory on Saturday, March 6, a blustery, late winter day to celebrate the opening of the new Salt Lake Theatre. Long before the 7 P.M. curtain the house was filled "from pit to roof." Young cautioned musicians and performers that if anything happened "contrary to the strictest virtue and decorum," offenders would have to leave the building.[22]

Constructed at a cost of $40,000, the new playhouse at First South and later State Street was the finest of its kind between the Missouri River and San Francisco. A talented artist, George Martin Ottinger, finished the interior for designers E. L. T. Harrison and William H. Folsom. Charles Millard, a Great Salt Lake tailor, made the scenery, and Flora Maddison Maben and other expert seamstresses created the costumes. Members of the Deseret Dramatic Association worked during the daytime and rehearsed until long after dark to prepare for the opening.

A delighted audience that night saw 30-year-old Margaret Gay Judd Clawson, second wife of Hiram B. Clawson, play the role of flower woman in James Robinson Planche's *The Pride of the Market.* The attractive actress would go on to achieve renown as "the mother of the drama" in Utah. Playing the villain was John T. Caine, 32, from the Isle of Man, destined to become Utah's fourth delegate to Congress. Between plays, William C. Dunbar, 39-year-old vocalist and bagpipe player, sang the comic number, "Bobbing Round."[23]

Featured in the second production, *State Secrets,* was Philip Margetts, a 33-year-old Englishman, who would win during a long acting career a reputation as "the dean of western drama." Sarah Ann Cooke, a gifted actress and wife of the first missionary to New Zealand; Joseph Simmons, a handsome 37-year-old New Englander; and Scotland's David McKenzie, 28, were among others who performed on opening night.

---

[22]*Deseret News,* May 14, 1862, 300.

[23]The farewell performance in the Salt Lake Theatre was staged on Saturday, October 28, 1928, before a capacity house. Despite the best efforts of Daughters of Utah Pioneers to save it, the historic building was soon after demolished. The theatre's main curtain was preserved and is now displayed at the DUP's Pioneer Memorial Museum in Salt Lake City.

MARGARET GAY JUDD CLAWSON
The "first lady of Utah drama"
in 1862 played the lead role in
the first play ever staged in the
Salt Lake Theatre on
First South and State Street.
*Courtesy, Manuscripts Division,
University of Utah Libraries.*

LOT SMITH RIDES AGAIN

For a brief time, issues of religion and politics were lost in a common love of the arts. Then came over the new telegraph line on April 28, 1862, a message direct to Brigham Young by order of President Lincoln that appeared to recognize Young's authority as governor of the sovereign state of Deseret. It authorized him to raise, arm, and equip a company of cavalry for service of ninety days to protect the overland mail and telegraph against Indian attack in the vicinity of Independence Rock on the Oregon Trail.

Such requests normally went to elected or appointed officials of states or territories. This time, the first in American annals, the authorization bypassed territorial officials and went directly to the head of a church and a theocratic form of government within the republic. It also usually took weeks to recruit and field a mounted company. In this case a fully equipped command of "one captain, two lieutenants, one first sergeant, one quartermaster sergeant, four sergeants, eight corporals," and seventy-two privates was ready to ride in only two days.[24]

Commanding the horsemen of Deseret was Capt. Lot Smith, the same cavalry officer who burned the U.S. Army's supply wagons in 1857. The

---

[24]*Deseret News*, April 30, 1862, 348.

first lieutenant was 39-year-old Joseph Sharp Rawlins from Illinois. John Quincy Knowlton, 26, completed the roster of commissioned officers as second lieutenant. That members of the command had responded as mercenaries to a church call rather than volunteered out of motives of patriotism is suggested by Young's personal orders to Captain Smith. "You will readily recognize the hand of Providence in our behalf, and place a secondary consideration upon the compensation you are entitled to," he said. "Let not a thought of pay swerve you from that high moral tone derivable only from an upright performance of all duties."[25]

With or without pay, Lot Smith's command guarded the Oregon Trail between the North Platte River and Fort Bridger before it was disbanded in mid-August. By then, it was clear the company's call did not imply recognition, and Young turned down an appeal for its members to serve three more months. Except for this single case, protestations of loyalty notwithstanding, Utah was the only state or territory to provide no soldiers to either side during the Civil War. But troops would be needed to deal with some trouble closer to home.

The Morrisite Affair

That Joseph Morris would be the one to provoke the use of military power was not apparent from his appearance or background. Born in England to "poor and respected parents," Morris was little educated, having gone to work at an early age in the coal mines, where he had been severely burned in an explosion.[26] He stood only about five feet six inches tall and wore his black hair long, but the spirit of God had seemed to attend him as he grew to manhood. At age 23, he had joined the Mormon church but had delayed coming to America "till I have finished paying all my debts."[27]

In 1853 Morris brought a wife and child to Utah, where he had difficulty adjusting to life in Mormon society. Farming did not suit him, nor did some of the doctrines he heard preached at Provo, Ephraim, and American Fork, where he lived for brief periods. He was vehemently opposed to polygamy but found it hard to keep only one wife happy. His

---

[25]Young to Smith, April 30, 1862, Lot Smith Collection.
[26]Eardley, *Gems of Inspiration: A Collection of Sublime Thoughts by Modern Prophets*, 7.
[27]Morris, *The "Spirit Prevails" Containing the Revelations, Articles and Letters Written by Joseph Morris*, 2.

first left him, then a second, on the advice of local authorities, and he became a resentful outcast, unable to find work sufficiently rewarding to provide even for himself.

At the time of the great reformation, Morris felt his spirit sorely tried. He "mourned and wept on account of the condition of the people" and devoted himself to constant prayer. In 1857 when he was "most utterly cast down," the word of God came to him and he received his first revelation. "Verily, verily, verily, thus saith the spirit unto thee, my servant Joseph: I, the Lord, have beheld thy afflictions," said the Almighty. "I have chosen thee from before the foundation of the world to be a mighty man, yea, to be a prophet in Israel."[28]

This visionary man soon after revealed "the Lord [h]as called me to be a prophet and to hould the keys of the last dispensation." He proclaimed the Second Coming of Jesus Christ and the millennium were at hand. Unlike Brigham Young, the prolific mouthpiece of God issued written revelations that began, "Thus saith the Lord," much like the faith's founding prophet. "i shall expect president Young to hould the presidency of the church as he [h]as dun be four," Morris said, "for it is not a prophets place to preside but to dick tate him that dus preside."[29]

"be hould," said the Lord, according to the prophet, "i am Jesus Christ, and i testefy unto all mankind that dwell upon the face of the hearth that i have hopened the Last seal by the Seventh Angel," as prophesied by John.[30] "and I wi[ll] give him power in a rod and he shall rule the nations of the hearth with it."[31] The prophet labeled the rod as the rod of Moses and not surprisingly identified the Seventh Angel who would rule the world as himself.

For some time Morris unsuccessfully asked in writing for a meeting with Brigham Young to arrange the reorganization of the church hierarchy. Conciliatory at first, his letters became more strident in tone. After failing in 1859 to gain an audience, he directed the Lord's will to the Mormon leader. "a Command ment i give unto you," the Almighty said

---

[28]Morris, *The Spirit Prevails*, 3, 9.

[29]Morris to Young, Brigham Young Collection, MS 1234, LDS Archives. Publisher George Dove later edited the revelations to correct punctuation and spelling errors.

[30]"The seventh angel sounded his trumpet, and there were loud voices in heaven, which said: 'The kingdom of the world has become the kingdom of our Lord and of his Christ, and he will reign for ever and ever.'" See Rev. 13:15.

[31]Morris to Young, June 15, 1859, Brigham Young Collection, MS 1234. For an edited version of this revelation, see Morris, *The Spirit Prevails*, 25, 26.

to Young through His prophet, "that you call my servent Joseph up to the head of my Church fourth with and linger not or you will be Cut of[f] for my time [h]as Come."[32]

To Utah authorities Joseph Morris was little more than an annoyance before he moved in 1860 to the Ogden area and converted religious leaders of South Weber, including Bishop Richard Cook. After that, his growing flock attracted attention at the highest levels. At a stormy meeting with apostles Wilford Woodruff and John Taylor at South Weber on February 11, 1861, some sixteen men and women who testified that Morris was a prophet and Brigham Young was not were cut off from the Mormon faith.[33]

As Morris issued Last Days prophecies, believers gathered at abandoned Kingston Fort, a tumbled down collection of log and mud houses in a ten-acre square, enclosed by a melting adobe wall, on the south side of the river near the mouth of Weber Canyon. Many of the arrivals lived in tents, covered wagons, or a few huts made of woven willows, mudded over. Built in 1853 and named after the first bishop, Thomas Kingston, the so-called "fort" was in fact an indefensible location, overlooked on the south and north by sandy bluffs.[34]

That the Morrisite movement was a millennial offshoot of its parent was demonstrated on April 6, 1861, the thirty-first anniversary of the founding of the Mormon faith, when Morris organized a new church and named it the Church of Jesus Christ of Saints of the Most High. Within a year, the number of converts or followers of the prophet had grown to nearly one thousand, or about two percent of Utah's citizens that year, many of them Scandinavians. Of this number, about five hundred were baptized members.[35]

The English prophet was now more than a nuisance, but little could be done about it while U.S. soldiers were stationed in the territory. Mor-

[32]The author of the recommended work on the Morrisite movement has edited these letters because "their complete lack of punctuation, erratic capitalization, and unique spellings render them almost unintelligible." See Anderson, For Christ Will Come Tomorrow: The Saga Of The Morrisites, 9.

[33]Kenney, ed., Wilford Woodruff's Journal, 5:549–50. Also see Howard, "Men, Motives, and Misunderstandings: A New Look at the Morrisite War of 1862," 112–31.

[34]While nothing remains today of the old Kingston Fort, Weber County historian William W. Terry has located the site on the southwest corner of 500 East and 6650 South in South Weber, Davis County. This would place it near Exit 85 of I-84, about two blocks south of the Weber River and 3.2 miles west of the U.S. Highway 89 and I-84 intersection at the mouth of Weber Canyon.

[35]Dove, Names of persons baptized during the administration of Joseph Morris, at South Weber, Utah Territory, in the years of 1861 and 1862.

ris knew the withdrawal of federal troops in the summer of 1861 put him in danger, but he received an assurance of divine protection. Having "dispensed with that army . . . I will now take the old church into mine own hands," the Lord promised. "When they make the attempt to kill, I will destroy them according to celestial law."[36] In a familiar pattern, the issue was brought to a head by dissenters within the movement.

Morris required his followers to consecrate their properties to the church with himself as trustee for the Lord. But when some of his millennial predictions failed, several decided to leave and take their belongings with them. For this, three were arrested and confined in Kingston Fort, although one managed to escape. Friends filed a complaint and Territorial Marshal Henry Lawrence sent his deputy, Judson Stoddard, to serve a writ for their release. He was told the paper was of no force since the Lord's chosen in the Last Days lived under a higher law.

Shortly after this, Joseph Morris revealed that Christ would come a few days after a pageant entitled the "Foreshadowing of the Kingdom of God Day," scheduled on May 10, 1862. In the ceremony, which took all day, Morris himself played the part of Jesus Christ, said one participant, "and was hailed as Lord over the whole earth, amid the shouts of the people and the blowing of the trumpets."[37] For the English prophet, the end was near indeed, but not in the way he envisioned.

On June 10 Chief Justice John Kinney ordered the release of the prisoners at Fort Kingston and the arrest of Morris and three of his principal followers. Since Marshal Lawrence, wanting no part of this business, had left the territory, the judge addressed the writ either to him or to Robert T. Burton, identified only as "acting marshal." Kinney then asked Frank Fuller, the territorial secretary, now acting as governor pending Dawson's replacement, to approve the use of the militia, which meant the Nauvoo Legion, as a *posse comitatus* to enforce the process. The judge later told Apostle Woodruff that he had "not taken any step without Counciling Preside[n]t Young and when the men came to sware out their Affidavit I told them they must ask Preside[n]t Young." They came back and said "they had done so & Preside[n]t Young told them to go to Judge Kinney & get out there Affidavits," he said.[38]

However it came about, an acting governor approved the use of military

---

[36]Morris, *The Spirit Prevails*, 123–24.   [37]Eardley, *Gems of Inspiration*, 23, 24.
[38]Kenney, ed., *Wilford Woodruff's Journal*, 6:58.

force by an "acting marshal" of questionable authority at the request of a judge who admitted he did nothing without checking first with Brigham Young. In addition, the man charged to execute the process was no ordinary sheriff or marshal. Col. Robert T. Burton was one of the Nauvoo Legion's top officers, soon to become a major general and Council of Fifty member. Nor did it bode well for followers of Morris that among Burton's lieutenants were Howard Egan, Judson Stoddard, and Lot Smith.

On Friday, June 13, an unlucky day for Morris, an imposing force of five companies of one hundred each appeared on the bluffs overlooking Kingston Fort from the south. Two companies came from Salt Lake County, two from Davis, and one from Weber, along with some five hundred volunteers. This small army moved up at least two cannons, one of them a twelve-pounder. At this unexpected sight, the prophet's followers, about one hundred men and three hundred women and children, gathered in their bowery to decide what to do.

Rather than execute the warrant himself, Burton sent a note into the fort with a Morrisite herdboy. Surrender Morris and the others named and release the prisoners within thirty minutes, it said, or send out the women and children. He stood by for an hour and a half, Burton later said, until he got tired of waiting and fired a warning shot from the twelve-pounder. The Morrisites claimed the herdboy with the ultimatum and a cannon ball arrived at about the same time.

Either way, the so-called "warning shot" landed in the midst of the congregation assembled in the bowery to hear the prophet's latest revelation and consider what course to take. It killed two women, one with a baby in her arms, and shattered the jaw of 14-year-old Mary Christofferson, a Danish girl. With the screams of the wounded girl in their ears and the fear of being massacred on their minds, the men ran for the few arms they had to defend their families. The battle of Kingston Fort was on.

For three days the fighting continued while a large crowd collected on the bluff north of the river to watch the unequal contest. On the first day, 19-year-old Jared Smith from Ogden raised up to get a better look and was fatally shot in the chest. On the third day, Sunday, June 15, another legion member, Peter Wahlin, 25, a recent German convert, was hit in the head by a ball that came "out near the crown," killing him instantly.[39] That day, Morris received his last revelation. It said: "When

---

[39]Journal History, June 16, 1862.

you see the ammunition of my people used up, and they have no means left to defend themselves, and mine enemies begin to make headway and force themselves into this camp, you may know that the time of my coming has arrived."[40] Not for the first time or the last did the Lord disappoint His people.

Charles F. Middleton, an onlooker on the bluff that day, described what happened next. "Between sunset & dark the white flag was run up & the rebels had came down onto the public square & stacked their arms," he said, "after which their leader started to lead them off when him & two or three others were shot down."[41]

Middleton's is probably as good as any of the contradictory versions of this tragedy. After the Morrisites had surrendered, Burton rode into the fort with a number of his men and personally shot Morris to death with a revolver at close range. It had the look of an execution. When Mrs. James Bowman protested, she, too, was shot and killed, as well as a second woman who threw herself on the prophet's body. Morrisite eyewitnesses claimed Burton himself killed the two women, but he steadfastly denied it to the end of his days.

John Banks, second counselor to Joseph Morris, was also shot in the back of the neck, but the gifted Englishman and former head of the British Mission's London Conference may have survived for a time. According to one report, he was poisoned that night by Salt Lake councilman, probate judge, and coroner "Dr." Jeter Clinton, a posse member. Another said that while a guard held Banks down, Clinton inserted a surgeon's knife into his neck, "turned the knife in the wound, unjointed the neck" and ended his life.[42] Whatever the cause, gunshot, poison, or knife, John Banks was surely dead by morning.

THE AFTERMATH

On June 16 the remains of Morris and Banks were delivered to Great Salt Lake where Apostle Woodruff examined the wounds before their bodies were washed, dressed, and put on public display in the City Hall.[43] Mockingly exhibited at the prophet's side were his emblems of

---

[40]Morris, *The Spirit Prevails*, 629–32.   [41]Journal of Charles Franklin Middleton, June 15, 1862.

[42]Howard to Devens, July 28, 1877, U.S. Justice Department Chronological File, Utah.

[43]Morris had been shot "with one ball through the Head & two in the breast & shoulders," Banks with "one ball through the neck." See Kenney, ed., *Wilford Woodruff's Journal*, 6:56, 57.

authority, a five-foot scepter, with a ball fifteen inches around, symbol of his calling to rule "over all the earth," two smaller scepters, and a tin crown "painted yellow, with red Cloth stuf[f]ed inside" and a tin tube to carry a stick or rod.[44]

"The whole Concern shows to what Extent fals[e] Prophets & fanaticism will go," Woodruff said.[45] Showing how far the English oracle's fame had spread, hundreds came in great excitement to see for themselves the body of the self-described prophet and marvel at the pathetic trappings of his authority.

Two days later nearly a hundred Morrisite prisoners were hauled before Judge Kinney, reported the *Deseret News* under the headline "The Davis County Bandits." Richard Cook was fined $50 and ordered confined thirty days for contempt, Peter Klemgaard and Christian Neilson were sent to prison, and ninety-five others were placed under bond to appear later for trial. In March 1863 seven were found guilty of second-degree murder and sentenced to prison for ten to fifteen years, two were acquitted, the rest fined $100 each.

Three days after that trial Governor Stephen S. Harding, who had been appointed in 1862 by President Lincoln, issued a proclamation, listing all of those convicted, and gave to each a "full and perfect pardon." He acted on petitions signed by non-Mormons in Utah, including all of the officers at the newly established Camp Douglas and new supreme court justices Charles B. Waite and Thomas J. Drake. The petitions featured at least one Mormon signature. The night before he issued the pardon, Harding received a late visitor who asked, "Has any Mormon signed?" The governor replied none had. The nocturnal caller then asked for the petitions, took up a pen, and wrote on both "in letters as large as John Hancock signed to the Declaration, his name—BILL HICKMAN." It was the start of a falling out between the self-confessed killer William A. Hickman and Brigham Young.[46] The pardon was also the final episode in the downfall of Utah's fourth governor.

Harding had already courted disapproval several months before by warning in his annual message against ignoring a new federal law banning polygamy. He had also rebuked territorial lawmakers over Utah's election law which deprived citizens of the right to cast their ballots in

---

[44]Ibid., 55, 56.   [45]Ibid.
[46]Harding to Beadle, December 23, 1871, published in Hickman, *Brigham's Destroying Angel*, 212–19.

secret. Moreover, like his predecessor, he had reproved legislators for failing to provide a common school system while "keeping up a quasi military establishment" beyond any real need for defense.[47]

Utah's delegate to Congress, William Hooper, soon found evidence that the governor and Associate Justices Waite and Drake had asked Congress to pass a law to (1) limit the powers of the probate courts to the probating of wills, (2) allow U.S. marshals to select jurors, and (3) give the governor authority to appoint all officers of the militia, or Nauvoo Legion, including major general. At this offense, directed at the foundations of theocratic rule, a mass protest meeting was called in the Salt Lake tabernacle. According to public reports, a brass band enlivened the March 3 event with "patriotic airs," such as the "Star Spangled Banner."[48] But one observer reported that Brigham Young called the governor a "black-hearted abolitionist" and told the assembly that if Harding, Drake, and Waite would not resign or be removed from office by the president, "the people must attend to it."[49]

"I will let him know who is Governor," Young reportedly said. "I am Governor. If he attempts to interfere with my affairs, woe! woe! unto him." The judges he called "perfect fools and tools" of Harding. "If they could get the power . . . to have the marshal choose juries of cutthroats, blacklegs, soldiers, and desperadoes of California, and if we are to be tried by such men, what would become of us?" he asked.[50] Resolutions were unanimously approved demanding that the three offending officials resign or be removed.

Refusing to be "driven away" or intimidated, Harding only a month later finally affronted the territory by issuing his pardon of the Morrisites. At this, the grand jury at Salt Lake likened him to "an unsafe bridge over a dangerous stream," or worse, "a pestiferous cesspool in our district breeding disease and death."[51] Non-Mormons in Utah reacted to this unfragrant blast by signing petitions supporting the governor and calling for Judge Kinney's removal.

With the Confederate Army of Northern Virginia moving to invade Pennsylvania, Lincoln had little time to worry about the continuing cold

---

[47]While the Legislative Assembly refused to appropriate funds to print Governor Harding's message on December 8, 1862, his remarks were published in full by the *San Francisco Evening Bulletin*, January 1, 1863, 1.

[48]Whitney, *History of Utah*, 2:88–96.

[49]*The War of the Rebellion: A Compilation of the Official Records of the Union and Confederate Armies*, referred to hereafter as *WOR*, Vol. 50, pt. 2, series 3584, 372–73.   [50]Ibid.   [51]Young, "The Morrisite War," 468.

Mary Christofferson Anderson, whose jaw was shattered by a cannon ball at Kingston Fort, in a rare photograph with husband, Niels, and eight grown children at Soda Springs.
Courtesy, Utah State Historical Society.

war with a western territory. Probably shaking his head, he sacked both Harding and the chief justice. Utah still had the last word in the controversy by electing, unanimously as usual, John F. Kinney as its first non-Mormon delegate to Congress.

Robert T. Burton, in 1862 the territory's "acting marshal," also prevailed sixteen years later when he was acquitted of the murder, not of Morris, but of Mrs. Isabella Bowman. A jury of Mormons and non-Mormons found Burton not guilty after a key witness, Samuel D. Sirrine, who had come from San Francisco to testify before the grand jury, elected not to show up for the trial and Morrisite witness Emma Just mistook Burton for his deputy, Judson Stoddard.

Meanwhile, terribly disfigured by Burton's "warning shot," Mary Christofferson, now 15, with eighty other Morrisite families was escorted in 1863 by federal troops to Soda Springs, where they established a thriving settlement near a new army post that protected emigrants on the Ore-

gon-California Trail. There she was married to Niels Anderson by Lieutenant Shoemaker of the Union Army's Third California Volunteers. The
couple raised a large family but she never joined another church.

Mary Christofferson Anderson's husband became known as the
leader of the "anti-Mormon" faction in Idaho, and her fifth child, Peter,
wrote the story of the Morrisites from their point of view in "The
Wound That Never Healed."[52] To make sure the episode is never forgotten, Peter Anderson also had this story cast on a large metal plate
anchored to the face of a solid granite block that stands over his parents'
grave in the Soda Springs cemetery, where it can be seen today.

THE MORRILL ACT

While the memory would die slowly, the battle of Kingston Fort and
its aftermath happened too late to have any impact on Deseret's 1862
bid for independence or statehood. Shortly before the Weber River confrontation, the newly elected senators, William H. Hooper and George
Q. Cannon, presented to Congress its constitution and memorial for
admission into the Union. The new state having been organized in
advance, they offered a choice between ratifying what had already been
done or seeing the new government go its own way. Ignoring either
course, Congress simply referred the memorial to committees on the territories in both houses, where it died. Nor did anything ever come of a
resolution to admit Hooper and Cannon to the Senate floor. Behind
such inaction was strong opposition to Deseret's bid. Leading anti-
admission forces was the delegate from Nevada Territory, John Cradlebaugh, whose blistering speech, "Utah and the Mormons," before
resigning from Congress to join the Union Army filled sixteen columns
of the *Congressional Globe*.[53]

The Republican Congress worked faster, however, when it came to a
bill dealing with the second of the "twin relics of barbarism" it had
vowed to stamp out. In April 1862, Congressman Justin S. Morrill of
Vermont introduced a measure "to punish and prevent the practice of

---

[52]Anderson, "The Wound That Never Healed," 28–48.

[53]See Cradlebaugh, "Utah and the Mormons," February 7, 1863, *Congressional Globe*, App. (37–3), X133,
119–25. The speech was later expanded to include an appendix with affidavits on the Parrish-Potter murders,
Aiken Party killings, and Mountain Meadows massacre and printed in pamphlet form under two titles, *Mormonism* and *Utah and the Mormons*.

polygamy in the territories of the United States." As states were then considered sovereign entities whose affairs were outside the reach of Congress, the act applied only to territories, which meant, in effect, Utah.

Even as Deseret's elected representatives argued its case for statehood, Congress that June approved the punitive new law which imposed a fine of up to $500 and a maximum of five years in prison for any person found guilty of bigamy. The bill also annulled the act of the Legislative Assembly incorporating the Church of Jesus Christ of Latter-day Saints and empowering the church to regulate and perform marriages. The measure further voided all other laws related to polygamy, "evasively called spiritual marriage," however disguised by legal or religious forms, such as "sacraments, ceremonies, consecrations, or other contrivances." It finally provided that no corporation or association for religious or charitable purposes in any territory would be allowed to acquire or hold real estate of greater value than $50,000.[54]

President Lincoln signed this bill into law on July I, 1862, but in keeping with his policy to "let sleeping dogs lie" when it came to Utah, he made no effort to enforce it. Holding the measure unconstitutional, the people of the territory just ignored it. But the Morrill Act would be for Utah like the fingers of a human hand that wrote on Belshazzar's wall, "God hath numbered thy kingdom."[55]

THE "GHOST" OF DESERET

In the meantime, a theocratic apparatus that historian Dale L. Morgan called "The Ghost Government of Deseret" operated for some eight years in Utah, largely out of sight.[56] It first came to life in 1862 when the independent state of this name was created and Brigham Young unanimously elected as its governor. And true to Governor Dawson's prediction, the spirit of Deseret lived on as if nothing had happened, even after Congress spurned its petition for admission into the Union.

So it was that members of the Legislative Assembly met in December 1862 to hear the message of Stephen S. Harding, the new governor of Utah Territory, and conduct its business. The same legislators then con-

---

[54]The Morrill Act in full is published in the *Congressional Globe*, App. (37–2), X131, 385.
[55]Dan. 5:26.   [56]Morgan, *The State of Deseret*, 91–119.

vened once more on the third Monday of January 1863, as scheduled the year before by the elected legislature of the state of Deseret, to receive the official message of Governor Brigham Young. It was enough to give an observer double vision.

Ignoring Harding's offering, the legislature for both bodies published only Young's message for public distribution. Not sent to the printer, however, were the Mormon leader's private remarks to the lawmakers. "We are Called the State Legislature but when the time Comes we shall be Called the kingdom of God," he said. "This body of men will give laws to the Nations of the Earth."[57] Publicly he professed loyalty to the Union, but in private he told to Deseret's legislators a somewhat different story. "Our Government is going to peaces [sic]," he said, "and it will be like water that is spilt upon the ground that Cannot be gathered." Joseph Smith, the founding prophet of their faith, had organized the Kingdom of God and promised it would "prevail over all our enemies," he went on. "We should get all things ready & when the time Comes we should let the water on the wheel and start the machine in Motion."[58] That the time was at hand for Deseret to rise and fulfill its destiny, he had already revealed.

While inspecting work on the Salt Lake Temple, Young several months before had confided to Apostle Woodruff and the venerable Isaac Morley that their people would shortly "go back to Jackson County which I expe[c]t will be in 7 years." Meanwhile he did not want "to quite finish this Temple for there will not be any Temple finished until the One is finished in Jackson County pointed out by Joseph Smith," he told them. "*Keep this a secret* to *yourselves*, he said, lest some may be discouraged."[59]

Over the period Young specified, the legislative body of the "ghost government of Deseret" held itself ready to come forth and fulfill its millennial mission to govern the nations of the earth. Its members convened each year and gave a higher stamp of approval to acts of the Utah Assembly, made up almost entirely of the same members, who had adjourned only a few days before. Then the ghost legislature quietly disappeared in 1870.

What eventually put it to rest was an armed obstruction placed in the road to independence and dominion by Abraham Lincoln.

[57]Kenney, ed., *Wilford Woodruff's Journal*, 6:92, 93.

[58] Ibid.   [59] Ibid., 6:71. Emphasis in the original.

GENERAL PATRICK EDWARD CONNOR
The Irish Catholic immigrant who trained his
cannons on Great Salt Lake City and
founded Utah's mining industry.
Courtesy, California State Library.

Chapter 11

THE CALIFORNIA VOLUNTEERS

Our course is onward to build up Zion, and the nation that has slain the Prophet of God and cast out his people will have to pay the debt. They will be broken in pieces like a potter's vessel; yes, worse, they will be ground to powder.

—Brigham Young

Traitors shall not utter treasonable sentiments in [the Military District of Utah] with impunity; but must seek a more genial soil, or receive the punishment they so richly merit.

—Col. P. Edward Connor

These sentiments, expressed in the same month, August 1862, would define the relationship between the two most important men in early Utah. One is virtually revered today; the other is almost forgotten. Yet Brigham Young's design to establish the Kingdom of God as an earthly state would be squarely challenged and forever changed by a vision of Utah's future advanced by his unremembered adversary, an Irish Catholic immigrant every inch as strong willed as the Mormon leader himself.

To Brigham Young, the start of the Civil War in April 1861 meant the fulfillment of a revelation given in 1832 by the faith's founding prophet. Joseph Smith that year visited New York City, where excitement ran high over South Carolina's refusal to accept a new federal tariff law and its threat to leave the Union. At this crisis, more than a quarter-century before the guns opened in Charleston Harbor, Smith foretold the punishment that lay ahead for the United States and the rebellious nations of the earth.

"Verily, thus saith the Lord, concerning the wars that will shortly come to pass, beginning at the rebellion of South Carolina, which will eventually terminate in the death and misery of many souls," the revelation began. It went on to predict a great war between Southern and Northern states that would spread around the world. With the sword, "famine, and plague, and earthquake, and the thunder of heaven," the inhabitants of the earth would feel the "chastening hand of an Almighty God, until the consumption decreed hath made a full end of all nations."[1]

So the guns that fired on Fort Sumter signaled to Young the start not only of civil war, but the fulfillment of prophecy. At hand was the chastening of the republic for its persecution of the saints of God and the pouring out of God's wrath on the nations of the world until all were destroyed. On the ashes would rise the Kingdom of God and Christ would return to introduce His millennial reign.[2] Young had already confided to Apostle Woodruff as they inspected work on the Salt Lake Temple that he expected this to come about within seven years.[3] Young professed loyalty to "the Constitution and laws of our once happy country," as he had in a message to the president of the Pacific Telegraph Company in 1861, and sent Nauvoo Legion troops to guard overland lines a year later.[4] But his policy was to take a neutral position and pray "for both parties in the States that they might both prevail." The United States had persecuted the people of God, said he, "and they will now get their pay for it."[5]

To 40-year-old Patrick Edward Connor, in contrast, the outbreak of war meant it was time to place his sword at the service of his adopted country. Born in Kerry County, Ireland, Connor had come to America as a teenager and, like many Irish immigrants, had joined the U.S. Army, serving five years in the First Dragoons. Later, he moved to Texas, where life on the Comanche frontier gave him a brutalized attitude toward warlike Indians. There he joined the Texas Volunteers during the War with Mexico.

---

[1]Revelation given through Joseph Smith, December 25, 1832, *The Doctrine and Covenants*, Sec. 87, 532–33.

[2]Apostle Woodruff put it this way: "This Nation is guilty of shed[d]ing the Blood of the Lords anointed, of his Prophets & Saints and the Lord Almighty has decreed their destruction. The Lord has Commenced a Controversy with the American Government and Nation in 1860 and he will never cease untill they are destroyed from under heaven, and the Kingdom of God Esstablished [sic] upon their ruins. Let the Gentiles upon this land prepare to meet their God." See Kenney, ed., *Wilford Woodruff's Journal*, 5:529.

[3]Kenney, ed., *Wilford Woodruff's Journal*, 6:71.

[4]Whitney, *History of Utah*, 2:30.

[5]Kenney, ed., *Wilford Woodruff's Journal*, 5:607.

Rev. John A. Anderson, chaplain,
Third California Volunteer Infantry,
reported the command's arrival in
Salt Lake Valley and its struggle
on Bear River.
Courtesy, California State Library.

Promoted to captain, Connor won the notice of General Zachary Taylor himself during the Battle of Buena Vista. "Captain Connor's company of Texas volunteers, attached to the 2nd Illinois Regiment, fought bravely," the future president reported, "its Captain being wounded and two subalterns killed."[6] After the war he moved to California to settle at Stockton and start a construction business. There he won the contract to build the foundation of the new state capitol at Sacramento, but his first love was always the military. So it was that when President Lincoln called on California to raise five regiments of infantry and one of cavalry, Connor hurried to enlist and accept a commission as colonel of the Third Regiment, California Infantry. He recruited his force from the Stockton area and nearby gold mining camps.[7] Named chaplain of the regiment was John A. Anderson of the Presbyterian church in Stockton, whose reports to the *San Francisco Bulletin* would make him a notable figure in Utah history during this period.

[6]"Appendix to Report of Secretary of War," Sen. Doc. 1 (30–1), 1847, Vol. 1, Serial 503.

[7]The latest work on Connor is Madsen's unsympathetic study, *Glory Hunter: A Biography of Patrick Edward Connor.* Also see Rogers, *Soldiers of the Overland, Being some account of the services of General Patrick Edward Connor & his Volunteers in the Old West.*

By late May 1862 the regiment was camped at Stockton, its tents, "high airy and commodious," covering the race course in neat rows. At the rear were eight tents for the women who did the washing for their husbands' companies and "received $1 per month from each soldier, and $3 from each officer on pay day."[8] To keep the command cleansed spiritually, the First Presbyterian Society of San Francisco gave Anderson a tent thirty feet long and six high as a mobile chapel large enough to seat three hundred in any weather.

That month General George Wright, Department of the Pacific commander, told the War Department he would send Connor's regiment to Great Salt Lake to protect, as ordered, the overland mail route. While the peril Connor was to guard against was presumably posed by hostile Indians, the Irish colonel and his commanding officer from the first appeared to perceive the real danger elsewhere. Even the notion to send a regiment of infantry to cover hundreds of miles of overland trails against Indians seemed inexplicable.

Whatever its mission, however, Wright was certain the command was ready. It "made a very fine appearance; the arms, clothing and equipments were in high order," he reported when it marched on July 12. Three weeks later the regiment was joined at Fort Churchill on the Carson River by several companies of the Second California Cavalry. At this post, some thirty-six miles east of present Carson City, Nevada, Connor took command of the Military District of Utah, made up of Utah and Nevada territories.

Following the overland stage route, the "Utah column" on September 1 arrived at the Ruby Valley station, some forty miles south of present Elko. While his troops built a new post, Connor rode ahead to inspect the remains of Fort Crittenden, formerly Camp Floyd, and see Great Salt Lake City, where he met with then Governor Harding. His visit was closely watched and surely showed the city "might not be unpleasant notwithstanding its desert location," the *Deseret News* believed.[9]

Anything but salutary, however, was Connor's first impression. Instead he found "a community of traitors, murderers, fanatics and whores," the latter an apparent reference to polygamy. Religious leaders "preach trea-

---

[8]*Daily Alta California*, May 31, 1862, 1.
[9]*Deseret News*, February 11, 1863, 261–62.

son from the pulpit," he reported, and federal officials "talk in whispers for fear of being overheard." With an eye for terrain, he had found during his inspection tour just the spot for a future military post in Utah where he could say to the inhabitants, "enough of your treason."[10]

Governor Harding and others were very anxious that he locate there, he told his commanding officer, "but if it is intended that I shall merely protect the overland mail and permit the Mormons to act and utter treason, then I had as well locate at Crittenden."[11] General Wright was aware that Brigham Young wanted the command to reoccupy General Johnston's old camp or some other remote location, but he decided "after mature consideration" the site Connor had chosen was best for "the accomplishment of the objects in view."[12]

Meanwhile, if the Californians were despised in Utah, the feeling was heartily mutual. On his return, Connor wired General Henry Halleck, the nation's top officer, the regiment would allow the withholding of pay then due, $30,000, if it was sent east, "and it pledges never to disgrace the flag, himself, or California." For the opportunity to stop a minie ball in northern Virginia, his men would even pay their own passage from San Francisco to Panama, said Connor. "We desire to strike a blow in this contest."[13]

In a prelude to later actions, Connor also dispatched from Ruby Valley a cavalry force under Maj. Edward McGarry to punish Indians at Gravelly Ford on the Humboldt River, about five miles east of today's Beowawe, for killing emigrants near the crossing, a hot spot every year for Indian trouble. McGarry had orders to "shoot every male Indian in the region of the late murders" that he carried out faithfully, killing some two dozen natives before rejoining the command via City of Rocks.[14]

---

[10]Connor to Drum, September 14, 1862, WOR, Vol. 50, pt. 2, Serial 3584, 119–20.

[11]Ibid.

[12]Ibid., Wright to Thomas, March 30, 1863, 369–70. His decision may have been influenced by the report of Maj. James H. Carleton who inspected the Mountain Meadows Massacre site in 1859 and later wrote among other things: "Suppose a crime—say a murder—has been committed by a Mormon upon a Gentile. Who compose the jury to find the indictment? The brethren. Who are the officers and jailers who have custody of the prisoner before and after the trial? The brethren. Who are the members of the jury before whom the trial takes place? Still the brethren. Who are the witnesses for the prosecution, and, more particularly, who are those for the defense? The brethren." For his entire report, see "The Mormons as a People," WOR, Vol. 50, pt. 1, Serial 3583, 549–51.

[13]Connor to Halleck, September 24, 1862, WOR, Vol. 50, pt. 2, Serial 3584, 133.

[14]San Francisco Evening Bulletin, October 4, 1862, 1.

CROSSING THE JORDAN

Given no release from its orders, the rest of the expedition marched east across the Great Basin over the Pony Express Trail. Nearing settlements, Connor stopped the column to warn his men to maintain stricter discipline from then on. "We are coming among a people whose customs were different from ours," he said, but every man must treat them "with the same courtesy and justice that he would show to his own people." He would not allow a few bad men to start a war and "sacrifice the lives of good men."[15]

On October 17 the colonel reported his arrival at Fort Crittenden, adding somewhat dramatically, "will cross the Jordan to-morrow."[16] While he expected no opposition, he knew the Nauvoo Legion outnumbered his force by nearly ten to one and his men stood little chance in any armed showdown. He may also have known that Brigham Young that year had said, also with a theatrical flourish, that "if armies are again sent here, they will find the road up Jordan a hard road to travel."[17] But Connor determined to advance.

At *reveille* the next morning, Sunday, a thrill of anticipation ran through the camp, said Chaplain Anderson, and never did cooks prepare breakfast "with greater alacrity." Carefully Surgeon Reid laid out "his abominable knives, saws and probes" and told every man who was able to carry a musket to do so. Out of forty-one on sick call, twenty-eight managed to shoulder their pieces, "and the remainder did not only because they could not."[18] When Connor asked about ammunition, the artillery officer said, "'Colonel, if you expect an attack to-day, I will overhaul those wagons and take more cannister,' with the same air that one calls for fried oysters in a restaurant." In the same casual tone of voice, Connor replied, "Not to-day; but to-morrow do so."[19]

To the disappointment of few, the force met no opposition at the Jordan River which it crossed that afternoon by the ford near the Jordan Narrows, just north of Lehi. It was a defensible place, too, Anderson

---

[15]"From our special correspondent," *San Francisco Evening Bulletin*, October 30, 1862, 1.

[16]Wright to Thomas, October 20, 1862, *WOR*, Vol. 50, pt. 2, Serial 3584, 187.

[17]Brigham Young, January 19, 1862, *Journal of Discourses*, 9:157.

[18]"From our special correspondent," *San Francisco Evening Bulletin*, November 1, 1862, 1–3.

[19]Ibid.

noted, "with a good-sized bluff upon the western side from which splendid execution could have been done."[20] Cavalry in front and no stragglers behind, the troops marched down the river to camp near the bridge below the mouth of Little Cottonwood Creek in the present limits of Murray.

Two miles from the capital, Connor formed his line of march: mounted color guard in front, followed by the colonel and staff. Then paraded the cavalry band, cavalry companies, light artillery, infantry field band, companies of infantry, commissary wagons, and infantry rear guard. With bands playing and flags snapping in the breeze, the column, some 750 strong, marched up today's Main Street to First South, then turned east several blocks to the governor's residence. Anderson described the scene:

"Every crossing was occupied by spectators, and windows, doors and roofs had their gazers. Not a cheer nor a jeer greeted us. One little boy, running along close to the staff, said— 'You are coming, are you?' —to which it was replied that we thought we were. A carriage, containing three ladies who sang *John Brown* as they drove by were heartily saluted." Except for the welcome of federal officials, "there were none of those manifestations of loyalty that any other city in a loyal territory would have made," he said.[21]

Much warmer was the reception at the governor's mansion, where Harding stood in Connor's wagon and welcomed the assembled command. Their mission was one of peace and security, he said, to everyone who lived in the territory. The people they had come among "will not disturb you, if you will not disturb them in their just rights, and in the honor and peace of their homes."[22] The troops cheered and then marched some three miles farther onto the bench near the mouth of Red Butte Canyon.

There, overlooking the city, Connor laid out a new military post covering four square miles and named it after Senator Stephen A. Douglas of Illinois, a fellow Democrat who had died the year before. The colonel's guns on the high ground, trained on the city below, announced the time was not yet for the stone of Daniel or the Kingdom of God to

[20]Ibid.   [21]Ibid.

[22]*San Francisco Evening Bulletin*, November 1, 1862, 1–3.

roll forth and break in pieces the authority of the national government. Hardly had his men constructed winter shelters than their courage was put to a severe test.

BATTLE OF BEAR RIVER

Even before Dimick Huntington, Brigham Young's personal agent, and Ogden Bishop West in 1857 had given them "all the Beef Cattle & horses" on the northern trail to California, the Indians of Cache Valley had been troublesome.[23] After that, this mixed Shoshoni and Bannock band had repeatedly attacked small emigrant parties along Snake River and Hudspeth's Cutoff from Soda Springs to the junction of the California Trail, near present Almo, Idaho. Some of these raids were reportedly led by whites.

Since the Indians, or "Lamanites," would become partners in the endeavor to build New Jerusalem, the first Mormon settlers of Cache Valley in 1856 were required to maintain peace at any price with the native inhabitants. This policy put white settlers virtually in a position of servitude, forcing them to feed warriors on demand and look the other way when they attacked parties on the road to California. At least some in the settlements no doubt also provided a market where stolen livestock was exchanged for arms and ammunition.

In early December Connor sent Major McGarry and two cavalry companies to recover stolen animals north of the Bear River ferry at present Collinston. Despite efforts to keep the move secret, someone tipped off the natives and most escaped after cutting the ferry lines. Even so, McGarry captured four warriors and vowed to kill them unless the stolen animals were returned. When they were not, he ordered the hostages shot. If the major meant to teach the Shoshonis a lesson, his action had the opposite effect.

A month later two men were reported killed by Indians on the road from Cache Valley to the new gold mines at Bannack City in present Montana. Vowing to kill every white man they met north of Bear River, the Shoshonis soon after attacked another small party and one John

---

[23]Journal of Dimick Baker Huntington, August 30, 1857, MS 1419 2, LDS Archives.

Henry Smith was killed. A companion then swore an affidavit before Judge John Kinney. In a process similar in some respects to the case of Joseph Morris, the judge issued a warrant for the arrest of chiefs Sanpitch, Sagwitch, and Bear Hunter. This task being easier ordered than accomplished, the judge instructed Isaac Gibbs, the territory's new U.S. marshal, to apply to Colonel Connor for military help. The colonel replied his plans were already made and did not include executing warrants or taking prisoners, but he said Gibbs could come along as an observer. The only other noteworthy civilian in the expedition was its volunteer guide, Porter Rockwell, the noted Mormon gunman and original member of the Council of Fifty.

The colonel's strategy was apparently designed to deceive local inhabitants and keep them from tipping off his quarry that he was coming. On January 22, 1863, infantry Company K, seventy-two men with fifteen wagons and two cannons, marched ostentatiously at midday through the city and headed north. The little force camped on January 25 at Empey's Springs, now Deweyville, on Hensley's Salt Lake Cutoff of the California Trail, some fifteen miles north of present Brigham City.

That night, covered by darkness and a violent snowstorm, a strike force of four full companies of cavalry, some 220 men, made a forced march of sixty-eight miles "in the teeth of the savage north wind" from Camp Douglas to Brigham City. The weather was "more intensely and bitterly cold" than the troops had yet found it. Their hands became so numb they could hardly hold the reins; ears and noses were made lifeless, while "whiskers and moustache were so chained together by ice that opening the mouth became most difficult," said Chaplain Anderson.[24]

On January 27 the two forces united at Mendon in Cache Valley, where more than a dozen frosted cavalrymen were left behind. After dark the infantry marched for the little settlement of Franklin on Bear River, where soldiers the next day found three Indians from Bear Hunter's band picking up bushels of wheat from the residents. From here Connor tried to time his departure so that infantry and cavalry would arrive at the Bear River ford at the same time, but the infantry was late starting and his horsemen came up first.

[24]"From our own correspondent," *San Francisco Evening Bulletin*, February 20, 1863, 1–3.

If the colonel had feared the enemy might get away, he was soon relieved of this concern. What he confronted instead looked like a carefully laid trap that found his force outnumbered by at least three to two. Less than a mile away, the Shoshonis held a fortified and almost unassailable position in a ravine some forty feet wide, six to twelve feet deep, and several miles long. This natural trench, formed by a dry waterway now named Battle Creek, was anchored on the north by hills and at its southern mouth by Bear River, whose waters were impassable on foot.

From this stronghold the Indians taunted Connor's troops. While one of the chiefs rode up and down in front of the ravine, "brandishing his spear in the face of the volunteers," warriors in front sang out: "Fours right, fours left; come on you California sons of b—es!"[25] If the invitation was extraordinary, coming from Indians, it was promptly accepted. Dismounting his troopers, Major McGarry sent them forward in a frontal assault over open ground. The Shoshonis responded with a deadly fire, and the Irish colonel saw his men fall "fast and thick around me."[26]

Finding he could not dislodge the natives "without great sacrifice of life," Connor ordered McGarry to turn the ravine on the north while he moved his infantry on horseback across the river in support. In desperate fighting, the troops outflanked the position and opened an enfilading fire as they advanced down both sides of the ravine. As their stronghold became a death trap, the Shoshonis fought "with unyielding obstinacy, often engaging the troops hand to hand until they were killed," Connor reported.[27]

Most who did escape from the ravine were afterward shot while trying to swim the river, "or killed while desperately fighting under cover of the dense willow thicket which lined the river-banks," he said.[28] To an admiring Chaplain Anderson, the colonel seemed not to hear the "snakish whistle of the bullets," but rode along the "banks of that vomiting volcano, often within ten paces of its edge, directing the movements of the troops and setting an example of cool gallantry."[29]

[25]*Deseret News*, February 11, 1863, 261–62.
[26]Connor to Drum, February 6, 1863, *WOR*, Vol. 50, pt. 1, Series 3583, 185–86.
[27]Ibid.
[28]Ibid.
[29]*San Francisco Evening Bulletin*, February 20, 1863, 1.

The fight Connor led has since been called either a battle or a massacre, perhaps depending on one's point of view, but in fact it was both, first a pitched struggle with no quarter asked and none given, followed by a one-sided slaughter. At the outset, it even appeared the Indians were prepared for an attack.[30] Connor was also accused of indiscriminately killing non-combatants and allowing his men to rape native women, but such charges are difficult to verify and even harder to square with his character. According to one participant, when the women saw the soldiers did not wish to kill them, they left the ravine and walked to the rear where they sat in the snow "like a lot of sage hens."[31]

THE BLOODIEST DAY

The Bear River struggle, waged from daylight to mid-morning near present Preston, Idaho, was the bloodiest in the history of America's Indian wars in the far West. For Connor the butcher's bill came to twenty-two men, all but two members of the Second California Cavalry, killed on the field or dead of wounds. The only officer slain was Lt. Darwin Chase, a former Mormon who had left Utah and gone to California.[32] More than forty men were wounded and nearly seventy were disabled by frozen hands and feet, some for life.

For the Cache Valley Shoshonis the cost was horrendous. As many as three hundred were killed fighting or trying to escape, including chiefs Bear Hunter and Lehi. Connor's body count of 224 probably included an unspecified number of women and children but not some fifty or more individuals shot in the river and carried downstream. The only survivors were the few warriors who managed to get away, including Chief Sagwitch, and about 160 women and children, who were given provisions out of the abundance found in the stronghold. By contrast, 130

---

[30]Besides Rockwell and Marshal Gibbs, an observer of the action was Sylvanus Collett, a former missionary at Fort Limhi to the northern tribes, who had visited the Indian camp "a short time" before the battle, allegedly to recover stolen animals. See Gardner, *History of Lehi*, 237–38. Collett in 1878 was acquitted of charges he acted as an accomplice of Rockwell in the 1857 Aiken Party murders. For more on this crime and trial, see Chapter 15.

[31]Statement of John Kelly, *Daily Bulletin*, Blackfoot, Idaho, January 19, 1929, published in Rogers, *Soldiers of the Overland*, 67–77. For other accounts of the conflict, see Madsen, *Glory Hunter* and *The Shoshoni Frontier and the Bear River Massacre*; and Schindler, *Orrin Porter Rockwell*.

[32]See Kenney, *Wilford Woodruff's Journal*, 6:96.

Cheyennes died at Sand Creek in 1864, 103 of the same tribe were killed in 1868 by Custer's Seventh Cavalry on the Washita River, and about 150 Sioux were slain at Wounded Knee in 1890. To the present, the Northwestern Shoshoni band has not fully recovered from losses suffered that bitterly cold January morning on Bear River.

Significantly Connor reported that on his march north he got no help from Utah settlers, who refused "to divulge any information regarding the Indians and charged enormous prices for every article furnished my command."[33] This failed to mention the assistance his hurt and frostbitten men received on the way back to Camp Douglas. "We are glad to learn the citizens of the settlements through which the wounded returned, contributed in every way they could to their comfort," the *Deseret News* said.[34]

RUMORS AND ALARMS

For inhabitants of Great Salt Lake, Connor's cannons on the bench took some time to get used to, and no one was sure what the combative colonel might try to do next. To get ready for anything, some three hundred men stood guard at Brigham Young's house, where a flag pole was raised to signal other forces, if needed. Arms and ammunition, including cannons, were moved from the Nauvoo Legion Arsenal on today's Capitol Hill to the Mormon leader's residence.

"Brigham just raised national colors on his house and called his people to arms," Connor reported to San Francisco on March 9.[35] To his amazement, some 1,500 men rallied that day at a rumor the colonel intended to arrest Young for bigamy. "Be prudent and cautious," instructed his superior on the West Coast.[36] More militant were the orders Connor received direct from General Halleck, the U.S. Army's commanding officer in Washington, D.C. "All arms and military munitions intended for use against the authority of the United States are liable to seizure," he said and told the Utah commander to exercise his

[33]Connor to Drum, February 6, 1863, *WOR*, Vol. 50, pt. 1, Serial 3583, 186–87.
[34]*Deseret News*, February 4, 1863, 253.
[35]Connor to Drum, March 9, 1863, *WOR*, Vol. 50, pt. 2, Serial 3584, 342.
[36]Ibid., 347.

discretion in making such moves. "You will be cautious and prudent, but when you act do so with firmness and decision," he ordered.[37]

On March 29 hundreds of armed men rushed to Young's defense and the entire city's teeth were set on edge when an eleven-gun salute at Camp Douglas announced Connor's promotion. The new brigadier general knew his troops stood little chance in any armed showdown with his far larger adversary, but he was also aware that behind him stood the full power of the government he represented.[38] Nor were his guns on the high ground the only provocation his force presented to Utah's capital.

In his zeal to take a commanding position, the officer failed to observe sanitary practices normally followed even in that day. He located his new military base on a watershed that served a large populated area, placing nearly a thousand men, enough horses for at least three cavalry companies, and hundreds of other animals on Red Butte Creek, the water source for the southeastern section of Great Salt Lake City. It was hardly any wonder Camp Douglas came under verbal fire from those exposed to its pollution. Some three thousand people in the city's first and fourth municipal wards relied on Red Butte Creek for water, not only for irrigation but for drinking and culinary purposes, reported the Third Judicial District grand jury. Connor's troops "fouled the waters of said stream and rendered the same extremely filthy and nauseous to the great annoyance of, and deleterious to the health of the people," it charged.[39] City councilmen branded the camp a nuisance and demanded its removal.

To reduce friction, General Wright for a time considered moving Connor back to the site of old Fort Crittenden but decided against it after asking the opinion of Utah's latest governor. He was James Doty, former Utah superintendent of Indian affairs, named by President Lincoln in June 1863 to replace Harding. Considered friendly to the Mormons, the 63-year-old Wisconsin Presbyterian nevertheless left no doubt in the Pacific Department commander's mind what he thought of that idea.

[37]Ibid., 358.

[38]Connor told Thomas Stenhouse he knew that "Brigham Young could use up this handful of men; but there are sixty thousand men in California who would avenge our blood," to which the Mormon editor responded, "Yes; and behind them there would be the whole nation." See Stenhouse, The Rocky Mountain Saints, 609.

[39]For the full text, see Journal History, April 9, 1864, 2–4.

"Your troops have displaced the Mormon power over these Indians, and it is of great importance to government at this moment that it be kept where it is for a year or two at least," he said. "This city is the seat of all power in this country," he went on, "and the only point from which the authority of the Government over the Indians or people can be, I think, successfully maintained."[40] Ironically, two cavalry companies from Nevada Territory, formerly part of Deseret and Utah Territory, joined Connor that fall.

BATTLE OF SPANISH FORK

If the site of Camp Douglas was ideal for keeping an eye on potential white troublemakers, it had one disadvantage. To reach any hostile Indians, Connor's troops had to "pass through Mormon settlements," he protested, and the inhabitants "notify the Indians of my approach."[41] His tactics in the Battle of Bear River showed that he had arrived early at that conclusion, but Connor had his opinion confirmed on April 12 when Indians attacked a small force from Camp Douglas right in the town of Pleasant Grove while hundreds of settlers looked on.

On April 11, Lt. Francis Honeyman, with five gunners and a howitzer, had apparently been sent as a decoy to the Utah Valley town to establish a base camp for operations against Utah Indians who had attacked overland stages between Salt Lake and Ruby Valley. The next day, a Sunday, Honeyman's little command came under attack by about one hundred Indians who "deployed into the town, skulking behind adobe fences, haystacks" and other cover until they had the Union volunteers completely surrounded. The soldiers took refuge in settler John Green's house, dispossessing the Greens and their six-week-old baby, where they hurriedly uncovered their piece and fired one shell with a short fuse down the street at their attackers. The blast cracked the adobe walls of their shelter and killed two U.S. Army mules. At this, the Indians replied from sunset to dark with an "incessant shower of balls" that riddled "stovepipe, pans, plates, and almost everything in the house."[42]

---

[40]Doty to Wright, August 9, 1863, WOR, Vol. 50, pt. 2, Serial 3584, 583–84.

[41]Ibid., Connor to Drum, April 28, 1863, 415.

[42]Report of Col. George S. Evans, Second California Cavalry, April 17, 1863, WOR, Vol. 50, pt. 1, Serial 3583, 205–08.

Arriving early the next day, Col. George Evans and two cavalry companies found the house wrecked, but the men inside miraculously unhurt. It was "a strange but stubborn fact," Evans reported, that this attack took place before the sight of "several hundred people calling themselves civilized and American citizens—God save the mark!" Not only had local inhabitants looked on, "apparently well pleased at the prospect of six Gentiles (soldiers) being murdered," they had actually helped the Indians steal government mules.[43]

Reinforced by a third company under Capt. George Price, the Second California Cavalry commander now set out to find and punish the hostile Utahs. At first he was apparently misled by settlers into thinking his quarry had retreated up Dry Canyon into Provo Canyon. Then he found a fresh Indian trail up Spanish Fork Canyon. On April 14 he camped on the southern outskirts of Provo and told the local inhabitants he would stay there until daylight. But at midnight his men silently saddled up and moved out.

Daybreak revealed the force about a mile above the mouth of Spanish Fork Canyon, where the troopers dismounted and deployed as flankers and skirmishers across the defile. For the Utahs, it was a complete surprise. When the Indians tried to stop the advancing line, Lieutenant Honeyman opened fire with his howitzer from a spur of the mountain and "dropped his shell among them." Resistance was broken in a ravine where the soldiers opened fire with revolvers. The California volunteers chased the fleeing Indians some fourteen miles up the canyon before Evans ordered his bugler to sound recall. By then, his force had killed some thirty natives, recovered stolen army mules, and captured horses, rifles, and other Indian provisions, he reported.[44] Probably more accurate was the count of a local settler who said, "there were four Indians killed and two wounded."[45]

Whatever the number, subsequent events appeared to vindicate Connor's brutal use of military force against Indians considered hostile in the territory. "Indians suing for peace," he exulted less than two months after the Spanish Fork Canyon fight. "My policy will win."[46] Connor

[43]Ibid.

[44]Ibid.

[45]Journal History, April 16, 1863.

[46]Connor to Drum, June 2, 1863, WOR, Vol. 50, pt. 2, Serial 3584, 470.

and Indian Affairs Superintendent James Doty early in June made a verbal peace treaty with some 650 Shoshonis at Fort Bridger, recovering dozens of stolen horses. Soon after they pow-wowed with Bannock and Shoshoni bands on Snake River, near Fort Hall, where only Pocatello, Sanpitch, and Sagwitch apparently wanted to keep on fighting.[47] At the request of Little Soldier, "chief of the Weber Utes," the two federal officers on July 7 "made a treaty of peace" with the northern Wasatch band.[48]

Ten days later Connor and now-Governor Doty with a cavalry escort went to the Spanish Fork Indian reservation, established in 1856 by Garland Hurt, where all of the leading Utah chiefs except Sanpitch gathered at the adobe farm building "surrounded by their warriors." There Connor told them the government would protect all "good Indians," but "severely punish all bad ones." The native leaders, including Antero, Tabby, Kanosh, and Black Hawk, expressed "regret for past bad acts and their hearty desire for peace."[49]

On the heels of this success came word from Pocatello, "the celebrated Snake chief," who asked for peace on Connor's terms. Offering to meet the general at Brigham City, the noted Shoshoni war leader said the chiefs of his Bannock allies also wanted to come and make a treaty. This pact was signed in October at Soda Springs. Two days before that the Tooele Valley Goshutes signed a compact after Capt. Samuel Smith and two cavalry companies that May had killed more than fifty members of the band.

In October 1863 Governor Doty reported that peace had been established "with all of the tribes in this country, and that no danger from them is to be apprehended by emigrants moving in trains or singly, nor of an interruption in future to the overland stage or telegraph lines."[50] In less than twelve months, Connor had restored an uneasy peace on the routes of travel across the Great Basin and present Idaho, but he had hardly begun to resolve Utah's own Indian problems to the satisfaction of all.

---

[47]The Shoshoni chief Sanpitch was not the same man as the Utah Indian leader of that name.

[48]Doty to Dole, June 20 and 26, July 18, 1863, House Exec. Doc. 1 (38–1), 1863, Serial 1182, 512–16.

[49]Connor to Drum, July 18, 1863, WOR, Vol. 50, pt. 2, Serial 3584, 527–31.

[50]Doty to Dole, October 24, 1863, House Exec. Doc. 1, 539–40.

THE BLACK HAWK WAR

The stage for trouble was set in May 1864 when Congress at the urging of Utah lawmakers opened the Spanish Fork Indian farm for settlement and created a "permanent" reservation in the Uinta Basin that President Lincoln had designated for the Utah tribe in 1861. Approved was $30,000 to prepare homes for the natives who would be moved there and to help them "in becoming self-supporting, by means of agriculture." The region encompassed the entire valley, considered "admirably adapted for the purpose of a large Indian reservation."[51] Ten months later Congress took the next step. It authorized the negotiation of treaties to extinguish "all Indian rights to all the agricultural and mineral lands" in Utah, except those set apart for Indian occupancy. Reservations should be as remote as possible from "present settlements in Utah Territory," the act provided. It also allowed $25,000 to buy presents for the Indians and defray the expenses of making the treaties.[52]

At first the leading chiefs of the Utahs, including Sowiette, Kanosh, Tabby, and Sanpitch, wanted none of the treaty proposed to them on June 7 at the Spanish Fork farm by the new Indian affairs head O. H. Irish. Only after a personal appeal by Brigham Young did most reluctantly agree to surrender their title to all Indian lands in the territory and move to the Uinta Basin, where they were to adopt the ways of white newcomers.

Not all the Utahs were ready to give up the life they had known in return for promises of annual payments of $25,000 during the first ten years and $20,000 a year for a decade thereafter, plus schools, mills, and other benefits. Sanpitch, possibly a half-brother of chief Walker, "lay on his face for about 2 days on his dignity," Apostle Woodruff said, "& would not speak to anyone."[53] Black Hawk did not bother to attend, probably because fighting had begun before some fifteen chiefs on June 9 put their marks on the treaty.

John Lowry, Jr., of Manti could never understand why everyone blamed him for that outbreak. After all, the 36-year-old former Indian

[51]Report of the Commissioner of Indian Affairs, Sen. Exec. Doc. 1 (38–2), 1864, Serial 1220, 159–61.
[52]Statutes at Large of the United States, 13:432.
[53]Kenney, ed., Wilford Woodruff's Journal, 6:227.

missionary had thrown natives out of his house and mistreated them before without causing an Indian war. "We had to do these things or be run over by them," he said. So when young "Jake" Arapene, son of the noted chief, interrupted a meeting he was having in town with other Indians, Lowry rode up, "turned him off his horse and pulled him to the ground."[54]

But this insult on April 9, 1865, had followed an imagined injury. Believing Sanpete Valley settlers had caused his father and others to die at Gunnison the winter before, the angry warrior, whose Indian name was Yene-wood, reportedly swore to take revenge. The day after the incident a small party from Manti went to round up the stock on Twelvemile Creek when one member, Peter Ludvigsen, was shot dead and the rest put to flight. Now growing in number, the hostile Utahs next swooped down on the herd at Salina.

In Salina Canyon, where they took the animals, an old friend of the tribe, Elijah Barney Ward, about 45, suddenly found himself for once in the wrong place at the wrong time. At age 15 Ward had run away from his Virginia home to take up the life of a mountain man and become the only mountaineer to make a lasting commitment to Mormonism, often serving as an interpreter. When a militia force reached Soldier Fork, where Ward and a companion, James Anderson, had camped, it found their bodies, scalped and horribly mutilated.

Riding up the canyon on April 12, the mounted company under Col. Reddick Allred ran into a carefully laid ambush and retreated in disorder after two men, William Kearns and Jens Sorensen, were killed. One of the worst atrocities by natives in Utah's deadliest Indian war occurred soon after in Thistle Valley, where John Given, his wife, and four children, John, Jr., 19, Mary, 9, Annie, 5, and Martha, 3, were massacred. The attackers made off with more than a hundred horses and cattle.

Even then the longest and most destructive of Utah's Indian wars might have been avoided if Congress had ratified the promises made that year at Spanish Fork. When it did not, the deadly series of atrocities and reprisals by both sides over the next three years claimed the lives of about seventy-five settlers and about the same number of Indians, and depopulated Sevier and Piute counties as well as some twenty-eight

---

[54]Lowry, *Wallace Lowry*, 54–56.

smaller settlements in Kane, Iron, Wasatch, Sanpete, and Washington counties. The war also exposed the decline in discipline and training of the Nauvoo Legion since the Walker War.

Led by Black Hawk and lesser chiefs, a collection of native freebooters, Utahs, Paiutes, and possibly a few Navahos, seldom more than a hundred in number, swooped down at will on cattle herds and killed unwary settlers in remote places during the summer months. Pursuing militia forces often ran into artfully laid ambushes. The raiders would then retreat to the Elk Mountain region, now the La Sal Mountains near present Moab, and live on stolen Mormon cattle and sheep over the winter.

One of the larger actions of the war came in September 1865 when Gen. Warren Snow and more than a hundred cavalrymen from Manti overtook Indian raiders and stolen stock at Fish Lake but suddenly came under fire, seemingly from every side. Hit in the shoulder, Snow cried out, "Boys, we've got to get out of here!"[55] Maj. James Guyman, a veteran Indian campaigner from Fountain Green, protested they had found the Indians and should stay and clean them out, but the force retreated, taking a few wounded with them.

General Snow had better luck the following year when his troops on April 12 surrounded some Indians camped in the open near Nephi. They shot one as he tried to get away. Of the rest, some twelve in number, four were tried for complicity in the raids and shot dead on the spot. Eight others, including Sanpitch, broke out of jail at Manti two days later, three dying in the attempt. Four of the remaining were slain in the mountains west of Fountain Green. Sanpitch was found hiding near Moroni and was killed.

Soon after, settlers at the new town of Circleville on the Sevier River committed the worst atrocity by either side in the war. They shot or cut the throats of at least sixteen captives, Paiute men and women, in a tragedy that has come to be known as the Circleville Massacre. Only four small native children were spared and placed in Mormon homes.[56]

Tired of war, Black Hawk, suffering from an old wound and accompanied only by his family, arrived at the Uintah Indian reservation late in

[55]Culmsee, *Utah's Black Hawk War, Lore and Reminiscences of Participants*, 56–58.

[56]For more on this, see Winkler, "The Circleville Massacre: A Brutal Incident in Utah's Black Hawk War," 4–21.

1867, where he had his hair cut like a white man and took up a new way of life. Scattered raids by lesser leaders went on for another year, but his surrender to the reality of a changing world would end the conflict that bears his name. The noted Utah chief died in 1870 and was buried in the mountains east of Spring Lake in Utah County.[57]

By then most Utah members of his tribe, including the Pahvant and Sanpitch bands, had moved to Uintah Valley. There they were joined in 1881 by the White River Indians and, a year later, by the Uncompahgre Utahs under Chief Ouray, both relocated from Colorado in the wake of the uprising known as the Meeker Massacre. Today, some three thousand Utahs live on the Uintah-Ouray Reservation in eastern Utah, including its Hill Creek extension on Green River.

At the start of of the Black Hawk War, General Connor at Camp Douglas had flatly turned down a request to arrest the marauders and protect central Utah settlers because he had been ordered to safeguard the overland trails. He could give no assistance to any settlement remote from the mail line, he said, a position that was later confirmed by Gen. William T. Sherman. This time, the bloody work fell to the territorial militia, or Nauvoo Legion.[58] Connor no doubt took some satisfaction in refusing to risk the lives of his soldiers to defend inhabitants he believed had refused to support his own command. Besides, he had another campaign in mind for the volunteers from the mining camps of California and Nevada who made up his little force. This new crusade was aimed at the heart of the Kingdom of God as a theocratic form of government and was intended to revolutionize Utah's culture from within.

---

[57]In 1919 a party of miners working near Santaquin located Black Hawk's grave and unearthed his remains. For some seventy years, the chief's bones were kept in the basement of the LDS Church Historical Dept. where they were found in 1995 by Pleasant Grove Boy Scout Shane Armstrong. They were then placed at the Brigham Young University's Museum of Peoples and Cultures at Provo, Utah, and later reburied near Pleasant Grove in keeping with the Native American Graves Protection and Repatriation Act. See *Deseret News*, Metro Edition, September 4, 1995, B:1, 2.

[58]In 1868 the Utah Legislative Assembly submitted a memorial to Congress, endorsed by then Governor Charles Durkee, requesting more than $1 million to pay for expenses incurred during the Black Hawk War, 1865–1867, but reimbursement was not approved. For a detailed accounting of such costs, see House Misc. Doc. 19 (41–1), 1869, Serial 1402.

Chapter 12

OF MINES, MURDER, AND LAND

I have considered the discovery of gold, silver, and other valuable minerals in the Territory of the highest importance, and as
presenting the only prospect of bringing hither such a population as is desirable or possible. The discovery of such mines . . .
in my opinion presents the only sure means of settling peace-
ably the Mormon question.

—P. Edward Connor

On November 20, 1863, General Connor opened his campaign to
promote a rush to the territory of a "new, hardy and industrious population" in a new newspaper, *The Union Vedette*, founded at Camp Douglas
by the California Volunteers. The first issue proclaimed Utah's hills
abounded in "rich veins of gold, silver, copper and other minerals."
Edited by Capt. Charles Hempstead, the opposition publication on January 27, 1864, became the *Daily Union Vedette*, Utah's first daily newspaper.[1]

The ingenious scheme to water down Utah's population with a flood
of "hardy, industrious, and enterprising" outsiders began after Mormon
workmen, including George and Alex Ogilvie, John Egbert, and Henry
Beckstead found silver ore in Bingham Canyon. They took a sample to
Connor, who helped form the Jordan Silver Mining Company. Soon
after, Mrs. Robert Reid, wife of the Camp Douglas surgeon, found
another rich vein in Bingham Canyon while picnicking with a party from
the post under Capt. Arthur Heitz.

Seizing the opportunity, Connor ordered his men to prospect for precious metals when it did not interfere with their duties and told his offi-

---

[1] *Union Vedette*, November 20, 1863. For the story of this paper, see Pedersen, "The Daily Union Vedette: A
Military Voice on the Mormon Frontier," 39–48.

cers to facilitate "the discovery of mines of gold, silver, and other metals." The men from California's gold mining camps, most experienced miners, hardly needed much encouragement. Whether the newcomers they would attract to the territory would have "the happiest effects," as Connor envisioned, however, was unclear to the existing inhabitants.[2]

If the belief that gold is wealth ever became widespread, Brigham Young said, discovery of the metal in Utah's mountains surely would bring "nakedness, starvation, utter destitution and annihilation." At the mere report gold was found in the Oquirrh mountains, he continued, "men left their threshing machines, and their horses at large to eat up and trample down" their crops and declared they "were now going to be rich, and would raise wheat no more."[3] To build the Kingdom of God required economic self-reliance, which could only come from wealth produced by farms and ranches, "the lumber from our saw mills, and the rock from our quarries," the Mormon leader believed. "Can you not see that gold and silver rank among the things that we are the least in want of?" he asked.[4]

As his words indicated, Young's objection to precious metals did not include the riches of the earth needed to build an independent economic base. After an 1849 exploring party under Apostle Parley P. Pratt found coal and iron ore in southern Utah, Apostle George A. Smith led a colonizing company to establish a pioneer ironmaking venture near present Cedar City.[5] About the same time, coal was discovered near the mouth of Chalk Creek and in Sanpete Valley, where the towns of Coalville and Wales were founded to exploit the finds. These early ventures ultimately failed due to the unsuitable quality of the raw materials and lack of transportation.[6] Nor did Young's dictum on mining cover everybody when it came to gold. Mormon leaders in 1848–50 had covertly sent as many as fifty of their adopted sons and other missionaries to California

---

[2]Connor to Drum, October 26, 1863, WOR, Vol. 50, pt. 2, Serial 3584, 655–57.

[3]Brigham Young, October 6, 1863, Journal of Discourses, 10:265–74.

[4]Ibid.

[5]For an account of this expedition, see Smart, "Over the Rim to Red Rock Country: The Parley P. Pratt Exploring Company of 1849," 171–90.

[6]The remains of early pioneer coke ovens and furnaces can still be seen about twenty-one miles west of Cedar City on State Highway 56. For the story of Utah iron ore mining, see G. D. MacDonald, III, The Magnet: Iron Ore in Iron County Utah.

to prospect new wealth for cash-starved Utah settlements.[7] And when Indian missionaries at Fort Limhi thought they had found gold in 1855, Lot Smith, an experienced prospector, had been quietly sent to check it out.[8] Some samples later delivered to Great Salt Lake proved to be "micaceous oxide of iron ore . . . mixed with quartz and mica,"[9]—fool's gold.

Whatever the earth held in store, outside prospectors were not welcome in the territory. Without bothering to inform Governor Doty, the lawful commander-in-chief of the militia, General Daniel Wells put the Nauvoo Legion on an emergency footing early in 1864, ready to move at "a moments notice, whenever a hostile intention or demonstration should manifest itself."[10] At least one report said there was more to the mobilization than any need to defend against "reckless savage or other lawless foe."[11] On May 20 the *Daily Union Vedette* published a letter from an "intelligent and reliable citizen (a Mormon)" who lived in "one of the outer settlements." It said the mobilization was ordered "to guard the hills canons, etc., and if a party of men should appear, to inquire of their business, order them to leave and make them do so." The unidentified writer gave his opinion that the purpose was "to try and prevent miners from prospecting the country."[12]

The Camp Douglas paper professed to doubt the accuracy of this report but took the opportunity to remind its readers that Utah's lands and mines belonged to the public at large. While the rights of settlers would be upheld, no one would be allowed to interfere with "the rights of those who desire to develop the mines," whether local residents or newcomers, said the editor. "Militia Captains and tinselled Generalissimos," referring to the Nauvoo Legion, were advised "not to trifle with so delicate a question."[13]

As it warned against interference, the *Vedette* trumpeted precious metal

[7]For more on this episode, see Davies, *Mormon Gold: The Story of California's Mormon Argonauts.*

[8]Biography and Journals of Benjamin Franklin Cummings, September 30, 1855.

[9]*Deseret News*, July 15, 1857, 149.

[10]Wells to Dame, April 5, 1864, Utah Militia Records.

[11]Ibid., General Order No. 1, April 25, 1864. This order was also published in *Deseret News* and can be found on this date in Journal History.

[12]*Daily Union Vedette*, May 20, 1864, 2.

[13]Ibid.

strikes in the Deep Creek Range, the mountains near Beaver, and along Bear River. "Silver in the Mountains—Silver in the Streets—Silver Everywhere" proclaimed the sheet on April 23 when silver was discovered in the mountains east of Rush Valley. And it assured farmers not to fear the impending mining boom since the prosperity it would generate "must find its way at last to the capacious pocket of the producer."[14]

Connor's promise of military protection probably ensured that the earliest strikes would be made along the Oquirrh and Wasatch ranges, both within easy reach of his command. Mining companies at first were organized under California law since Utah lacked its own mining statutes. When Acting Governor Amos Reed urged territorial legislators to remedy this problem, they drew up a bill that showed there were methods to defuse the hoped for mining bonanza besides interference by the militia.

If the lawmakers aimed to stop the opening of Utah's mineral wealth, Reed responded, he could think of no better way to do it than the act they sent him to sign. Unlike California, the measure proposed to put mineral development under a three-member governing board with dictatorial powers. It would also impose a heavy tax on the mines in violation of Utah's organic act, which ruled out any levy on property of the United States. The acting governor in January 1864 vetoed the bill.[15]

Rather than stifle the growth of mining, it was better to leave the whole subject under federal law or "the customs of the miners, which perhaps are sufficient for all practical purposes." editorialized the Vedette.[16]

More successful than laws were Mormon efforts to bring the mining boom under control by getting there first. When the West Mountain Quartz Mining District was created on September 17, 1863, West Jordan Bishop Archibald Gardner, a 49-year-old mill builder, was chosen president and recorder. And a party from Camp Douglas on arriving at Meadow Valley in southeastern Nevada found they had come too late. A colonizing party from St. George under Apostle Erastus Snow had already laid claim to the place.[17] "The whole mountain we found cov-

---

[14]"The Mines of Utah—A Word to Our Farmers," Union Vedette, November 27, 1863, 2.

[15]For Reed's veto message, see Daily Union Vedette, January 22, 1864, 2.

[16]Ibid.

[17]For the story of this settlement, see Lee and Wadsworth, A Century in Meadow Valley, 1864–1964.

ered and spotted with stakes . . . and so frequently did the St. George President's name appear stuck in the stakes, that it looked as though there had been a recent *snow* storm on that mountain," the disappointed arrivals reported. "Brother Snow, heedless of the maledictions denounced against treasure-seekers, had gone in with a vim."[18]

They also found the Mormons in earnest about their claims "and while they will not (wisely) neglect their farms and flocks, they propose to work the mines for themselves at proper times, and not let the new comers have it all." One Mormon dismissed reports that "Brigham and the Church are opposed to discovering and working the mines." Said he, "This whole party have taken up extensive claims on the Panacka lead, and we are going to work them too."[19]

Even so the soldiers from California and Nevada more than held their own in the race to put down stakes. On the east side of the Oquirrh Range they opened a number of mines and gave them such colorful names as Galena, Kingston, Empire, Silver Hill, and Julia Dean. They also established the Wasatch Mountain Mining District, which reached seventy miles or more from Weber Canyon to Provo, as well as the Rush Valley and Tintic mining districts. In 1864 Camp Douglas volunteers surveyed a new town on the site of Colonel Steptoe's 1854–55 encampment in Rush Valley, seven miles south of Tooele, and named it Stockton after Connor's home in California's San Joaquin Valley. Their commander put his own or borrowed money behind his mining campaign, investing $80,000 in a primitive smelter. In less than two years, Stockton boasted some four hundred inhabitants and more than five hundred claims were staked out on nearby hills and canyons.[20]

Unlike California, however, Utah's mineral wealth lay below the surface, not scattered in the gravel along creek beds, and was locked up in ore that took smelters to release. The cost to mine it and the lack of transportation to ship it to smelters held up for a time Connor's scheme to dilute Utah's Mormon population with a flood of newcomers. In six

---

[18]*Daily Union Vedette*, July 2, 1864, 2.

[19]Ibid.

[20]For one of the best reviews of early mining, see Arrington, "Abundance from the Earth: The Beginnings of Commercial Mining in Utah," 192–219. This issue of *Utah Historical Quarterly* was edited by Utah State Historical Society Director Everett L. Cooley and published in cooperation with the Utah Mining Association to mark the 1963 centennial of Utah mining.

years after his campaign began, the territory's mines yielded less than $600,000 in gold and silver.[21]

This total would sharply rise, however, after completion of the transcontinental railroad in 1869, followed a year later by the construction of the Utah Central Railroad from Ogden to Salt Lake City. Lead and silver discoveries near Parley's Park, now Park City, and establishment of the Tintic Mining District, centered on Eureka, both in 1869, would also go far toward making mining the foundation of Utah's economy for the next century or more.

Meanwhile an era of better feeling between the community and Camp Douglas seemed at hand in March 1865 when Great Salt Lake Mayor Abraham O. Smoot and the city council invited Connor and his men to take part in the celebration of President Lincoln's second inaugural. The general and Utah Governor James Doty shared the platform with the 50-year-old mayor and Apostle George A. Smith. Rev. Norman McLeod from the military base was chaplain of the day and Supreme Court Justice John Titus was the windy chief orator.

Connor seemed "greatly moved" by the parade of cheering Utah citizens and patriotism expressed by the speakers, reported Thomas B. H. Stenhouse, 41-year-old editor of the Mormon paper, *The Daily Telegraph*, established in July 1864 as a foil to the *Daily Union Vedette*. "He wanted differences forgotten," Stenhouse said, "and, with gentlemanly frankness, approached the author with extended hand and expressed the joy he felt in witnessing the loyalty of the masses of the people."[22]

After the ceremonies, the Nauvoo Legion's cavalry company from Great Salt Lake City under Col. Robert T. Burton escorted the Camp Douglas artillery unit back to its base. Lt. Col. Milo George, Nevada Volunteer Cavalry, and other officers were later treated by the city council to "an elegant repast" at City Hall, then located on First South

---

[21]Ibid. Also see Nelson, "The Mineral Industry: A Foundation of Utah's Economy," 178–91.

[22]Stenhouse, *The Rocky Mountain Saints*, 611–12. Born in Scotland, Stenhouse joined the LDS church in England where he married his first wife, Fanny, in 1850. Their first child, Clara Federata, became at 16 the fourth wife of Joseph A. Young, Brigham Young's oldest son. To the anguish of his first wife, Stenhouse in 1863 married 15-year-old Belinda Marden Pratt, Apostle Parley P. Pratt's daughter. He and Belinda had three daughters before they were divorced. His book, cited above, is one of the best on Utah history during this period. Believing her husband had not told the whole story, Fanny Stenhouse wrote *Tell It All: the story of a life's experience in Mormonism* and *A lady's life among the Mormons. A record of personal experience as one of the wives of a Mormon elder during a period of more than twenty years.*

between First and Second East. Toasts were openly exchanged by the members of both camps. "It was free, easy, hospitable and a most kindly interchange of loyal sentiment among gentlemen not wont often to meet over the convivial board," said the *Vedette*. "Like the procession, it was a union of the civil and military authorities of Utah, and passed off with eminent satisfaction to all concerned."[23] But conspicuous by their absence on this occasion were Brigham Young and his chief adversary, General Connor.

Only six weeks later the same parties joined hands again, this time to lament the president's death. More than three thousand mourners filled the tabernacle, "soldiers and civilians all uniting as fellow citizens in common observance of the solemn occasion." Apostle Amasa Lyman's eulogy was "all that could have been wished" and Camp Douglas Chaplain Norman McLeod "appealed direct to the hearts of his hearers."[24] City buildings were draped in black and flags everywhere were flown at half staff.

Improved personal relations with many Mormon leaders, however, never softened Connor's opposition to the theocratic political, economic, and legal institutions that made Utah society so distinctive during the territorial period. Less than a year later, he appeared before the House Committee on the Territories in Washington, D.C., to urge repeal of the territory's election law "so as to admit of the right of suffrage to American citizens."[25] He also recommended the indefinite stationing of two thousand regular troops in Utah to protect "dissenting Mormons and Gentiles" and urged an end to territorial laws that gave "special franchises to the leaders" to the exclusion of the poor and immigrants. Never did he give up his campaign to destroy the governing theocracy and make Utah like the rest of the American nation.[26]

MURDER OF DR. ROBINSON

With the end of the Civil War in 1865 many of the volunteers from

---

[23]*Daily Union Vedette*, March 6, 1865, 2.

[24]Ibid., April 21, 1865, 2.

[25]See "The Condition of Utah," House Report No. 96 (39–1), 1866, Serial 1272.

[26]According to Connor's biographer, Brigham D. Madsen, it is a remarkable fact that Connor and Brigham Young never met face to face.

California went back home while others, like Connor himself, remained in Utah to take up new careers in mining or other fields. The Union emerged from four years of conflict more powerful than before, not broken up or destroyed as prophesied. Conditions were now ripe for the first real breakthrough on an important front of the struggle between the United States and the theocratic territory—ownership of the land. But for one man it came at a terrible price.

Dr. John King Robinson, a native of Maine, came to Utah from California in 1864 to serve as assistant surgeon at Camp Douglas. After leaving the army, the young doctor early in 1866 married the daughter of a former Mormon, "a very respectable young lady," and began to practice medicine in Great Salt Lake. He also gave much time to the so-called "Gentile Sunday School," where he served as superintendent. He was outgoing and athletic, widely liked, and considered to be an excellent surgeon.

Robinson wanted to build Utah's first hospital on a location adjoining the Warm Springs about a mile north of town, outside of the city's occupied area but within its expanded limits. He thought he had figured out how to acquire the site under the 1862 Homestead and Preemption acts in spite of measures enacted by the territorial legislature to prevent private ownership of property, especially by outsiders.[27] Since federal laws exempted lands within municipalities from claim, Utah lawmakers had expanded the limits of cities and towns to make them large enough to encompass available farming land and control access by outside homesteaders.[28] They also passed a law requiring county recorders not to transfer land to anyone until "a certificate of survey has been approved and countersigned by one or more of the Selectmen of the county."[29] These and other measures effectively prevented outsiders from owning property.

---

[27]The 1862 Homestead Act allowed a qualified person to acquire title to a quarter section of public land, or 160 acres, on which he may have filed a preemption claim that allowed him to buy the property at a modest price. Congress also enacted that year a law allowing preemption claims on unsurveyed public lands even before Indian claims had been "extinguished." The latter measure established a land office in Colorado Territory. See "An Act to secure Homesteads to actual Settlers on the Public Domain," approved May 20, 1862, and "An Act to establish a Land Office in Colorado Territory, and for other Purposes," approved June 2, 1862, *Statutes at Large of the United States*, 12:392–93, 413.

[28]See Chapter 2, Note 28.

[29]"An ACT in relation to County recorders, and the Acknowledgment of Instruments of Writing," *Acts, Resolutions and Memorials, Passed at the Several Annual Sessions of the Legislative Assembly of the Territory of Utah*, 80, 81.

Robinson found a loophole, or so he thought, in the measures that kept him from acquiring his hospital site. The territory's organic act stated that all laws passed by the Legislative Assembly and governor shall be submitted to Congress, "and if disapproved shall be null and of no effect."[30] After some research the doctor discovered that the laws enacted in 1859–60, including one amending the incorporation of Great Salt Lake City, apparently had not been sent to Congress for approval. Viewing this as evidence that the city had no legal existence, Robinson built a construction shack on the place he wanted as proof of occupancy and prepared to enter a preemption claim at the land office in Denver.[31] When city police tore down his shed, he made the fateful decision to challenge the validity of the city charter in the Third District court and searched for a lawyer to press his case. This proved to be a brave but foolhardy act.

As Robinson must have known, non-Mormon Newton Brassfield, a veteran of the Nevada Volunteers at Camp Douglas, had been shot and mortally wounded earlier that year on the streets of the city while in the custody of the U.S. marshal. Brassfield had married the polygamous wife of a Mormon who was on a mission to England before she had obtained a church divorce, holding her polygamous marriage was illegal under the 1862 federal law.

Shortly before Robinson's case came before Judge John Titus, who replaced John Kinney in 1863, Brigham Young had something to say about alleged land-jumpers. "If you undertake to drive a stake in my garden with an intention to jump my claim, there will be a fight before you get it," he made clear. "If you come within an enclosure of mine with any such intent, I will send you home, God being my helper." By "home," Young probably did not refer to any earthly place.[32]

Perhaps that is why others had undergone harrowing ordeals after preempting public land on the west bank of the Jordan River. John Deaver and J. C. Emerson, who claimed adjoining sections, woke up one night with pistols in their faces. Deaver escaped, but the intruders, some

---

[30]Ibid. See "An Act to Establish a Territorial Government for Utah," Sec. 6, 26.

[31]In the absence of a Utah land office, the office for Colorado Territory was assigned during this period to handle any claims for Utah Territory.

[32]Neff, *History of Utah, 1847 to 1869*, 682.

forty in number, tied Emerson's feet and hauled him in and out of the river until he promised to leave the territory.

At about that time a former officer and a physician at Camp Douglas, named Brown and Williamson, respectively, were pounced on, wrapped in an old tent cover, and readied for drowning. Brown told his attackers to shoot him like a man, not drown him like a dog. On recognizing him, one of their assailants pleaded for their lives, which were spared on the condition they leave Utah forthwith. They did so.[33]

Not the least of such ominous signs was that General Daniel Wells, Nauvoo Legion commander and second counselor to Brigham Young, earlier that year replaced Kentuckian Abraham O. Smoot as mayor of Great Salt Lake City. The moderate Smoot, a noted plains captain, had served in this position to the satisfaction of most who knew him since the death of Jedediah Grant in December 1856.

So it was for good reason that no one besides Robinson's attorney, Robert N. Baskin, was brave enough to take the case. The 28-year-old Ohioan had come to Utah in 1865 on his way west and decided to remain and open a law office in the territory. He was part of "an influx of lawyers" who Brigham Young denounced as "birds of prey." Not intimidated, the prickly Baskin would go on to become one of the Mormon theocracy's most relentless enemies.

In the meantime, Justice Titus, chief of the territory's highest court, ruled against Robinson on the question argued by Baskin and city attorneys led by Hosea Stout. The heart of the issue, Titus concluded, was whether the legislative power of the Territory of Utah was adequate to complete legislation. And he decided, "An Act of the Legislature requires no further or other exercise of power to make it valid [and] binding."[34] Titus therefore refused to declare Great Salt Lake's charter null and void simply because the U.S. House Journal of 1860–61 failed to mention the Utah Legislative Acts for 1859–60 when the charter was amended. But he crafted his opinion carefully and gave it in writing because he knew it would be "reviewed and rectified by a higher tribunal, if erroneous."[35]

---

[33]For more on these events, see Roberts, *Comprehensive History of the Church*, 5:194–215; Stenhouse, *The Rocky Mountain Saints*, 618; and *Salt Lake City Directory, including a Business Directory, of Provo, Springville, and Ogden, Utah Territory*, 29, 30.

[34]The ruling of Judge Titus is published in full in *Deseret News*, October 24, 1866, 373.   [35]Ibid.

Robinson never got the chance to appeal. The next day the doctor went to the mayor's house to complain about the destruction of his bowling alley between Second and Third South by the city police. Mayor Wells asked him if he was the same man who was contesting the Warm Springs property. When Robinson said he was, Wells ordered him out of his house.

The following Monday, October 22, the young doctor returned to his residence near Third South and East Temple (now Main Street) at about 8 P.M., complaining of a headache, and went to bed. His sister-in-law, Mrs. Crosby, who lived with the Robinsons, turned in at about 10 P.M. but was awakened an hour later by a knocking at the door. Robinson from the front room called out, "Who is there?" A voice answered, "Doctor, come quick; my brother, John Jones, has broke his leg; a mule fell on it and smashed it all to thunder!"[36] Mrs. Robinson implored her husband not to go, but the doctor had no known enemies and a reputation for never refusing anyone who needed his services. No one inside saw the man who came to their door that night because he stayed outside in the dark and waited for Robinson to come out and go with him. Five minutes later the two women heard a shot.

Jacob Wimmer, who lived nearby, came home with some friends, Col. Kahn and Charles King, at eleven. Soon after, they heard "a very peculiar scream, which was repeated once." Then they heard a pistol shot. Raising the window, Wimmer saw three men running east toward City Hall but could not see their faces. Wimmer and King went out to investigate. At the corner of Third South and East Temple, they found Dr. Robinson lying on his face in a pool of blood.

Leaving King with the dying physician, Wimmer ran for the police but could not find them until he reached City Hall, where they made their offices. Nearly the entire professional force, Chief Andrew Burt and eight officers, reportedly had been at the circus until 11 P.M., when they returned to City Hall. Four officers went with Wimmer to the scene but made little effort to investigate. By 2 A.M. the policemen on duty that night had all gone to bed.

In the meantime, Robinson was placed on a board and carried for medical attention to Independence Hall, located on Third South

---

[36]Testimony of Mrs. S. Crosby, *Daily Union Vedette*, October 26, 1866, 2.

between East and West Temple, where he had supervised the Protestant Sunday school. Not until about I A.M. was his body delivered to his grief-stricken young wife. The broken hands of his heavy gold watch had stopped at 11:40 to register the time of the attack.

In sharp contrast to the unconcerned attitude of the police, the popular young physician's murder shocked the entire community, Mormon and non-Mormon alike. The city offered a reward of $1,000 for the capture of the killers, a sum matched by the county. To this was added $7,000 from private subscribers, including Brigham Young, who put up $500.

Trying to settle the uproar, Probate Judge Jeter Clinton, the city coroner, described by Stenhouse as "the most perfect type of Dogberry,"[37] requested Chief Justice Titus and Associate Justice McMurdy to assist him in the coroner's inquest. Some of Utah's most respected attorneys, both Mormon and non-Mormon, were brought into the case as special counsels, including Seth M. Blair, Hosea Stout, former *Vedette* editor Capt. Charles Hempstead, and John B. Weller, the ex-governor of California. On October 23 the jury viewed Robinson's body. His injuries were "a most horrifying sight." There was one deep slash over the left forehead made by the blow of a heavy hatchet or bowie knife, another cut on the back of the head, two stabs under the left eye, and a gunshot wound under the left eye, "passing through the skull, extending the skin behind the right ear." The fatal ball was described as a "large-sized slug, such as would come from a navy revolver or large derringer pistol."[38]

While looking at the mutilated body of his murdered client, Robert Baskin "mentally resolved" to do all he possibly could "to place in the hands of the federal authorities the power to punish the perpetrators of such heinous crimes."[39] He would never waver from this commitment.

Testimony before the coroner's jury revealed that while Great Salt Lake was protected by only nine regular policemen, each ward had its own police force, some five hundred or more in all, under captains who reported to the city's Chief Burt. Despite such coverage, there were no

---

[37]Stenhouse, *The Rocky Mountain Saints*, 619. Clinton was the same "Dr." Jeter Clinton who was accused by Morrisites of murdering John Banks, counselor to the self-proclaimed prophet, Joseph Morris. The character Dogberry is the pompous but comical constable in Shakespeare's *Much Ado About Nothing*.

[38]*Daily Union Vedette*, October 24, 1866, 2.

[39]Baskin, *Reminiscences of Early Utah*, 28.

witnesses to the murder and no real clues to the identify of the killers. After eight days the coroner's court ruled Robinson died "by the hands of some persons unknown to the jury," estimated to number from six to eight.

In vain the *Vedette* called on authorities "to ferret out and punish the evil-doers."[40] No witness came forward, no motive was found, and none of the assailants was ever identified. "To call a physician out of his bed in the night under the pretext of needing his services, and then brutally kill him in the dark is horrible," said Brigham Young. "I have not the least idea in the world who could perpetrate such a crime."[41]

But non-Mormons in the city had few doubts about where the guilt lay. They formed in a funeral procession at Independence Hall and marched slowly up the streets to pass in front of Young's house on their way to the Camp Douglas cemetery. The procession was outwardly calm, said Stenhouse, but there was not a man in that grim parade "who did not feel the inspiration of vengeance." It was a silent protest against "the deadly influences that then ruled in Zion."[42]

THE AFTERMATH

Dr. Robinson's bid to own property and its tragic outcome revealed more than anything else how much the theocracy's land monopoly rested on shifting sand. Squatters on the public domain had as much protection against unethical lawyers or the decisions of unfriendly judges as the settlers of Utah. Until the kingdom finally overcame its enemies, some accommodation had to be reached with the federal land laws. Earlier confrontations had only delayed and made more difficult this task.

Governor Charles Durkee made this clear less than two months after Robinson's death in his annual message before the Legislative Assembly. "It is of the highest importance to our settlers that they be enabled to speedily avail themselves of the beneficial provisions of the Homestead Act," the 61-year-old successor to the late Governor James Doty told

[40]*Daily Union Vedette*, October 24, 1866, 2.

[41]Brigham Young, December 23, 1866, *Journal of Discourses*, 11:281.

[42]Stenhouse, *The Rocky Mountain Saints*, 620. Dr. Robinson's grave can be seen today in the Fort Douglas Cemetery, where the center of the large stone marker has been defaced or broken away. Enough of the inscription remains, however, to show what it once said: "Vengeance is mine saith the Lord. I will repay."

lawmakers. A native of Vermont and a non-Mormon, the former U.S. senator said the title of those who had reclaimed the land must be "placed beyond legal question."[43] To achieve this, he urged lawmakers to join with him in asking Congress to appropriate money to finish the public surveys, appoint a surveyor general for the territory, and open an office in Utah "for the sale and entry of the public lands."[44] Too much time had already been lost in completing these three necessary steps to obtain title to public domain under federal law.

Soon after Utah became a territory, Congress had approved funds for a survey to prepare for the opening of a land office. David Burr, surveyor general, had come in 1855 to do this, but he reported his work had been constantly interrupted and surveyors beaten by local roughs who said *the country was theirs.*[45] After allegedly surveying nearly two million acres by June 1857, he had fled in fear of his life during the events leading to the ordering of a military expedition to Utah.

Burr's replacement, Samuel Stambaugh, came in 1859 but found evidence of surveys lacking. Either Burr had fraudulently charged the government for work he had not done, as Mormons alleged, or parties unknown had removed the stakes put down by his surveyors. Stambaugh recommended no more surveys be made until lands already measured had been sold and Congress had devised a policy "to induce other than Mormon emigration to the territory."[46] In 1861 the General Land Office told Utah's next surveyor general, Samuel R. Fox, not to undertake further surveys because there was no demand for land and Congress had not provided for an office to sell the land already surveyed. A year later the Utah surveying district was consolidated with the Colorado district and its records were removed to Denver.

Meanwhile Congress in a series of purposely punitive measures carved large sections from Utah's domain and gave them to Nevada, territory and state, and the territories of Nebraska, Colorado, and Wyoming. Not only was Utah cut back in size by more than half, but its people, who were the first to settle the Great Basin and upper Colorado

[43]"Governor's Message," December 12, 1866, *Daily Union Vedette*, 2.
[44]Ibid.
[45]Burr to Hendricks, February 5, 1857, House Exec. Doc. 71, 118. Emphasis in the original.
[46]Stambaugh's report is quoted in Larson, "Land Contest in Early Utah," 309–25.

River drainage, would become the last to be considered for private ownership of the land.

The way toward this benefit opened on March 2, 1867, when Congress approved a law that gave inhabitants of cities or towns the opportunity to acquire title to public land. This liberalized version of an earlier act allowed authorities of a city or town, if incorporated, or judges of the county court, if unincorporated, to enter claims on occupied public land on behalf of all inhabitants within their jurisdiction. How they disposed of the lots was left up to territorial or state legislatures to decide.[47] The law thus gave elected officials the right to enter public land on behalf of others and prescribe rules for handing out lots. Under Utah's election law, however, it also unintentionally ensured theocratic control over who received titles and who did not. Mayor Daniel Wells on October 3, 1867, declared his intention to enter a claim for Great Salt Lake which protected property within the city against land-jumpers while other issues were resolved. By year's end, some fifteen other Utah cities and towns had followed suit.

Not the least of remaining difficulties was that the new federal law, like the one before, was drafted to suit traditional agricultural towns where mainly merchants and tradesmen lived in the city while farmers lived on their homesteaded land on the outside. As such, it raised limits set by the earlier act but still imposed lids of 2,560 acres, or four square miles, on the size of a city and five thousand on the number who could enter claims for lots, averaging less than an acre in size, in the city.[48] This approach did not fit the millennial design of Great Salt Lake, which exceeded by about two and a half times both the limit on population and the area allowed by the new law. Surveyor General David Burr had noted this problem soon after his arrival in 1855 when he reported that special legislation would be required if the government desired "to give the residents (who have not surrendered their possessions to the church) the right of preemption to the lots they occupy."[49]

---

[47]See "An Act for the Relief of the Inhabitants of Cities and Towns upon the Public Lands," *Statues at Large of the United States*, 14:541–42.

[48]The earlier law, "An Act for the relief of the citizens of towns upon the lands of the United States, under certain circumstances, enacted May 23, 1844," allowed entry only to public land "actually occupied by the town," not to exceed 320 acres, or one-half square mile. See *Statutes at Large of the United States* 5:657.

[49]Burr to Whiting, September 30, 1855, House Exec. Doc. 71, 123.

Patterned after New Jerusalem in Jackson County, Missouri, Zion's Chief Stake had been laid out to comply with Joseph Smith's injunction: "Let every man live in the city."[50] Under this plan, drawn up to implement the law of consecration and stewardship, the people lived on 1.25-acre lots in the city and farmed land assigned to them on the outside. The communal concept, symbolized by the beehive, thus concentrated inhabitants within the extended limits of the city, exceeding ceilings imposed by the federal law.

Before addressing this problem, the Territorial Assembly on January 27, 1868, asked Congress to establish a land office in Utah to secure valid titles "to the land claims and improvements of the settlers."[51] National lawmakers did better than that. On July 16 they approved an act not only to provide a land office but also to appoint a surveyor general and extend "the pre-emption, homestead and other laws" to Utah.[52] Congress also appropriated $20,000 for surveys to supplement earlier surveys, but the amount was too little to overcome mistakes of the past. On February 15, 1869, Utah legislators reported to Congress that earlier surveys had been "so loosely and fraudulently made" that there was "hardly a township, section, or quarter section corner" in the territory that could be identified. They requested $60,000 for a re-survey, plus $55,000 to measure for the first time lands not covered in the initial effort.[53]

Despite uncertainties as to some corner locations, John A. Clark, the new surveyor general, and associates C. C. Clements, register, and Lewis S. Hill, receiver of public moneys, on March 9 that year opened the Utah land office. From the start they did a land office volume of business. By the end of the fiscal period, June 30, Utah settlers acquired 148,403 acres of which 51,683.26 acres had been purchased for $1.25 an acre and 96,764.65 acres had been taken up under the Homestead acts.[54]

---

[50]Smith, *History of the Church*, 1:357–59. Also see Schuster, "The Evolution of Mormon City Planning and Salt Lake City, Utah, 1833–1877."

[51]"Memorial of the Governor and Legislature of Utah," House Misc. Doc. 71 (40–2), 1868, Vol. I, Serial 1349.

[52]See "An Act to create the Office of Surveyor-General in the Territory of Utah, and establish a Land Office in said Territory, and extend the Homestead and Pre-emption Laws over the same," approved July 16, 1868, *Statutes at Large of the United States*, 15:91, 92.

[53]"Memorial of the legislature of Utah Territory," House Misc. Doc. 21 (41–1), 1869, Serial 1402.

[54]Report of Commissioner of General Land Office, 1869–70, House Exec. Doc. I (41–2), 1870, Vol. 3, pt. 3, Serial 1414, 230–43.

In the meantime Utah lawmakers asked Congress to amend the town site act of March 2, 1867, to make it apply to the size and population of the capital city, now named simply Salt Lake City,[55] and not "work a severe hardship" upon its people.[56] William H. Hooper, Utah's delegate to Congress, on March 16, 1869, introduced legislation to take care of this problem. As finally approved on July 1, 1870, it allowed all inhabitants of the city, not to exceed fifteen thousand, to enter collective land claims.[57]

A final problem was how to square a millennial design based on lots and ten-acre blocks with the U.S. public land survey system, created by Thomas Jefferson and followed by law elsewhere, founded on townships and sections. This was solved by a plan that combined both methods on land already surveyed in Salt Lake County, which is the reason Salt Lake City blocks have numbers, first assigned in 1847.[58]

After unsuccessful claims by Dr. Robinson's widow and others, some 5,730 acres on November 21, 1871, were at last entered on the General Land Office's townsite docket for Salt Lake City, and a patent for the land was sent to Mayor Wells. It was distributed under rules adopted by Utah lawmakers on February 17, 1869, which empowered mayors or county judges to dispense lots "to the persons entitled thereto." Parcels not claimed within six months were to be held for public purposes or sold for not less than $5 an acre.[59]

Action over three years to gain title to the land did not herald a sudden shift from collective to private ownership but announced instead an intended tightening of control as a theocratic territory moved to meet new pressures from the outside. Whether within a town or outside, the authority to decide who obtained land titles, and who did not, was

---

[55] The Legislative Assembly of Utah on January 29, 1868, gave Salt Lake City and Salt Lake County their present names, dropping the word "Great" from their titles.

[56] "Memorial of the Legislature of Utah Territory," House Misc. Doc. 22 (41–1), 1869, Serial 1402.

[57] See "An Act for the Relief of the Inhabitants of Salt Lake City, in the Territory of Utah," *Congressional Globe* (41–2), 1870, App., 676. Salt Lake City's population at this time was approximately 12,500.

[58] The compromise approach is followed today on land as far south as 45th South, as far east as Highland Drive and as far west as the Jordan River. See "Ten Acre A-B Big Survey, Showing Ties to Section Lines and Corners," September 5, 1952, Salt Lake County Surveyors Office.

[59] See "An ACT prescribing Rules and Regulations for the execution of the Trust arising under an Act of Congress entitled 'an Act for the Relief of the Inhabitants of Cities and Towns upon the Public Lands, March 2, 1867,'" *Acts, Resolutions and Memorials passed and adopted by the Legislative Assembly of the Territory of Utah, Eighteenth Annual Session, 1869*, 4–6.

covertly exercised by an organization known as the School of the Prophets, about which more to come.[60]

In 1879 L. S. Burnham of Bountiful, who identified himself as "a Mormon, but not a polygamist," told the Public Lands Commission that when the land office opened, "a multitude of filings" proved to be "simply forms" to prevent unwanted persons from gaining title to the land covered. "There was a multiplicity of fraudulent claims held over the whole country to keep the Gentiles from taking part of the land," he testified.[61]

It would take years for the theocratic land monopoly in Utah to be broken altogether. But once individual settlers acquired a title to their property, the process had begun and it would not be reversed even during the difficult days to come when a communal way of life would be imposed with renewed intensity.

---

[60]See Patrick, "The School of the Prophets: Its Development and Influence in Utah Territory," 89–91.

[61]See "Report of the Public Lands Commission," House Exec. Doc. 46 (46–2), 1879–80, Vol. 22, Serial 1923, 492–93.

Chapter 13

THE NEW SOCIAL ORDER

Through cuts in the mountains,
And over the fountains
He rides on a rail
With smoke for his tail,
And that's how the monster comes into our vale.
—Jabee Woodward
"The Steam Horse in Salt Lake Valley"

True to its charismatic creator, the Kingdom of God was a revolutionary ideal that looked to universal dominion within the lifetimes of those who advanced it. Its destiny was to prevail, not to compromise or co-exist. As established in Utah, it could never last long as a separate form of government or distinctive culture limited by the confines of the Great Basin.

From the first, the hope to roll the kingdom forth to world rule rested on a growing flood of converts to build the population and plant new settlements at a lower cost. For this reason, Utah lawmakers as early as 1852 had asked Congress to back construction of a railroad to the Pacific coast. In 1857 Brigham Young himself had personally investigated the potential to move people and goods up the Missouri River during his visit to Fort Limhi.

At the same time the transcontinental railroad carried the threat to corrupt the foundation of the kingdom's outward spread. As the iron rails drew closer, eventually to join on May 10, 1869, at Promontory, Utah, a drive began to purge the Chief Stake of Zion of outside influences and create a new social order, one destined to supersede all other social and economic systems throughout the world.

That year one of the Mormon hierarchy's most able leaders, 42-year-old Apostle George Q. Cannon, outlined the concepts behind the new economic order before the faith's April gathering. Less than a century after the founding of the American government, said the Liverpool, England, native, the "evils that have flourished so long in what is called the Old World have been transplanted to this land."[1] These evils he traced to a growing divide between the rich and poor, "an aristocracy of wealth," on one hand, and "another class in degradation and poverty." The chief cause of this disparity was an "incorrect organization of society" that prior efforts had failed to reform due to "a lack of union, and a lack of wisdom in the management of the affair." The power to address this evil, Cannon said, took "the restoration of the holy Priesthood to the earth."[2]

Under its authority, "you are to be equal," according to revelation, he told his listeners, with equal claims on property "for the benefit of managing the concerns of your stewardships, every man according to his wants and his needs, inasmuch as his wants are just." This would be done, he said, "that every man may improve upon his talent and every man may gain other talents, yea, even an hundred-fold, to be cast into the Lord's storehouse to become the common property of the whole Church."[3]

You may ask, Cannon said, "will not the careless and indolent share the blessings" of the industrious, and "will it not weaken the hands of the energetic?" Not in the least, he answered. "The man who is energetic and faithful" would receive his reward "in the day of the lord Jesus."[4]

The cooperative system, revealed to the church's founding prophet, Joseph Smith, was meant to apply not just to his church, but "ultimately to all society," according to early Utah historian Edward Tullidge, who said it would introduce the millennium. The spread of a communitarian gospel over the earth, bringing "the reign of righteousness," would be "the consummation of the Latter-day mission," he said. "Such was original Mormonism."[5]

---

[1]George Q. Cannon, April 6, 1869, *Journal of Discourses*, 13:97.

[2]Ibid., 97, 98.

[3]Ibid. See Sec. 82, *The Doctrine and Covenants of the Church of Jesus Christ of Latter-day Saints*, 132–34.

[4]Ibid., 101.

[5]See Tullidge, *History of Salt Lake City*, 385.

THE NEW SOCIAL ORDER

SCHOOL OF THE PROPHETS

To implement a unified move in this direction, Brigham Young on December 2, 1867, resurrected an organization from an earlier period of his church's history. He announced that day before an assembly of Mormon leaders that the University of Deseret, parent of the University of Utah, would be reorganized and "hence, it may properly be called the 'School of the Prophets.'"[6] Since it was founded in 1850, the university had seen few students but served mainly to publish and distribute the Deseret Alphabet.[7]

Established in 1832 at Kirtland, Ohio, under the apocalyptic "Olive Leaf Prophecy," the School of the Prophets had taught male priesthood holders "all things that are expedient for them" before it closed in 1837 when the church moved to Missouri.[8] As restored in Utah, it would instruct Israel's elders not only in the theology of religious communism, but in "all other matters which pertain to the temporal and spiritual lives of the Saints."[9] But it was more than a school in the customary sense.

In practical operation the organization served to implement a variety of policies, decided by the Council of Fifty and handed down to local groups, on a number of subjects, ranging from land claims to elections. At the grassroots level it would function as a town hall or legislature in resolving strictly local problems or disputes. Its larger purpose was to change the hearts of its members and make them willing subjects of a millennial economic and social order.[10] And its business was to be kept strictly secret.

Participation was generally broad based and included all male adults who held the priesthood and met the qualifications approved early in 1868. These included the faith's customary standards of personal clean-

---

[6]*Deseret News*, December 2, 1867, 2. While Young considered School of the Prophets to be the proper name and role of the University of Deseret, the institution's existing name remained the same. In 1872 the larger School of the Prophets was dissolved due to a lack of attendance and the inability of many to keep its affairs secret.

[7]See Chapters 2, 17, 18.

[8]Smith, *History of the Church*, 1:311.

[9]Brigham Young, February 8, 1868, *Journal of Discourses*, 12:159.

[10]See Patrick, "The School of the Prophets: Its Development and Influence in Utah Territory;" and Arrington, *Great Basin Kingdom*, 245–51.

liness, strict honesty, and obedience to the Word of Wisdom.[11] But they also required members not to do "anything to build up the world or any town or city thereof" and to refrain from "trading or trafficking with outsiders and or doing any other thing that will encourage them in our midst."[12]

The first School of the Prophets was organized in Great Salt Lake on December 9, 1867, when Brigham Young was chosen president and his counselors, Heber Kimball and Daniel Wells, were ratified as vice presidents, all unanimously. Soon after, separate schools were established in larger settlements throughout the territory to make ready for the opening salvo in the creation of a new economic order.

WAR AGAINST MERCHANTS

Following Dr. Robinson's murder nearly two dozen merchants, most of them non-Mormons, had offered to sell their merchandise to Brigham Young for cash at a twenty-five percent discount and leave the territory. "So far as we are concerned, you are at liberty to stay or go, as you please," Young had replied. "We have used no intimidation or coercion towards the community to have them cease trading with any person or class, neither do we contemplate using any such means."[13] But in 1868 Young dropped any pretense of tolerance toward outsiders who did business in Utah. Instead he opened that year a crusade to establish a closed, communal economy by declaring war on non-Mormon merchants. Listeners might ask him, "How tight are you going to draw the reins?" he said. "We are going to draw the reins so tight," he replied, "as not to let a Latter-day Saint trade with an outsider."[14] And if Mormon women did not stop buying from them, he said, "we are going to cut you off from the church."[15]

The drive to cleanse Zion of Babylonian influences was carried on mainly in the School of the Prophets, where members were told in meet-

---

[11]The Word of Wisdom was a revelation given to Joseph Smith in 1833 which advised church members to abstain from using alcohol, tobacco, and hot drinks (tea and coffee).

[12]Patrick, "The School of the Prophets," 145.

[13]Roberts, *Comprehensive History*, 5:213.

[14]Brigham Young, October 8, 1868, *Journal of Discourses*, 12:286.

[15]Ibid., Brigham Young, November 29, 1868, 315.

ings each week to "stop trading with our enemies & sustaining those who would destroy us."[16] Those who had "bought goods of our Enemies" were told to leave the School "& not come to the Communion Table no more for we do not fellowship you."[17]

"By and by there will be a gulf between the righteous and the wicked so that they can not trade with each other," Young said "and national intercourse will cease." He told his followers "to omit their wants for the present, and until we can manufacture what we want."[18]

ZION'S CO-OPERATIVE MERCANTILE INSTITUTION

As dismayed "gentile" merchants and uncooperative Mormon businessmen saw a precipitous drop in sales, LDS church leaders moved in October 1868 to circle the economic wagons still further and establish a full trade monopoly. "Convinced of the impolicy of leaving the trade and commerce of their Territory to strangers," they founded a new firm, named the Zion's Co-operative Mercantile Institution, the forerunner of today's ZCMI.[19]

The company offered up to 300,000 shares of stock at $100 per share to finance the enterprise, but restricted membership in the firm to those of "good moral character" who paid their tithing.[20] Merchandise to stock its shelves was furnished by Mormon merchants who were motivated to exchange their products for shares in the new venture by the fear of being boycotted along with outside traders. Brigham Young was named president of the firm, and Mormon religious and business leaders filled other offices.

No location was overlooked in the campaign, conducted by the School of the Prophets, to finance and spread the venture to every ward and town in Utah. Within six weeks after the first store opened, nearly eighty were in business and by 1880 the number had risen to at least 150. Keeping careful watch on the faithful from a sign over each store was the all-seeing eye of Jehovah. Above this daunting symbol arched the words, "Holiness to the Lord."[21]

[16]Kenney, ed., *Wilford Woodruff's Journal*, 6:382.   [17]Ibid., 426.

[18]Brigham Young, October 8, 1868, *Journal of Discourses*, 12:284–85.

[19]Tullidge, *History of Salt Lake City*, 725.   [20]Ibid., 727.

[21]Arrington's classic work, *Great Basin Kingdom*, 293–322, is still the best study of the cooperative movement.

It was hardly any wonder the enterprise became an immediate success and the model for a number of cooperative agricultural and commodity ventures. Yet home production could not begin to turn out at a competitive cost the articles people needed and wanted to buy. Goods still had to be purchased in the East for resale in the church-run stores, and an exception still made to the rule against doing business with non-Mormon merchants.

"This is the great secret we are teaching in the School of the Prophets," Brigham Young said, "be exclusive enough to sustain the kingdom of God . . . If we trade with outsiders at all we want it to be yonder at a distance, and not here."[22] Apostle Cannon further explained this course: "I would as soon deal with them in the eastern States as with anybody else; but it is because they are in Salt Lake City that I am opposed to them."[23]

This pragmatic policy also applied to construction of the transcontinental railroad. On May 21, 1868, Young signed a contract with Union Pacific to build the roadbed from the head of Echo Canyon, near present Wahsatch, either to Salt Lake City or to the north shore of Great Salt Lake, depending on which way the line went around the lake. Later, Apostle Ezra T. Benson, Lorin Farr, and Chauncey West undertook to grade the Central Pacific Railroad bed from present Wells, Nevada, to Ogden. To both projects the School of the Prophets sent workmen recruited in settlements as far away as Manti. For providing this employment, Young saw the hand of God, "thus keeping away from our midst the swarms of scalawags that the construction of the railroad would bring."[24] Protection from such influences would be necessary to make his followers ready for the transition to a higher economic and social design.

UNITED ORDER OF ENOCH

From the beginning, the School of the Prophets and ZCMI were only the first steps in a millennial design to get ready for "the day to come

[22]Brigham Young, November 29, 1868, *Journal of Discourses*, 12:314.

[23]Ibid., George Q. Cannon, October 7, 1868, 296.

[24]Patrick, "The School of the Prophets," 93.

when Jesus will descend in the clouds of Heaven." To make that day
come, "we must be prepared to receive him," the faithful were told. "The
organization of society that exists in the heavens must exist on the
earth."[25]

With his time running out, Brigham Young at age 72 moved to create
the social order that would usher in the millennium. Before leaving for
St. George, he told the Salt Lake City School of the Prophets in 1873
that he wanted a community of elders "willing to be one in Temporal
things"[26] to enter into the order that was given to Enoch and later
revealed to Joseph Smith, whose pseudonym at the time was Enoch.[27]
Finding willing followers at the southern Utah city, he founded the first
communal colony there.

On his return the following spring Young and company founded
more than two dozen communal orders at towns they visited along the
way. Church leaders soon after took the new social design to every Mormon settlement in the western United States, some 150 or more in all.
At Salt Lake City, separate orders were established in each of some
twenty wards. An over-all United Order board was organized with
Brigham Young "President over the whole Order throughout the
world."[28]

An individual United Order was much like an employee-owned enterprise, except that the surplus, or profit, would go to build the kingdom
rather than reward shareholders as bonuses, dividends, or enhanced value
of the firm. In theory it was a decentralized engine of perpetual economic expansion eventually encompassing the entire earth. Its success
depended on the unselfish devotion of its members to build the kingdom without regard for personal gain.

While operation of each unit varied to some degree, they were all alike
in that members contributed their property and pledged their time, labor,

[25]George Q. Cannon, April 6, 1869, *Journal of Discourses*, 13:99.
[26]"Salt Lake City Minutes," School of the Prophets, November 17, 1873, quoted in Patrick, "The School of the Prophets," 36.
[27]Apostle Orson Pratt in 1873 explained that the law of Enoch was the law given to Joseph Smith, Jr., (as Enoch). "Therefore, when I speak of the Order of Enoch, I do not mean the order of ancient Enoch; I mean the order that was given to Joseph Smith in 1832–3–4." See Pratt, August 16, 1873, *Journal of Discourses*, 16:156. Also see *The Doctrine and Covenants of the Church of Jesus Christ of Latter-day Saints*, Sec. 82, 83.
[28]Kenney, ed., *Wilford Woodruff's Journal*, 7:181.

and abilities. In return they received shares in the order and credit for work performed. They also agreed to abide by the constitution of the order, which closely followed the document initially drawn up at St. George, and placed themselves under the control of a board of directors.

Typical of most, except that it lasted longer, was the entity at Orderville in southern Utah where the members made a covenant by baptism to obey the rules of the community. Among other requirements, the covenant obliged them to patronize only those in the order, to devote themselves and all they had to the order and the building up of the Kingdom of God, to avoid foolish and extravagant fashions, and to live righteous lives. All lived from the general fund and all things were done by common consent. Each member's account was balanced at the end of the year with credit given for work done and charges entered for resources used. Those whose credits exceeded their debts gave the surplus to the company, while members whose debts surpassed their credits had their debts canceled, provided the shortfall resulted from a good cause, such as sickness or large family. All started out each year on an equal footing.[29]

"THE NEW MOVEMENT"

Even before the move toward communitarianism had reached its peak with the establishment of the United Order, some writers and merchants who called themselves Saints came out in opposition to Brigham Young's vision of society in the future.

William Godbe at age 36 was a tireless Mormon entrepreneur who had walked to Zion as a teenager rather than wait for a wagon party. He had become by 1868 one of Utah's richest men. Edward Tullidge and Elias L. T. Harrison, both in their thirties, were journalists who shared an interest in spiritualism. Others included 33-year-old Henry Lawrence, Salt Lake merchant and councilman; Eli Kelsey, 49, the lone American among the dissenters and operator of Bingham Canyon mines; and the Walker brothers, who came from England in 1852.

In 1864 Harrison and Tullidge had started the territory's first unsanctioned literary magazine, fittingly named *Peep O'Day*, which had

---

[29]See Seegmiller, "Personal Memories of the United Order of Orderville, Utah," 160–200. Also see Arrington, "Cooperative Community in the North: Brigham City, Utah," 198–217; and *Great Basin Kingdom*, 323–49.

peeped less than two months. Following this ill-fated venture, Harrison and Godbe in January 1868 teamed up as editor and publisher, respectively, to offer readers the *Utah Magazine*. At first this art and literary journal presented a curious blend of spiritualism and watered-down free market philosophy. But at the introduction of ZCMI, it came out in open opposition.

An editorial on October 16, 1869, noted that Utah was not a farming country, producing "not half enough to get us the money we need." Nor was it fitted for grazing as any "who have once looked on the rich pasturages of England and other countries" could see. Raising only enough for home consumption, it said, brought no money into the territory, "and we imperatively need something that will." What was that something? it asked. "The answer comes back from all parts of the territory, that it is MINERALS!"[30]

Vainly laboring "to bend the climate and soil" of a desert region while leaving untouched Utah's mineral wealth, it went on, was "to turn our backs on the open hand of God, and shut our eyes to that providential finger and voice, saying, 'this is the way walk ye in it.'" To this outspoken heresy, it added another: "It will pay to purchase the necessary skill for so important a purpose at almost any price."[31]

Two weeks later Harrison announced in his paper that he had been excommunicated for asserting "the Gospel gives me the freedom to differ with the leaders of the church."[32] The action by the Salt Lake High Council came on October 25 soon after Brigham Young had charged the editor and five sympathizers with non-attendance at the School of the Prophets "& other things."[33] Godbe, Tullidge, and the only culprit from Nauvoo days, Kelsey, were also cut off. Four others recanted and were restored to fellowship.[34]

In his account of the excommunication proceedings, Harrison said it was made clear that "it is apostacy to honestly differ with the Priesthood in any of their measures." Moreover, Daniel Wells had said that anyone who claimed the right to differ with Brigham Young "might as

---

[30]"The True Development of the Territory," *Utah Magazine*, October 16, 1869, 376–78.

[31]Ibid.

[32]Ibid., October 30, 1869, 406–12.

[33]Kenney, ed., *Wilford Woodruff's Journal*, 7:500.

[34]They were T. B. H. Stenhouse; George D. Watt, creator of the Deseret Alphabet; William C. Dunbar; and a "Brother Nesling."

well ask the question whether a man had the right to differ honestly with the Almighty," he reported.[35]

A month later the indignant editor and his associate, William Godbe, issued a "Manifesto" announcing a "New Movement," called the Church of Zion, in which, they said, the "Ordinances and Principles of the Gospel will remain intact as at present." At the same time, they said, "spiritual gifts will be encouraged in all their forms of manifestation."[36] Among the most popular of these were seances and spirit rapping.

With their magazine now boycotted in Utah, Godbe and Harrison on New Year's Day, 1870, published the first issue of a new weekly newspaper, *Mormon Tribune*. Lacking appeal to non-Mormon readers, the name was soon changed, first to *Salt Lake Daily Tribune and Utah Mining Gazette*, then to *The Salt Lake Tribune*, the title by which it is known today.[37] Under new owners, it would open in 1873 a relentless, continuing attack against the Utah theocracy.

UTAH'S "QUEEN CITY": CORINNE

In the meantime, like countless emigrants, starting with the Bidwell-Bartleson party, Union Pacific engineers had to answer the question posed by the dominant geographical feature of the region. Should they go to the south of the Great Salt Lake or keep to the north of the inland sea that covers a thousand square miles? In the growing quarrel between the Utah theocracy and its enemies, the answer was vital because the line of the transcontinental railroad would trace future economic growth and dominance.

To maintain control over the lines of transportation, Brigham Young fought to make the route go on the south side of the lake, via Salt Lake City, taking his case to Union Pacific's directors and federal officials. His opponents, on the other hand, wanted the route to go around the north side of the lake and by-pass the Mormon city. They wanted to create on the northern line a new, non-Mormon city to challenge the dominance of Zion's chief stake.

---

[35]*Utah Magazine*, October 30, 1869, 406–12.

[36]Ibid., November 27, 1869, 470–73. For more on the New Movement, see Walker, "The Commencement of the Godbeite Protest: Another View," 215–44, and "When the Spirits Did Abound: Nineteenth-Century Utah's Encounter with Free-Thought Radicalism," 304–24.

[37]See Malmquist, *The First 100 Years: A History of The Salt Lake Tribune, 1871–1971*.

The dream of a new metropolis in northern Utah to seize commercial control seemed fulfilled when the railroad, like most emigrants, decided in 1868 to build its line on the firmer ground to the north rather than cross the mud flats that ran for miles to the south. The approved route paralleled present I-80 and I-84 down Echo and Weber canyons to Ogden, then went north on the line of today's Utah Highway 83 to Promontory Summit and around the north end of the lake.

As the transcontinental line neared completion, opponents of Mormon rule began to promote a railroad construction camp on the west bank of Bear River as the future center of Utah commerce and trade, the new "Queen City" of the territory. Located on the well-paying freighting trail to Montana's mining camps, the town was first named Connor City after General Patrick Connor, then renamed after the daughter of its first mayor, Corinne.[38]

Brigham Young understood the logic of Union Pacific's move, but when its rails were joined with Central Pacific's at Promontory on May 10, 1869, an event then as historic as the moon landing, he did not bother to attend, going instead to southern Utah. To him a more important event arrived seven days after the gold spike was driven when Mormon workers broke ground for a new railroad to join Salt Lake City with the main line at Ogden.

Financing for the Utah Central came from stock sales, largely through the School of the Prophets, and returns from the Union Pacific contract. The construction superintendent was 35-year-old Joseph A. Young, son of Brigham Young, rescuer of the handcart companies, and sub-contractor on the transcontinental roadbed. Some fifteen thousand cheered a year later when the elder Young drove home the last spike to finish the thirty-eight-mile line. Not from gold was it shaped, but from southern Utah iron inscribed, "Holiness to the Lord."

STEAMBOATS VS. STEAM ENGINES

The new Mormon railroad put Salt Lake City back on the main line and made it the shipping point for commodities from the south, but its feisty competitor to the north was not ready yet to give up its dream of prominence.

---

[38]For the best treatment of this unique chapter of Utah's history, see Madsen, *Corinne: The Gentile Capital of Utah.*

In 1868 Patrick Connor had built the ninety-ton schooner *Kate Connor*, named after his wife, to deliver ties and other goods from the south side of Great Salt Lake to railroad builders on the north shore. The next year, the vessel tied up at Corinne with a load of ties, grain, and lumber from Tooele Valley after sailing across the Great Salt Lake from Black Rock. Alongside docked *Fillerbuster*, loaded with silver ore from the Stockton mines for shipment by rail to eastern smelters. More important than their cargo, however, was the hope these vessels bore that Corinne, already a shipping point on the railroad and Montana Trail, could be served from the lake's south side by a fleet of steamboats, bypassing the Mormon railroad.

To fulfill it, the *Kate Connor* was converted to steam and early in 1871 the Corinne Steam Navigation Company was formed to build and operate steamboats carrying sightseers and products between Corinne and Lake Point, near Tooele. Launched on May 23, the firm's first vessel was worthy of its name, *City of Corinne.* The new steamer was 138 feet in length with "handsomely furnished" cabins, capable of seating some sixty persons for dinner, with a "well-supplied bar."[39]

Cooling Corinnethian ardor three months later was another of Brigham Young's sons, 26-year-old John W. Young, who broke ground at Brigham City for a new railroad, the Utah Northern, from Ogden to Cache Valley and beyond. As it moved up the Wasatch Mountain front toward Hampton's, the narrow-gauge track promised one day to outflank Corinne's freight line to Montana. Work also began that same year to build the Utah Southern Railroad from Salt Lake City through central Utah towns, largely financed by Joseph A. Young.

In time steamboats on the lake and ox-drawn caravans proved no match for the iron horse. The choice of Ogden as the junction of the Central and Union Pacific railroads and the transportation genius of the Young family doomed Corinne's hope to become a lake port. The final blows fell when railroad builder John W. Young in 1875 bought the *City of Corinne* and Kaysville Bishop Christopher Layton acquired the *Kate Connor* and used its engine to run his grist mill.

If their dream of empire failed, Corinne's founders succeeded in establishing institutions that have lasted to the present time, including

---

[39] *Salt Lake Herald,* May 19, 1871, quoted by Madsen, *Corinne: The Gentile Capital of Utah,* 160.

the first free, or public, schools and first independent political party. Moreover, their city in 1869 became the beachhead of an invasion by Protestant missionaries bent on winning people of the territory back to the historical gospel of Jesus Christ. The ministers who came on the trains followed a faint but discernible tradition established soon after the first Mormon settlers arrived.

THE MISSION SCHOOLS

In 1859 Father Bonaventure Keller visited Camp Floyd where he offered the first Catholic mass. To Chaplain John Anderson of the Third California Volunteers goes the honors for holding one of the earliest Protestant services under roof, when he preached in 1862 at Camp Douglas in the tent chapel provided by the San Francisco First Presbyterian Society. But such early ministers served only the spiritual needs of small non-Mormon flocks. Not until 1865 did a preacher come to open a twenty-five-year evangelical challenge to Utah's major faith for the allegiance of its members.

An ordained Congregationalist and Presbyterian minister, Rev. Norman McLeod was an energetic, gifted preacher who was filled with the fire of the gospel. Within weeks after his arrival on January 16, he had "uplifted the banner of Christ for the first time in Utah," organized a new church, and begun to raise money for a building on the south side of Third South, west of East Temple (Main Street).[40] Completed in November 1866, the non-Mormon meeting place became known as Independence Hall.[41]

The tireless McLeod soon established two Sunday schools, one in the city, the other at Camp Douglas, attended by 250 or more children, many reportedly from Mormon families. At the request of General Connor, he became chaplain at Camp Douglas and appeared by Mormon invitation before combined memorial services at Salt Lake City for President Lincoln. Above all he was an ardent opponent of polygamy and other doctrines he deemed heretical. McLeod was the first to conclude that the only way to take the gospel successfully to Mormons

---

[40]Quote from Lyon, "Evangelical Protestant Missionary Activities in Mormon Dominated Areas: 1865–1900," 39, 40.

[41]The thirty-three by fifty-nine-foot building was torn down in 1889.

"would be through the operation of free schools, conducted by the mission boards of the churches, in which to educate the young people of the LDS faith."[42] Those who followed him would reach the same conclusion and move on a wide front to exploit the opening to Mormon society exposed by the state of education in the territory.

Every governor after Brigham Young had urged the Legislative Assembly in vain to upgrade Utah's schools by establishing a tax-supported system, then known as free schools, to replace the so-called "fee" system under which teachers collected their pay from parents. The inaction of lawmakers had yielded uneven educational standards, untrained teachers, an average school year of three months or less, and a level of attendance below fifty percent of enrollment.[43] Not only did Young oppose public schools, calling the system "taking away property from one man and giving it to another,"[44] in 1868 he also renewed his push, begun fourteen years before, to require Utah schools to use the Deseret Alphabet. On October 8 he told reluctant followers that thousands of first and second readers in the alphabet would be distributed throughout the territory. The radical new way to write the English language, he believed, would be "very advantageous to our children."[45]

Not sharing such views, Rev. McLeod in 1866 appeared with Connor before a House committee in Washington, D.C., to deliver a blistering assault on conditions in Utah. "As Gentiles and anti-Mormons," he testified, "we ask of Congress the rights of American citizens; the right to act as jurors; the right of the ballot; the right of liberty of speech." He also charged that armed assassins had violated the sanctity of "our place of worship" and said that "law-abiding citizens are threatened even by Brigham's police."[46] McLeod's aim was to oppose statehood and keep a force of two thousand troops in Utah after the Civil War, but his testimony soon would appear prophetic. On his way back the evangelist got word of the assassination of his Sunday school superintendent, Dr. John King Robinson, within a few feet of the church. Unwilling to trust his

---

[42]Lyon, "Evangelical Protestant Missionary Activities in Mormon Dominated Areas," 46.

[43]Ibid., 69–78.

[44]Ibid., 68.

[45]Brigham Young, *Journal of Discourses*, October 8, 1868, 12:298.

[46]For McLeod's testimony, see House Rep. 96 (39–1), 1866, Serial 1272, 14–25.

own life in God's hands, he chose instead to keep out of harm's way. Not for six years would he return.

Less contentious was 29-year-old Daniel S. Tuttle, the new Episcopal missionary bishop of Montana, with jurisdiction over Utah and Idaho. A peaceful man, but big enough in stature to discourage trouble-makers in his frontier mission field, the young bishop came to Great Salt Lake in July 1867 to review the work of Revs. George Foote and T. W. Haskins. They had taken over McLeod's Independence Hall Sunday school and established St. Mark's grammar school in Dr. Robinson's former bowling alley on East Temple. During his visit Bishop Tuttle also paid a courtesy call on Brigham Young, concluding afterward "that my policy will be to have as little as possible to do with him." Instead, like McLeod, the pioneer missionary over the next two decades would make education his first concern and emphasize "the truth that our great work in this Territory is with the young."[47]

Soon taking up this view were the other missionaries who came with the Union Pacific to Corinne, where they built churches on land donated by the railroads under an accord with the American Baptist Home Mission Society and other mission bodies. There Rev. Lewis Hartsough, Methodist missionary superintendent of the area, oversaw construction in 1869 of the first non-Mormon church chapel in Utah.

Hartsough's successor, Rev. Gustave Pierce, arrived in Utah the following year to organize in Faust's Hall the First Methodist Church of Salt Lake City. In 1871 he opened a new school named the Rocky Mountain Seminary with an enrollment within two years of well over two hundred. It would open a Methodist contribution to Utah education stretching over more than two decades.

To Presbyterians the opportunity offered by the shortcomings of Utah schools was especially inviting. Known for placing a high value on education, this reformed Christian body elsewhere favored tax-supported free schools at grade levels and placed its primary emphasis on secondary and higher education. In Utah, however, this policy was changed to allow the creation of grade schools wherever public education did not exist, which meant everywhere but Corinne.

---

[47]Beless, "Daniel S. Tuttle, Missionary Bishop of Utah," 359–78.

Leading the most costly effort by any of the churches was short, bewhiskered Sheldon Jackson, Presbyterian superintendent of missions for seven western states or territories, who in 1870 came at age 35 to build at Corinne the faith's first church in Utah. The era of rapid mission school growth began in 1875 when Jackson and Rev. Josiah Welch recruited Prof. J. M. Coyner to found the Salt Lake Collegiate Institute, forerunner of present Westminster College.[48] Extending his outreach to Utah's heartland, Jackson also sent Rev. Duncan J. McMillan, a former Illinois school superintendent, to Mt. Pleasant that year to open the Wasatch Academy, which is still in operation today, with thirty-four pupils. The young educator who had come west for his health soon faced fierce opposition that appeared at times to threaten it.[49]

Early in 1876, McMillan reported, Brigham Young came to Sanpete Valley and took "two turns at abusing me, pronouncing me a vile, godless man." Young warned his followers the Presbyterian missionary would "send sorrow and distress into many a mother's heart, and rob many a home of its virtue if he is allowed to remain here," he said. To this, Apostle George Q. Cannon reportedly added "he would rather his children should never know their A B C's than be taught by a Gentile."[50] But reports that McMillan carried arms to protect himself, even into the pulpit, were probably exaggerated for their fund-raising value in the East.

Even so, it was an exciting time for the missionary as well as for parents of his Mormon students. When the parents were told to take their children out of his school, they would usually obey just long enough for their leaders to look the other way, then send them right back. Opposition seemed only to spread the word and promote the demand for more schools. In 1880 McMillan replaced Jackson as mission superintendent and developed a plan for primary schools in every part of the territory.

Most of the teachers were single women who volunteered from a desire to minister to the children of polygamous families. "Night before last fourteen young ladies reached Salt Lake from the East," announced

[48]For more on this frontier missionary, see Stewart, *Sheldon Jackson: Pathfinder and Prospector of the Missionary Vanguard in the Rocky Mountains and Alaska.*

[49]Zimmerman, "The Long Journey," remarks on March 13, 1994, before the Presbyterian Church of Springville, Utah.

[50]For McMillan's account of his adventures in Mt. Pleasant, see *The Salt Lake Daily Tribune,* April 23, 1876.

The Salt Lake Tribune in 1880, "employed to come here by the Presbyterian Church Missionary Society." Describing them as "a most bright, earnest and winsome company," the paper said the new arrivals were to go directly to their assigned locations, "and ten new schools will at once be opened."[51]

By 1885 there were thirty-one Presbyterian day schools in Utah with fifty-three teachers and an attendance of about nine hundred, "75 per cent of them being of Mormon parentage," Rev. Robert McNiece told Governor Eli H. Murray. The schools were "practically free," McNiece said, and nothing of a denominational character was taught. "They are simply American schools."[52]

This approach was also followed in 1879 by the members of the Congregational Church, led by Col. C. G. Hammond of Chicago, who formed the New West Education Commission to renew the faith's push to plant schools in Utah. By 1885 more than 1,900 students, about two-thirds from Mormon backgrounds, were enrolled in twenty-eight New West Schools. There were also that year thirteen Methodist schools with 865 enrolled, five Episcopal with 795 students, four Catholic with 610, and two Baptist schools with 205 scholars.[53]

The magnitude of the evangelical Christian commitment to Utah education, prior to the establishment of free public schools in 1890, is shown by the estimate that some fifty thousand children, mostly from Mormon families, gained some education in mission schools.[54] Ironically, the returns from this twenty-five-year effort did not include many conversions by the churches that made it.

In 1894 Congregationalist Hammond spoke for all when he took an honest look at this mission side of the picture: "The major result of the Utah Christian schools appears to be that we are training Mormons to serve as Sunday school teachers, young folk leaders and bishoprics in the Mormon Church. They take our proffered education, but not our religion, and use it to strengthen their own institutions."[55]

---

[51] *The Salt Lake Daily Tribune*, September 17, 1880.

[52] "Annual Report of the Governor of Utah, 1885" in Annual Report of the Department of the Interior, 1885, House Exec. Doc. I (49–I), 1885, Serial 2379, 1043.

[53] Ibid., 1041, 1043.

[54] Lyon, "Evangelical Protestant Missionary Activities in Mormon Dominated Areas," 250.

[55] Ibid., 251.

At the same time, the work of the mission teachers and those who supported them raised the educational level in the territory and paved the way for passage of a true public school law in 1890. It also stimulated a Mormon response to improve education quality and prevent the faith's young members from having to attend schools of other churches.

Utah lawmakers in 1874 took a first step toward a free school system by allocating to schools $15,000 a year for two years. Two years later, they raised this amount to $20,000, created district schools, and empowered elected trustees to collect each year a tax of one-fourth of one percent on taxable property. The earliest territory-wide funding came in 1878 when a tax of "three mills on the dollar for the benefit of district schools," was levied.[56]

In addition, Brigham Young Academy, the forerunner of today's university, was founded at Provo and a similar institution started at Logan in 1875, the same year the predecessors of Westminster College and Wasatch Academy were opened. The educational challenge of the mission schools also buttressed the work of Dr. John Rockey Park, the 36-year-old Mormon educator and physician who became in 1869 president of the University of Deseret, renamed in 1894 the University of Utah, at Salt Lake City.

BIRTH OF POLITICAL PARTIES

On yet another front theocratic rule was contested when the dissident "New Movement" put up posters in Salt Lake City calling for a mass meeting on February 10, 1870, of the "People's Free and Independent Ticket" to name candidates for city elections four days hence. Unwisely, William Godbe's followers headed their announcement: "COME ONE, COME ALL." Hundreds, turned out by the School of the Prophets, invaded the meeting "with screams and yells jumping over and breaking the seats in the most reckless manner."[57] Led by Territorial Marshal John D. T. McAllister, the unruly arrivals voted the new party's regular chair-

[56]*Laws, Memorials, and Resolutions of the Territory of Utah, Passed at the 23rd Session of the Legislative Assembly, 1878,* 11. Also see Ivins, "Free Schools Come to Utah," 321–42; Moffit, *The History of Public Education in Utah,* 113–14; and "Annual Report of the Commissioner of Schools for Utah Territory, 1888," Sen. Exec. Doc. 87 (50–2), 1889, Serial, 2612, 2–4.

[57]*Mormon Tribune,* February 12, 1870.

man, Eli Kelsey, out of office and shouted their support for Bishop Jesse Little to replace him. They then proceeded to nominate the candidates already named by the School of the Prophets, headed by Mayor Daniel Wells. They also usurped the name, "People's Party," which afterward became the Mormon political arm, while the opposing movement would go forward as the Liberal Party.

According to one account, the unwelcome intrusion was merely "a practical joke," carried out "in a spirit of merriment" with no desire at all "to intimidate the new party."[58] Innocent or not, it failed either to amuse or frighten at least three hundred or so voters, out of 2,301 casting ballots, who voted for New Movement nominees and believed that "a gross outrage had been perpetrated by the Church officials."[59] Nor was it the first time the established order had faced a political challenge.

Soon after Brigham Young had refused their offer in December 1866 to sell out and leave, a small group of non-Mormon businessmen had decided that if they meant to stay in Utah they should organize and oppose Mormon political control. At the suggestion of Robert Baskin, they chose one of their number, William H. McGrorty, to run for election as delegate to Congress. The appearance of an opposition candidate was not the only reason the vote on February 4, 1867, was noteworthy.

The election that day was scheduled under an act passed by the Legislative Assembly and approved on January 10 by Governor Charles Durkee.[60] Afterward the same body had reconvened on January 21 as the sixth session of the General Assembly of the state of Deseret, created in 1862. After hearing Governor Brigham Young's message, lawmakers of the "ghost government of Deseret" had approved without Governor Durkee's signature a memorial asking Congress to admit the state of Deseret into the Union.[61]

During their session, Deseret's legislators also amended the theoc-

---

[58]Whitney, *History of Utah,* 2:385–86.

[59]*Mormon Tribune,* February 12, 1870.

[60]See "McGrorty vs. Hooper," House Rep. 79 (40–2), 1868, Serial 1358. Charles Durkee, a former U.S. senator from Wisconsin, was appointed governor in July 1865 to succeed James Doty, who died the month before.

[61]See "Memorial of the Legislative Assembly of the Proposed State, for the admission of the State of Deseret into the Union," House Misc. Doc. 26 (40–1), 1867, Serial 1312.

racy's constitution and approved acts to legalize the laws and resolutions they had passed earlier as a territorial body. These included the choice that February, not of a territorial delegate, the office McGrorty ran for, but of "a Representative to Congress," like those from any other state.[62] So the real purpose of the election, announced on January 26 by Daniel Wells as the secretary of state of the self-proclaimed state of Deseret, was to choose a congressman and approve changes in the constitution. The latter redrew the state's borders along present lines, except in the northeast, which was squared off to take in the southwest corner of today's Wyoming, including Evanston and Rock Springs. But looking ahead, the governor's powers still included "commander-in-chief of the naval and military forces."[63]

Again acting as Deseret's secretary of state, Daniel Wells on February 23 announced voter approval of the amended constitution by a margin of 14,005 to 30.[64] McGrorty's Mormon opponent, William H. Hooper, also won overwhelmingly, 15,068 to 105, with six votes going to an otherwise unidentified "Negro Sy."[65] Elected both as the delegate of Utah Territory and the representative of Deseret, Hooper prudently claimed his seat in the former capacity.

Despite his lop-sided defeat, McGrorty contested the election as a means of calling "the attention of Congress and the nation to existing conditions in Utah."[66] Before the U.S. House Committee on Elections, he charged that Hooper represented the institution of polygamy, that the votes cast had outnumbered the legal voters, and that ballots had been cast by proxy for aliens and minors.

While noting "the evils which now exist in this Territory," the committee could find little evidence that the "free exercise of the ballot by the citizens had been prevented by force or fraud."[67] But if Congress rejected McGrorty's attempt to win an election with less than one percent of the vote, it also ignored the theocratic state of Deseret's fourth bid for admission to the Union. And the challenge by the Salt Lake merchant would be only the first of many to come.

[62]Morgan, *The State of Deseret*, 105–07.
[63]House Misc. Doc. 26, 4.
[64]Ibid., 2–8.
[65]House Rep. 79.
[66]Baskin, *Reminiscences of Early Utah*, 23.

Undiscouraged by the outcome, on July 16, 1870, opponents of the Mormon regime, their numbers boosted by the railroad, organized at Corinne the Liberal Party and nominated Civil War veteran George R. Maxwell, register of the land office, to run for delegate to Congress. At its first convention the new party adopted a platform condemning polygamy, denouncing theocratic government, and calling for the development of Utah's mineral resources.

To give their creation the weight of Patrick Connor's national reputation, Liberal Party founders elected the retired general its first chairman, thus adding the title "father of Utah's first political party" to the honors later bestowed on him. But Connor himself would probably agree that the man more deserving the honor would have been the guiding spirit of the opposition political movement, Robert Baskin. Either way, the coming of the railroad and the formation of the Liberal Party introduced an intensifying struggle for political control between the defenders of theocratic and republican systems of government. This increasingly bitter confrontation would be waged for twenty years over polygamy, an issue of morality that would, as with slavery, make the outcome certain.

---

[67]House Rep. No. 79, 11.

Chapter 14

THE IMPENDING CONFLICT

The Lord has revealed the Law on the Patriarchal order of
Marriage & the Lord says we shall be damned if we do not obey
it & Congress says we shall be damned if we do. So it is the
Lord and Congress for it. I would rather obey the Lord than
Congress.

—Wilford Woodruff

No class of persons anywhere should be allowed to treat the
laws of the United States with open defiance and contempt.

—U. S. Grant

To the surprise of Congress, nearly six thousand women of all ages
filled every seat in the old tabernacle at Salt Lake City and stood in the
cold outside on January 13, 1870, to protest proposed legislation to
destroy polygamy and theocratic rule in Utah. Ten days later, Robert N.
Baskin, the former attorney of the slain Dr. John Robinson, testified
before the House Committee on Territories on the need for the draconian bill that he had largely written.[1]

The purpose of the measure, introduced by Congressman Shelby M.
Cullom, an Illinois Republican, was to insure enforcement of the federal
law prohibiting polygamy, the Morrill Act, already on the books.[2] To
accomplish it, the ingeniously crafted Cullom Bill took dead aim at the
theocratic political and judicial system that had allowed Utah courts and
law enforcers to ignore the federal statute ever since it was passed in 1862.

As explained by the sponsor, the proposed measure would, among its
thirty-four provisions:

[1] For Baskin's testimony, see "Execution of the Laws in Utah," House Rep. 21 (41–2), 1870, Serial 1436,
11–19.

[2] Cullom later served as governor of Illinois from 1877 to 1883 and as U.S. senator from that state until
1913 when he became a member of the Lincoln Memorial Commission. See Cullom, *Fifty Years in Public Service:
Personal Recollections.* Also see Neilson, *Shelby M. Cullom: Prairie State Republican.*

- Give the U.S. marshal and clerks of the district courts the authority to select grand and petit juries;
- Impose a sentence of five years in prison and up to $5,000 in fines for cohabitation with more than one wife;
- Allow the U.S. marshal to requisition military force to aid him in the performance of his duties;
- Empower the territorial governor to appoint and remove probate judges, justices of the peace, election judges, notaries public, and sheriffs;
- Abolish Utah's "numbered ballot" election law and guarantee that elections would be conducted by secret ballot;
- Repeal the territorial law giving probate courts original jurisdiction, both civil and criminal, and limit the authority of these tribunals to cases involving a maximum of $500;
- Cancel all Utah land laws, such as those giving large land grants to Brigham Young and other Mormon leaders;
- Require the U.S. president "to send a portion of the Army of the United States" to Utah to enforce the law, if necessary, and authorize him to call as many as 40,000 additional troops if needed to carry out this purpose; and
- Repeal "all acts and parts of acts of the United States or of the Legislature of Utah not consistent herewith," including the act creating the territory itself.[3]

Mormon women gathered at Salt Lake City heaped scorn upon such repressive proposals. Unanimously, they branded them "malicious attempts" to subvert religious and civil liberty. They declared themselves to be "united with our brethren" in sustaining polygamy as "the only reliable safeguard of female virtue and innocence." With "laudable womanly jealousy," they would simply ignore any act they deemed unconstitutional.[4] Significantly, they also resolved that should the Cullom Bill became a law, "by which we shall be disfranchised as a Territory," they would "exert all our power and influence to aid in the support of our own State government."[5] This vow reflected Brigham Young's view that if the territory's organic act was altered or repealed, Utah would revert to its original government created in 1849, the sovereign state of Deseret.

---

[3]For the text of the proposed bill and Cullom's explanation of each of its sections before the U.S. House of Representatives, see *Congressional Globe* (41–2), February 17, 1870, Vol. 160, 1367–73.

[4]Tullidge, *History of Salt Lake City*, 438–39.

[5]Ibid.

If public support of Mormon women for polygamy took Congress by surprise, it was not the only eye-opener the theocratic territory would deliver to the anti-polygamy crusaders who saw themselves as the saviors of Utah women from oppression and religious bondage. In 1869 Indiana Congressman George Julian introduced a bill "to discourage polygamy in Utah by granting the right of suffrage to the women of that Territory."[6] Predictable it was that women's suffrage societies in the East would quickly endorse the measure. But it was entirely unexpected when William Hooper, Utah's delegate to Congress, told the sponsor he, too, thought it might be a good idea. What happened next looked like an ingenious ploy to head off punitive federal legislation.

In their next session, Utah legislators enacted just such a law giving women the right at age 21 to "vote at any election." Territorial Secretary Stephen A. Mann signed the act on February 12, 1870, against the will of the newly appointed governor, J. Wilson Shaffer, who had not yet arrived in Utah but questioned Mann's authority to approve it.[7] Nine days later, it was adopted by the last known legislative session of the "ghost government" of the state of Deseret, which met in the City Hall, and approved by Governor Brigham Young.[8]

By this singular route Utah became only the second state or territory to give women the right to vote, trailing Wyoming by just two months. But it was first in the nation to provide the chance. Just two days after the act was approved, Seraph Young, a niece of Brigham Young, cast her ballot during municipal elections in Salt Lake City to become the first woman in the U.S. legally to vote.

While Utah was the first to open its polls to women, the right to vote came too late to head off passage of the Cullom Bill by the U.S. House of Representatives. When House members overwhelmingly approved the measure on March 13, they sent shock waves throughout the terri-

---

[6]*Congressional Globe* (41–1), March 15, 1869, Vol. 158, 72.

[7]Appointed governor in January 1870, Shaffer on July 7 urged that Mann be removed and told President Grant that his advisers were of the opinion that the office of secretary was vacant, "and all official acts performed by Mr. Mann are void." What this opinion was based on is unknown since Mann was notified of his appointment as secretary on June 1, 1869. See Shaffer to Grant, July 7, 1870; and Treasury Comptroller to Mann, June 1, 1869, Territorial Papers, Utah Series.

[8]For "Governor" Young's message to the General Assembly of the State of Deseret requesting lawmakers to "adopt and sanction the laws which have been enacted by the Legislative Assembly of the Territory of Utah, that the same may be valid and of full force in the State of Deseret," see *Deseret News*, February 23, 1870, 30.

tory and touched off a desperate effort to stop enactment of the unpopular measure by the U.S. Senate.

At the call of their leaders a great multitude gathered at Temple Square on March 31, filling every window, seat, and aisle in the tabernacle and spilling out over the spacious grounds. Chosen to preside was Daniel Wells. After speeches by Apostles Orson Pratt, John Taylor, George Q. Cannon, and others, a memorial to Congress was read and unanimously adopted by the vast assemblage.

More than ninety percent of the people in Utah were "members of the Church of Jesus Christ of Latter-day Saints, usually called Mormons," it began. They had settled the territory and "reclaimed the desert," Congress was reminded. In so doing, it went on, they had "brought into being a new State to add lustre to the national galaxy of our glorious Union."[9] Then came the crux of what seemed to be an unresolvable conflict: "The people who have done this, are believers in the principle of plural marriage or polygamy, not simply as an elevating social relationship and a preventive of many terrible evils which afflict our race, but as a principle revealed by God, underlying our every hope of eternal salvation and happiness in heaven."

"Let the revelation appear in the eyes of others as it may," it continued, "to us it is a divine command, of equal force with any ever given by the creator of the world to his children in the flesh."

The appeal denounced the Cullom Bill for violations of the Constitution, not only regarding the free exercise of religion, but of many other safeguards of individual rights. It protested, not without some irony, that the proposed law would create a "centralized despotism," leaving the "lives, liberties and human rights" of the people "subject to the caprice of one man, and that man selected and sent here from afar."[10]

Support for the campaign to stop the Cullom Bill came soon from an unexpected quarter. Members of the "New Movement," which numbered many former Mormons who had married more wives than one before they left the church or were excommunicated, took alarm at the severity of the measure Baskin had drawn up. At their urging, William Godbe went to Washington, D.C., to meet with President Grant and

[9]"Memorial Adopted by Citizens of Salt Lake City, Utah Territory," Sen. Misc. Doc. 112 (41–2), 1870, Serial 1408. Also see Tullidge, *History of Salt Lake City*, 458–63.
[10]Ibid.

congressional leaders, including Congressman Cullom, and actively lobby against the proposed law.

Despite majority support in the Senate, the bill that caused so loud an uproar quietly died in the Committee on Territories when Chairman James W. Nye, U.S. senator from Nevada, for reasons never revealed, failed to bring it before his panel.[11] What caused Nye's failure was "a matter of conjecture," Baskin said without offering an opinion years later.[12] But the author of the controversial bill would see to it that its provisions would be enacted piecemeal in other legislation over the next seventeen years.

DEMISE OF THE NAUVOO LEGION

Having subdued the South with military power, U. S. Grant in 1870 tried to bring a defiant territory under the control of the national government using the political power of his office as president. On January 17 he named as governor of Utah a former military officer who had some experience in dealing with rebellious people.

J. Wilson Shaffer of Illinois was 42 years old at the time of his appointment, an active Methodist, iron-willed and patriotic, but also "a brave and earnest man, unselfish and generous in his impulses."[13] During the Civil War he had served at New Orleans as chief of staff to Union General Benjamin F. Butler, better known to the people of that occupied city as "Beast Butler." He was also dying of tuberculosis.

Shaffer accepted the honor reluctantly but with resolve to fulfill a last opportunity of service to his country. Allegedly, he vowed, "Never after me, by God, shall it be said that Brigham Young is governor of Utah." If he actually said this, which is doubtful, he was soon disabused of any notions of his own importance in the place to which he was sent. Within two weeks after arriving on March 19, he informed Secretary of State Hamilton Fish that "unless something like the Cullom or Cragin bill

---

[11]Nye's public papers have never been found. The first governor of Nevada Territory, he was considered by some to be a "comic opera buffoon" but was also a shrewd politician and spellbinding storyteller who, it was said, "wore his principles lightly and honestly mistook his emotions for convictions." During the impeachment of President Johnson, it was also said his vote "was publicly offered for sale." See Samson, "Sagebrush Falstaff: A Biographical Sketch of James Warren Nye."

[12]See Baskin, *Reminiscences of Early Utah*, 30.

[13]Whitney, *History of Utah*, 2:488.

passes, the U.S. Officers will be powerless."[14] The governor had little
time left to act in his new office, and it was shortened still further when
his wife died that spring in Illinois, requiring him to go home for a
period of some weeks. On his return in July, he moved to strike a blow
in the only areas open to him.

First he asked President Grant to get rid of the offending secretary
who had signed the suffrage law, Stephen A. Mann, and the district
court justice who had commissioned him, Charles C. Wilson. Grant
replaced Mann with Vernon Vaughn of Alabama and named to take
Wilson's place as chief justice of the territorial supreme court a stiff
New Yorker, James McKean, who would become one of Utah's most
controversial figures.

Shaffer moved next to take control of the Utah theocracy's mailed
fist, the Nauvoo Legion. His opening came when General Wells on
August 16 scheduled a three-day muster before November 1 to drill and
complete rolls. Using his authority as commander in chief, Shaffer on
September 15 issued proclamations naming Patrick Connor major general of the command and prohibiting "all musters, drills or gatherings
of militia of the Territory of Utah," except by his orders.[15] In a letter
signed as "Lieut.-Gen. Com'g Militia, U. T.," Wells "respectfully"
requested Shaffer to suspend his proclamation until November 20 to
allow the completion of muster rolls as called for by law. He received a
biting response, literally dictated as the iron-willed Shaffer knew he was
dying.

"As the laws of the United States provide for but one Lieutenant-
General, and as the incumbent of that office is the distinguished Philip
H. Sheridan, I shall certainly be pardoned for recognizing no other," he
began. Pointedly addressing Wells as "Mr.," the governor went on to
stamp the Nauvoo Legion "an unlawful military system" that had
existed without authority and "in defiance of Federal officials." Without
his approval, Wells had issued an order in the "assumed capacity of lieu-
tenant-general," he said, and now you "virtually ask me to ratify it." This
he refused to do. But his hope that his reply would "supercede the neces-

---

[14]Shaffer to Fish, April 1, 1870, Territorial Papers, Utah Series.
[15]Tullidge, *History of Salt Lake City*, 483.

sity of any further exchange on the subject," only showed how little he knew about Utah.[16]

In a lengthy response addressed to the *Deseret News*, Wells mounted a verbal defense of his position. Correctly, he called attention to the federal law, enacted twenty-six years before, providing that all general militia officers "shall be elected by the people" in keeping with laws enacted by the legislatures of the states and territories. Since he had been chosen "by the unanimous voice of the people," under Utah's singular election law, Wells argued his rank was fully legitimate.[17]

His counterattack was meant for public consumption or the historical record, however, not the eyes of the man whose action had provoked it. Before it was published on November 2, Vernon Vaughn, Utah secretary and now acting governor, had sent a wire to President Grant. "It is my painful duty to inform you that his Excellency Governor Shaffer died at five oclock this morning," it said on October 31.[18] Shaffer drew his last breath less than four days after dictating his letter to Wells.

On November 12 Wells issued a general order postponing until further notice general musters in military districts where they "have not already been held." This directive was given over his signature as "Lieut.-Gen. Com'g N. L. Militia, U. T." to make clear the action was taken under his authority, not in compliance with an appointed governor's proclamation. But Shaffer's last official act would prove conclusive.

The following year, when plans for the July 4 parade in Salt Lake City included Nauvoo Legion marchers, Utah Secretary George A. Black, Shaffer's former scribe, acting in the absence of the latest governor, George L. Woods, renewed the ban against militia musters, drills, or parades. Moreover, Black asked Col. Regis de Trobriand at Camp Douglas to back the order with troops. The touchy French officer commanding the base had crossed verbal swords with Shaffer the year before over the misconduct of drunken soldiers at Provo but grudgingly complied.[19]

---

[16]Ibid., 484–85.

[17]For the reply by Wells and earlier correspondence, see *Deseret News*, November 2, 1870, 453–54.

[18]Vaughn to Grant, October 31, 1870, Territorial Papers, Utah Series.

[19]George Black was Governor Shaffer's former personal secretary. For more on the Provo disorder and clash between Shaffer and the French officer, see Grandstaff, "General Regis de Trobriand, the Mormons, and the U.S. Army at Camp Douglas, 1870–71," 204–23.

While some of its seven thousand or so officers and men kept it alive for a time, thus ended without fanfare one of the most unusual commands in American military annals. Over three decades of service, the Nauvoo Legion had fought the final battles around Nauvoo, protected the Mormon migration to Utah, stopped an American army on the high plains, fought three Indian wars and countless skirmishes, and marred an otherwise remarkable record at Mountain Meadows.

If the man who caused its eventual demise was uncompromising, every bit as determined, if somewhat less successful, was another of President Grant's appointees who came that same year.

Judge James McKean

Utah had taken a heavy toll on federal judges by the time James B. McKean, 49, arrived in Washington, D.C., in 1870 to tell President Grant why he hesitated to accept the appointment as chief justice of the territory's supreme court. "I am a man of positive character, Mr. President," he said. In trying to do his duty, he went on, he might become embroiled with the Mormons. "No means exist there to execute my decrees, and thus I may stir up trouble to no purpose and bring humiliation upon myself," he predicted truly.[20]

McKean was born in Vermont, the son of a Methodist clergyman, and educated in upstate New York. He had taught moral philosophy at a private high school and served two years in Congress before resigning to recruit a regiment, the 77th New York Volunteers, and serve as its colonel in the Civil War. Contracting typhoid fever on Virginia's peninsula, he had been sent home to die but managed to recover and take up the practice of law in New York.

Now, after listening impassively, Grant urged him to accept the Utah judicial post. The president had chosen McKean, he said, for his firmness of will. "Go there and make the laws respected," Grant vowed, "and if civil process will not restrain lawlessness, I will support you with the army of the United States." Supposing the promise, "coming from a soldier," amounted to something, McKean bitterly said later, he accepted the position.[21]

---

[20] *The Salt Lake Daily Tribune*, January 7, 1879.   [21] Ibid.

The Englebrecht Case

Shortly before he arrived, the long-standing jurisdictional feud between Utah's duplicating probate and district courts had been resolved for a time in favor of the district courts. Chief Justice Charles Wilson, McKean's predecessor, had ruled that U.S. Marshal J. Milton Orr, not his territorial opposite, J. D. T. McAllister, was the proper executive officer of the district courts. New associate justices Obed Strickland and Cyrus Hawley had decided the probate courts had no criminal jurisdiction and had set aside the territorial law on the selection of grand juries.

Under these rulings Judge McKean found a non-Mormon grand jury, impaneled by the U.S. marshal, when he opened the district court that September in Salt Lake City. The first case he would hear was a suit against Alderman Jeter Clinton and the city police brought by one Paul Englebrecht and his attorney, Robert Baskin, for malicious destruction of property. If the outcome would be historic, the case itself was commonplace. Englebrecht and his partners were wholesale liquor dealers in Salt Lake City who had stocked inebriants worth some $20,000 but disputed the levy imposed by the city for a license. Since they had no permit to do business, Police Chief Andrew Burt and as many as eighteen policemen invaded their store and smashed every bottle and barrel. The unannounced intruders poured the costly spirits, to the undoubted dismay of some, into the muddy street.

Defendants argued the grand jury had been chosen in violation of territorial law but were overruled. In keeping with earlier decisions by the associate justices, Judge McKean ruled the U.S. marshal was the only officer of the court with authority to select grand and petit juries.[22] With Mormons excluded, the latter panel in November 1870 awarded treble damages of $59,063.25. The case was appealed to the territorial high court where Judges Strickland, Hawley, and McKean predictably upheld their own earlier rulings.

As the case was being appealed to the U.S. Supreme Court, McKean's judicial crusade was put on hold by Territorial Auditor William Clayton, who refused to pay district court expenses. Utah law required such costs to be paid through the territorial marshal who had been ruled no longer

[22]For Judge McKean's ruling see *Deseret News*, September 28, 1870, 403.

an officer of the court. Without an appropriation by Congress, funds to keep the courts open had to be found from private sources. U.S. Marshal M. T. Patrick reportedly put up $8,000 of his own money.

Possibly inspiring such altruism was the confession about this time of the most feared man in the territory, 56-year-old William A. Hickman. This notorious killer surfaced to inform Robert Baskin about some of his crimes and implicate Brigham Young and others in murder. When Baskin handed a copy of Hickman's statement to U.S. Attorney Charles Hempstead, the former adjutant of the California Volunteers suddenly remembered what had happened to Dr. Robinson and prudently decided to resign. Judge McKean now named Baskin as his acting replacement.

When Baskin took this appointment, itself of dubious legality, the 33-year-old Ohioan was "frowsy, cool and red-bearded," according to one outside correspondent.[23] That he was also absolutely fearless was demonstrated by the shocking series of events he put in motion.

On October 2, 1871, Marshal Patrick put Brigham Young under arrest for "lewd and lascivious cohabitation." The indictment had been issued by a non-Mormon grand jury under a territorial law enacted in 1852. The Mormon leader was allowed to remain in his own home. The next day, Daniel Wells was also arrested on the same charge and released on $5,000 bail. Less than a week later, Apostle George Q. Cannon and Henry Lawrence, a member of the "New Movement," were also indicted.

If his tormentors expected the "Lion of the Lord" to roar at the impertinence of his arrest, they were disappointed. Brigham Young, apparently in ill health, on October 9 appeared quietly in McKean's court, which was on the second story of a livery stable on Second South, where proceedings were occasionally broken by a "bray of delight" by a "polygamous jackass."[24] He was attended by his attorneys who included, among others, Charles Hempstead and former "acting governor" Stephen Mann. Between interruptions from the stable, Judge McKean made the ruling for which he would be best remembered: "While the case at bar is called The People *versus* Brigham Young, its other and real title is Federal Authority *versus* Polygamic Theocracy."[25] While attorneys prepared for trial, another case involving polygamy came before the judge.

---

[23]Cincinnati *Commercial*, as quoted in Whitney, *History of Utah*, 2:623.

[24]Whitney, *History of Utah*, 2:622. Judge McKean had to hold court in the livery stable because he was unable to find anyone in Salt Lake City who would rent to him a suitable location.

[25]Ibid., 600.

Thomas Hawkins and his wife were married in England before join-ing the Mormon church and coming to Salt Lake City, where they had worked hard and saved their money to build a modest dwelling. There they had lived happily until he took a second wife. That was bad enough, but what made the new relationship truly intolerable to his first wife was that the wall that divided her bedchamber from the second's was so thin she had to listen to all that transpired at night between the loving pair. When the unhappy Englishwoman told her story to acting U.S. Attor-ney Baskin, he urged her to charge her husband with adultery under a different section of the same law he was bringing to bear against Young and others. She readily agreed to testify against her wayward spouse, as the territorial law allowed, even though the maximum punishment for this offense was twenty years in jail and a $1,000 fine. It took the non-Mormon jury just twenty-four hours to hear the case and find Hawkins guilty.

On the day Judge McKean imposed the minimum sentence of three years in prison and a $500 fine, October 28, 1871, the first Mormon was convicted, in effect, of polygamy, ironically under an obscure terri-torial law against adultery, not the federal act prohibiting bigamy. But this was not what stunned Mormons and non-Mormons alike on this eventful Friday and sent a shock wave spreading across the territory. That same day, Mayor Daniel Wells was arrested for the murder of one Richard Yates during the so-called "Utah War" of 1857. The indict-ment was based on the confession of William A. Hickman, who admit-ted killing the Green River trader for selling supplies to the U.S. Army.[26] Not to waste powder, the notorious killer had struck the trader in the head with an ax. But he said he did it on orders from higher authorities.

Among those implicated was Mormon attorney and Nauvoo Legion Adjutant General Hosea Stout, 61, soon after arrested and held at Camp Douglas. U.S. Marshal Patrick also took William Kimball into custody for alleged involvement in Hickman's murder of an Aiken party member in 1857. And Robert T. Burton was indicted for the murder of Isabella Bowman during his 1862 attack on the Morrisite camp in South Weber. Marshal Patrick even attempted to arrest Brigham Young himself in connection with these charges, but the Mormon leader, reportedly notified, had shortly before left the capital to spend time in

---

[26]For his full confession, see Hickman, *Brigham's Destroying Angel.*

the more congenial climate of Utah's Dixie. His departure did not slow
Baskin's judicial assault.

On November 30 new U.S. Attorney George Caesar Bates came from
Chicago to take over the prosecution. He soon announced that on January 9 he would try Brigham Young for murder and hired Baskin as an
associate. Right after that, Police Chief Burt, Officer Brigham Y. Hampton, and four others were arrested for the 1866 murder of Dr. Robinson. They were indicted on the word of a transient who would change
his story several times before being arrested and locked up himself for
alleged grand larceny.

Meanwhile at St. George, a source of inspiration referred to by
Brigham Young as "The Light," prompted the Mormon leader to come
back and face his accusers. After a wearing mid-winter journey, he
appeared quietly in January 1872 in McKean's court with his lawyers
and a number of friends. On the testimony of his physician, Dr. W. F.
Anderson, he was allowed to remain under guard in his own home,
pending trial.

By this time prosecutor George C. Bates had begun to lose his nerve.
"Had I dreamed what I should be called upon to do," he told the U.S.
attorney general, "I never should have come here."[27] To the disgust of
Baskin, who resigned, Bates asked the judge to put off Young's trial and
began to urge that McKean be replaced by a more moderate jurist. But
his change of heart was not the reason that charges against Young for
"lewd and lascivious cohabitation" and first degree murder would never
come to trial.

1872 BID FOR STATEHOOD

The rulings of appointed judges and the flood of indictments were
alarming reminders of how vulnerable to federal power was a theocratic
territory that was out of step with the rest of the nation. The compulsion to roll forth to universal dominion was giving way to the increasingly urgent need to gain independence and immunity from outside
oppression through statehood. So it was that as Young awaited trial,
Utah legislators in January 1872 enacted a bill calling for the election of
delegates to a fourth constitutional convention and approved an expen-

---

[27]Bates to Williams, January 5, 1872, quoted in Dwyer, *The Gentile Comes to Utah*, 84, n67.

diture of $50,000 to finance the gathering. Like his predecessor John Dawson, the territory's latest governor, 39-year-old George Woods, a raspy-voiced Missourian, vetoed both measures on the ground that it was up to Congress to confer such power through an enabling act.

"To become a State in the Union is not a *right*," the governor reminded territorial lawmakers, "but a *privilege*." He said that "before any convention should be called, Utah should place herself in harmonious relations with the General Government," presumably by obeying the law against polygamy.[28] But the convocation went ahead anyway on the basis of joint resolutions of the legislature.

On February 19 delegates from around the territory gathered at Salt Lake City to approve a constitution and ask Congress to enroll Deseret "as a free and sovereign state" in the Union of American states. Calling the territorial form of government a "colonial" system by its nature "inherently oppressive and anti-republican," the latest memorial included the signatures of nine respected non-Mormon delegates.[29] Based on Nevada's constitution, the latest founding document held out to Congress an invitation to insert a prohibition against polygamy. Its ordinance of adoption said that "such terms, if any, as may be prescribed by Congress as a condition for the admission," would become a part of the document, if approved by the people.[30] A delegation of three, George Q. Cannon, Thomas Fitch, a political opportunist from Nevada, and former Acting Governor Frank Fuller, was dispatched to Washington, D.C., to help territorial delegate William Hooper present the petition.

Not far behind this trio came another delegation bearing to Congress a counter petition, signed by more than 2,700 citizens of the territory, opposing statehood under the name of Deseret or any other. Calling the majority "antagonistic to the fundamental ideas of free government" because they "believe in one supreme *political* as well as religious head," the memorial held that most of Utah's people were "incapable of comprehending, much less of maintaining, a republican government."[31] The petition included three dozen affidavits of persons who had left the Mormon faith either by choice or excommunication. Of this number,

---

[28]Journal History, January 27 and February 15, 1872.

[29]See "Admission of Utah into the Union," House Misc. Doc. 165 (42–2), 1872, Serial 1526.

[30]Ibid., 5.

[31]See "Memorial of Citizens of Utah, Against the admission of that Territory as a State," House Misc. Doc. 208 (42–2), 1872, Serial 1527.

twenty-nine were foreign-born, with some twenty-two from England or Scotland. Common to many was the belief of 64-year-old Thomas Brown, former Southern Indian Mission clerk, who feared statehood would threaten the safety of "apostates" and non-Mormons and allow murderers to go free.[32]

Among other concerns, the Englishman named inferior schools, a university "existing in name only," and no "asylums, hospitals, or homes for the afflicted, aged, and poor." James Stevens, 45, said he and his wife had been cut off for providing room and board to a non-Mormon supreme court chief justice. Marsenas Cannon, 59, a native American, protested "the system of marking and numbering votes so that they can know how everyone votes." And 49-year-old John Groves claimed he had been excommunicated for voting against Mayor Daniel Wells after being told to do so.[33]

Significantly, "New Movement" member Eli B. Kelsey, who had joined the faith in England nearly thirty years before, swore that Mormon leaders were committed to "building up a 'kingdom of God' upon the American continent." This monarchy he described as "a literal kingdom," exercising "absolute power over the consciences and domestic affairs of its subjects."[34]

Whether it tipped the scales is unknown, but it is at least certain the opposing petition was among the reasons that Congress spurned Utah's latest bid for statehood.

Englebrecht Decision

The Liberal Party emissaries who carried the memorial to the nation's capital, Robert Baskin, Joseph Walker, and Henry Lawrence, arrived too late to join pro-statehood delegates on April 15 at the U.S. Supreme Court to hear the ruling on the Englebrecht case. But in the courtroom that day was Judge James McKean who sat stiff and stunned as the high court's pronouncement was given. In Utah, it touched off rejoicing as the news came in over the wire to the Salt Lake Telegraph Office:

> The judgment of the Supreme Court of Utah in the case of Englebrecht vs Clinton, Mormon test case, was reversed by the Supreme Court of the

[32]Ibid., 63–65.   [33]Ibid., 61–82.   [34]Ibid., 75, 76.

United States today. Jury unlawfully drawn, summonses invalid; proceedings ordered dismissed. Decision unanimous. All indictments quashed.[35]

In its unanimous ruling the U.S. Supreme Court held that the jury in the Englebrecht liquor case had been illegally selected by the U.S. marshal in violation of the 1859 territorial law, amended in 1870. This required the territorial marshal to summon members of grand and petit juries and specified the manner in which jurors would be chosen by the marshal and clerk of the county, or probate, court. That process, said the high court, was "obligatory on the district courts of the territory."[36] Moreover, in assuming it was a federal bench governed by acts of Congress, Judge McKean's Third District court had "erred both in its theory and in its action," the decision held. While conceding that territorial judges were appointed by the president under an act of Congress, the court said this did not make Utah's district or supreme courts "courts of the United States." Instead it ruled they were "the legislative courts of the territory."[37]

In any other territory the ruling would have made little more than a procedural difference. But in Utah it would disembowel for all intents and purposes the district courts and make it impossible ever to enforce the Morrill law against polygamy which had been in force and willfully ignored for ten years. That is why a Republican president and Congress, resolved to destroy the marriage practice, could never let the decision stand.

In the meantime U.S. Attorney Bates instructed his deputy to obtain a court order to discharge all defendants held by the U.S. marshal who according to the decision had been unlawfully arrested. Among those eventually set free were Thomas Hawkins, charged by his wife with adultery, and "Bill" Hickman, whose confession probably failed to mention at least a few of the men he had killed.

The first to go free was Brigham Young, who was being held at home. Probate Court Justice Elias Smith decided not to wait for a discharge order, but released the Mormon leader on a writ of *habeas corpus* under questionable legal powers bestowed by the territorial legislature. Even the U.S. Supreme Court had allowed it was not in the power of this legislative body "to confer judicial authority upon any other courts than those authorized by the organic law."[38]

---

[35]Whitney, *History of Utah*, 2:686.
[36]Salient points of the decision are quoted in Whitney, *History of Utah*, 2:681–85. [37]Ibid.

1872 Election Contest

Undaunted by the Supreme Court ruling, the Liberal Party in 1872 chose the registrar of the Utah land office, a crippled Civil War veteran, as its candidate in the August election for delegate to Congress. A colonel at age 22, George R. Maxwell of the First Michigan Cavalry Volunteers had been wounded seven times, five by minie balls, all in joints, and twice by saber cuts. His left knee was shattered in the war's last battle, at Five Forks, Virginia.[39]

Maxwell moved painfully with a limp, but he readily took on the Union's theocratic adversary in the political arena, where, like others, he found himself vastly outnumbered by votes for the Mormon People's Party candidate, George Q. Cannon, 20,969 to 1,942. Even so, the former "thunderbolt of Sheridan" refused to quit the field. Instead, he contested the election and claimed the seat in Congress on twelve grounds, starting with the charge that Cannon had not won "a majority of legal votes cast in a legal manner." In a written response the apostle rebutted each of these charges, except one. He frankly admitted ballots were "numbered and deposited in the ballot-boxes by the judges of the election, as they were received from the voters, and that the clerks at the several election precincts then wrote the name of the elector on the poll-list and opposite it the number of his vote." But he said this was done to conform with territorial law, not "for the purpose of intimidation." [40]

Cannon further denied that he was "now living with four wives, or that I am living and cohabiting with any wives, in defiant or wilful violation of the law of Congress of 1862, entitled 'An act to prohibit polygamy in the Territories.'"[41] If disingenuous, the statement may have been technically true since he then apparently had only three wives and did not again marry a fourth, the sister of his first wife, until a decade later.[42] But his words would come back against him in the future. Meanwhile the House committee accepted Cannon's defense at face value. It denied Maxwell's claim to a seat in the House of Representatives and

---

[38]Ibid.

[39]For more on Maxwell, see his obituary in the *Deseret News*, July 2, 1889, and the tribute in *The Salt Lake Daily Tribune*, July 3, 1889.

[40]"Contested Election, George R. Maxwell vs. George Q. Cannon," House Misc. Doc. 49 (43–1), 1873, Serial 1617.

resolved that "George Q. Cannon was elected and returned as a Delegate for the Territory of Utah."[43]

PRESIDENT GRANT ACTS

As the capable Apostle Cannon began his work in the nation's capital, on February 17, 1873, President Grant moved to overturn the Supreme Court's ruling on the Englebrecht case. In a special message to Congress, he warned of the "condition of affairs" in Utah and the dangers likely to arise from "a threatened conflict between the Federal and Territorial authorities."

Never was it intended to give the territorial legislature the power to increase the jurisdiction of probate courts and "take the administration of the law out of the hands of the judges appointed by the President or to interfere with their actions," he said. And if the selection of jurors was left to local authorities, he went on, it would be futile to enforce any laws "which interfere with local prejudices or provide for the punishment of polygamy or any of its affiliated vices or crimes." Further, Grant said, Utah lawmakers had "greatly embarrassed" U.S. courts and interfered with the administration of justice by conferring criminal jurisdiction and the power to issue writs of *habeas corpus* on the probate courts. "Manifestly the legislature of the Territory can not give to any court whatever the power to discharge by *habeas corpus* persons held by or under process from the courts created by Congress," he said.

President Grant made clear that the failure of lawmakers to address these problems might make "military interference necessary—a result I should greatly deprecate." He urged Congress to pass legislation that would enable Utah's district courts "to proceed with independence and efficiency in the administration of law and justice."[44] The issue would be joined in the courts.

---

[41]Ibid., 5.

[42]At the time, Cannon's wives included Elizabeth Hoagland, Eliza Lamercia Tenney, and Martha Telle, to whom he was married in 1854, 1865, and 1868, respectively. A fourth wife, Susanne De La Mare, returned to the Isle of Jersey where she died in 1862. He later defied anti-polygamy laws to marry Emily Hoagland in 1882 and Caroline Partridge Young, a daughter of Brigham Young, in 1884.

[43]House Misc. Doc. 49, 10.

[44]"Special Message by President U. S. Grant, February 14, 1873," Richardson, *A Compilation of the Messages and Papers of the Presidents, 1789–1897,* 7:208–11.

Englishman George Reynolds became "first among
the polygamous martyrs" when the U.S. Supreme
Court upheld the 1862 Morrill Act.
Courtesy, LDS Archives.

Chapter 15

A TIME OF TRIALS

Our crime has been: We married women instead of seducing
them; we reared children instead of destroying them; we desire
to exclude from the land prostitution, bastardy and infanticide.
—George Q. Cannon

To the disappointment of Liberal Party members, the initial response
of Congress to President Grant's call for new legislation was less than the
comprehensive assault on Utah's theocratic form of government they
wanted. Instead the new law appeared to reflect a continuing inability to
understand either the intensity of Mormon convictions or the differences
between this prickly territory and the rest of the nation. It did, however,
begin a time when unresolved issues were at last heard in the courts.

Introduced by Rep. Luke Poland, former Vermont Supreme Court
chief justice, the carefully crafted Poland Act, approved on June 23,
1874, overruled the U.S. Supreme Court's Englebrecht decision but did
little more. In so doing it enacted into federal law the opinions of virtually every appointed district judge to serve in Utah since the territory
was founded in 1850, including Judge Cradlebaugh and the troublesome
Judge McKean and his associates on the Utah Supreme Court.

Among its provisions the Poland Act stripped probate, or county,
courts of the powers so liberally bestowed by territorial lawmakers.
Restoring the intent of the organic act, the new law limited probate courts
to the settlement of estates and "like matters," and allowed the Mormon
benches "no civil, chancery, or criminal jurisdiction whatever." It made
clear that "exclusive original jurisdiction" belonged to the district courts.

The 1874 act additionally gave U.S. marshals and attorneys sole
authority to attend the district courts in serving all writs and process
and acting as prosecuting officers. A key provision allowed these federal

officers to appoint as many deputy marshals or assistant prosecutors "as may be necessary." Abolished were the duplicating territorial offices created to frustrate federal authority. Finally, to stop jury-packing by one side or the other, the Poland Act established a procedure for selecting grand and petit juries. District court clerks and probate judges in counties where court was scheduled to be held would alternately select the names of two hundred prospective male jurors "who can read and write in the English language." From this mixed pool, the U.S. marshal was to "fairly draw by lot" the names of grand and petit jurors, giving both sides balanced representation. [1]

Militant opponents of theocratic government in Utah saw the measure as too mild, but moved to make the most of whatever weapons it did give them. An opportunity came right away.

1874 ELECTION "RIOT"

Soon after the creation in 1870 of an independent political party, its chairman, J. Milton Orr, had requested Mayor Daniel Wells to include party members as judges and clerks at an upcoming election for city offices. The mayor's reply had been courteous but firm. The city council had already appointed election judges and clerks who "commanded the confidence of the entire people," he said. But he promised Orr that "every protection will be afforded for voters to vote their respective tickets without partiality or hindrance."[2]

Despite the mayor's assurance, Liberal Party losers in the 1870 and 1872 elections for delegate to Congress had contested the outcomes on the charge that illegal aliens and underage boys and girls had cast votes. With passage of the Poland Act, the party now took a more militant approach to the territorial election on November 3, 1874, to choose a congressional delegate, territorial legislators, and county officers. Leading its attack was newly appointed U.S. Marshal George R. Maxwell, the lame Civil War cavalryman whose instinct on beholding imagined enemies of his country was to sound the charge. Armed with an order from

---

[1]See "An act in relation to courts and judicial officers in the Territory of Utah," *Statutes at Large of the United States,* 18:253–56.

[2]Whitney, *History of Utah,* 2:386. Chosen election officials were Jesse C. Little, Seymour B. Young, and John Needham as judges and F. A. Mitchell and R. V. Morris, clerks.

Judge McKean, the marshal appointed, as the new law allowed, a small army of deputy marshals and stationed them at Salt Lake voting places to protect Liberal Party poll watchers, who loudly challenged the eligibility of those who came to vote.

At most locations the election was orderly, but at City Hall in the third precinct it became a daylong shouting and shoving match between city police and deputy marshals. As hundreds looked on or at times pitched in, opposing officers put each other under arrest and brandished their revolvers as they jousted for the right to enforce the law and ensure peace at the polls.[3]

Before it was over, Mayor Wells himself had been roughed up and Police Magistrate Jeter Clinton, Police Chief Alexander Burt, and officers B. Y. Hampton, Charles Ringwood, and J. Livingstone arrested for "resisting the U.S. Marshal and his deputies in the execution of their duties."[4] In turn, a marshal was jailed, and Clinton, also city judge of voter eligibility, ruled that Marshal Maxwell could not vote because he was not a taxpayer.

If the so-called riot was a portent of changes to come on the election front, no one was seriously hurt in the scuffles. Nor did the first real challenge to the eligibility of many voters seem to affect the outcome. George Q. Cannon of the People's Party buried the Liberal candidate, Robert Baskin, in the race for delegate to Congress by 22,360 to 4,513 votes. Baskin contested the election, alleging Cannon was a polygamist and not a citizen, but he was not successful.[5]

TRIAL OF GEORGE REYNOLDS

The election brawl was not the only event at this time that signaled changing times. Passage of the Poland Act introduced a period of sensational courtroom battles as greater judicial power encouraged U.S. prosecutors to become more aggressive in trying to impose justice for unpunished crimes. For Utah's future, the most notable of such trials

---

[3]It is noteworthy that the so-called "Mormon War" in Missouri began at a polling place in Gallatin when local settlers in 1838 tried to stop Mormons from voting.

[4]*The Salt Lake Daily Tribune*, August 4, 1874.

[5]See "Papers in the Case of Baskin vs. Cannon, as Delegate from Utah Territory," House Misc. Doc. 166 (44–I), 1876, Serial 1702.

was the case of 32-year-old George Reynolds, "the first among the polygamous martyrs."[6]

It is not clear why Reynolds, a private secretary to Brigham Young, was chosen for this distinction. Some later said he agreed to be convicted in return for a light sentence under a deal struck by the U.S. Attorney and LDS church heads to try the constitutionality of the Morrill Act. While evidence is lacking, this claim is not without conjectural support. Encouraged by the Englebrecht ruling, Mormon leaders may have hoped the U.S. Supreme Court would agree with their own belief and rule the measure unconstitutional. Nor was that all. While the law mentioned no statutory limitation, it failed to make clear whether someone who had married more than one wife prior to its approval could be legally prosecuted. Reynolds' marriage on August 3, 1874, to Amelia Jane Schofield—he had wed Mary Ann Tuddenham in 1865, the year he came to Utah—seemed to make him a likely candidate for a test case, since both marriages took place after passage of the Morrill Act in 1862. That he was indicted on October 23, 1874, by a grand jury of mostly Mormons lends credence to the claim of a trial by mutual consent.

The breakdown of the alleged agreement, if one existed, seemed to coincide with the sudden removal of the jurist who was expected to conduct the trial. In an unrelated case, the unpopular Judge McKean on March 11, 1875, apparently offended local sensibilities once too often by sending 73-year-old Brigham Young to prison for twenty-four hours for failing to pay temporary alimony to a young wife, Ann Eliza, who was suing him for divorce.[7] Five days later, President Grant sacked the controversial chief justice.

"Glory Halleluhah the Lord had he[a]rd and answered our Prayers and Judge J. B. McKean is removed out of his place," wrote Apostle Woodruff. "McKean has been the most unjust tyranical Judge ever sent to Utah, and we have prayed for his removal for a long time and the Lord has heard our prayers and answered them, and Praised be [the] name of the Lord."[8]

---

[6]The quote is from Tullidge, *History of Salt Lake City*, 145–48, which presents the story of George Reynolds and the trial from a Mormon point of view.

[7]The drawn-out divorce finally came to trial in April 1877, when the marriage was ruled invalid from the outset and all orders to pay alimony, not yet complied with, were revoked. Young was made to pay court costs.

[8]Kenney, ed., *Wilford Woodruff's Journal*, 6:221. McKean remained in Salt Lake City and practiced law until his death on January 5, 1879, of typhoid fever. He was buried in Mount Olivet Cemetery. For a sympathetic look at the man and his career, see *The Salt Lake Daily Tribune*, January 7, 1879.

Whatever the reason, when the trial opened before a new judge on March 31, there was little sign of any accord to cooperate on a test case, according to Attorney Robert Baskin, who disputed the claim from the beginning. Records of the two trials undergone by George Reynolds appear to support his contention that there was no deal, as do prosecutor William Carey's reports to the U.S. Justice Department. According to Baskin's account, he attended the Salt Lake City trial as an observer in company with Benjamin R. Cowen, assistant secretary of the Interior, who had been sent by President Grant on a fact-finding mission to Utah. During the trial, Cowen reported, Daniel Wells "swore positively" he could not recall performing any such marriage, Apostle Orson Pratt denied any knowledge of it, and the sister of Reynolds, who actually lived with the newlyweds, said she had no idea why the second wife resided in their house.[9]

At this point the prosecutor had exhausted his witnesses, and the trial seemed to be over almost as soon as it had begun. Just then, Baskin passed a card to Marshal Maxwell on which was written, "Tell him to call the second wife." The marshal left the courtroom and returned ten minutes later with Amelia Jane Reynolds. No one had expected her to be called. Said the Interior official, "The ghost of Joe Smith would scarcely have produced a more profound sensation."[10]

Everyone seemed to know that "here was a witness who was bound to tell the truth," Cowen said. And so she did. The defendant's second wife testified that she and Reynolds had been married that August in the Endowment House on Temple Square by Daniel Wells in person.[11] Not only that, said she, but Apostle Pratt had witnessed their marriage, and she had lived in the same house with Reynolds and his sister ever since.

It now appeared the U.S. attorney had surely won his case, except for one problem. If the eight or nine Mormons on the jury had been ordered beforehand to find the defendant not guilty, the surprise testimony of Amelia Jane Reynolds would not affect the verdict, no matter how convincing. As Carey pondered what to do, he was handed another note from Baskin. "Do not give the case to the jury tonight," it said, "but dismiss

---

[9]Cowen to *Cincinnati Commercial*, quoted in Baskin, *Reminiscences of Early Utah*, 64–68.

[10]Ibid.

[11]Ibid. Erected in 1854, the Endowment House was a two-story adobe building in the northwest corner of the Temple Block where marriages were performed prior to completion of the Salt Lake Temple. It was ordered torn down in 1889 by President Wilford Woodruff.

them to their homes."[12] Baskin reasoned the delay would give Mormon leaders a chance to rethink their strategy for the trial. Knowing an observer for President Grant had heard the second wife's persuasive testimony, he figured, they would hesitate to direct a finding of not guilty. Whether jury members had such instructions or received new ones is unknown, but a day later they returned a guilty verdict. Reynolds was sentenced to one year at hard labor in the Utah penitentiary and a fine of $300.

The erudite Englishman appealed his conviction, the first in thirteen years under the Morrill Act, to the Utah Supreme Court, which no longer included the uncompromising Judge James B. McKean. The tribunal, which counted two new justices, reversed the decision on June 19, ruling that the grand jury that indicted Reynolds listed more members than territorial law allowed.

By his second trial Reynolds no longer was willing to be the subject of a test case, if it meant prison, but it was now too late. Although he kept Amelia Jane out of sight, her prior testimony was allowed into evidence. Daniel Wells, Apostle Pratt, and other witnesses recovered their memories, and on December 21, 1875, the jury again found him guilty, a decision that the Utah Supreme Court upheld. This time his sentence, two years at hard labor and a $500 fine, was stiffer than the law allowed.

Even before the verdict was announced, 22,626 women of Utah had signed a petition in support of Reynolds and other polygamists of their faith. Sent on December 17, the memorial asked Congress to repeal the anti-polygamy act of 1862 and the more recent Poland Act. "As mothers and sisters," they entreated for this help "that our sons may be saved from drunkenness and vice and our daughters from the power of the seducer."[13]

Not only did they believe plural marriage, which most of them had adopted, was necessary "in remedying evils and producing good in our present existence," but without it "man cannot hereafter attain to a fullness of exaltation." In addition, they asked Congress to accept Utah as a state and to allow each married woman in Utah to homestead 160 acres in her own name. Their petition ended with the assurance: "Not one of the 22,626 signatures to this memorial has been obtained either by enticement or coercion."[14]

[12]Ibid., 67.

[13]"A Petition of 22,626 Women of Utah," House Misc. Doc. 42 (44–1), 1876, Serial 1698.

[14]Ibid.

THE REYNOLDS DECISION

Now convicted of bigamy, the unassuming husband of two wives became the subject of a sensational case before the U.S. Supreme Court whether he wanted to be or not. A target of intense public interest, he was reviled or praised across the nation when his case was argued on November 14, 1878, before the highest tribunal. Less than two months later, the court handed down its landmark decision, which is still cited today in cases involving the Constitution's "free exercise" of religion clause. The judges ruled unanimously that, first, it was within the legislative power of Congress to prescribe rules of action for the territories, including Utah. As for the First Amendment argument that the trial judge had failed to advise the jury that Reynolds could be acquitted if he had engaged in polygamy as a result of sincere religious conviction, the court went on: "Laws are made for the government of actions, and, while they cannot interfere with mere religious belief and opinions, they may with practices."

"Can a man excuse his practices to the contrary because of his religious belief?" the court asked. "To permit this would make the professed doctrines of religious belief superior to the law of the land, and in effect, to permit every citizen to become a law unto himself." The court's vaguely grounded position that polygamy was unprotected conduct because it was "subversive of good order" has been subject to criticism and debate for over a century.[15]

In keeping with the written opinion of Chief Justice Morrison R. Waite, the high court upheld the constitutionality of the first antibigamy law and sustained the first conviction under the act.[16] Providing a little comfort to Reynolds, it ordered Utah's supreme court to rescind the hard labor provision of his sentence that went beyond the punishment provided by the law. After the historic ruling, over thirty-two thousand citizens of Utah signed a petition to President Rutherford B. Hayes asking him to pardon Reynolds on the ground he had agreed to cooperate in return for the promise of a nominal sentence. An outspo-

---

[15]*United States Reports: Cases Argued and Adjudged in the Supreme Court of the United States,* 1878, 98:145–69. In the only dissenting opinion, Justice Field questioned whether it was proper to allow Amelia Jane's testimony at the first trial to be introduced at the second, but he did not disagree with the rest of the decision.

[16]For a scholarly analysis of the Reynolds decision, see Firmage and Mangrum, *Zion in the Courts, A Legal History of the Church of Jesus Christ of Latter-day Saints, 1830–1900,* 151–59.

ken enemy of polygamy, the president ignored the memorial, and Reynolds had to serve his full term, less 144 days for good behavior.

The U.S. Supreme Court gave the green light for an impending crusade to root out polygamy, but it did not begin to break Mormon resolve to obey a divine ordinance.[17] If Reynolds was punished, said Apostle Cannon, the world would know that in the United States the law is "swiftly invoked to punish religion, but justice goes limping and blindfolded in pursuit of crime."[18] The law would be defied in secret and so successfully obstructed that only one or two others would be found in violation over the next ten years.

DEATH OF BRIGHAM YOUNG

The high court's decision on January 6, 1879 came some twenty months too late for the man, other than Reynolds, who most wanted to learn the outcome of the first constitutional test of the anti-bigamy law that challenged the practice of polygamy.

As was his custom, Brigham Young spent the winter of 1876–77 in southern Utah, where he dedicated the lower story of the temple at St. George. On the way back, he also dedicated the site of the Manti Temple, performing the same ritual at Logan less than a month later. Apparently in good health, although at times weary, he kept a heavy schedule after his 76th birthday on June 1. Then on August 23 he was suddenly stricken with terrific pains in his abdomen accompanied by vomiting and purging. Frequent "laying on of hands" and the care of his physicians failed to arrest the Mormon leader's decline, and six days later he died of an illness diagnosed at the time as "cholera morbus." One student of medical history has since suggested his death may have come from a ruptured appendix, an ailment then unknown. Whether it was appendicitis or an unidentified bowel disorder will probably never be determined.[19]

According to his daughter, Zina, who attended him during his illness,

---

[17]As historian Gustive O. Larson has pointed out, the revelation on celestial and plural marriage was published for the first time in an 1876 edition of the LDS Church's *Doctrine and Covenants*, the same year the Reynolds case was appealed to the Supreme Court, to point up that the practice was a religious doctrine. See Larson, *The "Americanization" of Utah for Statehood*, 78, n34.

[18]Cannon, *A Review of the Decision of the Supreme Court of United States in the Case of Geo. Reynolds vs. the United States*, 52.

[19]See Bush, "Brigham Young in Life and Death: A Medical Overview," 92–103.

Young's last words as he gazed up from the open window by his bed were "Joseph! Joseph! Joseph!" and the look on his face seemed to show that "he was communicating with his beloved friend, Joseph Smith, the Prophet."[20]

While she alone of those present professed to hear him say this, her story rings true because his words so perfectly defined the life and character of the man himself. For Brigham Young was a devoted follower of his faith's founding prophet and considered himself to be an apostle of Joseph Smith, not his equal. While he left a will and instructions on his burial, he undoubtedly hoped to see Smith return with Christ in his own lifetime and believed his task to establish the Kingdom of God was a preparatory step toward this longed for day.

On Saturday, September I, more than twenty-five thousand mourners took a last look at their fallen leader in the tabernacle on Temple Square. As many as twelve thousand crowded the building and grounds the next day to hear Apostle Cannon eulogize him as "the brain, the eye, the ear, the mouth and hand for the entire people of the church." From the founding of territorial government to the shape of the seats the congregation sat on, Cannon said, "Nothing was too small for his mind; nothing was too large."[21]

Predictably, *The Salt Lake Daily Tribune* was less inclined to view such control favorably. Young's "unscrupulous use of the ignorance and credulity of his followers" not only silenced dissent within, the opposition paper said, but had "actually succeeded in preventing the execution of the laws." Still, even the dissenting daily had to concede that the Mormon chief "until the day of his death was *de facto* Governor."[22]

For three decades Brigham Young directed every aspect of the gathering of his people and the creation of hundreds of settlements in the American West. As a leader, he never doubted himself. In time of crisis, such as the migration west and the handcart rescue, his leadership was forceful and certain. Nor did he waver from his purpose to build the Kingdom of God. His drive for economic self-sufficiency revealed nat-

---

[20]This story from Susan Young Gates, *The Life Story of Brigham Young*, is quoted in the best of the faith-promoting biographies, Arrington, *Brigham Young: American Moses*, 399. Also see Whitney, *History of Utah*, 2:845–47, and Roberts, *Comprehensive History*, 5:517–18. An unbiased study of the Mormon leader by a biographer who is as qualified as Arrington and enjoys the same access to LDS church archives remains to be written.

[21]Roberts, *Comprehensive History*, 5:517–18.

[22]*The Salt Lake Daily Tribune*, August 30, 1877.

ural genius in the fields of transportation and communications. That Brigham Young never saw himself as the equal of Joseph Smith may account for possibly his most important legacy. Since the divine guidance he received after Smith's death depended on the faith and obedience of his people, Young introduced the element of reform that continues to strengthen the faith still today.

At the same time, it can be said that his thirty-year battle for supremacy with the national government cost Utah much of its area and delayed for decades its entry into the Union. His ideas on education, including his effort to impose a new alphabet, were harmful to the schooling of a generation or more, despite the work of the missionary teachers and many devoted Mormon educators. And his goal to create a socialistic agrarian economy could only keep many of his people on the edge of poverty.

If he should die anywhere in the mountains, Brigham Young had instructed, he wished to be buried on his own property overlooking the valley at about 140 East First Avenue (50 North), where his grave can be seen today. "But if I should live to go back with the Church in Jackson County," he said, "I wish to be buried there."[23]

A NEW LEADER

Sixty-nine-year-old John Taylor now became the head of the church due to his position as president of the Quorum of the Twelve Apostles, the same office Young had held in 1847 when he led the pioneer company to Salt Lake Valley. Ordained an apostle at age 30, the dignified Englishman had been with Joseph Smith in 1844 when an armed mob stormed Carthage Jail and shot the faith's first prophet to death. Taylor himself had been hit four times, but his life was saved when a fifth ball struck his watch. He would be sustained as the third president of his church on October 10, 1880.

Brigham Young's death came only six months after the execution by firing squad of John D. Lee for his part in the 1857 massacre in southwestern Utah of some 120 Arkansas emigrants on their way to California. Lee was the only one of the more than fifty participants in the horrendous crime ever brought to justice. His two trials in 1875 and 1876 at Beaver,

---

[23]Arrington, *Brigham Young: American Moses*, 399, 400. For the settlement of Young's estate, in which "church and private funds were almost inextricably intermingled," see Appendix D of Arrington's work, 422–30.

Utah, held the attention of the entire nation. At the first, a jury of eight Mormons and four non-Mormons deadlocked, eight against conviction, four in favor, after U.S. Attorney William Carey and his assistant, Robert Baskin, tried to implicate Brigham Young and other leaders. A storm of indignation swept the country at the stonewalling of witnesses and the refusal of Mormon jurors to return a guilty verdict.

Under growing pressure on both sides, a new U.S. attorney, Sumner Howard, met with Mormon leaders and struck a deal. As the second trial opened in September 1876, he announced he "had not come to try Brigham Young and the Mormon Church," but only Lee, and he dropped charges against others.[24] When an all-Mormon jury was chosen, Baskin knew "John D. Lee was doomed."[25] Witnesses now came forward to testify against Lee, but not against anyone else. On September 20 jurors took about one hour to find him guilty.

TRIAL OF SYLVANUS COLLETT

Only with the cooperation of his peers did Lee become the one man punished for the Mountain Meadows Massacre. Most of the time, U.S. prosecutors still faced obstruction and frustration in trying to win guilty verdicts under the Poland Act for polygamy or more serious crimes in Utah. The October 1878 trial of a 41-year-old Englishman for the murder twenty-one years before of John Aiken provides a revealing case study on the difficulties they encountered.[26]

As historian Harold Schindler has reconstructed their story from trial coverage and other sources, the six members of the Aiken party came from California in October 1857 intending to meet the U.S. Army expedition then approaching Utah from the east. They were a prosperous looking company, outfitted with pack mules, and well dressed, equipped, and mounted. And at least one wore a money belt full of gold eagles, six coins deep around his whole body. John Aiken and his brother, Thomas, Andrew J. "Honesty" Jones, Tuck Wright, John Chapman, and a man known only as Colonel Eichard were probably cattle

---

[24]Whitney, *History of Utah*, 2:805. Howard dropped charges against William Dame, Isaac Haight, John Higbee, and George Adair.

[25]Baskin, *Reminiscences of Early Utah*, 137.

[26]For the story of the Aiken party, see Schindler, *Orrin Porter Rockwell: Man of God, Son of Thunder*, 268–81. Also see *The Salt Lake Daily Tribune*, October 10–18, 1878.

buyers or gamblers. But when the federal army under Col. Albert S. Johnston failed to make it through the Wasatch Mountains into Salt Lake Valley that fall, their luck ran out.

Arrested in Weber County as spies by Lot Smith's command, they were taken to Great Salt Lake and held in the Townsend House on the corner of West Temple and First South. On November 20 Hosea Stout reported that the noted Mormon gunman, Porter Rockwell, with "3 or four others" started out that day to escort four of the captives back to California by the southern route now taken by I-15. Chapman and Jones were "permitted to go at large and remain till spring."[27] They were dropped off at Lehi.

At the trial a number of eyewitnesses named two other members of the escort as John R. Murdock, a Mormon Battalion veteran and a rescuer of the handcart companies, and his brother-in-law John S. Lott. A third, they said, was a tall 21-year-old Englishman with a "heroic physique," Sylvanus "Syl" Collett, the only one who ever came to trial. All three then lived in Lehi.

The mixed company, four Aiken party members and their escort, traveled on to Nephi, some eighty miles south of Great Salt Lake, where Bishop Jacob Bigler raised a second four-man party while the Californians slept at Timothy Foote's adobe hotel. The second party was sent that night to the Chicken Creek or the Sevier River crossing, where the two groups met the next day and decided to camp together. After dark, as they relaxed around the fire, the Nephi members created a diversion to allow each of the escorts to get in position and attack from behind the man assigned to him. Two of the murder attempts were successful, two were not. Badly wounded and on foot, John Aiken and Tuck Wright managed to stagger back to Nephi, where they were treated and kept again at Foote's house. Three or four days later, they started for Great Salt Lake in a loaned buggy for medical attention. They did not get far.

At Willow Creek, near present Mona, where the young drivers from Nephi stopped the buggy to water the horse, two men emerged from an abandoned herder's shack and shot-gunned Aiken and Wright to death as they begged for their lives. Their bodies were then weighted and dropped in the nearby deep springs. During the trial at Provo, William

[27]Brooks, *On the Mormon Frontier*, 2:645.

Skeen from Plain City testified that Collett had told him that he was one of the men who had pulled the trigger.

This the Englishman flatly denied. His defense was that he had left the Salmon River Indian mission at Fort Limhi, nearly four hundred miles to the north, on October 28, 1857, with a company headed for Utah with wagon loads of dried salmon. They had reached Great Salt Lake "about the last of November," he said, when he had gone home. He could not have murdered Aiken, his attorney argued, because "he was hundreds of miles away."[28]

Supporting this story was Mission President Thomas Smith, who had led a new party of colonizers north that fall to strengthen the settlement near present Salmon, Idaho. There he found Collett, he said, when he arrived on October 22. From his alleged diary, Smith read the Englishman's name as one of eleven men who left Fort Limhi on October 28 with ox teams and wagons loaded with fish.

A member of this party, Joseph Harker, former bishop of West Jordan, affirmed Smith's account, as did Richard B. Margetts, also then at Fort Limhi. Harker said the party with fish, including Collett, had encountered bad weather and difficult road conditions. It had taken thirty-four days, averaging less than twelve miles a day, for them to reach Great Salt Lake at the end of November, he said, when he and the defendant had parted and gone their separate ways.[29]

At the trial one of northern Utah's most respected citizens, Lewis W. Shurtliff, bishop of Plain City, also appeared reluctantly as a character witness against William Skeen. What Shurtliff did not say, however, was that he himself had been at Fort Limhi as a missionary at that very time and knew from personal experience what had occurred. He could have volunteered to support Collett's story if he had wished, yet he chose not to. A possible explanation for Shurtliff's reticence surfaces from documents that have come to light in recent years. These make it virtually certain that key defense witnesses deliberately testified falsely in an orchestrated performance.

Contrary to Thomas Smith's testimony, the Salmon River Mission Journal lists the names of those who left Fort Limhi on October 28

---

[28]See trial testimony, *The Salt Lake Daily Tribune*, October 15–17, 1878.
[29]Ibid.

with the wagon loads of fish. Collett's is not one of them. While they do include Harker, ten other names do not exactly square with those from Smith's professed diary.[30] Ironically, Harker himself tells why Collett was not one of those who left the fort on October 28. On October 16, twelve days before, he wrote in his own journal, "two of the brethren left here for Salt Lake to meet the company."[31] Which two he failed to say, but that blank was filled in three days later by two other journal keepers in Thomas Smith's northbound party.

At Market Lake on the big bend of Snake River, some fifteen miles north of present Idaho Falls, Milton D. Hammond on October 18 recorded, "S. Collet and A. Zanndel come into camp about 10 o'clock at night haveing been 3 days enrout from Ft. Limhi."[32] That same day, Charles F. Middleton from Ogden wrote, "In the night A. Zondel & S. Colet came into camp from Salmon River on their way home."[33]

So the truth was that Collett left Fort Limhi with the mail rider, Abraham Zundel from present Willard, Utah, nearly two weeks before Harker's wagon party pulled out. At the rate they covered the distance to Market Lake on horseback, forty-two miles a day, he would have reached home on October 24, more than a month before he said he did. Moreover, even if Collett had stayed with the wagon party, Harker's own journal shows he would have made the trip in twenty-one days, not thirty-four, at the rapid rate of travel for an ox train of nineteen miles per day, not less than twelve as testified. He still would have arrived in Great Salt Lake on November 17, in time for him to escort the Aiken party as it began its last journey three days later.[34] Had the jury known this, it might still have found Collett not guilty, as it did, but the lack of such information to counter the testimony of defense witnesses made the verdict virtually certain.

Whether the manipulation of witnesses and jurors, so apparent in the Lee and Collett trials, affected the outcome of other cases, including the trial of Robert T. Burton in 1879 for the murder of Mrs. Bowman at

[30]See Salmon River Mission Journal, October 28 and 29, 1857. The ten men who left Fort Limhi on October 28 were Thomas Bingham, W. Bailey Lake, Jacob Miller, Henry Nebeker, James Hill, Henry Cleveland, Jr., John Preese, Joseph Harker, William Burch, and David H. Stephens. Eben J. Robinson left the following day on horseback to catch up with the others.

[31]Journal of Joseph Harker, October 16, 1857.

[32]Journal of Milton D. Hammond, October 18, 1857.

[33]Journal of Charles F. Middleton, October 18, 1857. Also see Bluth, "The Salmon River Mission," 901.

[34]See Journal of Joseph Harker, October 28–November 17, 1857.

Kingston Fort in 1862, is not known. What is sure is that the practice obstructed the enforcement of laws in a place whose people lived under a higher form of jurisprudence. It also made the modest reforms of the Poland Act appear wholly inadequate to deal with the problem.

NEW ELECTION LAW

To prevent similar tampering with elections, members of the Liberal Party in 1876 asked Congress for legislation to guarantee a secret ballot. Utah's latest governor, George W. Emery, a New England moderate, added his voice to the growing demand. He told territorial legislators that year the existing law was "inimical to republican government, and in the interest of the church, so potent in Utah, and leaves church members no choice but to vote the ticket prepared for them."[35]

At last Congress forced the issue. On December 10, 1877, Sen. Isaac P. Christiancy of Michigan and Rep. John K. Luttrell of California introduced companion bills in both houses "to regulate elections and the elective franchise in the Territory of Utah."[36] Given a choice between reforming the law or seeing Congress do it for them, the Utah lawmakers wrote a new measure and abolished the marked ballot. It was approved on February 22, 1878.

For the first time in more than a quarter century, Utah voters enjoyed the right to make their choice at the ballot box in secret. But if applauded elsewhere, the new law still gave little hope or satisfaction to the opponents of theocratic rule who had done the most to force its passage. Liberal Party members protested that residency requirements of the act had been purposely crafted to make it difficult for miners and prospectors, their main constituents, to comply. Further, they complained, women who were not citizens were allowed to register if they were wives, widows, or daughters of someone who was a citizen, which gave alien polygamous wives the right to vote. They finally objected to provisions that put county assessors over registration and gave county courts the power to appoint election judges.[37]

[35]McMullin and Walker, *Biographical Directory of American Territorial Governors*, 305. Also see Roberts, *Comprehensive History*, 5:602.

[36]*Congressional Record* (45–2), Vol. 7, December 10, 1877, 81, 98.

[37]See "An Act Providing for the Registration of Voters and to Further Regulate the Manner of Conducting Elections in This Territory," 1878.

Less than a week after the act was signed, members of the territory's minority party declared their "unalterable opposition" and "undissembled grief" at a statute that gave the Mormon majority "power to provide the machinery to work the plan and the engineers to operate the machinery." Referring to miners, who moved often or lived in tents, they protested that the new law penalized most Liberal Party voters, but threw "wide open the doors to the wives, be they many or few or alien."[38]

GEORGE Q. CANNON DENIED SEAT

Even so, Liberal Party hopes were high on September 22, 1880, as its delegates gathered to choose a candidate to oppose People's Party incumbent George Q. Cannon in the November election for the office of delegate to Congress. The large, enthusiastic turnout in the Liberal Institute Building in Salt Lake loudly cheered activist speakers and patriotic music by the Camp Douglas military band. Delegates at the convention were energized by a new governor whose keynote speech was hailed as "a declaration of war" against the Utah theocracy. Few seemed more qualified than he to lead it. Eli Houston Murray, a native of Kentucky, had joined the Union Army as a private at 18 and risen to march through Georgia with William T. Sherman as a brigadier general. Appointed by President Rutherford B. Hayes just five days before the gathering, he was now ready to begin his own march through Utah.

Nominated for the seat in Congress was Allen G. Campbell from Beaver County, a wealthy mine owner, who waged a spirited campaign over the next six weeks throughout the territory. But as the votes were counted, the party's worst fears were realized. Not only did the blessing of a secret vote fail to shiver Mormon solidarity, but Cannon won by the widest margin ever, 18,568 to 1,357. His Liberal opponent captured less than a third as many votes as the party's last candidate, Robert Baskin, four years before.

In a shocking move, however, Governor Murray declared Campbell the winner, certifying him as Utah delegate to Congress, "being a citizen of the United States, having the greatest number of votes." He reversed the election outcome on the ground that Cannon was not a nat-

---

[38]Baskin to Hemingray, February 28, 1878, quoted in Dwyer, *The Gentile Comes to Utah*, 133.

uralized citizen and practiced polygamy in violation of law.[39] At the same time, another appointed official, the secretary of the territory, made his customary report on the canvass of the vote.

So it was that the U.S. House of Representatives received an official certificate from Governor Murray, as required by federal law, that named Allen Campbell as Utah's elected delegate, and a statement from the Utah secretary, also according to law, showing that Cannon won by far the most votes. House Clerk George Adams studied the federal statute and concluded to enter Cannon's name on the House payroll as the delegate from Utah.

Because of polygamy, the ensuing fight in courts and Congress between Cannon and his Liberal adversaries won front page coverage over the next sixteen months in newspapers across the country. The apostle headed off the claim he was not a citizen by coming up with records purporting to show he had been naturalized. It was not so easy at a time of growing opposition to polygamy for him to defend against the accusation that he was a polygamist who had publicly advocated the marriage practice.

No longer could he give the appearance of denying the charge, as he had in 1874 before the House Committee on Elections, because his tormentors were waiting with witnesses to refute him. Instead, he forthrightly admitted, "I have taken plural wives, who now live with me, and have so lived with me for a number of years and born me children." Moreover, he said, "as a teacher of my religion in Utah territory, I have defended said tenet of said church as being in my belief a revelation of God."[40] But this hardly squared with his denial, some seven years before, that he was "living with four wives, or that I am living and cohabiting with any wives, in defiant or willful violation of the laws of Congress," among other things. He also had denied at that time that he had ever declared "the revelation of polygamy paramount to all human laws, or that I would obey said revelation rather than the laws of any country."[41]

Early in 1882 the Elections Committee issued its report to the full House. Since Cannon had admitted "he practices, teaches and advises others" to practice polygamy, it said, "we feel it our duty to say to the people

---

[39]Whitney, *History of Utah*, 3:151.
[40]Roberts, *Comprehensive History*, 6:19.
[41]See House Misc. Doc. 49 (43–1), 1873, Serial 1617, 5.

of that Territory that we will exclude such persons from representing them in this House." In so doing, panel members desired "to cast no imputation" on Cannon personally. In every other respect, they said, his conduct was "certainly the equal of any other person on this floor."[42]

The House gallery was jammed on April 19 when the final vote was taken. Allowed first to address the body, Cannon spoke without notes for over an hour. For nine years he had served in Congress, he said, and "My right to my seat has been fully vindicated by the House." If it was now declared vacant, "fraud will be supplemented by this method of strangling, of murdering the representation of Utah Territory on this floor."[43] Eloquently the apostle professed the political system of Utah was the same as any other state or territory and defended "plural marriage" as a divine institution. Mormons were willing, he said, "to be placed on the same plane with Abraham, in whose 'bosom' all good Christians hoped to find eternal rest." Why should he now "be assailed, abused and denounced as I have been for lechery, because of marrying wives?" he asked.[44]

The answer came in the final vote, which reflected a groundswell of opposition to polygamy as the Cannon contest and Reynolds trials focused national concern on the issue. After dismissing Campbell's claim, the House voted 123 to 79 to unseat Cannon and declare the office vacant. Eighty-nine members abstained, most Cannon friends or sympathizers, not wishing either to vote against him or to go on record favoring polygamy.

Utah Territory was now without representation in Congress, but not for long. On November 7 that year, John T. Caine, 53, from the Isle of Man and former clerk of Brigham Young, manager of the Salt Lake Theatre, and father of thirteen children by only one wife, won the election as Utah's fourth delegate to Congress. He defeated U.S. Attorney Philip Van Zile, who had prosecuted Sylvanus Collett, by 23,039 to 4,884. Caine would serve for the next eleven years.

The man he succeeded had been unseated by a flood of petitions from across the nation demanding his removal and action by Congress to stamp out, once and for all, the practice of polygamy.

---

[42]For the committee report, see "Cannon vs. Campbell, Contested Election Case from the Territory of Utah," House Rep. 559 (47–1), 1882, Serial 2066.

[43]For a synopsis of Cannon's speech, see Whitney, *History of Utah*, 3:191–93.   [44]Ibid., 191.

Chapter 16

MARSHALS AND COHABS

McGeary searched McArthur's house
Good-bye, my lover, good-bye
And all he could find was the tail of a mouse
Good-bye, my lover, good-bye.

—A children's song

By 1882 the Morrill Act, which outlawed polygamy in Utah by name or under such guises as "legal or ecclesiastical solemnities, sacraments, ceremonies, consecrations, or other contrivances," had been on the books for twenty years.[1] Its constitutionality had been upheld by the U.S. Supreme Court. But in a dominion where people lived by higher codes of conduct, prosecutors and judges had found it virtually impossible to enforce.

Congressman Henry Morey voiced growing national frustration and outrage when he demanded stronger action to abolish polygamy. "The sentiment of the country, the Christian civilization of the time, demand it, and the Republican party is pledged to it," the Ohio lawmaker said. "They all demand that this Congress shall lay its hand upon this hideous vice that boldly and defiantly stalks in Utah and adjoining Territories."[2]

In December 1881 President Chester A. Arthur admitted the existing law against "this odious crime" was practically "a dead letter."[3] Among the obstacles U.S. officials faced in enforcing it, he told Congress, was the difficulty of procuring evidence "even in the case of the most noto-

---

[1] For the Morrill Act, see *Congressional Globe* (37–2), 1861–62, App., 385.

[2] *Congressional Record* (47–1), March 14, 1882, Vol. 13, pt. 7, App., 38.

[3] Arthur became president on September 20, 1881, succeeding James A. Garfield, who had survived the Civil War battles of Shiloh and Chickamauga only to be shot by a disturbed office-seeker on July 2, 1881, four months after his inauguration. Garfield died on September 19.

rious offenders."[4] He called for passage of new legislation to penetrate the secrecy that surrounded Mormon marriages and make it easier to win convictions.

Congress did that much, and more. Early in 1882 it stiffened the punishment for polygamy, which was hard to prove, but added a new offense, "cohabiting with more than one woman," which was less so. Named for its sponsor, Sen. George F. Edmunds of Vermont, the new law adding enforcement teeth to the 1862 act imposed penalties of as much as $300 and six months in prison for the misdemeanor of unlawful cohabitation. But that was only one provision of the bill signed on March 22. The Edmunds Act also denied to any "polygamist, bigamist, or any other person cohabiting with more than one woman" the right to vote or hold any public office within the United States. A simple expression of belief in the right to have more than one living and undivorced wife was also sufficient under the statute for one to be declared incompetent to serve on a jury.

Even more radically, the bill liquidated every office in Utah relating in any way to elections and vested all such duties in a board of five members appointed by the president. To this board it gave dictatorial powers over the registration of voters, conduct of elections, canvassing of ballots, and certification of election winners. The federal panel was charged to continue its work until a legislature, elected under its terms, enacted acceptable laws to carry out these democratic processes. At the same time, the Edmunds Act held out an olive branch to repentant believers in "celestial marriage." In a gesture of good will, it legitimized all children of the polygamous unions, "known as Mormon marriages," born before January 1, 1883, almost exactly nine months after the act was passed. It also gave the president power to grant amnesty to offenders under conditions he considered appropriate.[5]

Reaction in Utah to this latest attempt to crush the marriage practice was not long in coming. Two weeks after the measure was signed, John Taylor, the faith's third president, was as unbending as his predecessor, Brigham Young. His followers would "abide all constitutional law," he said, but they were not "craven serfs, and have not learned to lick the feet of oppressors." He and his people would fight "inch by inch, legally and

[4]Chester A. Arthur, "President's Annual Message," December 6, 1881, *Congressional Record* (47–1), Vol. 13, pt. I, 23–30.   [5]For the Edmunds Act, see *Statutes at Large of the United States*, 22:30–32.

constitutionally, for our rights as American citizens," he made clear, "and plant ourselves firmly on the sacred guarantees of the constitution."[6]

1882 STATEHOOD BID

The law Taylor objected to had not been passed before the threat of more repressive measures touched off yet another move to escape from federal domination by the avenue of statehood. While Congress in 1882 took up some two dozen bills and constitutional amendments to stamp out polygamy, Utah lawmakers in February that year adopted resolutions calling for a constitutional convention. Ignoring Governor Murray's veto, delegates came to Salt Lake from all parts of the territory on April 10 to adopt a constitution for "a republican form of government" as required by the nation's founding document.[7] Between the charter they produced and earlier versions, the only real difference was a significant one. Eliminated from the draft they unanimously approved on April 27 was the synonym for the Kingdom of God always proposed in the past as the name of the new state. No longer would it be Deseret, but from thence forward, Utah.

After a special referendum had ratified the constitution by 27,814 to 498, the convention reconvened in June and approved a memorial to Congress for statehood. The petition was respectful but forthright. Delegates considered statehood not only a right under the American constitution but one also assured by treaty with Mexico, possibly referring to the Treaty of Guadalupe Hidalgo in 1848 that ended the Mexican War, a hitherto unmentioned source of legitimacy. Moreover, in an apparent allusion to polygamy, the memorial held that benefits of statehood would "accrue not only to the new State but to the nation at large, in the settlement of questions that have frequently produced great and unprofitable agitation."[8] Seven delegates were chosen to deliver the initiative to Congress, where it soon died in committee.[9]

---

[6]John Taylor, April 9, 1882, *Journal of Discourses*, 23:67.

[7]See Sec. 4, Art. IV, of the U.S. Constitution, which states that the United States "shall guarantee to every State in this Union a Republican form of government." On this section rested much of the opposition to Utah's entry into the Union for some four decades.

[8]Whitney, *History of Utah*, 3:205.

[9]They were John T. Caine, William H. Hooper, James Sharp, William Riter, Franklin S. Richards, William D. Johnson, Jr., and David H. Peery.

THE UTAH COMMISSION

While the latest statehood bid was being ignored, the five-member board created by the Edmunds Act arrived that August to take charge of elections in the territory. If the newcomers appointed by President Arthur were unwelcome, they were anything but radical reformers bent on imposing their religious or political views on anyone else.

The chairman of the panel, now known as the Utah Commission, was Alexander Ramsey, a former U.S. senator and governor of Minnesota. He was described as a "kindly disposed, elderly gentleman, usually brimming with good nature, and without prejudice against the people among whom he came."[10] The remaining four, evenly divided between political parties, had been practicing attorneys who held positions of public trust in as many different states.[11]

To get ready for the November election, the commission named twenty-four county voter registrars, including eight Mormons, seven non-Mormons, and nine former Mormons. To the anger of inhabitants, this division disregarded Utah's population makeup, which in 1880 numbered 120,283 Mormons, 14,156 non-Mormons, and 9,524 ex-Mormons and all others. The board further chose, to the degree candidates were available, three election judges from both parties for each of some 750 polling places.

The commission's most controversial action aimed to implement the Edmunds Act's provision that no "polygamist, bigamist, or any person cohabiting with more than one woman" would be eligible to vote. To fulfill this mandate, the board arbitrarily added its own requirements to those already listed in the existing registration oath approved in 1878 by territorial lawmakers. Now, to vote, one had to swear out a two-part affidavit:

> I, _____, being first duly sworn (or affirmed), depose and say that I am over twenty-one years of age, and have resided in the Territory of Utah for six months, and in the precinct of   one month immediately preceding the date hereof, and (if a male) am a native born or naturalized (as the case may be) citizen of the United States and a taxpayer in this Territory, (or if female), I am native born, or naturalized, or the wife, widow or daughter (as the case may be), of a native born or naturalized citizen of the United States;

---

[10]Whitney, *History of Utah*, 3:222.

[11]They were former U.S. Senator A. S. Paddock of Nebraska, the most outspoken foe of polygamy, George L. Godfrey of Iowa, James R. Pettigrew of Arkansas, and Ambrose B. Carlton of Indiana.

And I do further solemnly swear (or affirm) that I am not a bigamist or a polygamist; that I am not a violator of the laws of the United States prohibiting bigamy or polygamy; that I do not live or cohabit with more than one woman in the marriage relation, nor does any relation exist between me and any woman which has been entered into or continued in violation of the said laws of the United States, prohibiting bigamy or polygamy; (and if a woman) that I am not the wife of a polygamist, nor have I entered into any relation with any man in violation of the laws of the United States concerning polygamy or bigamy.[12]

Two years later, the U.S. Supreme Court would throw out the commission's carefully worded test. Before then, estimates of the number it precluded from voting range from ten thousand to sixteen thousand, but in the end it made little difference. In the 1882 election for delegate to Congress, John T. Caine of the People's Party defeated Liberal Party nominee Philip Van Zile by about the same margin as usual, 23,039 to 4,884. The commission's work only legitimized Mormon control of the election process.

Unable to protest the outcome, as it had before, a frustrated Liberal Party blamed national lawmakers for not bringing the Mormon theocracy to heel. In a petition to Congress, it named the alleged evils of religious rule and said the 1862 Morrill Act, 1874 Poland Act, and 1882 Edmunds law had "failed to diminish the celebration of polygamous marriages" because the people of Utah "regard the Church [as] superior to the Government." Claiming to represent "30,000 loyal American citizens," the eighteen signers of the Utah Territorial Liberal Central Committee called on Congress to replace Utah's legislature with a legislative council of as many as thirteen members, appointed by the president. Only when the nation took "all political power from the Mormon people, then, and not till then, will the vexed problem be solved," they said.[13]

The Liberal leaders warned that if Congress refused to insure that the same laws could be made and enforced in Utah "as in other States and Territories of the Union," the opponents of theocratic government, "on this picket line of civilization," would reach the point "where discouragement must ensue."[14] Whether or not action as drastic was justified,

---

[12]See Annual Report of Utah Commission, 1882, House Exec. Doc. 1 (47–2), Vol. 11, No. 1, pt. 5, Serial 2100, 1003–08. Also see Whitney, *History of Utah*, 3:228.

[13]Liberal Party Petition to Congress, *Congressional Record* (47–2), December 7, 1882, 89, 90.

[14]Ibid.

change was in the wind, but on both sides those involved were too close to the struggle to see it coming.

JUDGE ZANE AND THE TRIAL OF RUDGER CLAWSON

It is a noteworthy coincidence that the two Republicans who did the most to fulfill the party's early platform to abolish "the twin relics of barbarism, slavery and polygamy," both came from the same law firm in Springfield, Illinois. When Abraham Lincoln left the office of Lincoln and Herndon to become president in 1861, his place was taken by 30-year-old Charles S. Zane, who later became a partner of Shelby M. Cullom, sponsor of the draconian 1870 statute, and was elected a circuit judge in Illinois.[15] Capping a successful career, the New Jersey native in 1884 accepted a commission by President Arthur to become chief justice of the Utah Supreme Court. At age 53, he was sworn into office on September 1 and assigned by Governor Murray to the Third District court at Salt Lake City, where he found himself presiding over the first polygamy case instituted under the Edmunds Act. If this was not challenge enough, the defendant was one of Utah's most admired young citizens.

Twenty-seven-year-old Rudger Clawson was the son of Brigham Young's former business manager, Hiram B. Clawson, and his second wife, Margaret Gay Judd, the attractive actress who had played the leading role in the first Salt Lake Theatre play. Not only did he have prominent parents, but young Clawson had won acclaim in 1879 for his courage in facing down a dozen armed mobbers who had shot a fellow missionary, Joseph Standing, near Dalton, Georgia. The murder had stirred excitement throughout the territory.[16]

In 1883 Clawson married as his second wife Lydia Spencer, 21, daughter of Mormon luminary, Daniel Spencer, in direct violation of the Edmunds law enacted the year before. For this he was indicted on April 24, 1884, by a grand jury, chosen under the new law, that did not include any member who believed it was right for a man to have more

---

[15]For an evaluation of Zane and his work, see Alexander, "Charles S. Zane . . . Apostle of the New Era," 283–314.

[16]Ignoring warnings his life was in danger, Clawson returned to Georgia in 1880 to testify against three men who had been arrested for the crime. Despite his testimony, a local jury found them not guilty. In 1898 Clawson was ordained an LDS apostle.

CHARLES S. ZANE (above)
The uncompromising judge sentenced
Rudger Clawson to prison as the first of
hundreds convicted under the Edmunds Act.
Courtesy, Utah State Historical Society.

Lydia Spencer (above, right), shortly before her marriage to Rudger Clawson.
She defied Judge Zane and went to prison rather than testify against her husband.
Courtesy, Roy Hoopes.

than one wife. Only a month after Zane had taken office, Clawson came
before the new judge from Illinois.[17]

As the trial opened on October 15, U.S. Attorney William H. Dickson and his assistant, Charles Varian, stacked the jury with members opposed to polygamy but ran into the same obstacles that had defeated prosecutors before them. Church leaders, including President John Taylor and Apostle Cannon, refused to reveal what they knew, while Clawson's alleged second wife could not be found. A deadlocked jury had just been sent home on October 22 when the break came.

---

[17]For a balanced presentation of Clawson's trial and the agonizing decisions faced by many Mormon men at this time, see Allen, "'Good Guys' vs. 'Good Guys': Rudger Clawson, John Sharp and Civil Disobedience in Nineteenth-century Utah," 148–74. For the most complete trial coverage from a Mormon point of view, see Whitney, *History of Utah*, 3:266–69.

That night Marshal Edwin Ireland's deputies discovered Lydia Clawson's hiding place, and Judge Zane at once ordered a new trial. When the clerk asked the young woman to take the oath, however, she refused. Asked to instruct the witness, Zane tried, but failed to shake her white-lipped resolve to keep silent. "You take a fearful responsibility in undertaking to defy the government," he told her and sent her off to the penitentiary to think it over.[18]

The night Lydia Clawson spent in prison apparently distressed her husband, who now urged her to tell the truth, more than it did her. Anxious and pale, she entered the crowded courtroom the next day to testify in as few words as possible that she indeed was the wife of the defendant. She then left with her father-in-law, then bishop of Salt Lake City's 12th Ward, a church unit similar to a parish. It took the jury only seventeen minutes to pronounce the younger Clawson guilty of both polygamy and unlawful cohabitation.

At his sentencing Rudger Clawson and Judge Zane measured the gulf between a theocratic territory and its parent in a dramatic confrontation. Asked if he had cause to show why judgment should not be imposed, Clawson on November 3 said without hesitation:

> I very much regret that the laws of my country should come in contact with the laws of God, but whenever they do I shall invariably choose the latter. If I did not so express myself I should feel unworthy of the cause I represent.
>
> The law of 1862 and the Edmunds Law were expressly designed to operate against marriage as practiced and believed in by the Latter-day Saints. They are therefore unconstitutional, and of course cannot command the respect that a constitutional law would.[19]

Somewhat surprised by this unrehearsed shot, Zane leaned back and thought for a few moments before he replied:

> The Constitution of the United States, as construed by the Supreme Court and by the authors of that instrument, does not protect any person in the practice of polygamy.
>
> While all men have a right to worship God according to the dictates of their own conscience, and to entertain any religious belief that their conscience and judgment might reasonably dictate, they do not have the right to engage in a practice which the American people, through the laws of their country, declare to be unlawful and injurious to society.[20]

---

[18]Whitney, *History of Utah*, 3:312.   [19]Ibid., 3:317.   [20]Ibid.

Zane then rewarded Clawson's defiant attitude with the full penalty provided for unlawful cohabitation, a $300 fine and six months in prison. To this he added three years and six months in prison and a $500 fine for polygamy, the maximum fine and only eighteen months less in prison than the law allowed for the latter offense. At first a lonely figure among the inmate population, Rudger Clawson, the first convicted under the Edmunds Act, was soon right at home among his own kind.

Before the future apostle was pardoned by President Grover Cleveland after serving, by his own reckoning, "three years, one month and ten days,"[21] the prison population would be transformed by about five hundred fellow believers who would follow his example, among them his own father, Hiram B. Clawson. Hundreds more would follow. Most would be sentenced by Judge Zane to six months in prison for unlawful cohabitation.

At the same time, Zane was as merciful toward violators who promised to obey the law as he was relentless in punishing to the fullest anyone who defied it. A small but growing number during this period pleaded guilty and vowed to obey the marriage laws in return for a fine, but no jail time. They included the venerable John Sharp, bishop of Salt Lake City's 20th Ward, who was stripped of his church office for his defection.[22]

RETURN TO MEXICO

In 1846 Mormons had begun an exodus from the United States to seek freedom to practice their religious beliefs and establish the Kingdom of God in the Great Basin of North America, then within the Republic of Mexico. Four decades later, as enforcement of federal laws against polygamy gained momentum, the story of the millennial movement began, once again, to repeat itself.

On January 8, 1885, three Mormon agents arrived at Corralitos, Chihuahua, Mexico, to rent or buy land for future settlement.[23] Later that month, John Taylor advised Arizona members of the faith to relocate on

---

[21]Jenson, *LDS Biographical Encyclopedia*, 1:174.

[22]Allen, "'Good Guys' vs. 'Good Guys': Rudger Clawson, John Sharp, and Civil Disobedience in Nineteenth-century Utah."

[23]They were Alexander F. MacDonald, Christopher Layton, and John W. Campbell.

the Mexican side of the border. The first party of some seventy members, under Edward A. Noble, soon after headed south from Snowflake, Arizona. A year later, Mormon colonizers raised a flagpole over their new village, named after the Mexican general, Juarez, in northern Chihuahua and saluted the Mexican flag. They were the vanguard of an extensive Mormon colonization over the next two decades in the states of Sonora and Chihuahua. At the same time, other organized parties headed north to plant new settlements in Alberta, Canada.[24]

TAYLOR'S LAST SERMON

The departure of polygamous families for more congenial soil was not the only sign that stepped up prosecution for having more than one wife would meet defiance. On returning from Arizona, John Taylor on February 1, 1885, took an uncompromising position against federal prosecutors. God had "revealed unto us certain principles pertaining to the perpetuity of man and of woman" and "He has told us to obey these laws," he said.[25] In his last public sermon, the courtly church leader said he could die for the truth, but he would not disobey God and "forsake my wives and my children." Striking a book on the lectern with his fist, he swore, "I won't do it, so help me God." This brought a loud "amen" from the capacity audience in the Salt Lake tabernacle. So what should they do? "If you were out in a storm," he advised, you would "pull up the collar of your coat and button yourself up, and keep the cold out until the storm blows past."[26]

In the meantime, he told his followers to forsake violence. They were not to "break the heads" of the "miserable sneaks" who were "crawling about your doors," or "spill their blood," he told them, "no rendering evil for evil." Instead, he said, they should avoid them, "just as you would wolves," and "get out of the way as much as you can."[27] Then Taylor and his capable first counselor, Apostle George Q. Cannon, took his own advice and vanished from public view.

---

[24]For more on the Mormon colonization in Mexico, see Tullis, *Mormons in Mexico*.

[25]John Taylor, February 1, 1885, *Journal of Discourses*, 26:152.

[26]Ibid., 152–55.

[27]Ibid., 155–56.

THE HALF-MAST INCIDENT

A manifestation of Taylor's policy of nonviolent resistance came on the nation's birthday that year when Salt Lakers on July 4 were surprised to see the American flag flying at half mast over City Hall, ZCMI, the Salt Lake Theatre, the *Deseret News*, and other buildings. Many asked if former President Grant, then in the last stages of terminal cancer, or some church leader had died.[28]

When they realized the lowered flag was a mute protest against polygamy prosecutions, angry non-Mormon citizens stormed City Hall and demanded it be raised. Said one demonstrator, the defiant act made him "as mad as when Fort Sumter was fired on."[29] Governor Eli Murray asked for troops to restore the affront to national dignity, a degree of involvement that Gen. A. McDowell McCook, like most of his predecessors at Fort Douglas, prudently avoided.

The *Deseret News* defended the flag-lowering as an exhibition of sorrow by Utah's people "over the decadence of their liberties." To cast it as an insult to the government, it said, was a "wilful aspersion" of this motive.[30] But the Grand Army of the Republic's Utah members branded it "a deliberate expression of Mormon contempt and defiance of the law which that flag represents."[31] Unimportant in itself, the incident was a true reflection of the divided state of Utah society at this time.

THE UNDERGROUND

Meanwhile the organized juggernaut of federal authority that replaced the half-hearted anti-polygamy campaigns of the past was bringing the territory to the brink of bloodshed. Joining Judge Zane on territorial benches were Jacob S. Boreman, former legislator from Jackson County, Missouri, and now in charge of the Second District, Beaver, and Orlando W. Powers of Michigan, First District, Ogden. To provide judicial fodder, U.S. Marshal Edwin A. Ireland, under powers granted by the Poland Act, deputized a growing army of federal marshals.

---

[28]The Civil War hero and former president died less than three weeks later at Mt. McGregor, New York, four days after finishing his two-volume work, *Personal Memoirs of U. S. Grant*.

[29]Whitney, *History of Utah*, 3:401.   [30]*Deseret Evening News*, July 7, 1885, 2.

[31]Whitney, *History of Utah*, 3:405–06.

To keep out of the way of these so-called "miserable sneaks" and their informants, as Taylor had instructed, Mormon leaders took to the "underground," an intricate web of hideouts and safe places, some under the noses of their pursuers. A communication network that included a Utah railroad, the telegraph, county sheriffs, and town police notified of approaching federal officers. The warning system in southern Utah included a "cohab code" in which Judge Zane was "Nero" and Justice Boreman, "Herod."

As marshals and "cohabs" played a grim game of hide-and-seek across the territory, inhabitants ridiculed the federal lawmen and found humor in the anti-polygamy prosecutions, despite the tragic consequences for many families. Charles L. Walker, while attending a Sunday school jubilee in the Salt Lake tabernacle, composed lines in 1885 "which were received with much enthusiasm":

> There's an underground railroad
> Evading the bail road
> Which ne'er was a jail road
>   in Utah.
>
> The girls still keep singing
> While washing and wringing
> There's none of them cringing
>   in Utah.
>
> The cows are yet eating,
> The sheep are still bleating
> While the lawyers are cheating
>   in Utah.
>
> While the marshals are slumming
> There's no thought of succumbing,
> For the babies keep coming
>   in Utah.[32]

So decentralized was church organization that its regular operations continued without significant interruption during this period. And so effective was the Mormon underground that only two members of the hierarchy were ever captured against their will. Less fortunate were hundreds of others. Convicted of unlawful cohabitation, they were sent to the territorial penitentiary, where they posed proudly in their striped

---

[32]Brooks, "Vignettes: Some Memories of Dixie," 294–96.

uniforms and revolutionized society inside the prison walls. Since their terms lasted only six months, there was a constant turnover of population.

ARREST OF GEORGE Q. CANNON

While lesser names filled the prison, the one offender federal officers wanted most was the able apostle who had served as Utah's delegate to Congress, rightly considered the real administrator of church financial and political affairs. On February 8, 1886, U.S. Marshal Ireland put up wanted posters in Salt Lake City offering a $500 reward for information leading to Apostle George Q. Cannon's arrest. "The names of any persons giving information will be held in strict confidence," he promised.[33]

As deputies watched his farm and questioned one of his wives, Emily Hoagland,[34] Cannon on February 12 slipped out of the city to buy land in Mexico for future settlement. Accompanied by Apostle Erastus Snow; Orson Arnold, Brigham Young's former bodyguard;[35] and Samuel Hill, he rode a freight car to Ogden, then went by carriage to Willard, where the party that night boarded the westbound train of the Central Pacific Railroad. As they entered the sleeping car "Santa Clara," the brakeman apparently spotted them. Alerted by telegraph, Humboldt County Sheriff Frank M. Fellows boarded the train at Winnemucca, Nevada. When the train stopped at Humboldt House for dinner, some thirty-eight miles farther west,[36] he entered the Mormon party's car and put the apostle under arrest. "I have got Cannon in custody," he wired Ireland, "when will you come after him." The U.S. marshal arrived on February 15 to take the captive on the next eastbound train back to Utah.

On his promise not to try to escape, Cannon was allowed to move about freely, but a few miles east of Promontory early the next morning,

[33]Whitney, *History of Utah*, 3:481.

[34]Following passage of the Edmunds Act, on July 11, 1882, Cannon married 44-year-old Emily Hoagland, the sister of his first wife, Elizabeth, who had died six months before. Emily Hoagland was the former wife of Jesse C. Little.

[35]At age 19 Orson Arnold had been accidentally shot in the left leg while serving in Lot Smith's command during the 1857 "Utah War" and walked with a limp. Despite this disability, the New Yorker was known for his courage during the Black Hawk Indian war and his skills as a frontiersman.

[36]Humboldt House is located on the railroad at Humboldt Exit 138 on present I-80 about six miles west of Imlay, Nevada. Before the trains added dining cars they made regular stops here to provide meals to passengers.

he jumped or fell from the moving train. Rearrested soon after while walking along the track, dazed and bleeding from a broken nose, he was put under a military escort and returned to Salt Lake City. The apostle claimed he fell off the train while getting some fresh air after a visit to the washroom, but the marshal thought otherwise. Charging that Cannon had not only tried to escape but had also tried to bribe the Nevada lawman, he and U.S. Attorney Dickson urged the judge to put bail at a high level, which Zane did. He imposed a total of $45,000, including bonds of $10,000 each on two counts of cohabitation. Even so, before his case came to trial on March 17, Cannon jumped bail and again took off.[37]

The only other leader caught unawares was Apostle Lorenzo Snow, the church's future fifth president, who became careless and was nabbed by federal deputies on November 20, 1885, at his home in Brigham City. Convicted on three separate counts of cohabitation, he was sentenced by Judge Powers to the maximum penalty for each, but the U.S. Supreme Court later ruled the judge had no power to compound punishments. Apostle Woodruff had a close call but was saved when "the Eyes of all the Marshals was Closed By the power of God."[38]

JOHN TAYLOR'S REVELATION

Hopes for relief from prosecution soared in Utah when Grover Cleveland became the first Democrat to win election as president since the Civil War. Inaugurated in 1885, the moderate son of a Presbyterian minister on April 21, 1886, appointed 41-year-old Caleb W. West from Kentucky, who had served as a teenager in Robert E. Lee's Army of Northern Virginia, to replace the contentious Eli Murray as governor. Otherwise, the new president did little to abate the crusade by Congress to exterminate polygamy.

In the Senate, new legislation by Judiciary Committee Chairman George F. Edmunds aimed to strengthen his 1882 law and crush Mor-

---

[37]Cannon later took advantage of a window of opportunity afforded by the brief term of Judge Elliot Sanford of New York, a moderate who was named in 1888 by President Cleveland to replace Charles Zane as chief justice of the Utah Supreme Court. Cannon surrendered voluntarily on September 17, 1888, pleaded guilty on two counts of cohabitation, and was sentenced to a total of $450 in fines and 175 days in the penitentiary. Other apostles who did the same included Moses Thatcher, who allowed himself to be arrested on September 4 at his home in Logan, and Francis M. Lyman, who gave up on November 12 and was sentenced to serve eighty-five days.

[38]Kenney, ed., *Wilford Woodruff's Journal*, 8:376.

Apostle George Q. Cannon, third from left, jumped bail, but later gave himself up
and went to prison with lesser church notables for cohabitation.
Courtesy, Manuscripts Division, University of Utah Libraries.

mon economic and political power. The Vermont politician's counter-part in the House of Representatives, J. Randolph Tucker of Virginia, although a states' rights Democrat, was drawing up legislation of his own that in economic terms was even more punishing.

As the two bills worked toward a single measure, Utah Delegate Caine and LDS church emissaries floated a proposed amendment in an attempt to head off the inevitable. Under it, implementation of the law would be delayed for six months while a constitutional convention was held in Utah. If the convention and voters approved a founding document prohibiting polygamy, they proposed that enforcement of the act would be further postponed until Congress had acted on a memorial for statehood.[39]

A friendly representative, William L. Scott of Pennsylvania, intro-duced this proposal as an amendment to the Tucker version of the anti-polygamy legislation. Church advocates in Congress now urged the Mormon president to give his blessing on the proposition. While the politicians argued in the nation's capital, on September 27, 1886, John Taylor laid the question before the Almighty.

"I the Lord do not change and my word and my covenants and my law do not," the answer came back. "And have I not commanded men that if they were Abraham's seed and would enter into my glory they must do the works of Abraham," it continued. "I have not revoked this law nor will I for it is everlasting and those who will enter into my glory must obey the conditions thereof."[40] Taylor would later relent, but only as a "political necessity" on the tacit understanding that "we neither yield nor compromise an iota on our religious principles."[41] This seemed to indicate that he would not oppose a prohibition of polygamy in the state charter as long as it was ignored, as the 1862 Morrill Act had been and as it is today, after Utah became a state.

Meanwhile all of the political maneuvering in Washington did little to protect one of Taylor's followers in southern Utah from more tragic consequences of the anti-polygamy crusade.

[39]For the story of political maneuvering during this period, see Lyman, *Political Deliverance: The Mormon Quest for Utah Statehood*. Also see Wolfinger, "A Reexamination of the Woodruff Manifesto in the Light of Utah Constitutional History," 328–49.

[40]See "A Revelation on Celestial Marriage given through President John Taylor at Centerville, Utah, on September 27, 1886," Collier, ed., *Unpublished Revelations of the Prophets and Presidents of the Church of Jesus Christ of Latter Day Saints*, 1:145–46.

[41]Taylor to Jack, February 27, 1887, quoted in Wolfinger, "A Reexamination of the Woodruff Manifesto in the Light of Utah Constitutional History," 343.

EMILY STEVENS DALTON
She was the English first wife of
"Young Ed" Dalton, who was
shot and killed by a
U.S. marshal at Parowan.
Courtesy, Utah State Historical Society.

THE KILLING OF ED DALTON

One of the first born in southern Utah's Parowan, 34-year-old Edward Meeks Dalton was a strapping six-footer who had two wives. When he was 20 and she 17, he had married Emily Stevens, a willowy English girl, who bore him three sons and a daughter. Eight years later, he married 18-year-old Delilah "Lila" Clark, by whom he had a son and a daughter. An athletic, free spirit, looked up to by youth in town, Dalton vowed he would never go to prison or pay a fine.[42]

Early in 1886 Dalton was arrested by Deputy Marshal William O. Orton from Beaver, who placed him in the temporary custody of the local sheriff. "Young Ed," as he was called, not wishing to embarrass the town's lawman, waited for a time for the federal marshal to return before making his escape, but at last he grew impatient, removed his boots, and took off. So fast a runner was he that no one could catch him. After spending the summer in Arizona, he came home in December for the winter.

Hearing of his return, Marshal William Thompson, Jr., from Beaver waited that month in a corner house on a Parowan crossroads as his

---

[42]There are many accounts of this episode, but one of the best is Dix, "Unwilling Martyr: The Death of Young Ed Dalton," 162–77.

quarry rode past driving some livestock. Then he rushed out and ordered the young man to halt. When Dalton turned and took off again, the marshal raised a borrowed rifle with a hair trigger and fired, he later claimed, "with the intention of shooting over him." Riding bareback, "Young Ed" pitched forward, grabbed at the horse's mane, and slid to the ground in agony, shot squarely in the back.[43] Bending over his victim, Thompson, a former Mormon, said, "I told you to halt; why didn't you stop?" The wounded man made no reply. He died less than an hour later as they carried him to his mother's house.[44]

Thompson and Deputy Orton were arrested by Sheriff Hugh Adams and held for their own safety as a coroner's jury stamped the deed "feloniously done" and excited townsmen gathered, many calling for the pair to be lynched. But the dead man's father, Edward Dalton, Parowan's mayor and a Mormon Battalion veteran, quieted the crowd. "Two wrongs won't mend one," he kept telling them.[45]

A significant sign of changing times and attitudes also came with word from Apostle Heber Jeddy Grant, then visiting at Cedar City. The son of the 1856 reformation firebrand, Jedediah Grant, and future church president, told local authorities to keep order and not let Dalton's friends "take the law into their own hands."[46]

A jury of non-Mormon miners at Beaver later acquitted Thompson of manslaughter, holding his use of deadly force justified, but the people of Parowan thought otherwise. Their judgment was pronounced for all time on an imposing monument over Dalton's grave: "He was shot and Killed December 16, 1886, in cold blood by a deputy United States Marshal, while under indictment for a misdemeanor under the Edmunds Anti-polygamy law."[47]

EDMUNDS-TUCKER LAW

The only polygamist killed by federal marshals, Edward Dalton

---

[43]Thompson to Dyer, December 16, 1886, quoted in Whitney, *History of Utah*, 3:531. Also see Roberts, *Comprehensive History*, 6:116–18.

[44]Ibid., 529.

[45]Dix, "Unwilling Martyr," 168.

[46]Roberts, *Comprehensive History*, 6:118.

[47]The stone monument over Dalton's grave can be seen today in the Parowan Cemetery.

became a martyr in the eyes of many as Congress was finishing work on
an even more punishing law against polygamy. Having rejected the Scott
Amendment, lawmakers early in 1887 passed the Edmunds-Tucker Act,
which became law on March 3 without the signature of President
Grover Cleveland. Among other things, the new statute:

- Disincorporated the Mormon church "in so far as it may now have or
  pretend to have, any legal existence" and ordered the U.S. attorney general to "wind up" its affairs;
- Dissolved the Perpetual Emigrating Fund Company and ordered that
  its assets in excess of debts and lawful claims, like those of its parent, be
  escheated, or returned, to the United States for the benefit of the territory's common schools;
- Prohibited secret marriages and required all weddings to be certified in
  probate courts by a license "subject to inspection as other public
  records";
- Gave to the U.S. marshal and deputies the power possessed by sheriffs,
  constables, and other local peace officers to enforce all federal and territorial laws;
- Abolished the right of females in Utah to vote;
- Required prospective voters, grand and petit jurors, and public office
  holders to swear an oath they would support the U.S. constitution and
  obey the Edmunds Act;
- Dissolved territorial laws providing for the election of probate, or
  county, judges and authorized the U.S. president to appoint such local
  magistrates;
- Liquidated existing election districts and ordered the Utah Commission to redistrict the territory and apportion representation according
  to population;
- Called it incest for first cousins or closer relatives to marry, cohabit, or
  have sexual intercourse and required punishment of not less than three
  years in prison for this offense; and
- Abolished the office of territorial school superintendent and gave the
  Utah Supreme Court the power to appoint a commissioner of schools
  with the authority to prohibit "any book of a sectarian character or
  otherwise unsuitable," a reference to Mormon works and the Deseret
  Alphabet.[48]

With approval of these and other sections, Congress completed by
piecemeal enactment almost all of the provisions of the failed Cullom

---

[48]For the full Edmunds-Tucker Act, see *Statutes at Large of the United States*, 24:635–41.

bill, introduced seventeen years before. Years after Utah became a state, the author of the proposed 1870 act, Robert Baskin, said its passage would have spared Utah much turmoil and produced needed changes at a much earlier day.[49]

1887 STATEHOOD CONVENTION

Passage of the Edmunds-Tucker Act was echoed by at least the eighth attempt by Utah Territory to take a sovereign position either through statehood or full independence from the rest of the United States.[50] If the motive was the same, this latest effort to escape from federal authority and laws, which applied only to territories, featured some noteworthy differences.

First, the sixty-nine delegates to the 1887 constitutional convention who gathered on June 30 in the Salt Lake City Hall had been chosen at mass meetings of the People's Party in twenty-two of Utah's twenty-four counties, not called by legislative resolutions or acts. One reason may have been that election changes, required under the Edmunds-Tucker Act, had resulted in the election of five Liberal Party members to the territorial legislature.

Moreover the Mormon political party had invited the fledgling Republican and Democratic parties to take part in the convention on the understanding they would be accorded "a fair representation." Both rejected the overture for the reason perhaps best expressed by J. B. Rosborough, chairman of the Democratic Territorial Committee. The claim of People's Party leaders "that all rightful political power is derived from God," rather than the people, was "repugnant to American institutions," he replied.[51]

Finally, most striking, delegates to the convention approved on July 7

---

[49]Baskin, *Reminiscences of Early Utah*, 28–31.

[50]Earlier bids for sovereignty included conventions or memorials under the name of Deseret in 1849, 1852, 1853, 1856, 1862, 1867, and 1872, a constitutional convention in 1882 in the name of Utah, direct moves to independence from the U. S. in 1857 and 1862, and introduction in Congress of enabling acts for a constitutional convention in 1874 and 1878.

[51]Rosborough to Winder, June 24, 1887, "Admission of the State of Utah," House Rep. 4156 (50–2), 1889, Serial 2675, 194–201. The replies of the territory's independent parties to the invitation to take part in the statehood convention are published in full in this document. They illustrate the political nature of the conflicts that existed in Utah at this time.

a founding document that forbade bigamy and polygamy as "incompatible with 'a republican form of government'" and provided stiff punishments "in the discretion of the court." Not only did they resurrect the Scott Amendment, killed earlier by Congress, they also adopted unanimously a provision ruling out any union of church and state in Utah.[52]

By special permission of the Utah Commission, the constitution was voted on during the August election by those who had not been weeded out of the election process by federal law. In a customary display of unanimity, voters approved it by 13,195 to 502 before it was submitted in December, with a petition for statehood, to Congress, where opposition had less to do with polygamy than it did with the territory's theocratic political system.

In the Senate the Committee on the Territories lost no time in resolving that statehood should be withheld until polygamy had been abandoned and it was "likewise certain that the civil affairs of the Territory are not controlled by the priesthood of the Mormon Church."[53]

At House hearings in January 1889, Utah Delegate Caine and Franklin S. Richards argued persuasively for statehood, but Governor Caleb West gave the most telling testimony. Described as "a thoughtful, intelligent man," untied to the Republican crusade against "the twin relics of barbarism," the moderate Kentucky Democrat said he had hoped on coming to Utah in 1886 to heal the division and hostility he found, calling it "as intense as existed in the border States" during the Civil War.[54] While some progress had been made, including formation of the Salt Lake Chamber of Commerce, the governor saw an "irreconcilable political difference, fundamental in character, between the Mormon system and the government established by the United States." Until the difference was settled, he said, "of necessity an irrepressible conflict will wage."[55] In the meantime, he opposed statehood.

For much the same reason, the Utah Commission also came out against Utah's bid. By a three to two vote, its members held that "no harmony in the Union could be maintained with a state ruled by a creed

---

[52]Report of the Utah Commission, 1887, House Exec. Doc. I (50–1), 1887, pt. 5, Vol. I, Serial 2542, 1317–57.

[53]See Resolution, Committee on Territories, Sen. Misc. Doc. 89 (50–1), 1888, Serial 2516.

[54]House Rep. 4156, 204.

[55]Ibid.

which claims all governments but its own to be illegal, and claims a 'separate political destiny and ultimate temporal dominion by divine right.'"[56]

Utah's neighbor on the north entered the debate with a similar, unfriendly expression. The Legislative Assembly of Idaho Territory resolved that "the admission of Utah and additional power thus given said church would create a dangerous condition of affairs in Idaho and would endanger the welfare of our social and moral institutions."[57] Idaho already had enacted a test oath for voters, office holders, or jury members that disfranchised LDS church members altogether, whether they practiced polygamy or not.[58]

Given such opposition, it was little wonder Congress turned down Utah's latest attempt to become a state. As if to add insult to rejection, national lawmakers gave approval for Montana, South Dakota, North Dakota, and Washington to enter the Union in 1889 and granted statehood to Idaho and Wyoming in 1890. All but one of the new states had been settled later than Utah.

DEATH OF JOHN TAYLOR

Defeat of the most determined of Utah's many assaults on the gates of the American Union would not be suffered in his temporal existence by the dignified leader who initiated it. John Taylor, distinguished in appearance, courteous in manner, had governed his church from the underground for two years and six months when after a brief illness he died at age 78 on July 25, 1887, at a private home in Kaysville. To the end, the silver-haired Englishman was true to the words he lived by: "The Kingdom of God or nothing."[59]

---

[56]Report of the Utah Commission, 1887, 1340.

[57]See House Joint Memorial No. 1, *Congressional Record* (50–2), January 14, 1889, Vol. 20, pt. 1, 760.

[58]Under the Idaho law, prospective voters, office holders, and jury members had to swear "that I am not a bigamist or polygamist; that I am not a member of any order, organization, or association which teaches, advises, counsels, or encourages its members, devotees, or any other person to commit the crime of bigamy or polygamy, or any other crime defined by law, as a duty arising or resulting from membership in such order, organization or association, or which practices bigamy or polygamy or plural or celestial marriage as a doctrinal rite of such organization; that I do not, and will not, publicly or privately, or in any manner whatever, teach advise, counsel or encourage any person to commit the crime of bigamy or polygamy, or any other crime defined by law, either as a religious duty or otherwise." See House Rep. 4156, 171. Also see Whitney, *History of Utah*, 3:275–76.

[59]See Taylor, *The Kingdom or Nothing: The Life of John Taylor*.

With his death the mantle of church authority fell to the shoulders of the senior apostle, an industrious son of Farmington Valley, Connecticut. Wilford Woodruff at age 80 took charge of his faith's affairs as president of the Quorum of the Twelve Apostles. He became LDS church president on April 7, 1889.[60]

Perhaps the most beloved Mormon leader of his day, the gentle farmer and devoted fisherman, at a time of unparalleled crisis, would shape the future of his church as no leader has done since the days of its founding prophet. But first, the millennial-minded apostle would look for divine intervention to preserve the faith from its oppressors.

---

[60]For the definitive biography of this important figure in Mormon history, see Alexander, *Things in Heaven and Earth: The Life and Times of Wilford Woodruff, a Mormon Prophet.*

APOSTLE WILFORD WOODRUFF
Woodruff received a revelation in the wilderness,
but as church president he turned his faith in a new
direction to end polygamy and theocratic rule.
Courtesy, Manuscripts Division, University of Utah Libraries.

Chapter 17

AMERICANIZATION OF THE KINGDOM

Prepare ye for the Coming of the Son of Man which is nigh at
the Door. No man knoweth the day nor the hour but the Signs
of Both Heaven and Earth indicate his Coming as promised by
the Mouth of my deciples [*sic*]. The fig trees are leaving [*sic*] and
the hour is nigh.

—Wilford Woodruff

At the LDS church's general conference in the unfinished temple at
Nauvoo, Illinois, on April 6, 1843, Mormonism's founding prophet had
at last answered the question uppermost in the minds of his followers:
When will Jesus Christ come again? While he earnestly prayed about
this, Joseph Smith said, a voice said to him, "My son, if thou livest until
thou art eighty-five years of age, thou shalt see the face of the Son of
Man."[1] Smith then announced "in the name of the Lord God, and let it
be written—the Son of Man will not come in the clouds of heaven till
I am eighty-five years old."[2] Since he was born on December 23, 1805,
this forecast was consistent with his earlier promise to the faith's first
apostles, made in 1835, that they would live to see Christ return in glory
and that "even fifty-six years should wind up the scene."[3]

If the exact day and hour were unknown, the two prophecies pointed
to 1890–91 as the time Christ would come to save the elect and punish
their enemies. In the hope they gave to a subjugated people, forgotten
were the disappointed expectancies of 1857–58 and 1861–67. For the
Kingdom of God in western America, the last days would be a season of
enduring oppression while preparing for its destiny to rule the world

---

[1]Smith, *History of the Church*, 5:324, 336.
[2]Ibid.
[3]Ibid., 2:182.

during Christ's millennial reign.[4] When the time arrived, "one government, one kingdom," said Apostle Orson Pratt in 1875, "everlasting in
its nature, will have dominion over the whole of our globe." As foretold,
it would be given "into the hands of the Saints of the Most High," a
scripture he believed referred to Mormon believers.[5] If all this smacked
of treason, said he, "perhaps it would be well enough for some of our
good judges to get out an indictment against the Prophet Daniel."[6]

DAY OF THE LAMANITE

Among sure signs the hour was nigh was a spiritual awakening that
year among the Lamanites, or Native Americans, believed to be children
of Jacob from the tribe of Manasseh. Before Christ came again, this
remnant of Israel, according to *Book of Mormon* prophecy, would learn of
the covenants God had made with their fathers and gather out of the
wilderness to build New Jerusalem, the City of Zion, in Jackson
County, Missouri.[7] This forecast seemed suddenly fulfilled when native
Americans at a time of deepening crisis for their own culture began to
flock in surprising numbers to the call of one man, who apparently
started the so-called Lamanite gathering all by himself.

George Washington Hill was the big, unsophisticated son of an Ohio
brickmason who became one of the most productive missionaries of any
faith to the western Indians. Sent to the northern tribes at age 33 during the great Lamanite missionary call of 1855, he had baptized Bannocks and Shoshonis at Fort Limhi by the dozens. Hill loved to talk,
and his good-natured bravado and gift for speaking in native tongues
were irresistible to Indians.

Called again in 1873 on a mission to the northern tribes, the Ohioan
by his own carefully kept records baptized nearly a thousand Shoshonis
over the next three years,[8] including the feared Sagwitch whose depreda-

---

[4]For an important article on this, see Erickson, "Joseph Smith's 1891 Millennial Prophecy: The Quest for
Apocalyptic Deliverance," 1–34. Another significant work is Reinwand, "An Interpretive Study of Mormon Millennialism during the Nineteenth Century with Emphasis on Millennial Developments in Utah."

[5]Dan. 7:27.

[6]Orson Pratt, "Second Coming of Christ, etc.," February 25, 1875, *Journal of Discourses*, 17:321.

[7]See *The Book of Mormon*, 2 Nephi 30:3–7. Also see McConkie, "The Lamanites and the Second Coming," *The
Millennial Messiah: The Second Coming of the Son of Man*, 206–19.

[8]Journal History, October 1, 1876, 2–6.

tions had led to the Battle of Bear River in 1863. In 1875 he established a farm on Bear River, some five miles from the new non-Mormon town of Corinne, where natives came from as far away as Fort Hall and the Wind River region of present Wyoming for food and instruction in the arts of agriculture.[9] According to one chief, they came in response to a vision in which three men told him that "the 'Mormons' God was the true God" and "the time was at hand for the Indians to gather."[10] Apostle Pratt named these mysterious messengers as the "Three Nephites" of *The Book of Mormon*, disciples of Jesus Christ in America "who lived eighteen hundred years ago." Promised they would never taste death "even until all things shall be fulfilled," they were to administer to the remnant of Israel before the Lord came again.[11]

"We have got to be sent forth as missionaries to all parts of this American continent," the apostle said, to the natives of "British America, to all the tribes that dwell in the Territories of the United States, also to all those who are scattered through Mexico, and Central and South America." After they are gathered, he said, "then shall the powers of heaven come down and be in the midst of this people."[12]

For citizens of non-Mormon Corinne, one Indian missionary like George Hill in the part of the world they called home was one too many. The gathering of some two thousand natives on the outskirts of town frightened them. Hardly comforting were rumors the Mormons called their Indian cousins, "The Lord's Battle Axes." Equally alarming were reports the Indians had been told "that the Bear River Valley belonged to them, and if the soldiers attempted to drive them away not to go, as their guns would have no effect upon them."[13] The latter was an apparent reference to the Mormon garment, which, the natives were allegedly told, "Gentile bullets would not penetrate."[14]

---

[9] See Christensen, "Sagwitch: Shoshoni Chieftain, Mormon Elder, 1822–1884," scheduled for publication.

[10] Hill, "An Indian Vision," 11, quoted in Christensen, "Sagwitch: Shoshoni Chieftain, Mormon Elder."

[11] Orson Pratt, "Redemption of Zion, etc.," February 7, 1875; and "Gathering of Israel, etc.," April 11, 1875, *Journal of Discourses*, 17:296–33, 18:19–21. Also see *The Book of Mormon*, 3 Nephi 28:1–10.

[12] *Journal of Discourses*, 17:301–02.

[13] Report of W. H. Danilson, U.S. Indian Agent, Annual Report of the Commissioner of Indian Affairs, 1875, House Exec. Doc. 1 (44–1), Vol. 4, pt. 1, Serial 1680.

[14] Madsen, *Corinne: The Gentile Capital of Utah*, 281. Mormons completing the temple or Endowment House rituals received a cloth undergarment with mystic markings to signify they had been cleansed of the blood of their generation and were prepared to receive the Bridegroom. Indians placed great store in mysticism, or medicine, and especially valued the assurance that garments would shield the wearer against harm.

FORGOTTEN KINGDOM

This volatile mix of mysticism and misunderstanding needed only a spark to blow the whole town into a full panic. It was struck on August 9, 1875, when the *Corinne Daily Mail* announced in big, black headlines: "Mormons Meddling with the Indians! Mountain Meadows to be repeated!! Corinnethians to be the Victims!!!"[15] The next day women and children holed up in the Central Hotel while men broke into a federal arms shipment at the railroad depot for weapons to defend the place. In a night of terror, pickets at the edge of town fired at shadows and warriors were seen skulking on every corner. The mayor demanded that soldiers be sent from Fort Douglas to protect the railroad town, but by the time they arrived, the big Indian scare was over.[16] Their captain told Hill to move his Indian camp away from the outskirts.

While the Ohioan gathered the "Lamanites" on Bear River, the new Mormon outreach to the tribes, starting in 1875, soon produced similar results in other places. "They are coming in by hundreds," reported Mormon Indian agent Dimick Huntington in June that year at Salt Lake City. "There has been 2,000 baptisms already."[17]

The spiritual uprising did not go unnoticed elsewhere. From the Moapa River Indian Reserve in southeast Nevada, U.S. Agent A. J. Barnes reported hundreds of natives were baptized that summer at St. George. Agent C. A. Bateman at Pyramid Lake in 1875 told the Indian Affairs commissioner that Paiutes from that reserve had been invited for reasons other than "simply religious" to come to Utah "and be washed." And Indians at Fort Hall had been told "they were the chosen people of God to establish his kingdom upon the earth," according to the agent there.[18]

THE GHOST DANCE

Such reports do not offer direct evidence that the work of Mormon

---

[15] *Corinne Daily Mail*, August 9, 1875.

[16] For more on the great Corinne Indian scare, see Madsen, *Corinne: The Gentile Capital of Utah*, 273–89; and Christensen, "Sagwitch: Shoshoni Chieftain, Mormon Elder."

[17] Huntington to Smith, June 6, 1875, published in *Millennial Star*, July 5, 1875, 426–27, quoted in Christensen, "Sagwitch: Shoshoni Chieftain, Mormon Elder."

[18] See Annual Report of the Commissioner of Indian Affairs, House Exec. Doc. 1 (44–1), 1875, Vol. I pt. 5, Serial 1680, 638–44, 760. Among other examples, also see reports of Commissioner of Indian Affairs, House Exec. Doc. 1 (45–2), 1877, Serial 1800, 182; House Exec. Doc. 1 (46–2), 1879, Serial 1910, 111, 168; House Ex. Doc. 1 (46–3), 1880, Serial 1959, 177; House Exec. Doc. 1 (47–1), 1881, Serial 2018, 63–64; and House Exec. Doc. 1 (48–1), 1883, Serial 2191, 54, 114.

Indian missionaries to redeem the remnant of Jacob before Christ came again influenced the birth of the new Indian millennial religion known as the Ghost Dance. The western tribes had known a number of prophets before a seer appeared about this time among the Paiutes, including Nakidoklini, the Apache medicine man; Smohalla from the Columbia River region; and the Paiute Wodziwob, who gave in about 1870 the forerunner of the Ghost Dance.[19]

Moreover, as historian Lawrence G. Coates has pointed out, it is highly improbable that Mormon missionaries ever took part in any of the native religious ceremonials.[20] The record suggests instead that they were as puzzled by the rituals as other observers on the frontier. For the Ghost Dance faith that swept through the tribes in the late 1880s was an authentic Indian religion that spoke to the hearts of Native Americans like no spiritual creation of white culture could ever hope to do.[21] Even so, the parallels between the two millennial movements are too striking to dismiss out of hand the possibility that one influenced the other. The most significant similarity, identified by historian Louis G. Reinwand, is that Wovoka, the Paiute prophet who introduced the Ghost Dance religion, taught his followers that Jesus Christ would come in 1891. This belief was advocated by no western religion other than the Mormons.[22]

Born in about 1856, Wovoka, meaning "The Cutter," was born in western Nevada's Walker Lake region, near present Yerington, where he was reared by a Protestant white family who gave him the name Jack Wilson. He was a full-blooded Indian, the professed son of Tavibo, also a dreamer who possessed supernatural powers. In about 1887, when "the sun died," Wovoka was taken up to the spirit world where he saw God and all the people who had died in a beautiful land full of game. God

---

[19]As early as 1857 natives in the Northwest told U.S. Army officers that "Choosuklee, Jesus Christ" had come east of the mountains to drive the whites out of the country. The story was thought to have been inspired by Brigham Young's meetings with the natives that year at Fort Limhi. See Clarke to Thomas, January 1, 1858, Sen. Exec. Doc. 1 (35–2), 1858, 335–36.

[20]Coates, "The Mormons and the Ghost Dance," 89–111. Also see Barney, *Mormons, Indians and the Ghost Dance Religion of 1890.*

[21]Studies on the Ghost Dance religion are many, but still the most authoritative source is Mooney, "Ghost-Dance Religion and the Sioux Outbreak of 1890," *Fourteenth Annual Report (Part 2) of the Bureau of Ethnology to the Smithsonian Institution, 1892–93.*

[22]Reinwand, "An Interpretive Study of Mormon Millennialism during the Nineteenth Century with Emphasis on Millennial Developments in Utah," 148.

told him to go back and tell His children they must live in peace with the whites, love one another, not lie or steal. If they obeyed, the messiah would come and they would be reunited with their resurrected relatives in a world where there would be no sickness, death, or old age.

To hasten the event, he was given a shuffling ceremonial dance for his people to perform in a circle, with no fire in the center, at night for five consecutive days at a time. The ritual was called the Ghost Dance because it would hurry the resurrection of the dead in a land full of game and no whites. It was an Indian vision of the millennium.

As the new faith spread like wildfire, converts added their own tribal beliefs and symbols until the variations were uncounted. A Sioux or Arapaho innovation may have been picked up from the Shoshonis and Bannocks at Fort Hall who had shown as early as 1858 an interest in the protective nature of the Mormon temple garment. This was the "Ghost shirt," a cloth garment in one piece, sewn with sinew, cut and ornamented in Indian fashion, that would safeguard its wearer from harm, including a speeding bullet.[23]

THE WILDERNESS REVELATION

Before a peaceful ritual turned into tragedy, early in 1880 Apostle Wilford Woodruff fled from St. George to a sheepherder's camp in the San Francisco Mountains of northern Arizona to escape from the federal marshal in the wake of the U.S. Supreme Court decision upholding the conviction of George Reynolds for polygamy. Like an Old Testament prophet in the wilderness, he became "rapt in vision" and on January 26 the word of God came to him.

"The hour is at the door when my wrath and indignation shall be poured out upon the wicked of this Nation," the Almighty said. "Cloth[e] yourselves in the robes of the Holy Priesthood," He told His apostles, and testify by name against those who had persecuted His people, "The Preside[n]ts of the United States, The Supreme Court, The Cabinet, The Senate & House of Con[g]ress of the United States The

---

[23]Following their attack on the Mormon mission at Fort Limhi in 1858, Bannocks and Shoshonis had stripped James Miller's body "and torn out the bloody spots in his garment and left the pieces on the ground." See Salmon River Mission Journal, February 26, 1858.

Governors of the States and Territories The Judges & Officers" and all the rest.[24]

"The Nation is ripened in iniquity and the Cup of the wrath of mine indignation is full, and I will not Stay my hand in Judgment upon this Nation or the Nations of the Earth," the Lord said. "Wo unto that Nation or House or people, who seek to hinder my People from obeying the Patriarchal Law of Abraham," He warned, referring to polygamy. "I will burn them up saith the Lord of Hosts."[25]

As instructed, on January 19, 1881, the First Presidency and apostles conducted "the first thing of the kind since the Creation of the world," recorded Woodruff. Donning their sacred robes, they performed "the ordinance of washing our feet against our Enemies And the Enemies of the Kingdom of God." Then they laid before the Almighty for punishment a list of the names of those who had "made war against Thee and thy kingdom and anointed ones."[26] In so doing, prayed John Taylor, recently ordained as LDS church president, "May the same spirit of Mercy love and Charity dwell in our hearts that dwell in the Soul of Jesus of Nazareth when he gave up the Ghosts [sic] upon the Cross."[27]

COUNCIL OF FIFTY RENEWED

While witnessing against the wicked, Taylor at the same time moved to revitalize the Council of Fifty, the millennial governing body, to prepare for world rule on Christ's arrival.[28] The name of the order, "the Living Constitution of the Kingdom of God," exposed the belief that a theocratic form of government, rule by revelation from God through inspired men, transcended the restrictions of a written document or manmade laws.[29]

When organized in March 1844, the council was a revolutionary body created to implement God's will that "my law, and my rule, and my

---

[24]Kenney, ed., *Wilford Woodruff's Journal*, 7:615–25. Also see Collier, *Unpublished Revelations*, 123–29.

[25]Ibid., 7:617.

[26]Ibid., 8:6, 7.

[27]Ibid., 7:621–25.

[28]See Quinn, "The Council of Fifty and Its Members, 1844 to 1945"; and *The Mormon Hierarchy: Origins of Power*, 105–41.

[29]Again, under this belief, the U.S. Constitution was considered inspired by God as a stepping stone to a higher form of government, not an end in itself.

dominion shall extend over the whole earth."[30] With world rule post-poned by the delay in Christ's arrival, it had gradually become less active in the theocracy's temporal affairs under the one-man rule of Brigham Young, who brought it back up to full strength only during the millen-nial expectancy of the mid-1860s.[31]

With Christ's coming again in sight, President Taylor in 1880 reorga-nized the council, retiring older members and ordaining over the next four years as many as thirty-four new ones.[32] On February 4, 1885, in obedience to revelation, members donned their "Priestly attire" and bestowed on the Mormon president the title, "King Priest and Ruler over Israel on the Earth," held by his predecessors.[33] With many mem-bers under siege by federal marshals, however, the covert body was by now little more than a standby apparatus, awaiting the Lord's arrival to become functional. The Council of Fifty in time would fade away alto-gether as millennial hopes waned and those who belonged failed to real-ize the assurance that came with membership that they would live to see Christ's return.[34]

CHURCH PROPERTY ESCHEATED

Undeterred by fears of divine retribution, enemies of the kingdom stepped up their campaign against polygamy and theocratic rule. Passage of the 1887 Edmunds-Tucker Act had placed in their hands destructive

---

[30]Collier, *Unpublished Revelations*, 1:132–136.

[31]Added in 1867 were Robert T. Burton, George Q. Cannon, Jeter Clinton, William H. Hooper, Edward Hunter, Charles S. Kimball, David P. Kimball, Heber P. Kimball, Parley P. Pratt, Jr., Joseph C. Rich, Heber J. Richards, John Sharp, Joseph F. Smith, Abraham O. Smoot, Hosea Stout, George J. Taylor, Brigham Young, Jr., John W. Young, and Joseph A. Young. See Quinn, "The Council of Fifty and Its Members, 1844 to 1945," 193–97.

[32]Ibid. They were William Budge, John T. Caine, Abraham H. Cannon, Angus M. Cannon, John Q. Cannon, Hiram B. Clawson, William W. Cluff, Lorin Farr, George F. Gibbs, Heber J. Grant, Leonard W. Hardy, Abram Hatch, William Jennings, Christopher Layton, Feramorz Little, Francis M. Lyman, John R. Murdock, John L. Nuttall, Charles W. Penrose, Canute Peterson, William B. Preston, George Reynolds, Franklin S. Richards, Lewis W. Shurtliff, John Henry Smith, Silas S. Smith, William R. Smith, William W. Taylor, George Teasdale, Moses Thatcher, John Van Cott, Junius F. Wells, John R. Winder, and Seymour B. Young.

[33]Franklin D. Richards Miscellaneous Papers, LDS Archives, quoted in Quinn, "The Council of Fifty and Its Members," 187.

[34]According to historian D. Michael Quinn, the Council of Fifty's last surviving member was church Presi-dent Heber J. Grant, who died in 1945. For more on the council's activities during the 1880s, see Quinn, *The Mormon Hierarchy: Extensions of Power*, 292–301.

new weapons, including the power to confiscate all church assets over $50,000. But that would prove to be more difficult than Congress may have figured.

Years before, anticipating just such a development, the far-sighted Brigham Young had shifted many church holdings under secret trusts to chosen members to keep them out of federal reach. As the punitive 1887 bill neared passage, wards and stakes were given all assets within their limits, except tithing property and receipts. Even after it became law, the temple block and buildings, the Gardo House,[35] and the Tithing Office were deeded to Robert T. Burton, William B. Preston, and John Winder, members of the Presiding Bishopric and Council of Fifty.[36]

Without realizing how difficult it would be just to find this property, much less to confiscate it, U.S. Attorney George Peters on July 30, 1887, waited until the day after John Taylor's funeral. Then be began proceedings before the Utah Supreme Court to escheat the church's assets. Appointed receiver, U.S. Marshal Frank H. Dyer on November 10 possessed without much trouble the Tithing Office. Taking courage from this success, he moved soon after to seize the ten-acre temple block and its buildings, including the tabernacle and unfinished temple, as well as the nearby Historian's Office and Gardo House. All of these properties were rented back to their former owner for amounts ranging from $1 a year for the temple block to $450 a month for the Gardo mansion, but work on the temple stopped.

Unfooled by transfers of property, Dyer and Powers over the next year ferreted out other church holdings. On October 9, 1888 the Utah Supreme Court took the temple block and its buildings off the forfeiture list because the law spared places of worship. But it rejected shifts of title made to hide assets and the argument by church attorney, Franklin S. Richards, that the Gardo House should be exempted because it was a "parsonage." These rulings and the federal act itself were now challenged in the U.S. Supreme Court.

---

[35]The Gardo House, also known as "Amelia's Palace" after Brigham Young's twenty-fifth and favorite wife, Harriet Amelia Folsom Young, thirty-seven years his junior, was a four-story mansion of three dozen rooms on the southwest corner of present South Temple and State Street. Finished just before Young's death in 1877, it served as the official residence of LDS church presidents before it was leased by Isaac Trumbo, a mining businessman and U.S. Senate aspirant, and later demolished.

[36]For a list of these properties, see Arrington, *Great Basin Kingdom*, 362–65.

RIGHT TO VOTE CURTAILED

Besides forfeiting the church's property, the 1887 federal law also took radical steps to curb Mormon political power, putting an end to woman suffrage and the practice of identifying ballots in Utah elections. As dictated, the Utah Commission also redistricted the entire territory to give greater weight to non-Mormon votes and imposed a test oath to disfranchise prospective voters who would not swear to obey the 1882 law.

To make manifest the government's "sovereign power," the Utah Commission further selected registration agents "from the Gentile or non-Mormon element of the population." Moreover, in appointing election judges, it chose two out of the three for each district, wherever possible, "from the non-Mormon element."[37] The election board in 1889 finally recommended a law to disfranchise Mormons altogether. Nor did measures to keep them from voting stop there.

When two foreign-born church members, John Moore and Walter J. Edgar, on November 9, 1889, tried to become naturalized citizens, eligible to vote, they suddenly found themselves under fire in the Third District court at Salt Lake City. Their citizenship quest was contested by Robert Baskin and other Liberal Party leaders on the charge they had sworn during the Endowment House ceremony to avenge upon the nation the blood of their faith's slain prophets, Joseph and Hyrum Smith. It was not a new allegation. As early as 1849, William Smith, Joseph's brother, had petitioned against statehood for Deseret on the same charge.[38] But over the next three weeks, it was fought over again as witnesses for both sides, loyal believers and the disaffected, stood before newly appointed Judge Thomas J. Anderson and told squarely conflicting stories. The truth of what they said seemed to rest largely on memory or semantic differences too subtle for the uninitiated to detect.

Judge Anderson weighed their testimony and on November 20 came down against the pair, denying citizenship on the ground they could not obey their Endowment House vows and oath of citizenship at the same

[37]Report of the Utah Commission, 1889, House Exec. Doc. I (51–I), Vol. 13, Serial 2726, 178. One commission member, Democrat John A. McClernand, commander of the Union Army's 13th Corps at the Battle of Vicksburg, dissented from the report's "general animus."

[38]See Chapter 2, note 10. That there was such an oath is beyond reasonable doubt. The question of whether such vengeance was to be taken against the nation or the murderers of the Smith brothers, or both, is open to debate.

time. Nine others who had not undergone the endowment ritual were also refused citizenship simply because they belonged to the church. The ruling was a heavy blow whose most immediate impact would be to keep foreign-born Mormons from voting in the future.

FIRST ELECTION DEFEATS

By 1887 the Edmunds-Tucker Act and an influx of outsiders had already begun to bite into the People's Party's margins of support. That year five non-Mormons won seats in the Legislative Assembly, three in the House and two in the Council. Encouraged, the Liberal Party in February 1889 scored a stunning reversal, taking control for the first time of city government in Ogden. The sweep touched off a wild celebration in the railroad center, but not the first of its kind that year.

Liberals in August won eight seats in the legislature, an increase of three. But the most shocking news that came out of the legislative election that month became apparent when the votes were counted in Salt Lake City, where city elections were to be held the following February. The totals showed that the Liberals had won forty-one more votes than the People's Party, which placed within the grasp of unbelievers the Chief Stake of Zion itself.

At this portent, rejoicing Liberals "made the night hideous with their yells, drums, tin pans, tin horns, cow bells, torch lights, and fire works and marching through the streets until after one o'clock in the morning," said L. John Nuttall, church President Woodruff's personal secretary.[39] The 55-year-old Englishman was also assistant to Utah's delegate to Congress, John T. Caine, and a newly ordained Council of Fifty member.

Not ready to join the Liberal celebration quite yet was Utah's new governor, Arthur L. Thomas, 48, appointed on May 6 that year by President Benjamin Harrison to replace the moderate Caleb W. West. A hard-liner, Thomas had been a Utah Commission member from 1886 to 1889 and had served as territorial secretary under former governors Emery, Murray, and West. No federal official had been as active in territorial political affairs.

It was a mistake to think "Mormon power was at an end in Utah,"

---

[39]Journal of L. John Nuttall, August 5, 1889.

CALEB W. WEST
The last territorial
governor, Dalton worked to heal
divisions and prepare for statehood.
Courtesy, LDS Archives.

Thomas told the U.S. secretary of the interior. "The time may come when the Gentiles will be in the majority," he continued, "but it will be many years hence." In the meantime, the governor said, Mormons viewed the "invasion of Utah soil by the Gentiles somewhat as the crusaders regarded the occupancy of the Holy Land by the Saracens."[40]

THE YEAR OF CHANGE

As the time of Christ's coming grew near, Wilford Woodruff was pressed by church attorneys to make concessions on polygamy and he inquired of the Almighty what to do. "Thus saith the Lord," the word came back on November 24, 1889, to the church president: "Let not my servants who are called to the Presidency of my church, deny my word or my law."[41] There would be no compromises on polygamy. Instead, warned the Lord, judgments were about to fall on "all nations under the heavens which include great Babylon," an apparent reference to the United States. "These judgments are at the door," He said. "Great events await you and this generation, and are nigh at your doors."[42]

[40]Annual Report of the Governor of Utah, 1889, House Exec. Doc. I (51–I), 1889, Vol. 13, pt. 5, Serial 2726, 473–502.

[41]"Revelation given to Wilford Woodruff," Kenney, ed., *Wilford Woodruff's Journal,* 9:67–69.

[42]Ibid.

To the Mormon leader it was manifest that "the word of the Prophet Joseph Smith is beginning to be fulfilled that the whole Nation would turn against Zion & make war upon the Saints," he told his diary on the last day of 1889. "1890 will be an important year with the Latter Day Saints & American nation."[43] One after the other calamities struck over the next twelve months like the sounds of a great bell ringing out the last days of the theocratic state in America's West, proving his prophecy true.

The first stroke was stunning. On February 3 the U.S. Supreme Court upheld the Idaho law disfranchising any person who belonged to an organization that "teaches, advises, counsels or encourages" its members to practice polygamy, whether he had more than one wife himself or not.[44] Right after the ruling came down, Robert Baskin boarded the train to Washington, D.C., to promote a federal version of the act.

The second stroke came just one week later. On February 10 the Liberal Party swept Salt Lake City offices after an election campaign marred by name-calling and accusations of illegal practices by both sides. The first non-Mormon mayor of Utah's capital was 54-year-old George M. Scott, a hardware retailer who came to Utah in 1871 to found the forerunner of Strevell-Patterson Company. A week later, Liberals took control of the city of fifty-two thousand and promptly raised their own salaries.

"The Year of Jubilee is Come," crowed *The Salt Lake Daily Tribune* over the wild Liberal celebration. "The struggle has been to Americanize Utah," the paper said, "and as the Central Stake of the Saint's kingdom passes out of Saintly control, the Americans are able to point proudly to their record here." It denied that opponents of Mormon rule have "ever attacked a religion or that they have ever sought to injure a Mormon in person or property."[45]

True or not, the boast looked somewhat hollow when Senator Shelby Cullom, right after Baskin arrived in the nation's capital, introduced a bill modeled after the Idaho law to disfranchise Mormons altogether. The next day, Isaac S. Struble of Iowa entered the measure's twin in the

---

[43]Ibid., 9:74.

[44]See "Admission of the State of Utah," House Rep. 4156 (50–2), 1889, Serial 2675, 171.

[45]*The Salt Lake Daily Tribune*, February 11, 1890.

House of Representatives. As a combined act moved through Congress, it posed a deadly threat to the source of Mormon political power.

Together, the LDS church's political and legal defeats were punishing, but potentially the most harmful blow fell on May 19 when the U.S. Supreme Court, with three justices dissenting, upheld the Edmunds-Tucker Act. Not only did Congress possess the power to confiscate the church's property, the court said, but the "organization of a community for the spread and practice of polygamy is, in a measure, a return to barbarism." It called the faith's history "one of patience on the part of the American government" and "of contempt of authority and resistance to law on the part of the Mormons."[46]

What made this ruling truly ominous was the appointment two months later of Henry W. Lawrence, a leader of the Godbeite schism, as receiver of church property. He replaced the moderate former U.S. marshal Frank H. Dyer, who had earlier agreed to keep hands off the church's temples under the provision of the law that exempted buildings used exclusively for "the worship of God." The Utah Supreme Court had approved this determination.[47] Now Lawrence and U.S. attorney Charles Varian, reappointed in 1889 by President Harrison, made it known they intended to overturn the agreement on the ground that temples in Logan, St. George, and Manti did not qualify for exemption since they were not places of *public* worship. If upheld, this move would lead to confiscation of the church's holiest places, where its most sacred ordinances were performed, including marriages.

WOODRUFF'S "MANIFESTO"

On November 24, 1889, Wilford Woodruff had sought the divine will and been told to stand fast and "be faithful until I come."[48] Just ten months later, he was still waiting for the Lord's promised arrival, but had reached the point where "I am under the necessity of acting for the Temporal Salvation of the Church."[49] No ringing, "Thus saith the Lord,"

---

[46]For this ruling, see *U.S. Reports, Cases Adjudged in the Supreme Court of the United States*, 1889, 136:1–68.

[47]See *Statutes at Large of the United States*, 24:637.

[48]Kenney, ed., *Wilford Woodruff's Journal*, 9:69.

[49]Ibid., 9:112–14.

was the statement dated September 25, 1890, and issued the day before. Instead it was an "Official Declaration," addressed "To whom it may concern."[50]

The Mormon leader began by denying reports that polygamous unions were still being performed. "We are not teaching poligamy [sic] or plural marriage nor permitting any person to Enter into the practice," he said. Then he came to the heart of the matter: "Inasmuch as laws have been Enacted by congress forbidding plural marriages which laws have been pronounced constitutional by the court of the last resort, I hereby declare my intention to submit to those laws and to use my influence with the members of the Church over which I preside to have them do likewise," he said. "And I now publicly declair [sic] that my advice to the Latter Day Saints is to refrain from Contracting any marriage forbidden by the Law of the land."[51]

Less than two weeks later, his "manifesto" was read before the church's semi-annual conference at Salt Lake City and sustained by the usual sea of uplifted hands that always greeted proposals from the pulpit. The almost unanimous acceptance produced "a sensation throughout the whole United States," Woodruff recorded, but came as little surprise to local observers who knew it would have been the same either way.[52]

At the October conference the Mormon president still seemed to hold out the promise of millennial deliverance. He reported to the faithful that in the temple he had met Joseph Smith, who said he was hurrying to prepare "to go to the earth with the Great Bridegroom." Smith had told him "the time was at hand for the coming of the Son of Man, for Christ to go forth in fulfillment of revelation, to meet the bride, the Lamb's wife, the Church and Kingdom of God upon the earth."[53]

As this and later events suggest, Woodruff may have intended his pronouncement only to deceive or stall for time. But it would prove historic, not only because it put an end to polygamy, which it eventually did, but because it accepted for the first time the supremacy of laws enacted by

---

[50]Ibid., 9:114–16.

[51]Ibid.

[52]Ibid., 9:117.

[53]Report of the Utah Commission, 1891, House Exec. Doc. I (52–I), Vol. 16, pt. 5, Serial 2935, 425, 427.

representatives of the people over laws revealed from God. Intentionally or not, his words signaled the end of the Kingdom of God as it had existed up to then and a turn in a new direction toward acceptance and growth.

While many treated the manifesto with skepticism,[54] one who took it at face value was the magistrate who had sent more men to prison for violating the marriage laws than anyone else. The day after it was sustained, Judge Charles Zane on October 7 said that he would record the church "opposed to polygamy hereafter, unless something happened to change my opinion," and he began only to fine violators, but not impose prison time.[55] His reversal was not the last of the notable changes that occurred that year.

LAST FIGHT OF THE SIOUX

On the morning of December 29, 1890, near Pine Ridge Indian agency in South Dakota, in a desperate bid to save their culture and hurry the millennium, Sioux warriors in Ghost Dance shirts exchanged fire with Seventh Cavalry troopers at Wounded Knee Creek. When the rifles and Hotchkiss guns ceased firing, more than one hundred and fifty Indians—men, women and children—and twenty-five cavalrymen lay dead or dying on the snow. In the murderous exchange, nearly one hundred others were wounded.

"Yes; take it off," one native woman replied when told her Ghost Dance shirt had to be removed in order to treat her wound. "They told me a bullet would not go through," she said. "Now I don't want it any more."[56] Nor did her Indian messiah come.

---

[54]In a pointed reminder that the manifesto was not issued as a revelation, Governor Thomas said that "we must not forget that they have been taught to believe and do believe that when their leader speaks with a 'thus saith the Lord' he but gives utterance to the will of the Divine Master." The Utah Commission in September 1891 reported eighteen alleged polygamous marriages over the prior year. See Report of the Governor of Utah, 1891, House Exec. Doc. 1, 412, 425.

[55]Journal of Charles S. Zane, October 7, 1890, quoted in Lyman, *Political Deliverance: The Mormon Quest for Utah Statehood*, 148.

[56]Mooney, *The Ghost-Dance Religion and Wounded Knee*, 790. The literature on the Wounded Knee massacre is extensive, but for balanced summaries see Utley, *Frontier Regulars: The United States Army and the Indian, 1866–1891*, 405–23; and *The Indian Frontier of the American West 1846–1890*, 253–60.

FREE EDUCATION

That same month Clarence E. Allen, one of six Liberal members of the territorial assembly, introduced legislation to create "free schools" in Utah as called for by Governor Thomas and every head of state since Brigham Young. At Allen's request, the governor took his proposed measures to Washington, D.C., where he asked Senator Edmunds to get them passed on a national level if all else failed.

After again refusing to act, People's Party lawmakers learned that Allen's measures had been introduced in Congress and demanded to know what this meant. "If your party does not care to pass these bills, or something similar to them, and have the credit for doing so, you can take the same legislation from the hands of the United States," he replied. "All at once," Allen said, "the committee on education became very active."[57] Allen's bills were forthwith combined, renamed after the majority party's committee chairman, and with a few minor changes approved. So it came about in this year of change, 1890, that Utah became the last state or territory to establish tax-supported, free elementary schools.[58]

PEOPLE'S PARTY DISBANDED

As millennial hopes died, still other freedoms were born. At Woodruff's direction, People's Party leaders in June 1891 dissolved the church's political party. Mormon officials were free to become Republicans or Democrats, but were instructed not to go in a block to either party. Instead, they were told to "divide about evenly between the parties, leaving an uncertain element to be converted to either side," which would produce "the best results."[59]

As 1891 drew to a close, time finally ran out on all possible interpretations of Joseph Smith's forecasts for the Second Coming. On December 19 Governor Arthur Thomas received a formal request for a

---

[57]Allen to Baskin, December 6, 1911, published in Baskin, *Reminiscences of Early Utah*, 198–201.

[58]For more on this topic, see Ivins, "Free Schools Come to Utah," 321–42. Also see Report of the Commissioner of Schools for Utah, 1888, Sen. Ex. Doc. 87 (50–2), 1889, Serial 2612.

[59]Journal of Abraham H. Cannon, June 11, 1891.

presidential amnesty, signed by the Mormon First Presidency and the apostles in Utah, for all who had been punished under the anti-polygamy laws. In the carefully worded petition, the "shepherds of a patient and suffering people" appeared to pledge on their "faith and honor" that their followers would obey Woodruff's manifesto and revealingly reminded their government, "When the men of the South, who were in rebellion against the Government in 1865, threw down their arms and asked for recognition along their old lines of citizenship, the Government hastened to grant their prayers."[60]

In transmitting the appeal, Governor Thomas and Chief Justice Zane told President Harrison they had "no doubt that it is tendered in absolute good faith" and recommended approval.[61] Early in 1893 the president issued a full pardon limited to all "who have since November 1, 1890, abstained from such unlawful cohabitation."[62] As the new spirit of cooperation took hold, some old enemies showed they could put the past behind them and work for the common good.

BASKIN ELECTED MAYOR

From the day in 1866 when he looked upon the body of his murdered client, Dr. John King Robinson, Robert N. Baskin had been the Mormon theocracy's most relentless foe. Fearlessly he had founded the Liberal Party, prosecuted John D. Lee for the Mountain Meadows massacre, and written much of the anti-polygamy legislation enacted by Congress. Now, on February 8, 1892, he found himself elected on the Liberal Party ticket mayor of Salt Lake City, charged to serve the welfare of all citizens. And he rose to the occasion.

Before Baskin took office, city utilities were vintage pioneer. Residents drew water from wells near old cesspools and privies that were "a

---

[60]A careful reading of the petition shows that while it suspends the obligation of church members to engage in polygamy as a divine commandment, it does not specifically promise to obey the federal anti-polygamy laws, including the ban on cohabitation. For the full text of this curious document and letter of transmittal to President Harrison from Governor Thomas and Chief Justice Zane, see Report of the Governor of Utah, 1892, House Exec. Doc. 1 (52–2), 1892, Serial 3089, 428–29.

[61]Ibid.

[62]Since President Harrison's proclamation was restricted to those abstaining from unlawful cohabitation, it apparently did not cover many church leaders. An original copy of the amnesty proclamation, signed by President Harrison, is located at the Harold B. Lee Library at Brigham Young University.

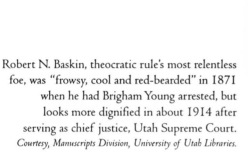

Robert N. Baskin, theocratic rule's most relentless foe, was "frowsy, cool and red-bearded" in 1871 when he had Brigham Young arrested, but looks more dignified in about 1914 after serving as chief justice, Utah Supreme Court. *Courtesy, Manuscripts Division, University of Utah Libraries.*

menace to public health."[63] Over the next four years, his administration issued long term bonds and built a modern water and sewer system, paved the streets of the business section, and laid miles of sidewalk. "From being one of the most unhealthy cities in the country," said *The Salt Lake Tribune*, the city was transformed "to one of the most sanitary."[64]

As Baskin pushed work on the City and County Building, another great edifice in the heart of the city neared completion. On April 6, 1892, a vast multitude gathered for the laying of the Salt Lake Temple's capstone. "Attention, all ye House of Israel, and all ye nations of the earth," called President Woodruff. "We will now lay the top stone of the Temple of our God." As the stone settled into place, thousands shouted: "Hosanna! Hosanna! Hosanna! to God and the Lamb!"[65] Thirty-nine years before, Brigham Young had laid the building's cornerstone.

---

[63]Baskin, *Reminiscences of Early Utah*, 26, 27.

[64]*The Salt Lake Tribune*, August 27, 1918, 14. Baskin was elected chief justice of the Utah Supreme Court in 1898. On his death in Salt Lake City on August 26, 1918, at age 81, the *Deseret Evening News* said: "He lived to see wonderful changes in the isolated country to which he came as a young man, and none will dispute the influential role he performed in affecting some of those changes, nor the prominence which he attained as a public character and a citizen." See editorial on August 27, 1918, 4.

[65]Roberts, *Comprehensive History*, 6: 232–33.

ROAD TO STATEHOOD

By the 1893 temple dedication, visions of the Kingdom of God as an earthly state had receded into the distant future, while the promise of statehood in the American Union was coming ever closer to fulfillment. Making prospects brighter was the inauguration that year of a Democratic president, Grover Cleveland, who reappointed the moderate Kentuckian Caleb W. West on May 4 as Utah governor.

When he first came to Utah in 1886, "conditions were vastly different commercially, socially and politically from those now existing," West said on taking office a second time. "Strife and contention prevailed throughout the Territory." Now, he continued, "peace prevails within our borders." He urged Congress to restore escheated property to the church. To this he added, "none should now be found to oppose Utah's entering the Union."[66] Governor West threw his personal support behind Utah's newly elected delegate to Congress, Joseph L. Rawlins, a fellow Democrat, who introduced on September 6 a statehood enabling act in the House of Representatives. Three days later, the 43-year-old native Utahn and future U.S. senator added to his proposed statehood measure a resolution to restore escheated property to the church.

So dramatically had the climate in Congress changed that the latter resolution passed both houses and was signed by President Cleveland in little more than six weeks. Under it, $438,174.39 was returned to the LDS church, but not until after statehood was real estate given back, including the Tithing Office, Historian's Office, and Gardo House. Even more remarkable was it that the House of Representatives approved the enabling act as early as December 5 with only five opposing votes. Yet another sign of the times appeared that December when the political body that had resolutely opposed the Mormon theocracy for more than twenty years followed the example of the People's Party and voted to dissolve. Most disbanded Liberal Party members joined the Republicans, only to find themselves increasingly working with leaders of the religious movement they had fought for so long.

Senate passage of Utah's Enabling Act stalled early in 1894, apparently out of concern over which political party the state's two new sen-

---

[66]Report of the Governor of Utah, 1893, House Exec. Doc. I (53–2), 1893, Vol. 15, pt. 5, Serial 3211, 389–405.

ators would represent or lingering doubts over the manifesto, but eventually was assured.[67] On July 16 President Cleveland signed the measure, which had been amended to delay, according to a revised timetable for completing the necessary steps, Utah's entry into the Union until 1896.

Under the old theocracy, constitutional conventions had been staged affairs that lasted just long enough to give the appearance of democratic proceedings. But the convention that opened on March 4, 1895, was unlike any ever held before. The 107 delegates from all counties in the territory, sixty Republicans and forty-seven Democrats, took more than two months to produce a state charter. They were presided over by the new Republican Apostle John Henry Smith, a member of the Council of Fifty.

CHARTER BANS POLYGAMY

The fruit of their labors was a new founding document similar in most respects to other state charters but with several notable differences. After much debate, often heated, delegates voted to return to the women of Utah their right to vote. Also vexing was the issue of polygamy. Since the federal laws prohibiting it in territories would no longer apply after statehood, the enabling act required the constitution forever to outlaw the marriage practice. Also as dictated by Congress, the constitution adopted on May 6, 1895, provided, "That perfect toleration of religious sentiment shall be secured, and that no inhabitant of said state shall ever be molested in person or property on account of his or her mode of religious worship."[68]

On August 27 the War Department ordered a new star to be added to the American flag, the forty-fifth. All that was left to do now was for voters to approve the new charter and elect state officers, a representative to Congress, and members of the legislature. But the election was nearly spoiled by charges of church interference in favor of the Republicans when two general authorities, Apostle Moses Thatcher and Seventies President B. H. Roberts, were denounced publicly by the First

---

[67]For more on the political maneuvering during this period, see Lyman, *Political Deliverance: The Mormon Quest for Utah Statehood*, 222–54.

[68]Roberts, *Comprehensive History*, 6:323–24.

Presidency for entering congressional races on the Democratic ticket without first getting permission.[69]

As if to verify tampering accusations, the Republicans swept all statewide offices. While the constitution was approved by a large margin, one in five voted against it, apparently reflecting a longstanding non-Mormon worry that statehood would bring a loss of federal protection against the religious majority, a fear that would prove unfounded.

Voters sent to Congress a non-Mormon Pennsylvanian, Clarence E. Allen, 42, father of Utah's free education law, who had come in 1881 as a teacher in the Salt Lake Academy. As the first governor, they chose 36-year-old Heber M. Wells, the independent-minded son of Daniel Wells, late Nauvoo Legion commander and Salt Lake mayor. The Republican legislature later named a non-Mormon lawyer, Arthur Brown, 53, of Michigan and the brilliant but unstable Frank J. Cannon, 36-year-old son of Apostle Cannon, as U.S. senators.[70]

A NEW DAY

At last, on January 4, 1896, President Cleveland signed a proclamation affirming that the necessary steps under the enabling act had been completed satisfactorily and Utah was now the forty-fifth state of the United States. As the news of statehood flashed over the wire, it touched off celebrations, bell ringing, speeches, gunfire, and dancing in the streets of cities and towns across the new state.

Not for years to come would the Mormon theocracy in America's West completely disappear, but with statehood its struggle with the federal republic was finally over. One of the first places to be settled west of the Missouri River had become one of the last to join the Union of sovereign states.

[69]The controversy produced a new declaration, known as "The Political Manifesto," which required higher church officials to obtain permission from the "proper authority" before taking on outside positions, "political or otherwise," that affected their religious duties. It also led to Thatcher's removal from his apostleship when he refused to endorse the policy on the ground, according to Roberts, it would lead to "ecclesiastic interference with the political affairs of the state." After some agonizing, Roberts accepted the new rule to maintain his church position.

[70]Neither of Utah's first U.S. senators would enhance the state's national reputation. After serving only one year, Brown was shot and killed in 1906 by a woman in Washington, D.C., who claimed to be the mother of his children. Cannon later switched parties and wrote a sensational exposé of Mormon rule entitled, *Under the Prophet in Utah: The National Menace of a Political Priestcraft.*

EPILOGUE

[W]e have not as a people, at all times, lived strictly to our agreements with the Government, and this lack of sincerity on our part goes farther to condemn us in the eyes of the public men of the nation than the mere fact of a few new polygamy cases.

—Reed Smoot

With the failed millennial expectation of 1890–91 and the coming of statehood instead, the most unusual form of government ever seen on American soil came to an apparent close after a life span of just under fifty years. If the covert apparatus of world rule, the mysterious Council of Fifty, still exists in any form, which is doubtful, it does so only on an inactive or standby basis.

Conceived in Nauvoo and established by Brigham Young and his followers in the Great Basin, the Kingdom of God was the literal fulfillment of Old Testament prophecy. It was the stone which the Prophet Daniel saw cut out of the mountain without hands that would break in pieces and consume all other kingdoms and stand forever.[1] It was an irresistible movement that would fill the whole earth as a condition of the Lord's coming again. With a zeal unknown to most faiths today, those who carried its banner created a society that, in its original form, resembled a determined effort to create so perfectly the conditions on which Christ's coming depended that the Lord would have no choice but to make His appearance. Later it would be continually transformed by the reverses suffered during its inevitable confrontation with the American republic.

In 1857 the Mormon theocracy under the name of Deseret began its march to universal rule by taking an independent position from the

---

[1]Dan. 2:28–45.

United States. But the stone described by Daniel rolled to a sudden stop when President Buchanan sent American troops to Utah to uphold federal law and the Almighty chose not to intervene, thereby signaling, once again, His own independence from human timetables. It would be a setback from which the fledgling "Theo-Democracy," as it was called by John W. Gunnison, would never recover.

Millennial hopes rose again when the American nation divided into North and South and from 1861–65 fought a terrible Civil War. Alone of all the states and territories, the Mormon kingdom stood on the sideline and prepared to rise on the ashes as the two sides destroyed each other, as prophesied, and then to go on to universal dominion. But President Lincoln sent the California Volunteers to Utah, the Union emerged from the war more powerful than before, and again the Lord did not come.

Afterward the Utah theocracy came under a growing attack as opponents used the moral issue of polygamy as a weapon to destroy its political and economic power through the enactment of federal laws against the marriage practice, beginning with the 1862 Morrill Act. But the real target was theocratic rule, "as great if not a greater evil than polygamy," said opposition leader Robert Baskin, "and as much opposed to our American institutions."[2] The removal of both, he said, would leave nothing objectionable to Americans.

Even then it took the disappointed messianic hope of 1890–91 for the Kingdom of God at last to give up outwardly its claim to rule on earth by divine right before Christ comes again. In the end, its demise came less from the blows of its enemies than from the decline of millennialism and the coming of a new generation, unscarred by wounds from Missouri and Illinois, that had adopted the democratic ideals of the American nation and wanted political freedom.

While the Kingdom of God as originally conceived ended with statehood, surprisingly more resistant to change proved the moral issue over which its quarrel with the United States was waged. A footnote to this story was written by the religious leaders who violated the solemn pledges they appeared to make and deceived men of good will on both sides of the issue who took them at their word.

---

[2]Baskin, *Argument against the Admission of Utah*, 1.

In his 1890 "manifesto," Wilford Woodruff said the LDS church "was not teaching polygamy or plural marriage, nor permitting any person to enter into its practice." He also declared his own "intention to submit" to the laws "forbidding plural marriages" and his advice to followers to "refrain from contracting any marriage forbidden by the laws of the land."[3] Yet from 1890 until statehood, couples were sent to the Mormon colony at Juarez, Mexico, where dozens of polygamous marriages were performed in secret in violation of the laws of both countries.[4] The careful wording of Woodruff's proclamation shows, too, that he never really intended to prevent cohabitation between a man and his polygamous wives, which was clearly prohibited by the same federal laws he referred to as constitutional.

In December 1891 the church First Presidency and apostles submitted a petition for an amnesty, affirming the Lord had given permission to tell church members "the law commanding polygamy was henceforth suspended."[5] On the recommendation of Governor Arthur Thomas, Judge Zane, and the Utah Commission, President Harrison granted this request. Yet a close reading of the petition shows that these leaders never pledged themselves specifically to obey the federal law. And most did not. Except for apostle and later church president Lorenzo Snow, all of them maintained connubial relations with more than one wife in direct violation of the 1882 Edmunds Act, which banned unlawful cohabitation. According to historian Kenneth L. Cannon II, eleven Mormon general authorities from 1890 to 1905 fathered seventy-six children by twenty-seven polygamous wives.[6] Moreover, the number of church-approved polygamous marriages from 1890 to 1904 came to at least 250, with the greatest increase coming after statehood.[7]

Amid growing national outrage, 40-year-old monogamous Apostle Reed Smoot on January 20, 1903, won election as a Republican to the U.S. Senate but found his right to take the seat contested on the charge he represented a religious hierarchy that exercised temporal and spiritual

---

[3]Kenney, ed., *Wilford Woodruff's Journal*, 9:214–16.

[4]For the story of post-manifesto polygamy, see Van Wagoner, *Mormon Polygamy: A History*, 153–63.

[5]House Exec. Doc. 1 (52–2), 1892, Serial 3089, 428–29.

[6]Cannon, "Beyond the Manifesto: Polygamous Cohabitation among LDS General Authorities after 1890," 24–36.

[7]Cannon, "After the Manifesto: Mormon Polygamy, 1890–1906," 31.

rule and still taught polygamy. At Senate hearings, Mormon church President Joseph F. Smith, son and nephew of slain prophets Hyrum and Joseph Smith, in March 1904 at age 66 admitted that he had fathered eleven post-manifesto children.[8] After being grilled for five days, Smith presented the following month a "second manifesto" before the church's annual conference. Noting reports that polygamous marriages had been performed since Woodruff's first pronouncement, he declared "no such marriages have been solemnized with the sanction, consent, or knowledge of the Church." He further announced that "any officer or member" who took part in such marriages would be excommunicated, but the husband of five wives pointedly failed to mention unlawful cohabitation.[9]

This seemingly forceful but disingenuous stand no doubt helped Senator Smoot keep his seat, despite embarrassing hearings that lasted for three years.[10] But within months, Rudger Clawson, the husband of Lydia Spencer and now an apostle, secretly took another wife in 1904. At age 47 he married the attractive Pearl Udall, 23. Not until 1910, when *The Salt Lake Tribune* published the names of more than two hundred men (including six apostles) who had taken wives after the manifesto, did the church begin resolutely to oppose the marriage doctrine.

Mormon splinter groups, known as Fundamentalists, claiming a higher priesthood authority still practice polygamy in Utah. But the reason it is no longer accepted by the mainline LDS church has less to do with manifestoes or laws than it does with the passive refusal of most church members, women and men alike, to accept the doctrine. From the beginning, it was viewed more as an onerous commandment than as a popular doctrine.

Estimates as to the percentage that engaged in polygamy range from ten to about thirty, but to most Mormons the practice was as unpopular then as it would be if it were reintroduced today. For this reason, it is safe to conclude that polygamy would have gone, with or without out-

[8]For the full report of these hearings, see Sen. Rep. 486, *Proceedings before the Committee on Privileges and Elections of the United States Senate in the Matter of the protests against the Right Hon. Reed Smoot, a senator from the State of Utah, to hold his seat*, (59–1), 4 vols., 1904–6, serials 2932–2935.

[9]See Roberts, *Comprehensive History*, 6:401.

[10]In a close call, the full Senate on February 7, 1907, voted to allow Senator Smoot to keep his seat, despite the recommendation of its Committee on Privileges and Elections that he be barred. Smoot went on to serve thirty years in the Senate, where he was co-sponsor in 1930 of the Smoot-Hawley Act.

side help, the way of other doctrines that were quietly resisted or simply ignored by most members of the faith. They included the law of consecration, marked ballots, the United Order, and the Deseret Alphabet, among others. As it happened, Wilford Woodruff's manifesto simply provided welcome relief.

Meanwhile the spirit of the Mormon Kingdom of God lives on today in the name Deseret and in attitudes that make Utah culture different from other parts of the country. In the political realm, it can be seen in opposition toward the federal government and such humanistic millennial movements as socialism and the welfare state. Ironically, this makes Utah conservative in political orientation, a bastion of the party that worked so hard for so long to destroy polygamy and the theocratic system.

Equally ironic is it that the state has gone from the communal economic ideal of its founders, so well symbolized by the beehive, to become a stronghold of entrepreneurship and free market economic thinking. Even so, echoes of the crusade to create an autonomous economic base still sound in values that actually complement a free enterprise attitude. They include such ideals as self-sufficiency, thrift, honesty, the obligation to care for one's own, and the duty to put more into one's work than one takes out of it, among others.

Perhaps less admirable are the exclusiveness and other social attitudes sometimes encountered by those who come to Utah and never quite become fully accepted members of their neighborhoods or true partners in society no matter how long they may live in the state. This fading reflection of earlier times still exists in a cultural divide that many Mormons appear unaware of.

Finally, when the heavens open and God again conveys His will through a prophet on earth, as He did in Old Testament times, the conditions of a theocracy will be established. Such convictions persist in the Mormon belief in a living prophet at the head of the church who is quite literally the mouthpiece of God. If the theocracy that existed in Utah from 1847 to 1896 is now largely inactive, many of the doctrines that gave it life during those years have not changed.

What is different today is that the millennium is no longer expected in the immediate future, tomorrow or next month, but as a more distant event. Gone, too, is the belief that Christ's return is conditional on the efforts of mankind to establish a theocratic system of government on earth in preparation for His appearance and universal rule.

With the decline of millennialism has come the opportunity for the Kingdom of God to become an active part of American society and to coexist in peace with the kingdoms of the world until the distant day, looked for by Christian believers, when the Lord in His own time will come again and before Him "every knee will bend."[11]

---

[11]Isa. 45:23.

BIBLIOGRAPHY
AND INDEX

BIBLIOGRAPHY

ABBREVIATIONS

CSmH	Henry E. Huntington Library, San Marino, California
CtY	Yale University, Yale Collection of Western Americana, Beinecke Library, New Haven, Connecticut
CU-B	University of California, H. H. Bancroft Library, Berkeley, California
DLC	Library of Congress, Washington, D. C.
DNA	National Archives, Washington, D. C.
GS	Genealogical Society of Utah, Salt Lake City, Utah
UAr	Utah State Archives, Salt Lake City, Utah
UHi	Utah State Historical Society, Salt Lake City, Utah
ULA	Utah State University, Logan, Utah
UPB	Brigham Young University, Harold B. Lee Library, Provo, Utah
USIc	Church Historical Department, Church of Jesus Christ of Latter-day Saints, Salt Lake City, Utah
UU	University of Utah, Marriott Library, Salt Lake City
SUU	Southern Utah University, Cedar City

BOOKS AND PAMPHLETS

Alexander, Thomas G. *Things in Heaven and Earth: The Life and Times of Wilford Woodruff, a Mormon Prophet.* S.L.C: Signature Books, 1991.

Allen, James B. and Glen M. Leonard. *The Story of the Latter-day Saints.* S.L.C: Deseret Book Co., 1976.

Anderson, C. LeRoy. *For Christ Will Come Tomorrow: The Saga Of The Morrisites.* Logan: Utah State Univ. Press, 1981. Second Edition printed as *Joseph Morris And The Saga Of The Morrisites,* 1988.

Andrews, Laurel B. *The Early Temples of the Mormons: The Architecture of the Millennial Kingdom in the American West.* Albany: State Univ. of N.Y. Press, 1978.

Arrington, Leonard J. *Great Basin Kingdom: An Economic History of the Latter-day Saints.* Cambridge: Harvard Univ. Press, 1958. Reprinted, S.L.C: Univ. of Utah Press, 1993.

—————. *Brigham Young: American Moses.* N.Y: Alfred A. Knopf, 1985.

———— and Davis Bitton. *The Mormon Experience: A History of the Latter-day Saints*. N.Y: Vintage Books, 1980.

Backus, Anna Jean. *Mountain Meadows Witness: The life and times of Bishop Philip Klingensmith*. Spokane, WA: Arthur H. Clark Co., 1995.

Bagley, Will, ed. *Frontiersman: Abner Blackburn's Narrative*. S.L.C: Univ. of Utah Press, 1992.

————. *The Pioneer Camp of the Saints: The 1846 and 1847 Mormon Trail Journals of Thomas Bullock*. Spokane, WA: Arthur H. Clark Co., 1997.

Bancroft, Hubert Howe. *History of Utah, 1540–1886*. San Francisco: History Co., 1889.

Barney, Garold D. *Mormons, Indians and the Ghost Dance Religion of 1890*. Lanham, MD: Univ. Press of America, 1986.

Bartholomew, Rebecca and Leonard J. Arrington. *Rescue of the 1856 Handcart Companies*. Provo, UT: Brigham Young Univ. Press, 1981. Revised edition, 1993.

Bashore, Melvin L. and Linda L. Haslam. *Mormon Pioneer Companies Crossing the Plains (1847–1868) Narratives: Guide to Sources in Utah Libraries and Archives*. S.L.C: Hist. Dept., Church of Jesus Christ of Latter-day Saints, 1989.

Baskin, R. N. *Argument against the Admission of Utah*. Wash., D.C: Judd & Detweiler, Printer, 1888.

————. *Reminiscences of Early Utah*. S.L.C: private printing, 1914.

————. *Reply by R. N. Baskin to Certain Statements by O. F. Whitney in His History of Utah Published in 1916*. S.L.C: Lakeside Printing Co., 1916.

Bean, George W. *Autobiography*, compiled by Flora Diana Bean Horn. S.L.C., 1945.

Benton, Thomas Hart. *Thirty Years' View; or, A History of the Working of the American Government for Thirty Years, from 1820 to 1850*, 2 vols. N.Y: D. Appleton and Co., 1856.

Berry, Robert, ed. *Western Emigrant Trails, 1830–1870, Major Trails, Cutoffs, and Alternates*. Independence, MO: Oregon-California Trails Assoc., 1991.

Bigler, David L., ed. *The Gold Discovery Journal of Azariah Smith*. S.L.C: Univ. of Utah press, 1990.

Biographical History of Eminent and Self-Made Men of the State of Indiana. Cincinnati: Western Biographical Publishing Co., 1880.

Bitton, Davis. *Guide to Mormon Diaries & Autobiographies*. Provo, UT: Brigham Young Univ. Press, 1977.

Black, Susan Easton. *Early Members of the Church of Jesus Christ of Latter-day Saints, 1830–1848*, 50 vols. Provo, UT: Religious Studies Center, Brigham Young Univ., 1993.

Bolton, Herbert E., ed. *Pageant in the Wilderness; the Story of the Escalante Expedition to the Interior Basin, 1776*. S.L.C: Utah State Hist. Soc., 1950.

Bonney, Edward. *The Banditti of the Prairies.* Chicago: Steam Press, 1850. New Edition, Norman: Univ. of Okla. Press, 1963.

Brodie, Fawn. *No Man Knows My History: The Life of Joseph Smith the Mormon Prophet.* N.Y: Alfred A. Knopf, 1945. Second Edition, 1973.

Brooks, Juanita. *The Mountain Meadows Massacre.* Stanford, 1950. Revised Edition, Norman: Univ. of Okla. Press, 1962. New Edition, 1970.

————, ed. *On the Mormon Frontier: The Diary of Hosea Stout,* 2 vols. S.L.C: Univ. of Utah Press, 1964. Reprint Edition, 1982.

————, ed. *Journal of the Southern Indian Mission, Diary of Thomas D. Brown.* Logan: Utah State Univ. Press, 1972.

————, ed. *Not by Bread Alone: The Journal of Martha Spence Heywood, 1850–1856.* S.L.C: Utah State Hist. Soc., 1978.

————. *John Doyle Lee: Zealot, Pioneer Builder, Scapegoat.* Glendale, CA: Arthur H. Clark Co., 1972. Reprinted, Logan, UT: Utah State Univ. Press, 1992. Second printing, 1994.

Brown, John. *Autobiography of Pioneer John Brown, 1820–1896.* S.L.C: private printing, 1941.

Bryant, Edwin. *What I Saw in California.* N.Y: D. Appleton & Co., 1848. Reprinted Palo Alto: Lewis Osborne, 1967.

Burton, Richard F. *The City of the Saints and Across the Rocky Mountains to California.* N.Y: Harper & Bros., 1862. Reprinted Boulder: Univ. Press of Colo., 1990.

Campbell, Eugene E. *Establishing Zion: The Mormon Church in the American West, 1847–1869.* S.L.C: Signature Books, 1988.

Cannon, Frank J. *Under the Prophet in Utah: The National Menace of a Political Priestcraft.* Boston: C.M. Clark Publishing Co., 1911.

Cannon, George Q. *A Review of the Decision of the Supreme Court of United States in the Case of Geo. Reynolds vs. the United States.* S.L.C: Deseret News Printing and Publishing Est., 1879.

Carter, Kate B., comp. *Heart Throbs of the West,* 12 vols. S.L.C., Daughters of Utah Pioneers, 1939–51.

————, comp. *Treasures of Pioneer History,* 6 vols. S.L.C: Daughters of Utah Pioneers, 1952–57.

————, comp. *Our Pioneer Heritage,* 18 vols. S.L.C: Daughters of Utah Pioneers, 1958–75.

Carvalho, S. N. *Incidents of Travel and Adventure in the Far West; with Col. Fremont's Last Expedition.* N.Y: Derby & Jackson, 1857.

Clayton, William. *The Latter-Day Saints' Emigrants' Guide.* St. Louis: Republican Steam Press-Chambers and Knapp, 1848. Reprinted St. Louis: Patrice Press, 1983.

Cleland, Robert Glass and Juanita Brooks, eds. *A Mormon Chronicle: The Diaries of John D. Lee 1848–1876*, 2 vols. San Marino: Huntington Library, 1955. Reprinted S.L.C: Univ. of Utah Press, 1983.

Collier, Fred C. *Unpublished Revelations of the Prophets and Presidents of the Church of Jesus Christ of Latter Day Saints.* S.L.C: Collier's Publishing Co., 1979.

————, ed. *The Teachings of President Brigham Young, Vol. 3, 1852–1854.* S.L.C: Collier's Publishing Co., 1987.

————. *Doctrine of the Priesthood: Adoption: Law of the Kingdom: Forgotten Doctrine of Mormonism.* S.L.C: Collier's Publishing Co., 1991.

Cook, Lyndon W., ed. *Aaron Johnson Correspondence.* Orem, UT: Center for Research of Mormon Origins, 1990.

Cooke, Philip St. George. *The Conquest of New Mexico and California, An Historical and Personal Narrative.* N.Y: G. P. Putnam's Sons, 1878. Reprinted Albuquerque, NM: Horn and Wallace, 1964.

Cooley, Everett L., ed. *Diary of Brigham Young 1857.* S.L.C: Univ. of Utah Library, 1980.

Cowley, Matthias F. *Wilford Woodruff, History of His Life and Labors, As Recorded in His Daily Journals.* S.L.C: The Deseret News, 1907.

Cradlebaugh, John. *Utah and the Mormons. Speech of Hon. John Cradlebaugh, of Nevada, on the admission of Utah as a state. Delivered in the House of Representatives, February 7, 1863.* Wash., D.C: L. Towers & Co., 1863.

Crampton, C. Gregory and Steven K. Madsen. *In Search of the Spanish Trail: Santa Fe to Los Angeles, 1829–1848.* S.L.C: Gibbs Smith, Publisher, 1994.

Crawley, Peter L. *The Essential Parley P. Pratt.* S.L.C: Signature Books, 1990.

Cullom, Shelby. *Fifty years in Public Service: Personal Recollections.* N.Y: Da Capo Press, 1967.

Culmsee, Carlton. *Utah's Black Hawk War, Lore and Reminiscences of Participants.* Logan: Utah State Univ. Press, 1973.

Daughters of Utah Pioneers. *An Enduring Legacy*, 12 vols. S.L.C: Daughters of Utah Pioneers, 1978–89.

Davies, J. Kenneth. *Mormon Gold: The Story of California's Mormon Argonauts.* S.L.C: Olympus Pub. Co., 1984.

DeLafosse, Peter, ed. *Trailing the Pioneers: A Guide to Utah's Emigrant Trails, 1829–1869.* Logan: Utah State Univ. Press, 1994.

DeVoto, Bernard. *The Year of Decision, 1846.* N.Y: Houghton-Mifflin Co., 1943.

Doctrine and Covenants of The Church of Jesus Christ of Latter-day Saints. S.L.C: LDS Church, 1970.

Dove, George S. *Names of persons baptized during the administration of Joseph Morris, at South Weber, Utah Territory, in the years of 1861 and 1862.* San Francisco: Geo. S. Dove & Co., 1886.

Driggs, Howard R. *Timpanogos Town: Story of Old Battle Creek and Pleasant Grove, Utah.* Manchester, NH: Clarke Press, 1948.

Dunbar, Seymour and Paul C. Phillips, eds. *The Journals and Letters of Major John Owen, Pioneer of the Northwest, 1850–1871,* 2 vols. N.Y: Edward Eberstadt, 1927.

Dwyer, Robert J. *The Gentile Comes to Utah.* Wash., D.C: Catholic Univ. of America Press, 1941. Revised Edition, S.L.C: Western Epics, 1971.

Eardley, John R. *Gems of Inspiration: A Collection of Sublime Thoughts by Modern Prophets.* San Francisco: Joseph A. Dove, Printer, 1899.

Esshom, Frank. *Pioneers and Prominent Men of Utah.* S.L.C: Western Epics, Inc., 1966.

Evans, Lucylle H. *St. Mary's in the Rocky Mountains: A History of the Cradle of Montana's Culture.* Missoula: Univ. of Montana, 1975. Revised Edition, Stevensville: Montana Creative Consultants, 1976.

Fales, Susan L. and Chad J. Flake. *Mormons and Mormonism in U.S. Government Documents.* S.L.C: Univ. of Utah Press, 1989.

Fielding, Kent. *The Unsolicited Chronicler: An Account of the Gunnison Massacre, Its Causes and Consequences, Utah Territory, 1847–1859.* Brookline, MA: Paradigm Publications, 1993.

Firmage, Edwin Brown and Richard Collin Mangrum. *Zion in the Courts: A Legal History of the Church of Jesus Christ of Latter-day Saints, 1830–1900.* Urbana and Chicago: Univ. of Ill. Press, 1988.

Flanders, Robert Bruce. *Nauvoo: Kingdom on the Mississippi.* Urbana and Chicago: Univ. of Ill. Press, 1965.

Ford, Thomas. *A History of Illinois from its Commencement as a State in 1818 to 1847.* Chicago: S.C. Griggs & Co., 1854. Lakeside Classics Edition, Milo Milton Quaife, ed., 2 vols., Chicago: Lakeside Press, 1945.

Franzwa, Gregory M. *The Oregon Trail Revisited.* St. Louis: Patrice Press, 1972. Fourth Edition, Tucson, 1988.

————. *Maps of the Oregon Trail.* St. Louis: Patrice Press, 1982; Third Edition, 1990.

Frémont, John C. *Report of the Exploring Expedition to the Rocky Mountains in the Year 1842, and to Oregon and North California in the Years 1843–'44.* Washington: Gales and Seaton, 1845. Reprinted as Allan Nevins, ed., *Narratives of Exploration and Adventure by John Charles Fremont,* N.Y: Longmans, Green & Co., 1956.

Furniss, Norman F. *The Mormon Conflict, 1850–1859.* New Haven: Yale Univ. Press, 1960.

Gardner, Hamilton. *History of Lehi.* S.L.C: The Deseret News, 1913. Revised Edition, Lehi, UT: Free Press Publishing Co., 1950.

Gibbs, Josiah F. *Lights and Shadows of Mormonism.* S.L.C: Salt Lake Tribune Publishing Co., 1909.

Goetzmann, William H. *Army Exploration in the American West, 1803–1863.* New Haven: Yale Univ. Press, 1959. Reprinted Lincoln and London: Univ. of Neb. Press, 1979.

Gottfredson, Peter. *History of Indian Depredations in Utah.* S.L.C, 1919.

Green, Nelson Winch. *Fifteen Years among the Mormons: Being the Narrative of Mrs. Mary Ettie V. Smith.* N.Y: H. Dayton, 1858.

Gowans, Fred R. and Eugene E. Campbell. *Fort Bridger: Island in the Wilderness.* Provo, UT: Brigham Young Univ. Press, 1975.

Gudde, Erwin G., ed. *Bigler's Chronicle of the West. The Conquest of California, Discovery of Gold, and Mormon Settlement as Reflected in Henry William Bigler's Diaries.* Berkeley and Los Angeles: Univ. of Calif. Press, 1962.

Gunnison, J. W. *The Mormons, or Latter-day Saints, in the Valley of the Great Salt Lake: A History of their rise and progress, peculiar doctrines, present condition and prospects, derived from personal observtion during a residence among them.* Philadelphia: Lippincott, Grambo & Co., 1852. Reprinted Brookline, MA: Paradigm Publications, 1993.

Hafen, Ann W. and LeRoy R. Hafen. *Handcarts to Zion, the Story of a Unique Western Migration, 1856–1860, with contemporary journals, accounts, reports; and rosters of members of the ten Handcart Companies.* Glendale, CA: Arthur H. Clark Co., 1960.

Hafen, LeRoy R., ed. *The Mountain Men and the Fur Trade of the Far West,* 10 vols. Glendale, CA: Arthur H. Clark Co., 1965–1972.

———— and Ann W. Hafen, eds. *Journals of Forty-Niners: Salt Lake to Los Angeles.* Glendale, CA: Arthur H. Clark Co., 1954.

———— and Ann W. Hafen, eds. *Old Spanish Trail: Santa Fe to Los Angeles.* Glendale, CA: Arthur H. Clark Co., 1954.

———— and Ann W. Hafen, eds. *The Utah Expedition, 1857–1858: A Documentary Account of the United States Military Movement under Colonel Albert Sidney Johnston, and The Resistance by Brigham Young and the Mormon Nauvoo Legion.* Glendale, CA: Arthur H. Clark Co., 1958.

Hallwas, John E. and Roger D. Launius. *Cultures in Conflict: A Documentary History of the Mormon War in Illinois.* Logan: Utah State Univ. Press, 1995.

Hammond, Otis G., ed. *The Utah Expedition 1857–1858: Letters of Capt. Jesse A. Gove, 10th Inf., U.S.A., of Concord, N.H., to Mrs. Gove, and special correspondence of the New York Herald.* Concord: New Hamp. Hist. Soc., 1928.

Hanks, Sidney Alvarus and Ephraim K. Hanks. *Scouting for the Mormons on the Great Frontier.* S.L.C: Deseret Book Co., 1948.

Hanson, Klaus J. *Quest for Empire: The Political Kingdom of God and the Council of Fifty in Mormon History.* East Lansing: Mich. State Univ. Press, 1967.

Harris, Sarah Hollister. *An Unwritten Chapter of Salt Lake, 1851–1901.* N.Y: private printing, 1901.

Hastings, Lansford W. *The Emigrants' Guide, to Oregon and California; Containing Scenes and Incidents of a Party of Oregon Emigrants; A Description of Oregon; Scenes and Incidents of a Party of California Emigrants; and a Description of California; with a Description of the Different Routes to Those Countries; and All Necessary Information Relative to the Equipment, Supplies, and the Method of Traveling.* Cincinnati: George Conclin, 1845.

Heitman, Francis Bernard. *Historical Register and Dictionary of the United States Army, from its Organization, September 29, 1789, to March 2, 1903,* 2 vols. Wash., D.C: Government Printing Office, 1903.

Hickman, William A. *Brigham's Destroying Angel; Being the Life, Confession, and Startling Disclosures of the Notorious Bill Hickman, the Danite Chief of Utah.* N.Y: George A. Crofutt & Co., 1872. Reprinted S.L.C: Shepard Publishing Co., 1904.

Hill, Marvin S. *Quest for Refuge: The Mormon Flight from American Pluralism.* S.L.C: Signature Books, 1989.

Hill, William E. *The Mormon Trail Yesterday and Today.* Logan: Utah State Univ. Press, 1996.

History of Nevada with Illustrations and Biographical Sketches of Its Prominent Men and Pioneers. Oakland: Thompson & West, 1881.

Houghton, Samuel G. *A Trace of Desert Waters: The Great Basin Story.* Glendale, CA: Arthur H. Clark Co., 1970.

Jensen, J. Marinus. *History of Provo, Utah.* Provo: New Century Printing Co., 1924.

Jenson, Andrew. *Church Chronology. A Record of Important Events Pertaining to the History of the Church of Jesus Christ of Latter-day Saints.* S.L.C: Deseret News Press, 1899.

——————, ed. *Latter-day Saint Biographical Encyclopedia,* 4 vols. S.L.C: Andrew Jenson History Co., 1901. Reprinted S.L.C: Western Epics, 1971.

Johnston, William Preston. *The Life of Albert Sidney Johnston, Embracing His Services in the Armies of the United States, the Republic of Texas, and the Confederate States.* N.Y: D. Appleton and Co., 1878.

Jones, Daniel W. *Forty Years Among the Indians, A True Yet Thrilling Narrative of the Author's Experiences Among the Natives.* S.L.C: Juvenile Instructor's Office, 1890.

Journal of Discourses, 26 vols. London: Latter-Day Saints Book Depot, 1854–86.

Kelly, Charles. *Salt Desert Trails.* S.L.C: Western Printing Co., 1930. Third Edition, Peter H. DeLafosse, ed., S.L.C: Western Epics, 1996.

——————, ed. *Journals of John D. Lee, 1846–47 & 1859.* S.L.C: Western Printing Co., 1938. Reprinted S.L.C: Univ. of Utah Press, 1984.

—————— and Maurice L. Howe. *Miles Goodyear, First Citizen of Utah.* S.L.C: Western Printing Co., 1937.

Kenney, Scott G., ed. *Wilford Woodruff's Journal,* 10 vols. Midvale, UT: Signature Books, 1983.

Kimball, Stanley B. *Historic Sites and Markers along the Mormon and Other Great Western Trails.* Urbana: Univ. of Ill. Press, 1988.

————. *Heber C. Kimball: Mormon Patriarch and Pioneer.* Urbana: Univ. of Ill. Press, 1981.

Knight, Hal and Stanley B. Kimball. *111 Days to Zion.* S.L.C: Deseret Press, 1978.

Korns, J. Roderic and Dale L. Morgan, eds. *West from Fort Bridger: The Pioneering of Immigrant Trails across Utah, 1846–1850.* S.L.C: Utah State Hist. Soc., 1951. Revised and updated by Will Bagley and Harold Schindler, Logan: Utah State Univ. Press, 1994.

Larson, Carl V. *A Data Base of the Mormon Battalion.* Providence, UT: Kieth W. Watkins and Sons Printing, Inc., 1987.

Larson, Gustive O. *The "Americanization" of Utah for Statehood.* San Marino, CA: Huntington Library, 1971.

Larson, Stan, ed. *Prisoner for Polygamy: The Memoirs and Letters of Rudger Clawson at the Utah Territorial Penitentiary, 1884–87.* Urbana and Chicago: Univ. of Ill., 1993.

Lee, John D. *Mormonism Unveiled; or The Life and Confessions of the Late Mormon Bishop, John D. Lee. Written by Himself.* St. Louis: Bryan, Brand & Co., 1877.

Lee, Ruth and Sylvia Wadsworth. *A Century in Meadow Valley, 1864–1964.* S.L.C: Deseret News Press, 1966.

LeSueur, Stephen C. *The 1838 Mormon War in Missouri.* Columbia: Univ. of Missouri Press, 1987.

Linforth, James. *Route from Liverpool to Great Salt Lake Valley,* ed. by Fawn Brodie, illus. by Frederick Hawkins Piercy. Cambridge: Belknap Press of Harvard Univ. Press, 1962.

Linn, William Alexander. *The Story of the Mormons: From the Date of their Origin to the Year 1901.* N.Y: The Macmillan Co., 1923.

Long, E. B. *The Saints and the Union: Utah Territory during the Civil War.* Urbana, Chicago, London: Univ. of Ill. Press, 1981.

Lowry, Walker. *Wallace Lowry.* Stinehour Press, 1974.

Ludlow, Daniel, ed. *Encyclopedia of Mormonism,* 4 vols. N.Y: Macmillan Pub. Co., 1992.

Lyford, C. P. *The Mormon Problem, An Appeal to the American People.* N.Y: Phillips & Hunt, 1886.

Lyman, Edward Leo. *Political Deliverance: The Mormon Quest for Utah Statehood.* Urbana and Chicago: Univ. of Illinois Press, 1986.

MacDonald, G. D., III. *The Magnet: Iron Ore in Iron County, Utah.* Cedar City, UT: private printing, 1990.

McConkie, Bruce R. *Mormon Doctrine.* S.L.C: Bookcraft. Second Edition, 1966.

————. *The Millennial Messiah: The Second Coming of the Son of Man.* S.L.C: Deseret Book Co., 1982.

McMullin, Thomas A. and David Walker. *Biographical Directory of American Territorial Governors.* Westport, CT: Meckler Publishing, 1984.

Madsen, Brigham D. *Corinne: The Gentile Capital of Utah.* S.L.C: Utah State Hist. Soc., 1980.

————. *The Shoshoni Frontier and the Bear River Massacre.* S.L.C: Univ. of Utah Press, 1985.

————, ed. *Exploring the Great Salt Lake: The Stansbury Expedition of 1849–50.* S.L.C: Univ. of Utah Press, 1989.

————. *Glory Hunter: A Biography of Patrick Edward Connor.* S.L.C: Univ. of Utah Press, 1990.

Malmquist, O. N. *The First 100 Years: A History of The Salt Lake Tribune, 1871–1971.* S.L.C: Utah State Hist. Soc., 1971.

Marcy, Randolph B. *Thirty Years of Army Life on the Border.* Phila. and N.Y: J. B. Lippincott Co., 1963.

Mattes, Merrill J. *The Great Platte River Road.* Lincoln: Neb. State Hist. Soc., 1969.

Moffitt, John Clifton. *The History of Public Education in Utah.* private printing, 1946.

Mooney, James. "The Ghost-Dance Religion and the Sioux Outbreak of 1890," *Fourteenth Annual Report (Part 2) of the Bureau of Ethnology to the Smithsonian Institution, 1892–93, by J. W. Powell, Director.* Wash., D.C: Government Printing Office, 1896. Reprinted, N.Y: Dover Publications, 1973.

Moorman, Donald R. with Gene A. Sessions. *Camp Floyd and the Mormons: The Utah War.* S.L.C: Univ. of Utah Press, 1992.

Morgan, Dale L. *The Humboldt: Highroad of the West.* N.Y: Farrar & Rinehardt, 1943.

————. *The Great Salt Lake.* Indianapolis: Bobbs-Merrill Co., 1947.

————. *Jedediah Smith and the Opening of the West.* Indianapolis: Bobbs-Merrill Co., 1953.

————. *Overland in 1846: Diaries and Letters of the California-Oregon Trail,* 2 vols. Georgetown, CA: Talisman Press, 1963.

————. *The State of Deseret.* Logan: Utah State Univ. Press and Utah Hist. Soc., 1987.

Morris, Joseph. *The "Spirit Prevails" Containing the Revelations, Articles and Letters Written by Joseph Morris.* San Francisco: George S. Dove & Co., 1886.

Mulder, William. *The Mormons in American History.* S.L.C: Univ. of Utah Press, 1957.

———— and A. Russell Mortensen. *Among the Mormons: Historic Accounts by Contemporary Observers.* N.Y: Alfred A. Knopf, 1958.

Mumey, Nolie. *John Williams Gunnison (1812–1853) The Last of the Western Explorers: A History of the Survey Through Colorado and Utah with a Biography and Details of His Massacre.* Denver: Artcraft Press, 1955.

Neff, Andrew Love. *History of Utah, 1847 to 1869.* S.L.C: Deseret News Press, 1940.

Neilson, James. *Shelby M. Cullom: Prairie State Republican*. Urbana: Univ. of Ill. Press, 1962.

Paul, Rodman W. *The California Gold Discovery: Sources, Documents, Accounts and Memoirs Relating to the Discovery of Gold at Sutter's Mill*. Georgetown, CA: Talisman Press, 1966.

Penrose, Charles W. "Testimony of James Holt Haslam," in *Supplement to the Lecture on the Mountain Meadows Massacre: Important Additional Testimony Recently Received*. S.L.C: The Juvenile Instructor Press, 1885.

Poll, Richard D. *Quixotic Mediator: Thomas L. Kane and the Utah War*. Ogden, UT: Weber State College Press, 1985.

Powell, Allan Kent. *Utah History Encyclopedia*. S.L.C: Univ. of Utah Press, 1994.

Quaife, Milo Milton, ed. *The Diary of James K. Polk During His Presidency, 1845 to 1849*, 4 vols. Chicago: A. C. McClurg & Co., 1910.

Quinn, D. Michael. *The Mormon Hierarchy: Origins of Power*. S.L.C: Signature Books, 1994.

——————. *The Mormon Hierarchy: Extensions of Power*. S.L.C: Signature Books, 1997.

Reavis, Logan Uriah. *Saint Louis: The Future Great City of the World*. St. Louis, 1875.

Reinfeld, Fred. *Pony Express*. N.Y: The Macmillan Co., 1966. Reprinted Lincoln/London: Univ. of Neb. Press, 1973.

Remy, Jules. *A Journey to Great-Salt-Lake City*, 2 vols. London: W. Jeffs, 1860.

Richardson, James D. *A Compilation of the Messages and Papers of the Presidents, 1789–1897*. Wash. D.C: Published by Authority of Congress, 1900.

Ricketts, Norma Baldwin. *The Mormon Battalion: U.S. Army of the West, 1846–1848*. Logan: Utah State Univ. Press, 1996.

Roberts, Brigham H. *A Comprehensive History of The Church of Jesus Christ of Latter-day Saints*, 6 vols. S.L.C: Deseret News Press, 1930.

——————, ed. *History of the Church of Jesus Christ of Latter-day Saints. Period II. Apostolic Interregnum. From the Manuscript History of Brigham Young and Other Original Documents*, Vol. 7. S.L.C: Deseret News, 1932.

Robertson, Frank C. *Fort Hall, Gateway to the Oregon Country*. N.Y, 1963.

Rogers, Fred B. *Soldiers of the Overland, Being some account of the services of General Patrick Edward Connor & his Volunteers in the Old West*. San Francisco: Grabhorn Press, 1938.

Salt Lake City Directory, including a Business Directory, of Provo, Springville, and Ogden, Utah Territory. S.L.C: G. Owens, 1867.

Schindler, Harold. *Orrin Porter Rockwell: Man of God, Son of Thunder*. S.L.C: Univ. of Utah Press, 1966. Revised Edition, 1983.

——————, ed. and comp. *Crossing The Plains; New and fascinating accounts of the hardships, controversies and the courage experienced and chronicled by the 1847 pioneers on the Mormon Trail*. S.L.C: The Salt Lake Tribune, 1997.

Sessions, Gene A. *Mormon Thunder: A Documentary History of Jedediah Morgan Grant.* Urbana: Univ. of Ill. Press, 1982.

Simpson, James H. *Report of Explorations across the Great Basin of the Territory of Utah for a Direct Wagon-Route from Camp Floyd to Genoa, in Carson Valley, in 1859.* Wash., D.C: Government Printing Office, 1876. Reprinted, Reno: Univ. of Nev. Press, 1983.

Slater, Nelson. *Fruits of Mormonism or A Fair and Candid Statement of Facts Illustrative of Mormon Principles, Mormon Policy and Mormon Character, by More than Forty Eye-Witnesses.* Coloma, CA: Harmon & Springer, 1851.

Smith, George D., ed. *An Intimate Chronicle: The Journals of William Clayton.* S.L.C: Signature Books, 1991.

Smith, Joseph, Jr. *History of the Church of Jesus Christ of Latter-day Saints. Period 1. History of Joseph Smith, the Prophet, by Himself,* 6 vols. S.L.C: Deseret News, 1902–1912.

Sonne, Conway B. *World of Wakara.* San Antonio: Pub. House of the Southwest, 1962.

Stansbury, Howard. *Exploration and Survey of the Valley of the Great Salt Lake of Utah, including a Reconnaissance of a New Route through the Rocky Mountains.* Philadelphia: Lippincott, Grambo & Co., 1853.

Stegner, Wallace. *The Gathering of Zion.* N.Y: McGraw Hill Book Co., 1964.

Stenhouse, Fanny. *Tell It All: The story of a life's experience in Mormonism.* Hartford, CT: A.B. Worthington & Co., 1874.

—————. *A Lady's life among the Mormons. A record of personal experience as one of the wives of a Mormon elder during a period of more than twenty years.* N.Y: Russell Brothers, 1872.

Stenhouse, Thomas H. B. *The Rocky Mountain Saints: A Full and Complete History of the Mormons, From the First Vision of Joseph Smith to the Last Courtship of Brigham Young.* N.Y: D. Appleton & Co., 1873.

Stewart, George R., Jr. *The California Trail: An Epic with Many Heroes.* N.Y: McGraw-Hill Book Co., Inc., 1962.

Stewart, Robert Laird. *Sheldon Jackson: Pathfinder and Prospector of the Missionary Vanguard in the Rocky Mountains and Alaska.* N.Y: Fleming H. Revell Co., 1908.

Stott, Clifford L. *Search for Sanctuary: Brigham Young and the White Mountain Expedition.* S.L.C: Univ. of Utah Press, 1984.

Taylor, Samuel W. *The Kingdom or Nothing: The Life of John Taylor, Militant Mormon.* N.Y: Macmillan Pub. Co., Inc., 1976.

Thrapp, Dan L. *Encyclopedia of Frontier Biography,* 4 vols. Glendale, CA: Arthur H. Clark Co., 1988, 1994.

Townley, John M. *The Overland Stage: A History & Guidebook.* Reno: Jamison Station Press, 1994.

Tullidge, Edward W. *Life of Brigham Young; or, Utah and Her Founders.* N.Y: Tullidge & Crandall, 1876.

——. *History of Salt Lake City.* S.L.C: Star Printing Co., 1886.

——. *Histories of Utah Volume 2: Northern Utah and Southern Idaho Counties.* S.L.C: Press of the Juvenile Instructor, 1889.

Tullis, F. LaMond. *Mormons in Mexico.* Logan: Utah State Univ. Press, 1987.

Tykal, Jack B. *Etienne Provost: Man of the Mountains.* Liberty, UT: Eagle's View Pub. Co., 1989.

Tyler, Daniel. *A Concise History of the Mormon Battalion in the Mexican War, 1846–1847.* S.L.C., 1881. Reprinted Glorieta, NM: Rio Grande Press, Inc., 1980.

Utley, Robert M. *Frontier Regulars: The United States Army and the Indian, 1866–1891.* N.Y: Macmillan Pub. Co., 1973.

——. *The Indian Frontier of the American West, 1846–1890.* Albuquerque: Univ. of New Mex. Press, 1984.

Van Wagoner, Richard S. *Mormon Polygamy: A History.* S.L.C: Signature Books, 1986.

Whitney, Orson F. *History of Utah,* 4 vols. S.L.C: Deseret News Press, 1892.

Whittaker, David J., ed. *Mormon Americana: A Guide to Sources and Collections in the United States.* Provo, UT: Brigham Young Univ. Studies, 1995.

Winther, Oscar Osburn, ed. *The Private Papers and Diary of Thomas Leiper Kane: A Friend of the Mormons.* San Francisco: Gelber-Lilienthal, Inc., 1937.

Wise, William. *Massacre at Mountain Meadows, An American Legend and a Monumental Crime.* N.Y: Thomas Y. Crowell Co., 1976.

PERIODICALS

Alder, Douglas D., Paul J. Goodfellow, and Ronald G. Watt. "Creating A New Alphabet For Zion: The Origin Of The Deseret Alphabet," *Utah Historical Quarterly,* 52:3, 1984.

Alexander, Thomas G. and Leonard Arrington. "Camp in the Sagebrush: Camp Floyd, Utah, 1858–1861," *Utah Historical Quarterly,* 34:1, 1966.

——. "Charles S. Zane . . . Apostle of the New Era," *Utah Historical Quarterly,* 34:4, 1966.

Allen, James B. and Ted J. Warner. "The Gosiute Indians in Pioneer Utah," *Utah Historical Quarterly,* 39:2, 1971.

——. "'Good Guys' vs. 'Good Guys': Rudger Clawson, John Sharp and Civil Disobedience in Nineteenth-century Utah," *Utah Historical Quarterly,* 48:2, 1980.

Anderson, Peter. "The Wound That Never Healed," *Frontier Times*, 39:4, New Series 36, June–July 1965.

Arrington, Leonard J. "Abundance from the Earth: The Beginnings of Commercial Mining in Utah," *Utah Historical Quarterly*, 31:3, 1963.

—————. "Cooperative Community in the North: Brigham City, Utah," *Utah Historical Quarterly*, 33:3, 1965.

Auerbach, Herbert S. and J. Cecil Alter, eds. "The Journal of Albert Tracy," *Utah Historical Quarterly*, 13, 1945.

Bagley, Will. "Lansford W. Hastings: Scoundrel or Visionary?" *Overland Journal*, 12:1, 1994.

Beless, James W., Jr. "Daniel S. Tuttle, Missionary Bishop of Utah," *Utah Historical Quarterly*, 27:4, 1959.

Bigler, David L. "The Crisis at Fort Limhi, 1858," *Utah Historical Quarterly*, 35:2, 1967.

—————. "Garland Hurt, The American Friend of the Utahs," *Utah Historical Quarterly*, 62:2, 1994.

Bitton, Davis and Linda P. Wilcox. "Pestiferous Ironclads: The Grasshopper Problem in Pioneer Utah," *Utah Historical Quarterly*, 46:4, 1984.

Bluth, John V. "The Salmon River Mission," *Improvement Era*, 3:11, 12, 1900.

Brooks, Juanita. "The Deseret Alphabet," *Utah Historical Quarterly*, 12, 1944.

—————. "The Mountain Meadows: Historic Stopping Place on the Spanish Trail," *Utah Historical Quarterly*, 35:2, 1967.

Bush, Lester E., Jr. "Brigham Young in Life and Death: A Medical Overview," *Journal of Mormon History*, 5, 1978.

Cannon, Kenneth L., II. "Beyond the Manifesto: Polygamous Cohabitation among LDS General Authorities after 1890," *Utah Historical Quarterly*, 46:1, 1978.

—————. "After the Manifesto: Mormon Polygamy, 1890–1906," *Sunstone*, 8, January–April 1983.

Carter, Lyndia McDowell. "The Mormon Handcart Companies," *Overland Journal*, 13:1, 1995.

Christian, Lewis. "Mormon Foreknowledge of the West," *Brigham Young University Studies*, 21:3, 1981.

Christy, Howard A. "Open Hand and Mailed Fist: Mormon-Indian Relations in Utah, 1847–52," *Utah Historical Quarterly*, 46:3, 1978.

—————. "The Walker War: Defense and Conciliation as Strategy," *Utah Historical Quarterly*, 47:4, 1979.

Coates, Lawrence G. "The Mormons and the Ghost Dance," *Dialogue: A Journal of Mormon Thought*, 18:4, 1985.

Cooley, Everett L. "Report of an Expedition to Locate Utah's First Capitol," *Utah Historical Quarterly*, 23, 1955.

Dix, Fae Decker. "Unwilling Martyr: The Death of Young Ed Dalton," *Utah Historical Quarterly*, 41:2, 1973.

Ehat, Andrew F. "'It Seems Like Heaven Began on Earth': Joseph Smith and the Constitution of the Kingdom of God," *Brigham Young University Studies*, 20:3, 1980.

England, Eugene. "'Lamanites' and the Spirit of the Lord," *Dialogue: A Journal of Mormon Thought*," 18:4, 1985.

Erickson, Dan. "Joseph Smith's 1891 Millennial Prophecy: The Quest for Apocalyptic Deliverance," *Journal of Mormon History*, 22:2, 1996.

Fleming, L. A. and A. R. Standing. "The Road to 'Fortune': The Salt Lake Cutoff," *Utah Historical Quarterly*, 33:3, 1965.

Fletcher, Jack E. and Patricia K. A. "The Cherokee Trail," *Overland Journal*, 13:2, 1995.

Fowler, Catherine S. and Don D. "Western Shoshonis," *Utah Historical Quarterly*, 39:2, 1971.

Gibbs, Josiah F. "Gunnison Massacre, Indian Mareer's Version of the Tragedy," *Utah Historical Quarterly*, 1:3, 1928.

Grandstaff, Mark R. "General Regis de Trobriand, the Mormons, and the U. S. Army at Camp Douglas, 1870–71," *Utah Historical Quarterly*, 64:3, 1996.

Harris, Henry, Jr., an Interview by Floyd O'Neil, "The Walker War," *Utah Historical Quarterly*, 39:2, 1971.

Hill, George Washington. "An Indian Vision," *Juvenile Instructor*, 12, January 1877.

Howard, Gordon. "Men, Motives, and Misunderstandings: A New Look at the Morrisite War of 1862," *Utah Historical Quarterly*, 44:2, 1976.

Irving, Gordon. "The Law of Adoption: One Phase of the Development of the Mormon Concept of Salvation, 1830–1900," *Brigham Young University Studies*, 14:1, 1974.

Ivins, Stanley S. "Free Schools Come to Utah," *Utah Historical Quarterly*, 22, 1954.

Janetski, Joel C. "Utah Lake: Its Role in the Prehistory of Utah Valley," *Utah Historical Quarterly*, 58:1, 1990.

Kelly, Charles. "The Salt Desert Trails," *Utah Historical Quarterly*, 3:2, 1930.

————. "We Found the Grave of Chief Walker," *The Desert Magazine*, 9:12, October 1946.

————. "Forgotten Trail of the Old West," *The Desert Magazine*, 13:12, October 1950.

————. "Charles Kelly Discovers Chief Walker's Grave," *Utah Historical Quarterly*, 39:4, 1971.

Kimball, Solomon F. "Belated Emigrants of 1856," pt. 4, *Improvement Era*, 17:4, February 1914.

Larson, Gustive O. "Land Contest in Early Utah," *Utah Historical Quarterly*, 29:4, 1961.

Linford, Lawrence L. "Establishing and Maintaining Land Ownership in Utah Prior to 1869," *Utah Historical Quarterly*, 42:2, 1974.

Logan, Roger V., Jr. "New Light on the Mountain Meadows Caravan," *Utah Historical Quarterly*, 60:3, 1992.

Loving, Ron, ed. *Mountain Meadows Newsletter*, June 1990. UU, UHi.

Luce, W. Ray. "The Mormon Battalion: A Historical Accident?" *Utah Historical Quarterly*, 42:1, 1974.

MacKinnon, William P. "125 Years of Conspiracy Theories: Origins of the Utah Expedition of 1857–58," *Utah Historical Quarterly*, 52:3, 1984.

Mattes, Merrill. "The Northern Route of the Non-Mormons: Rediscovery of Nebraska's Forgotten Historic Trail," *Overland Journal*, 8:1, 1990.

Miller, David E., ed. "Peter Skene Ogden's Journal of his Expedition to Utah, 1825," *Utah Historical Quarterly*, 20:2, 1952.

Morgan, Dale L. "The Administration of Indian Affairs in Utah, 1851–1858," *The Pacific Historical Review*, 17:4, 1948.

Nelson, Elroy. "The Mineral Industry: A Foundation of Utah's Economy," *Utah Historical Quarterly*, 31:3, 1963.

O'Neil, Floyd A. "The Reluctant Suzerainty: The Uintah and Ouray Reservation," *Utah Historical Quarterly*, 39:2, 1971.

————. "Of Pride and Politics: Brigham Young as Indian Superintendent," *Utah Historical Quarterly*, 46:3, 1978.

Parry, Keith. "Joseph Smith and the Clash of Sacred Cultures," *Dialogue: A Journal of Mormon Thought*, 18:4, 1985.

Pedersen, Lyman C., Jr. "The Daily Union Vedette: A Military Voice on the Mormon Frontier," *Utah Historical Quarterly*, 42:1, 1974.

Quinn, D. Michael. "The Council of Fifty and its Members, 1844 to 1845," *Brigham Young University Studies*, 20:2, 1980.

Rogerson, Josiah. "Martin's Handcart Company, 1856," *Salt Lake Herald*, serialized weekly, Oct. 13 to Dec. 8, 1907.

Rollins, George W. "Land Policies of the United States As Applied to Utah to 1910," *Utah Historical Quarterly*, 20:3, 1951.

Seegmiller, Emma Carroll. "Personal Memories of the United Order of Orderville, Utah," *Utah Historical Quarterly*, 7:4, 1939.

Smart, Donna T. "Over the Rim to Red Rock Country: The Parley P. Pratt Exploring Company of 1849," *Utah Historical Quarterly*, 62:2, 1994.

Spedden, Rush. "Who Was T. H. Jefferson?" *Overland Journal*, 8:3, 1990.

————. "The Fearful Long Drive," *Overland Journal*, 12:2, 1994.

Topping, Gary. "Overland Emigration, the California Trail, and the Hastings Cutoff," *Utah Historical Quarterly*, 56:2, 1988.

Walker, Ronald W. "The Commencement of the Godbeite Protest: Another View," *Utah Historical Quarterly*, 42:3, 1974.

————. "When the Spirits Did Abound: Nineteenth-Century Utah's Encounter with Free-Thought Radicalism," *Utah Historical Quarterly*, 50:4, 1982.

————. "'A Banner is Unfurled': Mormonism's Ensign Peak," *Dialogue: A Journal of Mormon Thought*, 26, Winter, 1993.

Whittaker, David J. "Mormons and Native Americans: A Historical and Bibliographical Introduction," *Dialogue: A Journal of Mormon Thought*, 18:4, 1985.

Wills, John A. "The Twin Relics of Barbarism," *Publications of the Historical Society of Southern California*, I, 1890.

Winkler, Albert. "The Circleville Massacre: A Brutal Incident in Utah's Black Hawk War," *Utah Historical Quarterly*, 55:1, 1987.

Wolfinger, Henry J. "A Reexamination of the Woodruff Manifesto in the Light of Utah Constitutional History," *Utah Historical Quarterly*, 39:4, 1971.

Young, Richard W. "The Morrisite War," *The Contributor Magazine*, 11, June 1890.

NEWSPAPERS

California Star, Yerba Buena and San Francisco, California.

Corinne Daily Mail, Corinne, Utah.

Corinne Reporter, Corinne, Utah.

Daily Alta California, San Francisco, California.

Deseret News, Salt Lake City, Utah.

Frontier Guardian, Kanesville, Iowa.

Latter-day Saints' Millennial Star, Liverpool.

Mormon Tribune, Salt Lake City, Utah.

Nauvoo Expositor, Nauvoo, Illinois.

Salt Lake Herald, Salt Lake City, Utah.

Salt Lake Tribune, Salt Lake City, Utah.

San Francisco Evening Bulletin, San Francisco, California.

Times and Seasons, Nauvoo, Illinois.

Union Vedette, Camp Douglas, Utah.

Utah Magazine, Salt Lake City, Utah.

Valley Tan, Great Salt Lake City, Utah.

THESES

Carter, D. Robert. "A History of Commercial Fishing on Utah Lake." M.A. thesis, Brigham Young Univ., 1969.

Christensen, Scott R. "Sagwitch: Shoshoni Chieftain, Mormon Elder, 1822–1884." M.A. thesis, Utah State Univ., 1995.

Christian, Lewis Clark. "A Study of Mormon Knowledge of the Far West prior to the Exodus." M.A. thesis, Brigham Young Univ., 1972.

Jack, Ronald C. "Utah Territorial Politics: 1847–1876." Ph.D. diss., Univ. of Utah, 1970.

Lyon, Thomas Edgar. "Evangelical Protestant Missionary Activities in Mormon Dominated Areas: 1865–1900." Ph.D. diss., Univ. of Utah, 1962.

Miller, David Henry. "The Impact of the Gunnison Massacre on Mormon-Federal Relations: Colonel Edward Jenner Steptoe's Command in Utah Territory, 1854–1855." M.A. thesis, Univ. of Utah, 1968.

O'Neil, Floyd A. "A History of the Ute Indians of Utah until 1890." Ph.D. diss., Univ. of Utah, 1973.

Patrick, John R. "The School of the Prophets: Its Development and Influence in Utah Territory." M.A. thesis, Brigham Young Univ., 1970.

Peterson, John A. "Warren Stone Snow, A Man in Between: The Biography of a Mormon Defender." M.A. thesis, Brigham Young Univ., 1985.

Peterson, Paul H. "The Mormon Reformation." Ph.D. diss., Brigham Young Univ., 1981.

Reinwand, Louis G. "An Interpretive Study of Mormon Millennialism during the Nineteenth Century with Emphasis on Millennial Developments in Utah." M.A. thesis, Brigham Young Univ., 1971.

Samson, Jud. "Sagebrush Falstaff: A Biographical Sketch of James Warren Nye." Ph.D. diss., Univ. of Maryland, 1979.

Schuster, Stephen William IV. "The Evolution of Mormon City Planning and Salt Lake City, Utah, 1833–1877." M.A. thesis, Univ. of Utah, 1967.

Yurtinus, John F. "A Ram in the Thicket: The Mormon Battalion in the Mexican War." Ph.D. diss., Brigham Young Univ., 1975.

Manuscripts

Bigler, Jacob G. Diary. UPB.

Billings, Alfred Nelson. Elk Mountain Mission Diary. USIc; UPB.

Borrowman, John. Journal, 1846–1860. UHi.

Brown, Lorenzo. Journal, Vol. I. UPB.

Bullock, Thomas. The Council in the Grove on Little Sandy River with Mr. Bridger. USIc.

Bunker, Edward. Autobiography. UPB.

Burr, David A. Map of a Survey of the Indian Reservation on Spanish Fork Cr., Utah Territory, Showing its Connection with the U. S. Survey of the Territory. DNA; UPB.

Burr, Frederick H. Journal, 1857–58. CtY.

Butler, John. Autobiography, 1808–1861. UHi.

Cannon, Abraham H. Journal. UPB.

Cedar City Ward Records, 1857. USIc.

Cedar Stake Journal. Palmer Collection. SUU.

Clements, John Moon. Diary. USIc.

Collected statements on Mountain Meadows Massacre. USIc.

Cumming, Alfred. Papers. Duke University, Durham, North Carolina; UHi.

Cummings, Benjamin Franklin. Autobiography and Journals. UPB.

Dame, William H. Papers, 1838–1884. USIc; UPB.

Evans, David. Papers. UHi.

Haight, Isaac C. Biographical Sketch and Diary. UHi; UPB; USIc; UU.

Hammond, Milton D. Journal, 1856–1858, and Autobiography. UHi.

Harker, Joseph. Journal, 1818–1895. UPB.

Hill, George Washington. Autobiography. GS.

Huntington, Dimick Baker. Statement on Battle Creek Fight. USIc.

——————. Journal, August 1857 to May 1859. USIc.

Ivins, Stanley S. The Moses Thatcher Case. UHi.

Jones, Nathaniel Vary. Papers, 1856 and 1859. General Orders No. 1, Nauvoo Legion, Great Salt Lake City, March 6, 1858. USIc.

Journal History of the Church of Jesus Christ of Latter-day Saints. USIc.

King, Hannah Tapfield. Journals. USIc.

Kinney, John F. Biography. UU

List of donations toward fitting out Soldiers for the Army of Israel 1st ward ogden City, Weber Co., 1st February 1858. USIc.

Lansdale, R. H. Journal, 1856–58. CtY.

Lee, Rachel. Diary. CSmH.

Letter, George A. Smith to Mr. St. Clair, Nov. 25, 1869. USIc.

Lincoln, Robert T. Collection. DLC.

Love, Andrew. Journal, 1852–1880. USIc; author.

McBride, Heber R. Autobiography. UHi.

Mass Quorum of Seventies, Nephi, Utah. Minute Book. UPB.

Middleton, Charles Franklin. Journal. USIc; author.

Moore, David. Salmon River Mission Journal. CU-B; UHi; UPB.

Nuttall, John L. Journal. UPB.

Pace, William B. Elk Mountain Mission Diary. UPB; UHi.

Pitchforth, Samuel. Diary, 1857–1868. UPB; USIc.

Pratt, Parley P. Pratt Family Correspondence. USIc.

Prince, Maj. H. Ground of the Mountain Meadow Massacre, Mountain Meadows, 17th May 1859. DNA.

Savage, Levi. Journal. UHi.

Shurtliff, L. W. Life and Travels of Lewis Warren Shurtliff. Idaho Hist. Soc., Boise.

Smith, Albert. Journal. USIc; author.

Smith, Azariah. Journal. USIc; author.

Smith, George A. George A. Smith Typescript Collection. USIc.

Smith, Lot. Collection. Univ. of Arizona, Tucson.

Woodruff, Wilford. Wilford Woodruff Collection. USIc.

Young, Brigham. Collection. USIc.

——————. A Series of Instructions and Remarks by President Brigham Young at a Special Council, Tabernacle, March 21, 1858. USIc, UU.

——————. Proclamation by the Governor, Territory of Utah, April 23, 1853. UU.

Zane, Charles S. Journal. Ill. Hist. Soc., Springfield.

Zimmerman, Josephine S. The Long Journey. Presbyterian Church of Springville, Utah; author.

Public Documents

U.S. *Congressional Globe.* [37th through 41st Congress].

U.S. *Congressional Record.* [45th through 50th Congress].

U.S. House. *Executive Documents.* [32nd through 53rd Congress].

U.S. House. *Miscellaneous Documents.* [31st through 44th Congress].

U.S. House. *Reports.* [34th through 50th Congress].

U.S. House. "The Utah Expedition," Exec. Doc. 71 (35-1), 1858, Serial 956.

U.S. Senate. *Executive Documents.* [30th through 50th Congress].

U.S. Senate. *Miscellaneous Documents.* [36th and 50th Congress].

U.S. Attorney General. "Records relating to the appointment of Federal judges, attorneys, and marshals for the Territory and State of Utah, 1853–1901." DNA; UHi; UU.

U.S. Interior Dept. "Letters Received by the Office of Indian Affairs, 1824–81, Utah Superintendency, 1849–90." DNA; UHi; UU.

————. "Indian Office Letterbook, Records of the Office of Indian Affairs, Letters Sent." DNA; UHi; UU.

U.S. Justice Dept. "Chronological File, Utah." DNa; UHi; UU.

U.S. State Dept. "Territorial Papers, Utah Series," Vols. 1 and 2. DNA; UHi; UU.

U.S. War Dept. "Selected Letters from Col. E. J. Steptoe, 1854–55." DNA; UHi.

————. "Army of Utah, Letters Sent, 1857–61." PNA; UHi.

————. *The War of the Rebellion: A Compilation of the Official Records of the Union and the Confederate Armies.* Series I, Vol. 50, in two parts, serial nos. 3583, 3584 (Wash. D.C., 1897).

Statutes at Large of the United States, Vols. 5, 12–15, 18, 22, 24 Boston and Wash., D.C., 1850, 1859–69, 1875, 1883, 1887.

U.S. Reports: Cases Argued and Adjudged in the Supreme Court of the United States, 1878, Vol. 98 (Boston: Little, Brown, and Co., 1879).

U.S. Reports: Cases Adjudged in the Supreme Court of the United States, 1889, Vol. 136 New York & Albany: Banks & Brothers, Law Publishers, 1890.

Missouri. *Document Containing The Correspondence, Orders, &c. In Relation To The Disturbances With The Mormons; And The Evidence Given Before The Hon. Austin A. King* (Fayette, MO: Office of the Boon's Lick Democrat, 1841).

Utah Territory. *Acts, Resolutions and Memorials, passed at the Several Annual Sessions of the Legislative Assembly of the Territory of Utah, from 1851 to 1870 Inclusive* (S.L.C: Joseph Bull, Public Printer, 1870). UAr; UHi.

Utah Territory. *Laws, Memorials and Resolutions of the Territory of Utah, Passed at the 23rd Session of the Legislative Assembly, 1878* (S.L.C., 1878).

Utah Territory. *An Act Providing for the Registration of Voters and to Further Regulate the Manner of Conducting Elections in This Territory* (S.L.C: Star Book and Printing Office, 1878). UHi.

Utah Territory. Militia Records. Uar.

INDEX

Church of Jesus Christ of Latter-day Saints (Mormon): 21; history of, 26-29; 179, 208, 210; disincorporated by Morrill Act, 218; 284, 308; disincorporated by Edmunds-Tucker Act, 335; 339, 341; property of escheated, 349; 354; requests presidential amnesty, 358; 365. *See also* First presidency; Quorum of the Twelve Apostles; Presiding Bishopric

Church of Jesus Christ of Saints of the Most High (Morrisite): 210

Church of Zion (Godbeite): 268

Churchill County, Nev: 194

Cimarron River forks: 32

Circleville, Utah: 239

Circleville Massacre: 239

City Creek Canyon: 39, 54

City of Corinne (steamboat): 270

City Hall: 283, 301, 327

City of Rocks: 33n4, 165, 225

Civil War: 48, 82, 199, 208; as fulfillment of prophecy, 221, 222; end of, 247, 272; 285, 288, 296, 300, 317n3, 330, 337, 364

Clark, John A: 256

Clark, Thomas: 81

Clarkston, Utah: 33

Clawson, Hiram B: 143n8, 206, 322, 324, 325, 348n32

Clawson, Lydia Spencer: 13, 322-324, 366

Clawson, Margaret Gay Judd: 206, 207, 322

Clawson, Moroni: 203, 204n11

Clawson, Rudger: trial of, 322-325; marries Pearl Udall, 366

Clay, Henry: 48

Clayton, William: 23n, 36n42, 205, 289

Clements, C. C: 256

Cleveland, Grover: 325, 330, 330n, 335; reappoints Caleb W. West, 360; signs enabling act, 361; proclaims statehood, 362

Clinton, Jeter: 13; reportedly kills John Banks, 213; holds inquest on Dr. Robinson, 252; sued by Englebrecht, 289; arrested, 301, 348n31

Clover Creek (Mona), Utah: 72, 78

Cluff, Harvey: 115

Cluff, William W: 348n32

Coalville, Utah: 196, 242

Coates, Lawrence G: 345

Collett, Sylvanus: 13, 191n31, 231n30; murder trial of, 309-13, 316

Collinston, Utah: 228

Colorado: 25, 44, 46, 48, 63; 161, 240, 248

Colorado River: 31, 72, 84, 93-95, 178, 254

Colorado surveying district: 254

Columbia River: 29, 97, 345

Comanche Indians: 32, 222

Compromise of 1850: 48

Comte, Auguste: 185

Congregational Church: schools of, 275

Congressional Globe: 217

Connor City (Corinne): 269

Connor, Patrick Edward: 17, 220, 221; in War with Mexico, 222, 223;visits Great Salt Lake City, 224; punishes Indians, 225; crosses Jordan, 226; lays out Camp Douglas, 227; 228; in Battle of Bear River, 229-232; promoted, 233; 234, 235; makes peace with Indians, 236; refuses to protect settlers, 240; orders troops to prospect, 241; 242, 244, 245; invests in smelter, 245; 246, 247; 248; introduces steamboats on lake, 270; 271, 272; 278, 286

Conover, 184n

Conover, Peter W: in Provo River battle, 70; 77

consecration, law of: revealed, 38; restored, 55; 211, 256, 367

Continental Army: 183

Continental Divide: 25, 115, 137, 143, 144, 158

Cook, Richard: 210, 214

Cooke, Philip St. George: 155, 199

Cooke, Sarah Ann: 206

cooperative movement: 260

Corinne, Utah: 268, 269, 270; 273, 274, 278; Indian scare at, 343, 344

Corinne Daily Mail: 344

Corinne Steam Navigation Company: 270

Corn Creek: 63n, 90; Indian farm at, 99; 167; ox allegedly poisoned at, 175

Corps of Topographical Engineers: 53, 54, 196

Corralitos, Chihuahua, Mexico: 325

Council Bluffs, Iowa: 22, 29, 109

Council of Fifty: 11; pioneer company members of, 23; 24, 36n41; rulings of, 37; 41; 45, 47, 49n15; members control resources, 54; 58, 75, 102, 122, 164, 165, 212, 229, 261; renewal of, 347, 348; 349, 351, 361, 363. *See also* Kingdom of God

Cowen, Benjamin R: 302

Coyner, J. M: 274

Cradlebaugh, John: arrival of, 189; and Mountain Meadows massacre, 190-93; and creation of Nevada Territory, 194, 195; elected to Congress, 195; wounded at Vicksburg, 195n50; 198, 217, 299

Cragin Bill: 285

Crittenden, John J: 199

Crosby, Mrs: 251

Crosby, H. R: 59n43; fired on, 202, 203

Crow Indians: 93

Cullom, Shelby M: 281, 285, 322, 353

Cullom Bill: 281, 282; provisions of, 282; 283; 284, 285; provisions of enacted, 335, 336

Cumming, Alfred: appointed governor, 146; 147;

THE AUTHOR

David L. Bigler is a native of Provo, Utah, a naval veteran of World War II and Korea, and a graduate of the University of Utah, where he earned a B.A. degree in journalism in 1950. He received an honorary Doctor of Letters degree in 1979 from Southern Utah State College, now Southern Utah University, at Cedar City. He is the retired director of public affairs for U.S. Steel, now USX Corp. Since 1986 he has devoted full time to the study of Utah and western American history.

Bigler is past president of the Oregon-California Trails Association; a founder and first president, Utah Westerners; former member, Utah Board of State History; former director, Friends of University of Utah Libraries; and member, Utah State Historical Society, Gold Discovery Park Association, and Sacramento Westerners. He is also a former officer or director, Utah Manufacturers Association, Utah Mining Association, and Salt Lake Area Chamber of Commerce.

He is editor of *The Gold Discovery Journal of Azariah Smith*, recently reissued by Utah State University Press, and author of articles and reviews on Utah, Mormon, and western American history for *The Salt Lake Tribune, Utah Historical Quarterly, Overland Journal*, and other publications. His Spring 1994 paper, "Garland Hurt, the American Friend of the Utahs," won the Utah State Historical Society's Dale L. Morgan Award for best scholarly article published that year by its quarterly journal.

He and his wife, Evah, now reside in Roseville, California.